HEGEL AND THE PROBLEM OF MULTIPLICITY

SPEP Studies

in Historical Philosophy

General Editors David Kolb
John McCumber

HEGEL AND THE PROBLEM OF MULTIPLICITY

Andrew Haas

Northwestern University Press
Evanston, Illinois

Northwestern University Press
Evanston, Illinois 60208-4210

Printed in the United States of America

ISBN 0-8101-1669-3 (cloth)
ISBN 0-8101-1670-7 (paper)

This book's index was made possible by a grant from the University of New South Wales.

Library of Congress Cataloging-in-Publication Data

Haas, Andrew.
Hegel and the problem of multiplicity / Andrew Haas.
p. cm. — (SPEP studies in historical philosophy)
ISBN 0-8101-1669-3 (alk. paper) — ISBN 0-8101-1670-7 (pbk. : alk. paper)
1. Hegel, Georg Wilhelm Friedrich, 1770–1831—Contributions in philosophy of the many. 2. Many (Philosophy)—History—19th century.
I. Title. II. Series.
B2949.M32 H23 2000
119—dc21 00–008843

The paper used in this publication meets the minimum requirements of the American National Standard for Information Sciences—Permanence of Paper for Printed Library Materials, ANSI Z39.48-1984.

With respect and gratitude, this book is dedicated to the forgotten friends and remembered enemies, beloved teachers and learned lovers, with whom I have had the privilege of thinking, speaking, writing, and not just:

David Allison, Thomas J. J. Altizer, Babette Babich, Amy Baehr, Jeremy Barris, Peter Baumanns, Ken Baynes, Benjamin Binstock, Seyla Benhabib, Sam Binkley, Matt Biro, Marcos Bisticas-Cocoves, Christophe Bourot, Melissa Bolyard, Burke Brown, Victoria Burke, Jeff Bussolini, Ed Casey, Pierre Chapel de la Pachevie, Jean-François Courtine, Françoise Dastur, Heather Delilo, Jacques Derrida, Andreas Drewer, Mark Driscoll, Katsu Endo, Eileen Finkelstein, Eva Geulen, Susan Goldman, Avery Gordon, Irving Haase, Richard Haase, Stacy Haase, Sybil Haase, Lisa Handler, Shari Hartline, Robert Harvey, Holly Haynes, Rudolf Heinz, Andrew Herman, Jhan Hockman, Torsten Höpfner, Drew Hyland, Hester Ijsseling, Christiane Jaeger, Sandra Joshel, Fouad Kalouche, Julia F. Karnick, Irene Klaver, Arthur Kroker, Marilouise Kroker, Sarah Kofman, Armin Köstlich, Julia Kristeva, Helen Lang, Rainer Liesendahl, Pierre Macherey, Eduardo Marx, Teresa Mathern, John McCumber, Josef Mendoza, Andrew Mitchell, Scott Mobley, Christian H. Möller, Pablo Nagel, Diane Nelson, Esther von der Ostensachsen, Katrin Pahl, Kim Paice, David Pettigrew, Stephan Pfohl, Teresa Podlesney, Daniel Puissant, François Raffoul, Mary Rawlinson, William Richardson, Anna Riek, Sabine Rosenthal, Ron Scapp, Dennis Schmidt, Susanna Schmitz, Leander Scholz, Brian Seitz, Zarlasht Sharif, Art Simon, Josef Simon, Shilpi Sinha, Max Statkiewicz, Eric Steinhart, Kieran Suckling, Isabelle Tardé, Tim Walters, Marek Wieczorek, Manni Wollner, Norbert Wollner . . .

Contents

	Abbreviations	ix
	Preface	xiii
	Introduction	3
1	Interrogation of Metaphysics	27
2	Difference of Absolute Particularity	58
3	From Science to Speculation	82
4	Being Multiple	94
5	Quality of Quantity	112
6	Measure of Multiplicity	138
7	Conceptual Subjectivity	165
8	Conceptual Objectivity	203
9	Idea of Totality	215
10	Metaphysics of Multiplicity	246
	Conclusion	275
	Notes	293
	Selected Bibliography	341
	Index	349

Abbreviations

Fichte

UBW — *Über den Begriff der Wissenschaftslehre* (1794)
GW — *Grundlage der gesamten Wissenschaftslehre* (1794)

Hegel

BS — *Berliner Schriften* (1818–31)
Diff — *Differenz des Fichteschen und Schellingschen Systems der Philosophie* (1801)
Enzy — *Enzyklopädie der philosophischen Wissenschaften* (1830)
FVC — *Fragmente über Volksreligion und Christentum* (1793–94)
GCS — *Der Geist des Christentums und sein Schicksal* (1798–1800)
GPR — *Grundlinien der Philosophie des Rechts*
JS I — *Jenaer Systementwürfe I: Das System der spekulativen Philosophie*
JS II — *Jenaer Systementwürfe II: Logik, Metaphysik, Naturphilosophie*
JS III — *Jenaer Systementwürfe III: Naturphilosophie und Philosophie des Geistes*
PhG — *Phänomenologie des Geistes* (1807) [*PhS: Phenomenology of Spirit*]
PN — *Philosophy of Nature*
VA I — *Vorlesungen über die Ästhetik I*
VA II — *Vorlesungen über die Ästhetik II*
VA III — *Vorlesungen über die Ästhetik III*
VGP — *Vorlesungen über die Geschichte der Philosophie* [*LHP: Lectures on the History of Philosophy*]
WLB — *Wissenschaft der Logik: Die Lehre vom Begriff* (1816) [*SL: Science of Logic*]
WLSa — *Wissenschaft der Logik: Das Sein* (1812)
WLSb — *Wissenschaft der Logik: Die Lehre vom Sein* (1832) [*SL: Science of Logic*]
WLW — *Wissenschaft der Logik: Die Lehre vom Wesen* (1813) [*SL: Science of Logic*]

Heidegger

GA 5 *Holzwege* (1950)
GA 9 *Wegmarken* (1919–61)
GA 13 *Aus der Erfahrung des Denkens* (1951–69)
GA 14 *Zur Sache des Denkens* (1969)
GA 15 *Seminare* (1969)
GA 21 *Logik: Die Frage nach der Wahrheit* (WS 1925/26)
GA 24 *Die Grundprobleme der Phänomenologie* (SS 1927) [*The Basic Problems of Phenomenology*]
GA 26 *Logik (Leibniz)* (1928) [*The Metaphysical Foundations of Logic*]
GA 28 *Der Deutsche Idealismus (Fichte, Hegel, Schelling) und die philosophische Problemlage der Gegenwart* (SS 1929)
GA 32 *Hegels Phänomenologie des Geistes* (WS 1930/31)
GA 42 *Schelling: Über das Wesen der menschlichen Freiheit* (SS 1936)
GA 68 *Hegel* (1938/39, 1941, 1942)
BW *Basic Writings*
DT *Discourse on Thinking*
EGT *Early Greek Thinking*
EM *Einführung in die Metaphysik* (SS 1935) [*An Introduction to Metaphysics*]
EP "Europa und die deutsche Philosophie" (Rome, April 8, 1936)
FD *Die Frage nach dem Ding* (WS 1935/36) [*The Question of the Thing*]
ID *Identität und Differenz* (1957)
PLT *Poetry, Language, Thought*
QIV *Questions IV*
SG *Der Satz vom Grund* (WS 1955/56)
SZ *Sein und Zeit* [*Being and Time* (1927)]
US *Unterwegs zur Sprache* (1959)
VA *Vorträge und Aufsätze* (1954)
WD *Was heisst Denken?* [*What Is Called Thinking?* (1951–52)]
WP *Was ist das—die Philosophie?* (August 1955)

Kant

KU *Kritik der Urteilskraft* [*Critique of Judgment*]
KrV *Kritik der reinen Vernunft* [*CPR: Critique of Pure Reason*]
KprV *Kritik der praktischen Vernunft* [*Critique of Practical Reason*]
MS I *Metaphysik der Sitten: Metaphysische Anfangsgründe der Rechtslehre*
MS II *Metaphysik der Sitten: Metaphysische Anfangsgründe der Tugendlehre*
Proleg *Prolegomena zu einer jeden künftigen Metaphysik*
Ref *Reflexionen zur Metaphysik*

Nietzsche

KGW	*Kritische Gesamtausgabe*

Schelling

DSP	*Darstellung eines Systems der Philosophie* (1801)
PB	*Philosophische Briefe über Dogmatismus und Kriticismus*
SI	*System des transzendentalen Idealismus* (1800)
SP	*Stuttgarter Privatvorlesungen*
UWF	*Über das Wesen der menschlichen Freiheit* [*Of Human Freedom*]
VMS	*Vorlesungen über die Methode (Lehrart) des akademischen Studiums* (SS 1802)

Miscellaneous

PP	*The Presocratic Philosophers*

Preface

Lysander. One turf shall serve as pillow for us both;
One heart, one bed, two bosoms and one troth.
Hermia. Nay, good Lysander; for my sake dear,
Lie further off yet, do not lie so near.
Lys. O, take the sense, sweet, of my innocence!
Love takes the meaning in love's conference.
I mean, that my heart unto yours is knit
So that but one heart we can make of it;
Two bosoms and a single troth.
Then by your side no bed-room me deny;
For lying so, Hermia, I do not lie.

—*Shakespeare*[1]

Must I begin then with a lie?" Already this question is even more of a lie than I had hoped—for it is no lie at all, but lies, a pack or far more a tissue of lies for a glorifying of liars, and that may be a lie as well. If you ask me, then, to account for myself, I can only bear false witness; if you demand that I speak the whole truth, I can only produce perjury; if you instruct me to respond clearly and distinctly, I can only prevaricate. And when confronted directly with my own lying, with the mendaciousness and untrustworthiness, the blatant improbity, Janus-faced, double-dealing, pass-the-buck, Iscariotic-sell-down-the-river, thief-in-the-night, cock-and-bull-canard and Trojan-horse-treachery of my own words, I can only begin again with another lie, more lies—for beginning itself is a lie: not only because the beginning has always already begun, nor because the end is the actual beginning; but rather, because beginning is far more beginnings, and not just. Here, necessity is precisely not paradoxical—for this possibility already assumes only true lies and lying truths; and the necessity of lying lies elsewhere. Now, I, too, the teller of lies, am not just the liar—for I am far more liars, a pack of liars, and not just.

The lie with which I begin, then, is that of multiplicity. And it shows itself as a question, as the question: What does multiplicity mean? This is perhaps the question—yet if I answer with a single definition, a statement of essence, a true description, a particular formulation, then I cannot address the multiplicity of the meaning of multiplicity, cannot but contradict myself in a single, self-identical meaning. And if I respond with multiple meanings, then, too, I have thought multiplicity under the sign of one meaning, that is, as *a* multiplicity. Even if I answer the question of multiplicity with a double-answer, by saying that it is both multiple and non-multiple, then I still have not addressed the question multiply. How then is it possible to respond at all to the question of multiplicity multiply?

To begin, once again, this time not with the question of multiplicity, but with the answer, with the place where the answer to the question of multiplicity lies, with the history of answers known as the history of philosophy as metaphysics, that is, a history of the lie of multiplicity, a lying history of multiplicity, a history of multiple lies. Here, the question of multiplicity has never become a question, has never become questionable—for it was, however non-multiply, always already answered. What, then, has multiplicity meant for metaphysics? The following hypotheses have been maintained:

1. Multiplicity is *pluralization:* for example, "addition" of a simple "-s" or multiplication of subjects or predicates, or an original, *archē*-multiplicity that shows itself after the "subtraction" of unity. Here, the question "What is? What is x? What is there? What exists?" is superficially answered by "many things, dogs, cats, books, philosophers, ideas, numbers, words, signs, etc." The simple fact *that* there are beings, however, the actuality or reality of entities—rather than nothing—leaves the enigma of multiplicity intact. The observation of multiplicity explains nothing. And the assertion that there are many things, or that things are multiple in themselves, says nothing—for the meaning of many is far from self-evident, and multiplicity remains meaningless. Indeed, the question for multiplicity is far more: How does the possibility of pluralization *lie* in multiplicity?

2. Multiplicity is *infinite:* the multiplicity of multiplicity of multiplicity, and so on. Here, only the continuous "multiplication" of things, ideas, beings, predicates, subjects, and so on, of identities and differences and multiplicities, attempts to address the question of multiplicity. The infinity of multiplicity is either successive or simultaneous, spatial or temporal. Yet what does it mean to think multiplicity as a process, as unending multiplication, permutation, production, reproduction? Can a multiplicity that is just infinite (or finite—or in some way both) address the problem of multiplicity itself? Or is an infinite multiplicity no longer

multiple? And does the reduction of multiplicity to that which is infinite or finite not far more mean that its meaning remains obscure?

3. Multiplicity is *indefinable:* any single definition is inadequate insofar as it is no longer multiple. Yet to what extent is the answer of "inescapable aporia," of inevitable "double-bind," dependent upon a certain somehow motivated skepticism or refusal of the problem of multiplicity itself? A skepticism that is itself only possible on the basis of an unthought multiplicity? A skeptical multiplicity that cannot even explain its own skepticism? And how must a multiplicity of definitions, in all their multiplicity, fail to address the problem of multiplicity itself?

4. Multiplicity is an *idea:* abstracted from, prior to, or contemporary and co-constituted with things. Yet how can ideal multiplicity, in its identity with (and difference from) the real, hope to remain multiple? Or is the simple ideality or reality of multiplicity not far more another way of posing the question of multiplicity so as to deny, refuse, conceal, forget, repress, negate, the very question itself?

5. Multiplicity is a *predicate:* it is either a real quality, quantity, and so on; that is, something particular that a being *has* (or, reverting to pluralization, multiplicity is many predicates, qualities, quantities, etc.); or something universal, for example, everything is, is one, is many; everything that is, is thinkable, is made up of parts, is not made up of parts, is multiple, and so on. In other words, beings are multiple or being is multiple; or more precisely, multiplicity is more universal than universals, the most universal universal. Yet how can predication in general, however real or universal, assuming that judgment means connecting subjects to predicates, address multiplicity? How does the reduction of the question of multiplicity to one of "being" or "having" precisely mistake multiplicity for that which it is not? Or even further, to what extent must the question of multiplicity lie elsewhere?

6. Multiplicity is a *substantive,* or substantives, that is, a multiplicity that is itself created, invented, produced, generated, or abstracted, and made up of multiple identities, an idea, form, or schematism. Here, if beings are already multiple, then predicating multiplicity of them would add nothing but only serve to make explicit the identity of the thing in itself. Rather, if every single representation already contains a manifold, then it is only because multiplicity itself functions as the condition of the possibility of the multiplicity predicated of things. Or, if substantive multiplicity is material, an empirical construct, a thing, then everything is a multiplicity, and its singularity, identity, unity, oneness, wholeness, is an effect, a result of a reductive process. To what extent, however, does the resolution of the problem of multiplicity in terms of substantiality (and that means subject and predicate once again) rest upon some

fundamental or original non-multiplicity? And then, how does this split (between words, predicate and substantive, or original and copy), serve to paralyze multiplicity?

7. Multiplicity is a *modality* (either/or): a possible or impossible multiplicity, being or not-being (really, truly) multiple, necessarily or contingently multiple. Here, modality marks the (disjunctive) way(s) in which subjects and predicates relate, or more specifically, their way of being (ontological status): a subject is possibly/impossibly multiple, is or is not really/truly multiple, is necessarily/contingently multiple. In other words, the cynic cries that multiplicity cannot be or be thought, that the multiple is nothing, an illusion, phenomenon, or reality effect at best and a deceptive simulation or false multiplicity at worst. Yet how must modes, to the extent that they fall back upon the double-choice of on/off, something/nothing, reality/illusion, phenomenon/real, phenomenal/noumenal, possible/impossible, true/false, and so on, fail to ask the meaning of their own modal multiplicity, of the multiplicity they claim as their ownmost, and never approach the problem of multiplicity? Indeed, how must cynical multiplicity, insofar as it presupposes the logic of identity and difference in order to assert its "no," in order to refuse that which does not compute, to label the question of the multiple a non-question and the problem of multiplicity unproblematic, to dismiss the inquiry into the many as "much ado about nothing," in order to insist that philosophy would better spend its time investigating things that matter—how must all this not always already assume a non-multiple multiplicity and a non-multiple logic of negation/affirmation? Does the superficial dismissal of multiplicity, its reduction to an illusion or non-problem, not serve to support the positions of those who would prefer it to remain unquestioned? And does the dismissal not far more miss or mistake even the very possibility of multiplicity in the event of dismissal itself? For is the questioning and non-questioning, the acceptance and refusal, of illusory or real multiplicity, not itself a refusal of multiplicity?

8. Multiplicity is a *relation,* or relations: ways of connecting that are themselves either qualitative or quantitative or both. Relationality is the work of verbs: the copulative function of the "to be" ("God is dead"), of the "to speak" ("Language speaks"), "to love," "to eat," of the "to think," "to affirm," "to deny," "to dream," and so on. Here, multiplicity means to multiply, multiplication. As relation, multiplicity always also has a modality. The difference between relation and modality of multiplicity is the ontological difference, the gap between the two senses of *ens* (*essentia* and *existentia*), the distance between "whatness" and "howness." But does relationality, insofar as it follows a connectionist/disconnectionist logic and remains always dependent upon a modality, not limit its ability to think multiplicity?

9. Multiplicity is a modal relation and a relational modality: or rather, it is a *concept*. With the identity and difference of the identity and difference of modality and relation, multiplicity is no longer logical. Here, in order to approach multiplicity, the law of identity and non-contradiction is superseded; and multiplicity is quantitative and qualitative, a substantive and a predicate, subject and substance, a one, and a many. Yet to what extent must conceptuality, at the precise moment that it attempts to think and be multiple, lie about its own multiplicity? And does this lie come any closer to even raising the question of multiplicity as such?

A multiplicity of multiplicities then—but in all this, the question has not even become a question: What is the multiplicity of these multiplicities? What does multiplicity itself mean? What are its ramifications for a reflection on being, truth, time, space, subject, object, identity, difference, and multiplicity? What could multiplicity mean for philosophy? And how is it that multiplicity has become so multiple? What constitutes the multiplicity of multiplicity? Does multiplicity itself not lie elsewhere? And do these multiplicities not attest to yet another multiplicity?

The question of pluralization, multiplication, multiplicity as predicate or substantive, the multiple versions of multiplicity, is that of the multiplicity of multiplicity; and this multiplicity is itself multiple; however, it cannot remain just multiple—for then it would no longer be multiple. Multiplicity then must also be self-identical, self-differentiating, and so on, that is, a multiple multiplicity or multiplicities.

It is always possible to think these multiplicities by both returning and not returning to the traps of metaphysics; yet here philosophy remains subject to the logic of being and nothing, of determination via negation, remains dependent upon the discourse of identity and difference. Thought must, rather, become multiple—but if becoming is thought as a simple change in state, or a mediation on being and nothing, then it remains within the tradition of western metaphysics as onto-theology or dialectic, as philosophy of presence or absence, that is, as the logic of identity and difference. If philosophy, however, becomes multiple in the sense that its becoming, too, is multiple, is far more becomings, then it can no longer be called metaphysics or non-metaphysics. The becoming multiple of philosophy has no name because metaphysical nominalism is incapable of becoming multiple. Yet if philosophy could become multiple, if it could shift over into a multiplicity of languages, logics, ways of thinking, the times, spaces, places, the beginnings and ends—and not just—then it might begin to name and question its own multiplicity.

In fact, it is perhaps not surprising that from the inception of Greek philosophy, the *philosophos* was marked by an inquiry into the many. As Heraclitus knew: "those who love wisdom must be good inquirers into *many* things indeed."[2] In asking about the meaning of philosophy then, it is also critical to ask about the many. Yet the tradition of western metaphysics has never posed the question of the many, or of the manyness of the many. Thus, the question of and for philosophy remains to be asked: What is the many? What would it mean to think the many as many? The multiplicity of metaphysics own multiplicity as multiple? What would philosophy become if it finally took the question of its own "many" seriously?

Regardless, in approaching the problem of multiplicity at least three warnings are necessary. First, the danger of *forms and matters*—neither a simple shift in construction, the production of a form, the creation of a mechanical system or multiple logic, nor a pluralization of things, beings, subjects, cultures, opinions, differences, or identities, and so on will allow philosophy to think the many as many. Second, the danger of *identities and differences*—many cannot be thought simply through identity, multiple identities, or the identity of multiplicity; nor through difference, the double, the other of identity; nor through the combination of both, that is, via a discourse of identity and difference, being and non-being, revealing/concealing, one/many, and so on. In fact, if identity and difference are unable to think multiply, then it is precisely because they belong together, co-constitute and imply one another, because they are the same if not identical, and thereby, not multiple. Third, the danger of *multiplicity as multiplicity*—if multiplicity is just multiple, then multiplicity constitutes its identity, and its difference from the non-multiple. Thus, multiplicity can only be thought through a multiplicity that is not just multiple and identical and differential.

The approach to multiplicity, however, can also not just be one of "thinking" that which is multiple, of cognizing, understanding, or conceptualizing being, as a subject thinks its object. Philosophy must itself become multiple if it is to make multiplicity into a problem, or rather, problems. No longer satisfied with mere thinking (although thinking must become multiple as well), philosophy must become reading, writing, speaking, eating, sleeping, sweating, and so on—and not just. An interpretation of the history of philosophy that sets forth the ways in which multiplicity has been thought opens up the possibility of a way for philosophy to become multiple—and then philosophy can no longer simply interpret multiplicity; rather, it must begin to improvise a philosophy become multiple. Here, philosophical language itself becomes multiple: no longer upholding the self-censor of logic or the identity of truth, being, subject, substance, cause and effect, *logos,* and so on, or the difference of legitimate or illegitimate connections and consequences; "philosophy as improvisation" means that the multiplicity of discourse emerges, and that philosophy itself becomes terrifyingly multiple.

Operating against this multiplicity, however, is the control mechanisms of two thousand years of metaphysics in general, and the metaphysics of identity and difference in particular. For this reason chapter 1 interrogates metaphysics itself. Here, success is failure: by thinking multiplicity as non-multiple, the question of multiplicity as answered never becomes a question. An interpretation (not yet an improvisation) of the history of philosophy then can establish "that" and "how" multiplicity has been thought as non-thought.

For Aristotle, for example, the aporia of the many must be asked and answered in response to Plato, Parmenides, and the Pythagoreans (without falling into Democritan Atomism): thinking many as a real predicate, they cannot explain, on the one hand, how substance (*ousia*) is substances, on the other hand, how substance itself is multiple—nor can they explain the relation between substance and substances. For the *Metaphysics,* everything in the objective world of nature (*physis*) has being and is one—and the one's double-status (as a category and a universal predicate) is the clue to the many. Aristotle's radicality consists in the way in which many, like being and one, is thought as a universal. If being (as the being of beings) can be spoken in *many* ways, then it is not simply because many is a category (opposed to one)—for being and one are not genera, but equivocals, even wider than Platonic Ideas. The split between substance and substances is overcome just as that between being and beings: universals are always particular, and they can be so because that which is one is always also many. However, the logic of identity and difference means that the categorical many is dependent upon its relation to the one—as with species and genera, all identification is differentiation, and the many is pre-categorical. Thus, substance is Aristotle's answer to the question of the meaning of being because substance is always the substance of substances. The metaphysics of many that philosophy forgets means that everything has being, is one and is many. If metaphysics, however, thinks multiplicity as a universal predicate of things, then that which is multiple in multiplicity, the many qua many, remains unthought.

After Aristotle then, Kant marks the next radical re-articulation of ontology in the history of metaphysics: just as being is pure position, copula, and no longer a predicate, multiplicity becomes a substantive. Here, against Empiricism, Kant argues that non-manifold unities cannot be given in intuition; rather, they must be synthesized in order to become objects of knowledge. Intuition of the manifold would mean: the thoughtless leading the conceptless—for "thoughts without content are empty, intuitions without concepts are blind."[3] Yet if synthesis of the manifold rests upon the original-synthetic unity of apperception, and ultimately on the schema of time, that is, the homogeneous third thing that, as two-sided, mediates the heterogeneity of inner and outer, transcendental and empirical, then the manifold may only appear under the condition that it is unified, as non-manifold, no-longer-manifold. In other words, the manifold appears insofar as it does not appear, is included qua excluded. As such, the manifold is beyond the limit of human understanding. The manifold, however, must be given if intuition and knowledge are not to remain merely empty, if time is not to be simply the formal condition of sense. In fact, the manifold is the other and unthought condition of the possibility of the intuition and thought of objects for us. Yet if multiplicity is a substantive, and never knowable as such, then the multiplicity of multiplicity is not simply un-thought, but unthinkable.

With Hegel, as I argue in chapter 2, the history of the metaphysics of multiplicity reaches a kind of completion: predicative and substantial multiplicity are superseded in the logic of multiplicity, a multiplicity of logics, a multiplicity of multiplicities. The problem of multiplicity is solved by the logic of "the identity and difference of identity and difference": the concept of multiplicity is both multiple and non-multiple, subject and substance, universal and particular.[4] Philosophy itself, is double: on the one hand, it is the scientific exposition of a living system; on the other hand, it is the speculative thought of the identity and difference of the motions of consciousness and absolute spirit. For Hegel, multiplicity is *the* concept, and the concept is *multiple.* Here, concept no longer means an idea that, in corresponding to an object, is true; rather, it signifies a double-movement: on the one hand, subject and substance are destroyed, annihilated, taken care of, exterminated in identity, difference disappears in abstract negation; on the other hand, they are not-destroyed, but maintained, saved, preserved, remembered, cared for. In the concept, the one-sidedness of thought and/or being is superseded; they are both identical and different.

Yet what is the multiplicity of the concept? The supersession of predicate and substantive implies the supersession of subject and object, potential and actual, abstract and concrete, transcendental and natural, ideal and real, that is, of all the double-philosophemes of metaphysics. On the one hand, multiplicity cannot remain merely ideal, a function of the subject, for example, a Cartesian *cogito* certain of its existence or a Fichtean pure self-positing of the self-identical, absolute "I"—for then its reality is inexplicable. Nor can multiplicity be only potentially real or objective, an infinite ought-to-be multiple, a striving toward multiplicity;

for then it is worthless, a promise never to be fulfilled, a debt never to be paid, the bad credit of bad infinity, a never multiple multiplicity. On the other hand, multiplicity cannot be simply real (e.g., metaphysical pantheism from Heraclitus to Spinoza), a substance or substances, things or objects—for then it repeats the mistakes of idealism in reverse. Nor can multiplicity mean just the identity of ideal and real multiplicity: the one-sided unification of all, the totality within which multiplicity is obliterated; the indifference to difference is the death of multiplicity, a multiplicity that is no multiplicity at all—if everything is multiple, then nothing is multiple; and if multiplicity is everything, then everything is no longer multiple.

For this reason, already in the *Differenzschrift,* Hegel thinks the supersession of realism and idealism through an understanding of multiplicity conceptualized as absolute particularity, that is, the identity and difference of universality and particularity, ideality and reality, thinking and being. Here, antinomical terms are not merely connected, linked, placed next to one another; rather, their relation is both synthetic and analytic; they are absolutely identified and differentiated. The concept is absolute insofar as contradiction remains contradictory and is resolved; it is neither a product of human reason nor a fact of nature—but the movement of both, the self-production/destruction of what Hegel in the *Phenomenology* calls "the Bacchanalian revel in which no member is not drunk; yet because each member collapses as soon as he drops out, the revel is just as much transparent and simple repose."[5] Here, if multiplicity is to be thought, then neither the deductions of critical philosophy nor the productions of natural philosophy will suffice—another logic of the phenomenon of multiplicity, and of the multiplicity of phenomena, is necessary.

Logic, however, from Aristotle to Kant, was understood as the science of all thought, a priori or empirical, of the laws of reason (for example, of identity, non-contradiction, the excluded middle, etc.), a "closed and completed body of doctrine," only disfigured by attempts at improvement. Here, as in mathematics, freedom was equated with abstraction, independence from concrete objects. And truth meant correspondence of thought and thing, idea and object. For Hegel, however, as I argue in chapter 3, if logic has not suffered any changes since Aristotle, then it is all the more in need of total revision. Indeed, the *Science of Logic* revamps the dead bones of classical logic by revealing that logical truth (and validity) only veils the truth of the concept, that is, the dialectical movement of thought and being, form and content, the double-element wherein subject and substance, ideal and real, transcendental and empirical, show themselves as essentially in relation to one another, as both dependent and independent, as identical to and different from one another.

Following Spinoza's *omnis determinatio est negatio,* Hegel's logic of multiplicity then functions via a kind of negation that is both abstract (forgetting that which is negated) and determinate (superseding—destroying and preserving, taking care of and for—that which is negated). And the moments of the dialectic, in conformity with the concept, are multiple as well as non-multiple in the specificity of their contents and forms. In fact, the negative often *seems* to serve as the horizon, boundary, or limit of Hegel's ability to think multiplicity—its mark bears witness to a logic of multiplicity that is just as multiple as non-multiple. And the logic is both necessary and contingent: on the one hand, "how" it is negated remains content specific; on the other hand, "that" and "that which" is negated remains fixed. The substance (no longer essence or object) is the subject's own: for example, to the subject "body" belongs the substance "extension." Throughout the *Logic,* multiplicity determines itself via negation—but negation must, if Hegel is taken seriously, be negated as well, and multiply.

The logic of multiplicity then, as multiple, shows itself as a multiplicity of logics: not only are there multiple multiplicities, there are multiple ways in which they are and are thought. And Hegel thinks the logic of multiplicity in a double-movement; that is, he thinks it scientific-speculatively. On the one hand, scientific thought, following a linear or teleological narrative, allows the essence of multiplicity to show itself, explicates an always already implicit multiplicity—and here the concept is a result, end, or goal of the dialectical process. Speculative thought, on the other hand, as circular, sees that science does not think, realizes that its advance is actually a retreat into the ground, a step back into its truth, from whence it came.[6] Being (i.e., that which is, is there, as a fact, as given, at the beginning) is far more a product of the process of abstraction—the beginning is the end. The purity of the beginning is, thereby, contaminated with its other; and insofar as science begins with that which is immediately given without calling it into question, it does not think (speculatively). The logic of multiplicity then has two beginnings: scientifically, that which shows itself as first, as immediate indeterminacy in the *Logic* or sense-certainty in the *Phenomenology;* speculatively, that which appears last, the absolute idea and absolute knowing—the end is the beginning. The two directions of thought mark the multiplicity of logics, the multiplicity that is as infinite as it is finite—for the circle is the image of the multiplicity of logics themselves.

Yet what is, and is Hegel's thought of, multiplicity? What is multiplicity in the *Logic?* In order to answer these questions, I undertake a reading of the *Science of Logic:* from the beginning to the end and then to the middle, from the "Doctrine of Being" to the "Doctrine of the Concept" to the "Doctrine of Essence"—for the limit of Hegelian multiplicity is to be found at the very center of the *Logic.*

In chapters 4 through 6 then, I interrogate Hegel's "Doctrine of Being." Here, as a science, logic begins with that which shows itself as immediate and indeterminate, with "*being, pure being,*—without any further determination."[7] In fact, the first sentence of the first chapter of the *Science of Logic* is no sentence at all, that is, it lacks a verb—for Hegel cannot even say that being *is.* Lacking all qualities, not even being here and now, present or absent, being is (strictly speaking) nothing; but then, nothing in some way must be. And then nothing and being are; or more precisely, being and nothing are the same, and the priority of being or nothing is an impropriety. Being has become nothing and nothing has become being; they have become one another, have meaning only in their relation—in fact, the truth is that they are, that which they are, only in becoming one another. The movement from being to nothing, and from nothing to being, Hegel names "becoming." And in the concept of becoming, the truth is not simply that being and nothing do not pass over into one another—but that being has passed over into nothing, and nothing into being.

Becoming, then, is the concept that resolves and preserves the contradictions of being and nothing. The speculative truth of becoming, however, can no longer be expressed via predication; rather, as Hegel writes, being and nothing *is* the same. Yet the grammatical failure is not the fault of thought, but the failure of grammar when confronted with the task of thinking both identity and difference, contradiction and resolution. The multiplicity of predicates cannot be thought as multiple when reduced to the form "S is P." Hegel, therefore, supersedes the laws of classical logic in order to think the multiplicity (of the multiple determinations) that always also supersedes the singularity of predication. Yet if the language of the two-sided concept is designed to express becoming, then to what extent must it fail to allow multiplicity to show itself? And what would it even mean to think the multiplicity of the *Logic?*

First of all, for science, multiplicity means the multiplicity of being, that is, a quality of being: to be means to have qualities—for contrary to Musil, there is no "man without qualities." For its part, however, quality *is* as well; it has being and quality cannot not be. The multiplicity of being then does not simply mean *having* many predicates, qualities, sides, perspectives; rather, multiplicity is itself the quality of being, the way of being from which predication (however multiple) is a reduction. Being is multiple—but as such, as only multiple, being is no longer multiple;

it is just *one* quality of being, that is, not multiple. What is, however, the essence of the conceptual relation between being multiple and being one? It cannot be an *ideal* unity, since it must be just as real; rather, if the quality of being multiple is one insofar as it is not multiple, then its multiplicity is the negation of the one. In fact, this multiplicity is far more void of multiplicity, the void of multiplicity, the Atomistic one in which multiplicity dis-appears. Yet this, too, cannot be the quality of being multiple—for it is de-void of multiplicity, and thereby incapable of becoming multiple. Only through recognizing that multiplicity is one by not being multiple can being multiple show itself as the concept that is as multiple as it is one, that is, the one that becomes multiple and the multiplicity that becomes one. Here, being multiple and being one (non-multiple) show themselves in a relation of mutual repulsion and attraction: the quality of being many is one, and of one, many, many ones, one many, or in Hegel's language, "many one"—and the truth of both is their becoming one another.

The quality of being multiple, then, shows itself in multiple ways: many and one, included and excluded, repulsed and attracted, and so on. Yet how is it possible that the quality of being multiple becomes both multiple and non-multiple? For Hegel (as for Aristotle), quality alone is insufficient for determining being: for example, cinnabar and rose are both red—their difference is one of degree; their relation is one of intensity or quantity. Here, being multiple means becoming delimited as a particular quantity, a magnitude or number. Yet how can the concept of multiplicity be numbered? It cannot be by using numbers as abstract forms—for a purely ideal number can never think the materiality of being, and a symbolic logic is no logic at all. Nevertheless, the will to quantification thinks at least one side of the concept of multiplicity. And quantity is multiple insofar as it counts the many ones, the amounts of quality, insofar as quanta determine being as units. The concept of quantity, however, is just as qualitative as quantitative: not only is a number a number of somethings, not only does geometry originate with beings; and not only does a being not have a quantity of being; but quantity itself is a limit—a quantum has a limit; its other is its limit (e.g., degrees on a scale), and limitation is qualitative. Quantitative multiplicity, then, is a qualitative limit as well: a number is not only a number; rather, a degree's double-identity means that it is what it is insofar as it negates other degrees; a magnitude contains a multiplicity inside and excludes a multiplicity outside itself. In other words, multiplicity is limited, has another as its limit, is a limit for an other—but only insofar as limit shifts. And the truth of the quantity of being multiple is its movement, its becoming always another limit.

Is multiplicity then infinite? An infinite deferral or displacement? A mere should-be-multiple for an ever receding beyond? As Zeno knew, the paradox of infinity means if infinity is only potential, then it is no infinity at all; however, if it is actually infinite, then it is no longer infinite. Quantification solves the aporia of infinity by thinking it not as a number, but as a pure limit concept, that is, that above which there is no greater; however, it thereby forgets both its origin and the qualitative side of quantity. Indeed, for Hegel the quantity of being infinite is also a quality, namely, negation of finitude, that which gives a quantity meaning, fixes or determines it as opposed to others: even a mathematical term is what it is in relation to other terms. Quantitative multiplicity then is not only pluralization (just as multiplication is not simply accelerated summation); rather, as simultaneously qualitative, it is also conceptual transition, that is, heterogeneous alteration, self-externalization, supersession: for example, the difference between a point and a line is not one of magnitude; the difference between a line and a plane is not one of quantity—there is only a leap to another kind; between water and ice, there is only a shift in type or species, in quality. At the limit of calculation, the quantity of being multiple, like quality, shows itself as a qualitative-quantitative concept. The truth of infinity then, for Hegel, is neither just qualitative nor quantitative; rather, it is the concept of the relation of both. Being infinite, multiplicity is also finite; it is an infinite/finite concept, a relation in which infinity and finitude appear and dis-appear as dissociable and indissociable. Alone, infinity can no more respond to the problem of multiplicity than finitude—for without finitude, infinity is meaningless.

Yet what does it mean to be in multiple relations? Or multiple relation? No longer just a kind of being or a number of beings, multiplicity shows itself as measure. Yet what is the measure of being multiple? For Hegel it is not, as Protagoras would have it, simply human being—for that would return science to one-sided subjectivism; rather, the concept is the measure of all things. Here, being multiple means not only the multiplicity of measure, the polyvalent quality and quantity of political, social, chemical, aesthetic measures, but also measuring being multiply. The measure of being multiple shows itself in a multiplicity of ways: as a specific quantity through which quality (via identity and difference) is determined; as a real—not only ideal—multiplicity; a series in which multiplicity masks as a series, the boring repetition of mechanical reproduction; as a choice to the exclusion of a multiplicity of other partners (be they chemical or sexual); or as many knots on one line. Yet the immeasurable other(s) through which a determinate measure is multiple (and the particularity of "this" material multiplicity, "here and now") always also escapes measurement. Being then is multiple not because it has a multiplicity of measures, but because multiplicity is the measure of being—and being multiple is the being of beings.

If the beginning of the *Logic*, however, in the multiplicity of the concept of being is a result, then it is to the end, to the "Doctrine of the Concept," that I turn, in chapter 7 through chapter 9, to find its origin and truth. Here, multiplicity becomes subjective: the universals of reason and the particularities of nature are superseded in the individual as multiple. For Hegel, however, subjective multiplicity means far more that the concept of subjectivity itself is essentially conceived as multiple. In order to express this multiplicity, the concept must be spoken as multiple: "to be multiple" means, on the one hand, "to be named as multiple," and "multiply named," "to name multiply," on the other hand, "to be judged multiple" and "multiply judged," or "judge multiply"—but names and judgments are only moments torn out of language, abstracted out of the multiplicity of languages or language, language as multiple and language's multiplicity.

Yet language (however multiple), for Hegel, is not supposed to be merely subjective; on the contrary, it should express something about things themselves. With a real Copernican revolution in thought, truth becomes objective, that is, conceptual correspondence: subjective multiplicity agrees with the multiplicity of objects, and the object's multiplicity—for the objectivity of the object is itself multiple; it is the mechanical, chemical, teleological, natural object. Truth then is a function of the relation of subjective and objective multiplicities—and in this sense, it is far more truths. If the subjectivity of subjects and the objectivity of objects, however, can correspond, then it is because their relation is essentially conceptual. What then is the concept's multiplicity and the multiple concept itself?

For Hegel the concept is never simply the concept of another (of being, essence, universality, particularity, individuality, of subjectivity and objectivity); on the contrary, it is always also the concept of itself, the concept of the concept. And the relation of both the concept of the concept and the concept of concepts Hegel names the absolute idea. Here the *Science of Logic* comes to an end: the concept takes on a life of its own and comes to know itself as itself (and as another)—for the absolute idea is the totality of itself and its others. The end of the *Logic*, however, is not simply the end of a book, but the completion of the dialectical movement that began with being. And if the absolute idea (as the totality of multiple moments) is being, then it is because being was always already essentially conceived as multiple.

Being then is multiple—but how can multiplicity belong to being?

In order to answer this question, I turn in chapter 10 to Hegel's "Doctrine of Essence," that is, to the meaning of being as essence, and to the logic of identity and difference that makes the relation of being and concept possible. Here, at the very center of the *Logic,* lies the problem of multiplicity itself—for if multiplicity is only a question of the concept and conceiving multiply, or of being and being-multiply, then thought has been indifferent to the essence of multiplicity, to the essence that is identical to (and different from) being and concept. And here being is essentially multiple being: the question of "howness," that it is and/or is not, of the becoming of being, implies the question of "whatness," of the *essence* of being and the *being* of essence. The concept is essentially conceived multiply—but what then is the essence of the concept? How can the essence of multiplicity be conceived? And to what extent does the logic of identity and difference circumscribe how multiplicity can be conceived?

For Hegel essence is not Aristotelian substance, nor a definition or form with reference to matter, nor a particular mark of identification or differentiation; rather, it is that which makes identification and differentiation first possible—namely, identity and difference themselves, and the concept of their contradiction. Indeed, the metaphysical arch, which begins with Parmenidian being and comes to completion in Hegel, congeals and continues to operate today in the ubiquitous discourse and "philosophy of identity and difference." Here, multiplicity lies un-thought in metaphysics; or rather, it is that which is thought precisely in remaining un-thought. And if Hegel demonstrates how the philosophy of identity and the philosophy of difference, as essentially two sides of the same conceptual coin, co-constitute each other, work together to legitimate and support one another, then it also shows how the logic and discourse of identity and difference forms the most effective mechanism in the history of philosophy for taking care of the problem of multiplicity before it becomes problematic. Yet if philosophy is to become multiple, then it must think the logic of identity and difference to its logical conclusion; it must ask for the essence of identity and difference.

What then is the essence of identity? For symbolic logic, the formula for identity reads A = A, a body "is" a body; but this is (as the saying goes) "the night where all cows are black," the abstraction that takes difference as fodder for self-identification. Yet here identity is self-contradictory: subject and predicate are supposed to be different, but they are identical—something is supposed to have been said, but nothing has been said. For Hegel, however, identity only shows itself as negation of difference: the identity of identity is determined insofar as it is not-difference. The essence of identity then is not just identity; rather, since it is founded upon the difference between identity and difference, it has become the concept of identity, that is, the identity that is non-identity, that is difference, the identity that is (and is not) always also in relation to difference. And the truth of identity is the identity of identity and difference—for abstract identity is the most superficial of thoughts.

In this way identity is identical to and different from being: the essence of a being is its identity because the essence of being is identity. The essence of the question "What is being?" is the question "What is identity?" Being, however, cannot simply mean "presence"—for non-presence belongs to being as much as difference to identity. If Hegel is a philosopher of presence, then he is just as much a philosopher of absence. And the essence of identity shows itself in expression, in the movement from implicit being to explicit essence. Here the copula of being marks the essential identity and difference of subject and predicate, antecedent and consequent, far more than their essence.

The problem of the logic of conceptual identity then is also one of language. If predication can only think identity, then another language is necessary in order to think difference as well—for predication of identity is only possible to the exclusion of other predicates. Only by superseding the laws of grammar is philosophy able to express the essence of identity that includes difference: for Hegel identity and difference *is* the same. And the problem of language is also one of logic. Grounded upon the law of identity, classical logic cannot think its integration with difference: for example, a tree is a tree insofar as it is also not a non-tree, different from cars and people, and different in itself. Speculative logic then thinks identity as a movement: identity is always "more" than identity, always in reference to that difference which exceeds it. Hegel's concept of identity then means both identity and difference—for the logic and language of identity think the identical essence of identity and difference.

And if difference merely falls under the concept of identity, it is no difference at all. What then is the essence of difference? For Hegel difference cannot be simply different, abstract difference—for then it is self-identical and no longer difference; rather, the concept of difference means the difference of identity and difference. The determination of difference is that which is identical in difference. On the one hand, difference is non-identity, difference; on the other hand, its non-identity is its identity—and the essence of difference is the difference of the difference and identity of difference. Difference then is the concept of the opposition of difference and identity. And the logic of difference as opposition positions identity and difference as both opposed and non-opposed; it is a logic of blood—I kill you, you kill me—a bloody logic, or a "blood logic."

If identity and difference, however, are merely opposed to one another, radically different from each other, then their identity has been forgotten. Simple opposition, the reversal of positions, a revolution in thought or power, essentially serves to maintain the given logic, the status quo and hegemonic order. If thought assumes a logic of identity and difference, then the "philosophy of identity" and the "philosophy of difference" are, once again, identical. Yet the essential difference of identity and difference, lost in opposition, can be thought, and the logic of contradiction makes thinking the identity and difference of identity and difference possible—for the concept of contradiction is double: positive and negative, inclusion and exclusion, like and unlike, and so on are as identical as they are different. In other words, identity and difference *are* the same.

With Hegel then, the concepts of identity and difference imply a radical re-interpretation of the laws of classical logic. First, the law of identity becomes the law of non-identity in order to think its "more," the difference that has always already exceeded it. Second, the law of the excluded middle becomes the law of the included middle in order to think the multiple "and-so-ons" or "etceteras" from which identity and difference are abstracted. Third, the law of non-contradiction becomes the law of contradiction: "*all things are in themselves contradictory.*"[8]

If speculation, however, thinks contradiction as the essence of being and the concept, what has happened to multiplicity? With the identity and difference of identity and difference, multiplicity disappears. The Hegelian supersession of classical logic, however, simultaneously opens philosophy to the necessity of the logic of identity and difference, and the possibility of a logic of multiplicity. First, the law of identity/non-identity becomes the *law of multiplicity:* "all things are multiple" means not only the schizophrenic plurality of identities or the double-entendre of multiple differences, but always "more" than identity and difference, always also multiple multiplicities. Second, if predicates are multiple, then the law of the excluded/included middle becomes the *law of multiple predication:* not only multiple subjects and predicates, but predicative language itself becomes multiple—the copula becomes copulations, and verbs of "being" or "having" lose their priority. Third, the law of non-contra-diction/contra-diction becomes the *law of multi-diction:* no longer just identity and/or difference, logic becomes logics, poly-logics. In reworking logic as logics then, the work of philosophy becomes that of philosophies: no longer simply a question of thinking or being, or both, philosophy becomes a question of multiply eating, sleeping, drinking, seeing, smelling, thinking, being, and so on, and not just—for the difference between multiplicity and the multiple implies that yet another "multiplicity" lies prior to this onto-epistemological difference.

Yet has Hegel, with the concept, with the logic of identity and difference, not already thought this multiplicity? If multiplicity is subject to the logic of identity, to a self-identical, self-same absolute spirit, in spite of all difference; if it is subjective, one-sided (in spite of a multiplicity of personalities), or objective, or both; if it is onto-epistemological, that is, a question of being that forgets nothing and becoming, or if it remembers them; if multiplicity both appears and disappears; if it is an effect of difference, a mechanical reproduction of differences; if it is a totality; if it is only thinkable as negation, abstract or determinate, or as affirmation; if it is a question of expression and intention, explication and implication; if it is a problem of meaning what I say and saying what I mean, or of the relation between predicative and pre- or non-predicative structures of language; if it is an idea or a thing; transcendent and/or immanent; transcendental or empirical; if it is identical and different, or multiple and non-multiple—if multiplicity is any of these things, or none of them, then Hegel is the philosopher of multiplicity as multiplicity par excellence. However, if multiplicity means precisely that which is not just double, then to what extent must the concept of multiplicity mis-take the multiplicity of multiplicity?

The problem of multiplicity, then, shows itself when the philosophy of identity and difference completes the metaphysical arch that stretches from Parmenides to Hegel. Here, the question of multiplicity itself fails to become multiple. A double-*logos,* a division of all things into being and non-being, in itself and for another, a split of all being into things and ideas, a determination of determination as negation, a defining of definition as sense or non-sense, limiting of meaning to expression or subsumption, a thinking that has or does not have a twofold concept—all this can never think multiplicity, can never become multiple itself. Indeed, Hegel solves the problem of ontological difference, overcomes the chasm between ideal and real, subject and substance—but the price of this re-solution is that the question of multiplicity never becomes a question, that which is most questionable never becomes questions. And if making Hegel into a straw man, a superficial one-sided thinker of identity, a picture-thinker of difference, only serves to leave the threat of dialectic intact, then interpretation brings metaphysics' own question of multiplicity to a metaphysical answer: under the name of Hegel, multiplicity is both multiple and non-multiple, is thought multiply and non-multiply. Yet is this name not the most effective of non-namings? Is this multiplicity not the very height of non-multiplicity?

At the horizon of the interpretation of metaphysical multiplicity then, another multiplicity emerges: What if multiplicity and thinking multiply were not identical and/or different, but multiple? The concepts and philosophies of identity and difference would remain possibilities for thought and being, but would they not become possibilities among possibilities? What would happen to these possibilities if they became multiple? What would it mean for the two-sided concept to become many-sided? This "many" would no longer be and be thinkable as just "many"; it would need to be designated by another name—for as the becoming many of many, this "many" is too many; and it could perhaps be called "manys."

Manys, then, would be the name of a becoming multiple of being and thought to the point where they can no longer just be or be thought. Here, the "s" of "manys" cannot mean superficial pluralization—for many is already plural and "manys" is just too many; nor does it imply possession—for manys does not belong to many, and it is no longer simply a question of the being of *be*-longing, nor of a metaphysical genitive or "of-structure"; rather, the "s" marks the place where multiplicity becomes too much for metaphysics, where language and logic can no longer just be, be thought and be expressed. For Hegel, if it is impossible to say what you mean and mean what you say, then the multiplicity of language must be controlled by the two-sidedness of the concept. If the multiplicity of language can be heard, however, if logicians can "lie" with lovers, can share the same semiotic bed, then it is not just because they speak the same or different language, or languages, but because language, too, becomes multiple, because yet another multiplicity lies at the core of language. In fact, the inability to control language marks the possibility of multiple signification. And here philosophy becomes multiple as well—for the history of philosophy is no longer just the history of thought, of being or "Being," of *logos* or absolute spirit; rather, it is histories, and histories of philosophies. Thus, the "s" of manys is not just the sign of redundancy, not only a grammatical error or transgression of the laws of thought, not simply a slip of the tongue (and cheek)—for it is the mark of a multiplicity become multiple, and multiple to the point where it is not just multiple.

Manys, then, is the becoming multiple of philosophy itself, and not just the being and thinking of the "multiplicity of multiplicity." And at this point interpretation becomes improvisation in order to think, be, speak, write, read, hear, act, doubt, feel, deny, hate, ignore, know, and so on, multiply. A philosophy become multiple means that philosophy is no longer simply philosophy; logic is no longer merely logic, many is no longer just many—rather, philosophy becomes an improvisation on the multiplicity that lies at the core of the metaphysical interpretation of the (ontological) difference and on the conceptual identity of multiplicity and on that which is multiple.

Perhaps now, the lie with which I began has made me even more of a liar, at the end of this preface, than I had hoped at the beginning. And yet maybe, it may be that, like Socrates at his defense, I know at least that I cannot but lie. Yet once again, against myself, I bear false witness (*pseudo-logos*)—for the question of the lie, "to tell the truth," is no longer *one* of truth or lies, but of telling, accounting, of counting and recounting, that is, of *logos*. In fact, if *logos* has a multiplicity of meanings (word, expression or saying, report, an account, conversation, discussion, and also narrative, story, fable, rumor, writing, both the speech and that of which is spoken, language, reason, thought, reflection, deliberation, making sense, calculation and reckoning, relation, proportion, analogy, and a ground or condition, gathering, laying), if *logos* has all these meanings, and if it is rooted in *legein,* in the verbs "to lay, lay asleep, to lie, lie down, to lay in order, arrange, gather, to reckon, count, to recount or tell," then the question of the multiplicity of *logos* lies in metaphysics. Yet that which language speaks, however, that which can be heard in *logos* as a way of lying (that is, not merely replacing one truth for another, masking, concealing or revealing), is a way of lying that is a way of lying. *Logos* then opens the possibility for philosophy to become multiple, but not just—for it, too, lies in wait.

HEGEL AND THE PROBLEM OF MULTIPLICITY

Introduction

> If there are many things, it is necessary that they are just as many as they are, and neither more nor less than that. But if they are as many as they are, they will be limited.
>
> If there are many things, the things that are, are unlimited; for there are always others between the things that are, and again others between those. And thus the things that are, are unlimited.
>
> —*Zeno*[1]

What if Zeno's antinomies are not designed to end in absurdity, but to demonstrate the inappropriateness of the infinite and the finite themselves for posing the question of the many? Then "if there are many things, then they are both limited and unlimited" means that the many is foreign to the categories, anathema to this type of choice, to the possibilities of identity and the differences of logic. In the moment that it receives its mark, its interpretation, in the moment that it enters into the house of difference as its one and only guest (*zenos*), the many remains a stranger (*zenos*) to the host's *logos*—for the price of friendship is the denial of oneself, the refusal of a many that cannot be thought between two, myself and a friend.[2]

But what does many (*polla*) mean? Is it merely a collection of units, wholes, things? Must it find its meaning in dialogue or dialectic, or in the one?[3] And what would it mean to take *polla* seriously? How can it be thought as such, as many (*polla he polla*)? Here the very posing of the question becomes problematic—for if the problem of *polla* can even be thought, then it is because it is not only the problem of *polla*.

Manys

> Tell me, Muse, [the story of] the man of *many* moves, who very often was driven off course after he sacked the sacred town of Troy. He saw the cities of many men and understood their outlook, at sea he suffered much anguish in his heart struggling for his own life and for his companions' homecoming.
>
> —*Homer*[1]

> [I]n fact, the great form of life has always shown itself on the side of the most thoughtless *polytropoi.*
>
> —*Nietzsche*[5]

To "many," there is no plural—for "many" is already plural, and "manys" are too many. Yet here the grammatical error is far more the error of grammar. And if pluralization seems redundant, then it is because "manys" does not mean just more "many," does not name the very many of many. The question then is the question of "manys"—but first, the question of the many.

Polla—from here, more than two thousand years, two millennia that constitute the history of a problem, a problem that is no problem at all, that as a problem, as such, never becomes problematic. More than two thousand years of translating *polla,* as "many," and as plurality, multiplicity, manifold, diversity, difference, frequency, variety, and so on—these terms are used constantly, without a problem, until they become a problem. The goal then is to make this problem into a problem, or rather, to make problems, many, many problems. In other words, a goal that is itself no goal at all; rather, the making of problems as the making of goals—for these goals and problems of *polla* are not only those of *polla.*

Making problems then but not in the sense of logical or computational problems, that is, exercises to be mechanically answered, analytically worked out or figured; rather, making problems for philosophy, problems that are philosophical, that are of thinking, writing, speaking, acting, and so on. On the one hand, if philosophy can only be understood by doing philosophy, so too can the making of philosophical problems only be done within philosophy, within the history or histories that call themselves philosophy; on the other hand, as problems *of* philosophy are radically different from problems *for* philosophy, and as the latter are perhaps essentially non-philosophical, that is, only thinkable with respect to some kind of philosophical horizon; the making of philosophical problems must, apparently, be done from both inside and outside philosophy. Yet interiority and exteriority, as positions from which philosophical problems can be made, already assume a certain structure or logic, a certain practice, that is, from the very start, unsuitable for the problems of "many." Thus, the making of philosophical problems has become the making of trouble, trouble making.

If the problem of *polla,* however, can make trouble today, then it is because it has been making trouble for some time—trouble in the sense of no trouble at all—since the question of *polla* has already been answered. And precisely because it has been answered, and re-asked, and answered again, and re-answered, and re-posed, and answered once again, can it be posed now. Yet this re-posing, if it is to do anything other than merely reposing, repeating (with or without a displacement or difference), if it is to make trouble for philosophy in any way that has not already been identified, described, analyzed, located, differentiated, classified, contained, and then diffused or harmlessly detonated, it must come out of the history of the answering of the question of *polla,* that is, out of the history of philosophy. The history of philosophy then as an account of problems, questions, answers, and so on, that is, as the fate with which philosophy threatens all potential trouble makers.

The history of the problems of *polla* then under many names: Parmenides' insistence that there are *many* signs on the "way of truth" that being is and that nothing is not; Plato's discussion of *polla* or *multiplicities* and the one;[6] Aristotle's reflection on the many senses of being "in relation to one," a reflection that simultaneously implies, necessitates, assumes, a reflection on the one (*hen*) and the many, that is, on how it is possible to speak the many;[7] Descartes's cogito, itself a multiplicity, upon which the certainty of diverse experience is grounded; Leibniz's claim that the simple substance of the monad is also a multiplicity;[8] Kant's original-synthetic unity of apperception in relation to the manifold or the object that unites the "multiplicity of our representations";[9] Hegel's "many [that] are, however, the one that is the other; each is one or also one of many," or the image of a "slow-moving succession of spirits";[10] Heidegger's multiplicity in unity of being-in-the-world or his insistence that "multiplicity belongs to Being itself."[11] The history of the problem of multiplicity, in other words, occurs under many names, in many forms, that can be reduced neither to any single, ahistorical problem to which a number of philosophers have responded, nor to a simple displacement of problems, that is, to the difference between a given response and an earlier one. Must philosophy not multiply the consideration of the multiplicity of problems as multiple, *polla* as *polla?* Not merely add another concept, idea, thing, reflection, interpretation, and so on to the pile, but multiply that which is already there? How is multiplicity possible and what could it mean? How must the question of the multiplicity of *polla* itself be addressed before that of *polla* itself, of the philosophy of multiplicity?

And yet, not just the addressing and/or non-addressing of philosophical histories—for once again, this falls away from the stated goals, falls into a language that already circumscribes and delimits, forms the horizon, of how the stories of histories are recounted. The problem of address as a problem of language, of languages and their histories, of etymological connections, of aural slides, glossolalia, translation, and so on, and their relations to thought, to philosophical problems. Making trouble for language then, as the questions of *polla* in many languages, is the possibility of addressing histories of philosophy. The questions of *polla* are simultaneously the question of history, of the history of philosophy, of histories, but these questions themselves cannot yet be addressed—and cannot not be addressed.

The shift to multiplicity, however, has secretly, without announcing itself, without making itself present (or remaining absent), already begun, already started without warning, preparation, without reflection or the time and space of questioning: from *polla* to multiplicity, to multiplicities, to a multiplicity of problems, a polyphony of questions (history, language, philosophy, etc.) to the problems and questions of multiplicities and polyphonies. How is it possible to think *polla he polla?* And what could that mean? If philosophy has already thought *polla* under the sign of the one, identity, unity, dialectic, difference, then why has it not thought it as multiple? Is it not because when multiplicity is thought as such, it is no longer multiple? And is it merely a problem of structure? Or is it that the thinking of multiplicity qua multiplicity, the attempted or perhaps feigned—but not just—determination of essence, is itself then not enough, that the problems themselves, their names (not name, but also) have been multiplied, that they are out of control precisely because they are multiple?

What began with *polla* ends with *polla he polla.* The science of the question of multiplicity qua multiplicity takes multiplicity as multiple. Metaphysics is the name of the science that studies multiplicity: not only *if* multiplicity is multiple (*quid facti*) but how, with what right (*quid juris*) it is multiple. Metaphysics poses the question of multiplicity as a question: What is multiplicity? And it answers that multiplicity is spoken in many ways: (1) it is self-identical, one multiplicity, a whole or totality, and multiple only insofar as it is not multiple; (2) it is a predicate assigned to being in order to allow it to be as beings, that which must already belong to being, be "of" being; (3) it is a substantive itself, that which is given and appears "as" identity or difference; (4) it is self-differentiating, always already in relation to an other, constituted through that which it is not, the product, effect, or result of some process of identity and/or difference. Thus, a certain kind of multiplicity always belongs to multiplicity itself.

And *polla* is the name that metaphysics uses for the multiplicity of multiplicity, said in many ways. However, either (1) the many ways lead back to one primary/primordial/unifying way or (2) they can be divided into two specific ways (multiplicity as multiple, and multiplicity as non-multiple) or (3) they must remain multiple. For metaphysics only the first two ways seem understandable (and perhaps, therefore, suspect): taken together, in many combinations and permutations, they have determined the history of the metaphysics of multiplicity; the third remains problematic; in fact, it is the problem of *polla*. And for metaphysics, that which is problematic about this problem is that the problem of multiplicity, if it is to be and to be thought multiply, must be problems. Yet if multiplicity remains multiplicity, the multiple remains multiple, the many remains many, only or purely many, then it returns to the other two ways; it is no longer many. The movement of *polla* from identity to difference to multiplicity, the thought of many both as many and not as many, is metaphysical to the core.

Polla he polla then is a type of conclusion or closure of a certain metaphysical arch, a certain instinct or will, a curvature that shows itself to be part of a circle, a digression that completes itself in the return of metaphysics to itself. More precisely, the metaphysical horizon of *polla he polla* always waits on the horizon as that which can never be reached but which always remains incommensurable with metaphysics, always receding and yet always presenting itself; it is the way in which metaphysics fixes itself with respect to a limit in motion, a movement of delimitation, a determination relative to position. Yet in the moment when metaphysics deploys the philosophemes of "horizon" or "limit" to explain that which remains unfixed, indeterminate, open in closing, it betrays the very *polla* that it sets out to contain. *Polla he polla* remains outstanding or unthought, a metaphysical debt, but a debt that has always already come due, and that has also been paid. The multiplicity of metaphysics is the success in failure and the failure in success to think multiplicity as multiplicity.

Yet how is it possible that metaphysics answers the question "What is multiplicity?" in many ways? Only if the ways themselves are many, and not just. The many that becomes *polla* is itself many—but this many is even "more" many than the metaphysical many. This many is not named by metaphysics; it is not simply the many of the many as many—but the becoming multiple of that which is already many to the point of "manys."

Manys is not, however, once again, just the pluralization of plurality, the making multiple of that which is already multiple, an addition or supplementation, the production of multiplicities; nor is it the discovery, removal, or extraction of that which always already was multiple, the retraction or subtraction of some mask, veil, shield, and so on—for this procedure is far more the work of metaphysics; rather, manys is the act of becoming multiple, an action that is far more than actions, a becoming that is far more than becomings. To metaphysics, manys appears illegitimate (or a legitimate illegitimacy)—for metaphysics thinks multiplicity without ever becoming multiple, and because it marks manys as non-sense, outside of sense, meaning-less. Yet what if metaphysics itself was already a reduction of multiplicity to legitimate/illegitimate, the determination of thought according to categories, the definition of philosophy upon the ground of identity and difference? For metaphysics, manys appears as an abyss, a non-ground, groundless ground, shows itself before, with, or after, many—but it is far more that which can become the distinction of ground/non-ground, the determination of pluralization (however legitimate or illegitimate). Manys can become many, can become its result, simultaneous with it, co-constitutive with many, can become behind, next to, under, and over many—for the direction of manys is far more directions, and not just.

How must manys become the "many as many" and as "not many" in order to function? What are the relations between manys and many? How is manys not simply the next attempt to articulate the most universal of universals, the widest of concepts, the condition of the possibility of many, that which is prior to many? How is it not the answer to the quest for a first principle or origin—and as such is manys not the most metaphysical of names? Indeed, if manys is posed as a question or answer, thought as a problem or solution, then it is metaphysical to the core.

In order to approach manys then a shift in approach is critical; a rethinking of thought, experience, perception, awareness, instinct, drive, direction is necessary—for manys is that which cannot simply be reduced to the options of metaphysics, of many or not-many. For its part, however, metaphysics will always lay claim to manys as metaphysical or non-metaphysical, and thereby as that to which metaphysics must expand in order to take account of that which it could not have thought, to include that on which it had not calculated. A reading of the history of philosophy as a history of *polla,* an interpretation of the ways in which metaphysics has thought multiplicity, the multiplicity of multiplicity, that which is multiple about multiplicity, is designed to show how the metaphysical possibility of *polla he polla* emerges. Interpretation, however, will never reach manys—a shift to improvisation is necessary. Here the "s" of manys is no longer more or less, no longer a priori or a posteriori; thought is no longer a thought or not a thought, no longer a thought of that which is and/or is not thought, nor is it merely many thoughts—

for improvisation neither simply obeys nor transgresses the law of metaphysics; rather, it is that which first opens thought to becoming manys itself. The movement from multiplicity as non-multiple to multiplicity as multiple, to the multiplicity that is both multiple and non-multiple, to the multiplicity that is neither multiple nor non-multiple, and so on, is interpretation; but the way to manys lies in improvisation. Now, however, philosophical improvisation can show itself only in the form of a question mark, unknown, a shadow, glimpse or inclination, an instinct or desire, a bet, wager or under the guise of the hypothetical: What if it were possible to multiply multiplicity, to go multiple—what then? What if this multiplicity were no longer just many, but far more manys?

Yet first, in order to approach the problem of multiplicity, one, single, solitary, and preliminary question, the question of the interpretation of *polla*. Thus, how is multiplicity a question of structure, that is, to what extent does philosophy drive toward a logic, construct a paradigm or frame? And how can the subject matter of thought be multiple? To what extent is it necessary to multiply the subject or object of philosophical investigation? Can this becoming multiple bring philosophy any closer to even posing the question of multiplicity as multiple? Or how can multiplicity be thought if it does not resort to the difference of form and matter? To what extent can difference serve to think multiplicity? Then what is multiplicity as such? And what does it mean to think the multiplicity of multiplicity, that is, that which in multiplicity itself is multiple? Finally, how is multiplicity not just a question of making or re-making, finding or re-finding (and re-fining) that which is sought, of interpreting or reinterpreting a multiplicity saved, but of improvising a language, or rather, languages of multiplicity, of a multiplicity of languages, of polyphonies and of philosophies, of ways of thinking, reading, speaking, writing, and so on?

Seduction of Structure

> The multiple *must be made,* not by always adding a higher dimension, but rather in the simplest of ways, by dint of sobriety, with the number of dimensions one already has available—always $n - 1$ (the only way the one belongs to the multiple: always subtracted). Subtract the unique from the multiplicity to be constituted; write at $n - 1$ dimensions. A system of this kind could be called a rhizome.
>
> —*Deleuze and Guattari*[12]

If philosophy today cannot think the problems of multiplicity, then it is because it is too simple. The question here is not *if* philosophy thinks, but *how* it thinks. The continual reduction of multiplicities and denial of polyphonies through their juxtaposition, negation, opposition, unification, and so on signifies that a new structure is needed, one that responds to multiplicity, that is multiple—or rather, not simply one: the multiplication of structures. The questions then: Can philosophy restructure itself in order to think polymorphously? Can it reform the *morphe* of *poly-morphe,* transform itself into something multi-formed in order to create other forms of thought (*Denkformen*)? And if thought-forms are expressed as logic, then what can it mean to think with logics? Is it the multiplication of ahistorical, Aristotelian logic? It is the de-delimitation of Kantian logic as a "closed and completed body of doctrine," that is, as "an exhaustive exposition and strict proof of the formal rules of all thought (whether it be a priori or empirical, whatever be its origin or its object, and whatever hindrances, accidental or natural, it may encounter in our minds)?"[13]

Here Hegel's speculative logic is revolutionary, but a revolution that is no longer merely Copernican (like Kant's in thought) nor merely transcendental: (1) a revolution in the science of logic—the "formal rules of thought," the laws of identity, non-contradiction, and so on, insofar as they remain inadequate to the dynamics of thought, to the life of the mind in motion, are rethought as the concept (*Begriff*), as circular, what Hölderlin in *Hyperion* calls "an eccentric track [*exzentrische Bahn*]," as the movement out *from* itself that returns *to* itself, through dialectic (*via negation*), as a totality of philosophemes that are *in-and-for-themselves,* identical/different to/from themselves; (2) a revolution in phenomenology where the contents of logic must be seen as the forms of thought, as logics that metamorphose themselves in relation to their content, that are bound to (not, as in Aristotle and Kant, abstracted from) the necessary moments of spirit as both subject and substance in the living, immanent contradiction (*innerem Widerspruch*) of the speculative idea, the unity that is simultaneously concrete and spiritual (*konkrete, geistige Einheit*), that is, that is not only identity, but just as much difference; (3) a revolution in the speculative phenomenologic that provides a structure for the thought of multiplicity qua multiple. Thus, if the form of thought is the content of logic, and if the content of thought is phenomenological, then the deformation of thought entails the transformation of both logic and phenomenology.

The necessity for a structural shift then, in order to think the problem of multiplicity, to ask about that which is problematic in the problem, enables the expression of the problem itself, makes explicit the way in which explication is possible. In Hegel's concept, multiplicity and its negation are thought together and separately, as the togetherness of their separation and the separation of their togetherness—the concept is the logical structure that takes care of the holding and releasing of both. And phenomenology makes the implicit explicit, allows the content of thought to show how it has, in determining itself, always already submitted itself to the necessity of negation, and to the concept that always already made it possible. Here multiplicity is first structured as identity: being, the beginning of science, is the end, the being that is the origin, source, or beginning (here the connection, however non-etymological, *pas à la l'être:* "being" appears anagramatically as "begin") is the end result of an abstraction that has always already happened, the product of a happening. And multiplicity is also structured as difference, that is, relation, the difference of (*genetivus subjectivus* and *objectivus*) subjective and objective, subject and substance, idea and thing, being and beings, and of identity and difference themselves. The logical forms of multiplicity then are ways of closing off, determining, of cutting up being as identities, differences, triads (or triangles? cf. Plato, *Timaeus*), fours, fives, and so on; in other words, infinity, the infinite possibility of determining that which is, being or nature (*physis*), the possibility that belongs to being itself. Yet is there a structure capable of thinking infinity? Or is all infinite structure a *contradictio in adjecto?*

Indeed, the deformation of logic and of thought entails the re-forming of multiplicity, a multiplicity that has almost exclusively (i.e., traditionally, canonically, normally) been structured under the name of either identity or difference. Structural multiplicity then is a deformation that reveals the normal forms to be themselves merely normalized deformations: the hierarchic split, the priority of identity and of difference, is a normalized (and normalizing) function as the norm's condition of possibility (or purported necessity). No longer the norms of identity/difference, nor merely a deformation or aberration—for multiplicity means that the normal/abnormal has itself been multiplied—the multiplication of categorical possibilities in polymorphic logics means that thinking is no longer logic, that an illogical form must be invented, an a-logical frame must be found.

On the one hand, Hegel's formation/deformation of multiplicity is important here because it completes a functional metaphysics and closes off or concludes a certain logical trajectory: either identity, that is, multiplicity as totality, as tolerated within a unified organism (e.g., the multiple moments, and moments of moments, of absolute spirit), within the horizon of a "realized infinity," a totalizing system (e.g., the *Logic* as the system of thought-forms or the *Encyclopedia* as the system of science in general) that avoids a bad infinity (*schlechte Unendlichkeit*); or difference, that is, multiplicity as dialectic, as contained within one or both sides of a movement or within the identity and difference between the "one" and the "both." As Schelling did in his identity-philosophy, Hegel appears to have developed a sophisticated containment system for multiplicity as uncontrolled/uncontrollable polymorphism. Yet identity and difference are tied to, determined through, the ways in which they bind multiplicity, a multiplicity that is neither singular, identical, unified, individual, totality, and so on; nor double, split, divided in two spheres, realms, perspectives, appearances, and so on. These ways of formalizing are neither false nor inadequate; they do not hide or conceal multiplicity as it is—on the contrary, if the formal (logical) techniques operate the *technomorphisms* of identity and difference, then it is because truth is not simply structural. Thus, identifying the forms of identity, differentiating the forms of difference, tracing the deformations of their forms, is an essential propedeutic in thinking the multiplicity of logics, polylogocentrism.

On the other hand, the completion, closing off, or limitation of the metaphysics of multiplicity is possible because it is simultaneously an opening up of thought as dialectical. The motion of the concept then is not only a way (*met-hodos*) of thinking identity, one that groups multiple traits or parts together, parts that are themselves complex, multiple parts in multiple wholes, multiple strands bound together forming a woven tissue (com-plex, *plexus*), that have no smallest part to which they can be broken down, examined, analyzed (except provisionally) and then rebuilt, re-constructed, that cannot be un-knotted, one from the other, without losing the texture of their constitution, cannot be extricated from each other since they are not joined through a simple mixture; nor is it a way of thinking only difference, the split or gap (or lack) between beings, the distance between being and beings, the space between subject and object, the doubling, repetition with a difference, or displacement. Rather, the concept is the opening up of a way to think both identity and difference (and neither): by seeking out those differences within/without of which identity and difference are thought, in the identity of identity and the difference of difference, that is, the condition of the possibility of difference (and identity), and the "possibility of the possibility" of the "difference of difference." Here the concept is the logical conclusion (*Vollendung*) of structural multiplicity because its permutations, under the duel sign of identity/difference, are finally exhausted (identity of identity, identity of difference, identity of identity and difference, difference of identity and difference, difference of identity, difference of difference)—and this is the opening for multiple philosophical structures, for *polyphilomorphisms,* multiple because they *could* simultaneously be thought in identary-differential logics (along with their acceptances/rejections, affirmations/negations, inclusions/exclusions, etc.), multiple because their tropes (*tropos,* way, manner, character, rooted in a turning, turn of mind or speech) are that of multiplication.

First warning: the seduction of structure, of simplicity as the problem and complexity as the solution, of form and formalism, of hylemorphism, of calculation, prediction, absolute control, of logical certitude, machine dreams and technological fantasies, one-sided empiricism, radical constructivism, of the progressive refinement of philosophical practice that imagines either metaphysical perfection, mastery through systematics or (ironically, or not) an escape from metaphysics, transcendence and the desperate faith in a structure, another way of framing (however multiple) with magical (or emancipatory) possibilities—the pot of gold at rainbow's end—all these cannot begin to think multiplicity. For here, under the signs of identary-differential logic, the identity and/or difference between identity and multiplicity (even if it is a difference perhaps only discernible by the dogs of Plato's *Republic*) resides a metaphysical logic of blood, a bloody logic: either/or, I and thou, subject and other, male/female, substance/accident, and so on are the logics of "with us" or "against us," friend/enemy, of kill or be killed: as if philosophy should content itself with merely outlining borders, drawing frontiers, *Grenzbegriffe,* limits, horizons, with only creating new (old) metaphysical concepts or methodologies, with simply reinventing structures within which canonical problems can be thought, within which the history of philosophy can reproduce itself. Structuralism will not save philosophy from metaphysics, it cannot respond to multiplicity, cannot even raise the question of the meaning of *polla;* rather, it re-inscribes the difference of form/content or structured/non-structured. The search for a better system, a more effective thinking machine, a philosophical construct or technology will not lead out of metaphysics. The simple multiplicity of forms is not multiple—and polymorphism is not manys.

Manipulation of Matters

The matter at hand then, or rather, the matters at hand, what matters to multiplicity, is the manipulation of matter for philosophy: at the limit of formal multiplicity, at the logical conclusion of structural polymorphism, lies the question of subject matter, of a multiplicity that makes problems for philosophy, history, language—and their combinations: history of philosophy, language of philosophy, philosophy of language, philosophy of history, history of language, language of history—and their permutations: philosophy as speculative, as phenomenology; or as history, as the history of absolute spirit coming to know itself, as the "history of the forgetting of the question of Being," and so on. What matters is the multiplication of substances and subjects (not in the psychoanalytic sense—no romanticism for the pain or pleasure of schizophrenia) of philosophy as not simply a matter of form, but essentially of content, thing, object, interest, and so on.

What matters is precisely that which classical logic does not grasp, the place into which it cannot reach, that which eludes structural considerations, mere formal multiplications. The matter of Hegel's *Logic,* for example, is the multiplication of forms. In other words, formations and deformations, thought-structures and logics, are themselves the matter at hand, the moments and their concrete contents, the ways in which they come to themselves through an other that is their own (not simply *any* other). And the matter of the *Phenomenology,* for instance, is the radical individuality of absolute spirit's historical unfolding, the specific ways in which it shows itself precisely because logic as phenomenologic means that form shifts with its content. In consciousness's education, Aristotelian logic is only a moment on the way to the point of absolute knowledge—for it is only a precursor to philosophy, only the beginning point in the development of the philosophy of spirit.

The question then is the multiplicity of matters, not how many senses can be united under one concept or idea, not how some being can be revealed or concealed in many (not just one) ways; it is about the *meaning* of the multiplicity of things, of beings. In what does the multiplicity of multiple matters consist? Is it a number, combination or quantity of components, constitutive parts, aspects, sides, perspectives, and so on? Or is it a quality of material that shows itself in the moment of its individuation? Or are quality and quantity not already too non-multiple for that which matters, the matter of multiplicity? And if a single, self-identical thing is present as self-identical and self-differentiating, then how can the multiple matters be approached or thought, by a single or double form? Must not the concept itself, in order to take account of multiplicity, be multiple? And not just be or not be multiple, but understand its being as beings and its non-being as nothings? At the moment that the matter of a multiple thing is determined as matters, the thing cannot be thought as categorical; for it is also non-categorical, and not just—since it is multiple, matters. At the moment that the truth (that matters) of multiple matters is determined, fixed, it becomes radically unsuitable to the multiplicity it should explain. Phenomenologic, then, thinks the matter of thought as multiple, and as constitutive for structure, form, logic: beings determine being, things determine ideas; and a thing is always things, a being always beings—as much as a thought (the formal matter of logic) is always thoughts.

After formal multiplication, identary-differential form, a form to which it is indifferent, or rather, a (transcendent or transcendental) form that is, strictly speaking, badly informed, the priority of matters shows itself as the immanence or pure empiricism that resists abstract formalization (or formations), as the "given real" that remains radically misunderstood, necessarily mis-formed, reduced, constrained, by the scientists of structure, the technocrats of polymorphism, the logicians and their architectonics, the systems analysts and their metaphors. What matters for a philosophy of multiplicity are philosophical matters, the matters of philosophy, those ideal or real substances that it finds itself unable to formulate, when it comes to what matters.

Second warning: the multiplicity of matters, the sheer increase in subjects, disciplines, factors, cultures, races, genders, differences, identities, and so on (or of forms, deformations, structures), however multiple, will not "escape" the constraints of metaphysics—for metaphysics is a way of constraining, controlling, or reducing multiplicity: as if philosophy should content itself with merely more matters, with an ever increasing field of possible research, with more subjects, substances, activities, with even more mandates, manifestos, methods, and ever more words. The instinct to include more ideas, opinions, truths, facts, disciplines, peoples, bodies, and so on is unsuitable for the question of multiplicity and the flip side of the seduction of structure, the quest to build a better construct, a more efficient form. The sheer multiplicity of matters, however, is not multiple—and the possibility of manys is here not even a possibility.

Indifference of Identity and Difference

> It inscribes difference in the heart of life. . . . [N]umerical multiplicity does not sneak up like a death threat upon a germ cell previously one with itself. On the contrary, it serves as a pathbreaker for "the" seed, which therefore produces (itself) and advances only in the plural. It is a singular plural, which no single origin will ever have preceded. . . . [I]f this in itself were intended to mean something, it would be that there is nothing prior to the group, no simple originary unit prior to this division through which life comes to see itself and the seed is multiplied from the start; nothing comes before the addition in which the

> seed begins by taking itself away, before what *Drama* announced as "a proliferation which would never have begun," before what *Logics* set down as a swarm of bees, a division at work.
>
> —*Derrida*[14]

The question of multiplicity, of forms and matters, then, is first played out within the metaphysics of identity and difference. On the one hand, defined by a particular type of dominant philosophical instinct, the discourse of identity is no longer only the search for a particular structure, one structure, a totality through which differences can be filtered, connections and transitions made, between subject and object, possible and actual, form and matter; it is not only the assumption of a whole or unity by which the problems of multiplicities can be solved—for it is also the rejection of the gap between structure and substance, subject and object: "and if western philosophy until Hegel, fundamentally does not come out of Parmenides' proposition: being is one [τὸ ὄν τὸ ἕν], despite all changes, then this implies no lack; rather, a preference, and the sign that it, despite everything, remains strong enough to preserve its first truth."[15] Insofar as the metaphysics of identity has been effectively able, under the sign of the "one," to think multiplicity for over two thousand years, it is there that an investigation must first turn if it wants to ask the meaning of multiplicity as multiple, to the questions: In what does the strength of western philosophy consist? To what extent, and at what price, is its "first truth" preserved? How does this truth think multiplicity, and how can it never hope to think it? And if the one of being, the being of the one, is philosophy's origin, then what is "being" and what is "one"?

On the other hand, opposed to the metaphysical instinct for being and one, at its limit or horizon, an other instinct can be discerned: the metaphysics of difference, the difference of forms and matters (however multiple), of form/matter (and the entire philosophy of difference that assumes difference in order to destroy it, to think beyond or against it—but only as difference; that thinks multiplicity insofar as it submits it to the difference and displacement between one and an/its other, the "difference of," and so on, in order to think multiplicity qua difference, as radical otherness, its absolute incommensurability or transcendence) makes no difference at all; that is, it is itself indifferent to the difference of multiplicity, to the very difference it sets out to know, see, hear, conceive, and so on, or rather, in its difference/indifference from/to multiplicity, it can only differ.

Metaphysics then implies a radical failure in success, the success of identity and difference in their most sophisticated forms, their most powerful avatars, to think multiplicity—but a multiplicity that is not multiple, that is no multiplicity at all. The identity of multiplicity is not multiple identities, and the difference of multiplicity is indifference to multiplicity. What then is multiplicity? What is meant by multiple, by many?

For metaphysics, multiplicity is an identity (a source, origin, *archē*—or identities), or it is a difference, negation, that which is not-identity, that is, it is an identity/non-identity. Or it is some combination, repetition, or permutation of identity and difference: for example, multiplicity as an effect of differentiation, as the product of the difference of being from itself, self-differentiation; or the multiplicity that emanates from an absolute identity, that participates in a self-same idea, and so on. Yet are these the only ways in which philosophy can think multiplicity? What if philosophy sought to think multiply, that is, without falling into the familiar (albeit functional) philosophemes of identity and difference? Indeed, how do the questions of identity and difference make the very posing of the question of an other multiplicity impossible? To what extent must multiplicity as multiple relapse into the discourse of identity and difference—and how is the logic of "relapse" even possible? Why is it, in fact, that multiplicity constitutes no problem at all for metaphysics?

Multiplicity as Such

"Neither a doubting or proofing, nor a provisional *epochē,* a turning-off or turning-down, nor a shedding of skin, a thinning-out, weeding and harvesting and sowing, counting or recounting; but rather, a loosening-up, an unfixing of a history, tradition, language, of multiplicity, in order to provide a quick taste, or whiff, of a "many" that cannot be avoided for much longer.

Multiplicity as multiple is neither an empirical concept nor a necessary a priori representation; neither a (pure) transcendental form of intuition nor a discursive or general concept produced, abstracted, created, constructed from a number of particular instances; nor is it a particular instance deduced from a general concept. It is not a condition of possibility—for multiplicity as such cannot be thought within the logic of possible/actual or ground/grounded. It is not, strictly speaking, definable—for it cannot be grasped as multiple in the semantic formula S is P, nor conceived of as a *logos*—for it cannot be determined via dialectic, negation, or affirmation, by answering the ontological doubled-question of what is it/what is it not; but nor is it simply indefinable, mystically inaccessible, beyond, transcendent. And it does not imply relativism—for it cannot be thought under the relativist/absolutist difference. Neither is it numerical, merely quantitative—for multi-*pli*-cation, multiple-folds is the logic of identity (a single fold, line, crevasse, crack, etc.) and difference (two sides, halves, etc.), nor the intricacies and intrigues of some sort of intellectual origami, the combinations of some calculating *combinatoire*. Nor is it merely multi-culturalism, multi-colored, multi-faceted, multi-purpose, multi-tasking, or multiple choice, and so on, that is, not in the computational sense of multiplication, not in the sense of multitudinous, anything between infinity and more than one (e.g., of the Platonic seven hundred and twenty-nine that indicates the difference between the just and the unjust man with respect to pleasure and pain),[16] nor in the sense of a mere increase in the quantum of terms, concepts, problems, and so on considered through the sheer velocity of multiplication to the point of simultaneity, high-speed addition or supplementation, permutations or simply mutations; rather, multiplicity is the becoming multiple of questioning to the point where the logic of calculation (and the logic of questioning itself) no longer functions, the point where predication via identity and difference no longer accounts for thought—and further, to the point where they continue to function, and therefore permit another logic to emerge.

Multiplicity as multiple, strictly speaking, *is* none of these things because it *is not;* it cannot *be* them, if being is understood according to the laws of identity and difference. If being is defined as a predicate joined to a subject through the copula of possession, having, giving, taking, and so on; if it is taken as the copula of subject and predicate or pure positionality; if it is understood as disclosedness, presence, unfolding—multiplicity as multiple *is* none of these, and it *is not* none of these—for being and non-being (nothing) are dependent upon the discourse of identity and difference, a discourse that by definition cannot think multiplicity as multiple. And only through the becoming multiple of multiplicity can multiplicity as such show itself.

Becoming multiple then is the way of thinking multiplicity as multiple—but not in the sense of some "original" act or fact, not some transcendent or transcendental ground, not as an uncovering of what lies always already present or absent (or both), no revealed abditories, *archē*-ological finds or buried treasure: for this leaves intact the difference of ground/grounded, as well as temporality and history, along with a certain foundationalism, constructivism, and creationism or vitalism and its creator/created difference (e.g., being as reality, *Wirklichkeit*), nor the ex-statics of inside/outside, of ex-pressionistic logic. And not as method—for in application, a non-multiple logic is assumed, and the limits of investigation between subject and object, scientist and specimen, artist and work, are determined. Nor as immanent critique—for remaining immanent, it can never get out, and more important, because it always already assumes an inside/outside not in order to reassert transcendence (or itself as transcendental, as a transcendental immanence, pure interiority), but to re-inscribe the difference on the basis of which it re-totalizes. Indeed, all that remains insufficient for multiplicity as such.

Multiplicity then is not just the negation of difference, nor its affirmation, nor both simultaneously, nor some between stage, gray zone, or spectrum—for these remain indebted to differential horizons, between two poles—for if negation and affirmation are two ways of differing, of articulating difference, then they carve out their identities (and differences) by reducing the multiple ways of speaking to specifically two. Neither the simple multiplication of affirmations or negations, but rather, if the language of affirmation and negation remains differential, then multiplicity is the becoming multiple of languages.

Yet multiplicity as multiple is not simply chaos, not merely a metaphysical tower of Babel—for absolute indeterminacy is equivalent to absolute identity, convertible to indifference, a "night where all cows are black"; and it is not the uncountable of some unformed stuff or substance, the material of sensations, appearances, or representations, that must be ordered, reduced, delimited. It cannot be thought as representation or resemblance (e.g., the walnut's semblance to the brain and the corresponding "scientific" conclusion that madness can be cured by nuts)[17] because this form of displacement assumes a linearity or temporality that falls once again into the identity and difference of original and copy; nor as simulation and its radically identary logic that copies the copy while denying any trace of difference; nor can it be drawn (via metaphor or analogy) from an event, thing, phenomenon, or experience. Nor is it simply a place or non-place, sense or nonsense, that is, neither there or not there, present or non-present (absent), neither materialized, fixed in a place, concretized as a thing, nor non-materializable, non-fixable, nor a combination thereof. And multiplicity as multiple is not thinkable as non-thinkable, in its non-presence, absence, in the space of its appearance or non-appearance—negative onto-theo-logics, negative theologies, can never think multiply. It is neither active, middle, or passive—for these categories can only reduce the grains of the voice, only restructure the vibrations of vocal cords, the movements of tongues, configurations of muscle tissues, teeth, phlegm, diaphragms, and so on. And multiplicity is not the movement of infinite or finite, not merely a question of numbers or kinds—for it is neither merely quantity, that is, abstract number or logic; nor quality, that is, category or categories, specific determination, a kind of thing, being, idea, and so on (nor quality as kinds of things, i.e., quantified quality); rather, multiplicity is not only multiple—for that is the logic of identity, and of difference.[18]

If the paradigms of metaphysics, therefore, by which multiplicity is thought (as identity and difference) are refused by multiplicity as such, then the question of multiplicity becomes more urgent—the problem of multiplicity becomes a problem. As a universal predicate or a substantive, multiplicity is not yet multiple. Only if thought is a motion can it begin to think multiplicity as such: only through the movement of multiplicity, through the movement of that which is no longer of "that which is or is-not" (for this is a return to the discourse of identity and difference), are thought and multiplicity the same—and not the same—or rather: multiplicity and thought multiply."

Third warning: if, in fact, multiplicity is thought as such, then it is the multiplicity of multiplicity, multiplicity as multiple. Here, dialectics gives multiplicity as such an other. And the othering of multiplicity constitutes its submission to metaphysics. Insofar as the concept remains dependent upon determination as negation, the full force of multiplicity will be contained. Multiplicity sunders itself into a multiplicity of moments, opens itself to becoming multiple because it is multiple (multiplying)—but the supersession of multiplicity is always also non-multiple. Here multiplicity is never "as such," never only multiple; and this is the first loosening of the identary logic through which metaphysics has thought multiplicity. With dialectic, multiplicity is never simply a single word, a non-multiple definition or essence; rather, unfixing *logos,* multiplicity as such shows itself in/as the moment (*Augenblick*), as the product of a prior reduction: if the truth of multiplicity is not multiple, then it is because pure multiplicity does not exist. If multiplicity as such is to be thought, then another a-dialogical logic is called for, a living, moving, self-transforming logic that thinks multiplicity as neither mediate nor immediate, neither quantity nor quality. Multiplicity demands another logic, one capable itself of becoming multiple.

And if multiplicity has a multiplicity of meanings, meanings that cannot be articulated within the identities assigned to it by metaphysics, if they cannot be restricted to the "ontological difference between Being and beings" as it shows itself in the difference between being as substantive and as verb, idea and thing, essence and existence, and so on, in the difference, forgotten by metaphysics, that reduces multiplicities to difference, then another language is necessary. If multiplicity can only be thought through language (by language), then to speak of multiplicity is no longer to speak in one way, to speak clearly and distinctly, nor in only two ways, with forked tongues, 1/0, merely antinomies or paradoxes, per se or *per accidens.* Multiplicity demands the becoming multiple of language, and of languages.

The problem of multiplicity then shows itself as that which precisely does not just mean "multiplicity as multiplicity" (*polla he polla*), not simply "multiplicity as multiple" or "the multiplicity of multiplicities." The becoming multiple of multiplicity means that the questioning of multiplicity's identity, which brings identity out of itself, implies non-identity, difference, must be put into question—this is the becoming multiple of identity. And the question of the difference through which identity becomes self-grounding in seeking another ground must be put into question—this is the becoming multiple of difference. Now, the question of the multiplicity of identity, difference, and multiplicity must itself become multiple.

The becoming multiple of multiplicity then implies a multiplicity of strategies, processes, actions (verbs—but not just) of thinking, reading, writing, speaking, eating, sleeping, sweating, and so on multiply. If philosophy is thinking, then it is no longer merely thinking a thought, or its negation, or both, or neither; rather, philosophy is thinking thoughts. Yet philosophy, if it is to think multiply, can no longer just think—for it must also read, write, speak, eat, sleep, sweat, and so on. Will the becoming multiple of thought, however, not find yet another limit? Fall into the logics of multi-*pli*-city, that is, fold along the lines of identity and/or difference? Would the brain not have to call on the ears, throat, fingertips, thigh, the spleen, ass, pineal gland, and so on in order to approach multiplicity—as Nietzsche writes: "in the theme of the body, an horrific *multiplicity* shows itself"?[19] What could the becoming multiple of metaphysics do to the philosophical body and the body of philosophy, to the horror that shows itself in the body, the body that, multiplied, is no-body at all? And to the philosophy that is not just a question of the body?

Here, the question of multiplicity, insofar as it remains inside/outside metaphysics, prepares, makes ready, for yet another question of multiplicity, one that is not simply multiple and/or non-multiple: If to "many" there is no plural, then what could it mean to multiply many? To multiply it to the point not simply of its becoming multiple, but where multiplicity itself breaks down? To pose the questions, problems, answers, solutions, for the paradoxes, ambiguities, homologies, homographs, metaphors, analogies, for the discomforts, queasiness, and pains, the heated laughter and the dangerous speeds, of a many that is far more "manys?"

From Interpretation to Improvisation

If traditional systems and structures are unable to deal with the problems of becoming multiple, with a multiplicity that is not just a philosophical form or matter, not just a question of identity or difference or multiplicity, then how is it possible to speak, write, think, and so on multiply? And how is it possible to even prepare for manys?

First, the becoming multiple of interpretation as the interpretation of multiplicity: that is, a reading of the history of philosophy of multiplicity, a re-reading of that which has been read, in order to show "that" the history of philosophy is multiple, that it is far more histories of philosophies. Here interpretation is no longer the task of identifying the truth of the text; rather, it is the irritation of reinterpretation, a rubbing of the metaphysical text, a rasping of its skin, beyond the point of pleasure. Reading then, no longer within the logic of passivity/activity, but as the explication of what it means to be read, or rather, to be red: becoming red then, but not as a sign of embarrassment (unless it is an embarrassment of riches), shame at the body of the text, humiliation (or mort-ification) before a secret concealed (or revealed, or both)—rather, as the red of blood. Reading as bleeding, the application of leeches, the fattening of ticks, parasitic, vampiral: the semantics of reading, that is, the becoming multiple of meaning without reference (but not just without return, reserve) to one determinate meaning—for blood is never just a question of meaning, and language is not satisfied with mere expression. Interpretation has been bloodied: it is no longer the gathering nor the explosive dissemination (splatter-interpretation) of meanings (however multiple); rather, words cut, syllables violate, are repulsive, bring on nausea, and grammars soothe, syntax seduces. Reading, therefore, is not just a question of black on white, of the materiality of writing, nor of its ideality, of the connections between words and things. In other words, if the irritation of the philosophical text scratches at flesh in order to demonstrate that philosophy is multiple, it is because interpretation qua multiplicity chips away at bone in order to read splinters.

Yet interpretation (and here, another warning) remains strapped to western metaphysics despite all centering, re-centering, de-centering of origin; despite all refusal of the safety of the interpreted text, the forsaking, losing, forgetting, of the *ur*-text; despite claims that the origin has always already been for-saken (a forsaking that is prior, temporally or essentially, as well as a warning, and *vor*- and teleological); despite a destruction of ground or *archē* of interpretation, the referent, thing, or an immanent critique that leaves other (traditional) interpretations intact as possibilities; despite attempts to bring metaphysics to its limit or logical conclusion (since it has already finished, where it began); and despite methodologies that seek to allow the weight of one kind of interpretation to follow its course, its own trajectory, to work, to elicit its "ownmost" truth in order to demonstrate that other kinds are possible. The quid pro quo, however, by which a single interpretation is elevated to the level of truth, is not the end of negotiations; it is the beginning of war, a hematic war of interpretations, of meanings, of readings—yet a war that is not between two opponents, but among many—for "the battle-field of these endless controversies is called metaphysics," and interpretation is always metaphysical.[20]

Interpretation then, as preparation, making-ready (inter-*prêt*-ation), but not as rote repetition, not as practice, the boring re-circulation of canonical readings, the simple gathering of provisions, skills, facts, figures, forms, and so on, not as merely education, maturation, sophistication, certification, legitimation, normalization; nor as the inter-, the mediation between text and reader, object and subject, things (in themselves) and us—for the interpreter knows that translation, for example, breaks down at the point where it attempts to reproduce a word's multiplicity. Indeed, interpretation means that the multiplicities of languages (not just connections, interconnections, disconnections, and not just within language, a language, or between languages) are sacrificed in the identary-differential exigencies of translation.[21] Preparations then, not made in the name of a more refined form or method, not under the sign of the newest interpretation, the latest model, nor for the sake of some quest for the source, some search for a presumed lost origin, some expedition to a beginning or first principle, return to some primal ground, nor simply to satisfy a "will to nostalgia" for the things in themselves, or a fantasy of thinking their essential truth—but preparations for a forgetting: the remembering of identity and difference, quality and quantity, of totality, of one, of metaphysics, and of the many as many, *polla he polla,* precisely in order to forget it. In other words, remembering that the a priori is far more posited a posteriori, after presupposing the logic of identity and difference whereby metaphysics asserts its power (or its limit and lack of power) to know the truth, origin, ground, and essence of things in themselves. Forgetting then is for getting ready for multiplicity, for letting it run, a letting loose or opening up of multiplicity. Yet the becoming multiple of memory, of mimetic relations, is neither limited to remembering and/or forgetting, nor to the borrowing of that which lends itself to interpretation, that which pays; and interpretation multiplied is not just the becoming multiple of interpretations—for it is not just a question of meanings or readings. Rather, interpretation is the stretching of a metaphysics on the verge of becoming multiple, as the tightening of philosophemes, of metaphysical multiplicities, to the point where they too becoming multiple, where they multiply their multiplicity, shows that philosophy is no philosophy at all—for it is philosophies.

Yet in what does this multiplicity consist? If philosophy is multiple, then what does multiplicity mean if not form or matter, quality or quantity, identities or differences? How can philosophy think multiplicity if it remains subject to the forms of question and answer, problem and solution, text and interpretation, and so on?

Indeed, the multiplicity of philosophy demands a change of ways. The meanings of multiplicities demand a shift in means: a way of doing philosophy, or rather ways, possibilities for thought, speech, writing, and so on that are no longer within the confines of metaphysical language (its words, parts of speech, ideas, subjects, objects, etc.), and that function not only according to the "science" of semantics, nor solely against them (e.g., false etymologies, slang, puns, harmonic interconnections, etc.); not simply diachronic or synchronic, consonant or dissonant, tonal or atonal, legitimate or illegitimate—rather, the instigation of a rash of polyphonies within a given language, but not just within one language—for the demand is for polylinguistic, hearing, writing, thinking, speaking, in many tongues. Thus, the questions: What if philosophy acted in many ways (thought, read, wrote, spoke, heard, etc.), with many faculties (sound, touch, taste, sight, smell, etc.), and synesthetically wrote with its tongue, thought with its nose, heard by feeling the voice, tasted the blood as a logic is carved out, saw a concept in neither light nor dark, black nor white, and not just in colors? What if philosophy took multiplicity as multiple seriously—and not just?

The decomposition of the language of philosophy is the composting of metaphysics: a loosening-up of "nots" that have become "needs" (*Not*-s), by listening to notes, the tones of notes, the one tone, the tone's own (but not just), the tone that has not yet been noted, the tonnage that has not yet been weighed, nor its age yet *betoned* in *beton,* written or noticed, the no that turns on, the on that says no, oh no! In other words, what is philosophy if not the hearing of that which can also be heard? How can it instigate the landslide of signifiers, cause a catastrophe for thought? For is this disaster of signifiers not always already underway? Is philosophy not precisely an expression of the need to stem the flow of language by imposing difference (and/or identity), by distinguishing legitimate and illegitimate? The making audible of that which tickles in what is whispered: not by merely turning up the volume, nor through a more rigorous technology of sound reproduction, and not simply as the parlamblings of the *figura etymologica,* or the superficial mask of *Sprachmagi.* And here touch also becomes more susceptible to stimulation, the skin taut, in order to wonder: Is teaching philosophy not the making of the taught? And is writing not a tightening of the text, a wrapping in trappings? If philosophical language then, in determining its meaning, in fixing a semantic field, drags other meanings along with it, carries the seeds of its own discontent, its own undoing, if the body of the text is in continual decomposition, then what would happen if it was taken seriously, was thought, heard, smelled, and so on, as multiple? And not just—for how is the question of multiplicity not only a question for philosophical anthropology, not just an issue "for us" (whoever or whatever we may be), not just a problem of the body or the mind, physiology or psychology?

The decomposition of philosophy as language is no longer just a question of textuality, of linguistic objects, of a determinant *eidos* (e.g., genus, species); nor simply non-linguistically, as that which eludes, that is, transcends, the word; nor of simply increasing the number of languages; nor of merely deconstructing genre. Metaphysics has already both remembered and forgotten multiplicity. In order to think multiply, however, philosophy must leave the metaphysical body of work, tightly bound, strapped together, a togetherness or a to-gather-ness, the action (verb) that operates to get truth (and if truth is a women, then metaphysics wants to-get-her, that is, multiplicity as identity and difference). And the questions multiply themselves: Is it possible to hear the cacophony of thoughts, if it is not only a question of listening? How is philosophy as text multiple, not merely text, and not simply text or non-text? How is it possible to think the multiplicity of this multiplicity?

Regardless, from interpretation, from the question of how multiplicity is thought, of how it plays itself out in a particular text in multiple irritations, configurations, consternations, from the injection of dissonance in metaphysical harmonics, hinting at what could be thought in what is thought, a becoming multiple of interpretations emerges—for this multiplicity works, produces. Interpretations of things as themselves or not themselves (as others) can be exchanged, distributed and redistributed, consumed, digested and expelled. Yet the becoming multiple of interpretation engenders its other, refers to that which it is not, namely, anti-interpretation, the back-lash that screams "Back to the things themselves," or the scientism (or technological fetishism) that insists on facts, figures, and formulas, or proclaiming the necessity of that which remains uninterpretable, beyond interpretation, re-inscribes transcendence and immanence, that is, once again the logic of identity and difference.

Now, improvisation neither fights for or against interpretation, for/against an interpretation of multiplicity or the multiplicity of interpretation—for it is neither an action performed on a concept nor a concept of action, neither impressionism nor expressionism, not just a question of the ear, nor of a way of speaking or a being spoken, neither a gathering nor a dissemination, contraction nor expansion, not merely a practical deployment or utilization of that which is at hand, not simply a means of introducing chaos into order, chance into necessity (or possibility, or vice versa), not leading back to a primary meaning, nor sustained in a totality or frame. Rather, the interpretation of thoughts and things comes out of improvisation (*ek tōn autoschediasmatōn*).[22] And even further, thoughts and things themselves can be made only by improvising—for making itself (*poiein*), the creation of concepts, the production of ideas, the invention of systems, as well as the shaping of stone or the growth of flowers, is always improvisational.

No longer simply many then, manifold, multiple, multiplicities, or many as such, philosophical improvisation acts out manys. Of course, improvisations are susceptible to interpretation and reinterpretation—but they can be eaten raw, sinuous, and heavy with blood, so that philosophy can hear in the languages of manys, listen to the instruments of surgery or war, the gaspings for words and gropings for air, can smell the acidity of a printed letter as it brushes against reason and can suffer the seductions of philosophical surfaces. As Nietzsche knew, the happiest (like Homer) are also the most susceptible to suffering (while running the danger of not being able to solve foolish little riddles because they have become too refined in pain), and the improviser is one of two who are happy.[23] Yet even here the question of improvisation does not yet become a question as such. And this is perhaps because the artists tell us that "in order to improvise we must stop thinking." But we say: "Thinking means improvising." To this end then, improvisations are ways of doing philosophy for which there is, strictly speaking, despite all preparation, no preparation possible: impromptu writings, extemporaneous readings, makeshift thoughts, speaking ad hoc, and neither with nor without warning, neither with nor without control—or rather, philosophy improvises manys, and not just.[24]

First, however, before improvisation, if metaphysics has thought *polla* from its inception, then *polla* interpreted, decomposed, shows itself at the inception (and logical conclusion) of metaphysics. Thus, after the simple reductions of form and matter, speaking and spoken, writing and speech, after many, multiplicity, multiplicities, at the source, as condition of the possibility of reduction, as delimitable, subsumable, and so on, after the usual transcendental ruses, the ploys, clichés or feigns (or even truths) of origin (temporal or essential), after the negation of an *archē* (and an *an-archē*), and the negation of negation—after all this, a return to the question: How does metaphysics think many objects, their identities as many, as well as their differences? Now, or still, before going multiple—one, single, solitary, and perhaps terribly ironic question, the question of the interpretation of *polla*.

1

Interrogation of Metaphysics

> But what, therefore, am I? A thing that thinks. What is a thing that thinks? That is, a thing that doubts, that conceives, that affirms, that denies, that wants, that does not want, that also imagines, and that senses.
>
> —*Descartes*[1]

I *am, I exist* (*ego sum, ego existo*): a single, clear, and distinct proposition that is constantly and "necessarily true, every time that I pronounce it, or that I conceive of it in my mind." Yet I cannot stop here; the danger of infinite regress is too great, the threat "that there is nothing certain in the world."[2] I must continue: What is this "I" that "is," that "exists"? Not a human—for what is a "human"? If I answer with Aristotle's "rational animal," then I am merely embarrassed—for I must investigate "what is an animal, and what is rational, and thus from one single question, we fall imperceptibly in an infinity of others more difficult and embarrassing."[3] My cogito must be self-grounding, foundational, pronounced in such a way that it avoids infinite regression (or rather, embarrassment), that it needs no further explanation; but at the moment of its articulation, do I not reach beyond myself and find my ground in another?

I am, I exist (*je suis, j'existe*): I should be at the end of questioning, the skeptical project should have found the one indubitable point from which the world, through analytic geometry, can be reconstructed, restructured—I should be the "master and possessor of nature"! Yet I must continue, I must continue until this definition "needs no further explanation."[4] I must solve the problem of meaning itself, stop the infinite regress of definitions, find the ground of subjectivity: the "I" is a "thinking thing," and the "thinking thing" is a "thing that doubts, conceives, affirms, denies, wants, doesn't want, imagines and senses"—but here a "thinking thing" is a thing that is multiple. The "I," the fixed point of my Archimedian meditation, the cogito's truth, its independence, self-grounding status for the being and thinking of subjectivity, is dependent upon another, upon others. As a "thinking thing," I am clear and distinct because I am grounded on a multiplicity that is clear and distinct. Now, if I am certain of anything at all, I am certain that I am multiple.

Thus, I need not go on. I have found what calls for no further definition, namely, that clearly and distinctly, I am multiple. And this multiplicity is multiplying: "I am a thinking thing," that is, something "that doubts, that affirms, that denies, that knows few things, that ignores many, that loves, that hates, that wants, that does not want, that imagines also, and that senses."[5] Even further, as Nietzsche writes:

> Let us be more careful than Descartes, who remains hanging in the snare of words. *Cogito* is admittedly only *one* word: but it means something multiple: something is multiple and we crudely grab after it, truly believing, that it is *one*. In that famous *cogito* hides (1) it thinks (2) and I believe that I am that there which thinks, (3) but also (supposing that this second point remains suspended as a belief) that first "it thinks" also contains yet another belief: namely, that "thinking" is an action for which a subject (at least an "it") must be thought—and further, the *ergo sum* means nothing![6]

From *Meditation* to *Meditation* then, from Latin to French, I exchange my determinations—yet I remain something multiple. And this multiplicity, this non-defined definition, remains the unstable ground of my subjectivity. Yet how is it possible that I posit the *cogito* on multiplicity? Can I only determine myself, become a thinking thing, by denying myself? By refusing my own multiplicity? How is it possible that I am multiple? And what do I mean by the multiplicity that I am?

Histories of Philosophy

> The multiplicity of rules often derives from the ignorance of the master, and that which one can reduce to a single general precept is less clear when we divide it in a great number of particular precepts.
>
> —*Descartes*[7]

Now, the multiplication of questions, of multiplicities in the history of philosophy, a history that serves to incite histories, stories of philosophy, yet one that must remain provisional (not yet even multiple) insofar as it remains true to the familiar logic of identity and difference, settles for immanent critique and the boredom of metaphysics, precisely in order to trace its limits and horizons. A history of multiplicity in philosophy and not yet the multiplicity of the history of philosophy, a questioning of the philosophical tradition that is a questing or searching for multiplicity that is denied—often simply denied, as when Leibniz insists that "reason wants us to avoid multiplicity in hypotheses or principles, like when the simplest system is always preferred in astronomy."[8] Here multiplicity is denied precisely insofar as it is acknowledged, affirmed, employed, insofar as it is insisted upon as that which it is not. If multiplicity must be thought in relation to the history of philosophy, then it is not only because it has been thought as a non-thought, because it has not been thought at all, but also because of the ways in which it has been thought, ways that remain, always remain, possibilities for multiplicity (however metaphysical). How then could the thinking of multiplicity, the placing or re-placing, the re-positioning of the question, the possibility of the questioning of multiplicity, through the becoming multiple of the question itself, think multiplicity? What could this becoming do to metaphysics—and to the becoming itself?

In fact, the multiplicity of the history of philosophy is particular to the philosophical work. The becoming multiple of a philosophical project is the multiplication of its relations with a multiplicity of other projects, and thereby, a multiplication of the history of philosophy itself—for as an object of inquiry, multiplicity can only be approached through a multiplicity of readings (of multiplicity—but not just). Indeed, the becoming multiple of the history of philosophy remains a metaphysical project: multiplying the multiplication of the multiplicity of multiplicity for philosophy, that is, for philosophies. Thus, the question: How could the multiplication of the history of philosophy, and the multiplication of the historical questions of philosophy itself (e.g., truth, being, thinking, unity, subjectivity, language, history, power), shift philosophy's self-understanding?

The history of philosophy then, as that which is itself already multiple: no longer the history of the thought of just one idea, of just one question or subject in different forms of thought, for example, "the history of the discovery of *thoughts* about the absolute, that is its object."[9] Philosophy's subject is not truth, it is not the history of the forgetting (i.e., remembering) of the "Being of beings," nor the search for the origin (*archē*); its objective is not merely the exposition or deduction of the a priori condition of the possibility of knowledge, experience, and so on—for "philosophy" has no single name. How then could the becoming multiple of philosophy transform what can be thought and what can be named?

Yet first, before this question, a history of philosophy that is the history of multiplicity in and for philosophy in preparation for histories of philosophies, not in the hope of presenting new philological research, rather, read as a place, or places, where the questions of multiplicity can be asked—and Aristotle, Kant, and Hegel (but also Parmenides, Heraclitus, Plato, Plotinus, Spinoza, Leibniz, Nietzsche, Heidegger, Derrida) as thinkers, writers, speakers, names, personae, signs, labels, markers, not only for the multiplicity of answers, but also for the posing of questions. Reading the history of metaphysics then, first in order to find that which has been refused, that is, the critical role that multiplicity has played for thought, for the history of western philosophy as metaphysics, in order to understand how its philosophemes have seamlessly solved the questions of multiplicity. The questions of multiplicity then, of a terminology: What has multiplicity meant for metaphysics? How has the language of multiplicity, multiplication, multiplying, and so on become multiple?

Before the act of the becoming multiple of multiplicity, and of philosophy—and before manys: delimiting the specific solutions, within the history of philosophy, to the problems of multiplicity; demonstrating how they function (not dysfunction), *that* and *how* they *do* work, perform perfectly, and simultaneously immunize themselves to critique. A preliminary acquiescence to the method of working inside/outside the tradition in order to prepare for a *working of* (no longer inside nor outside) the tradition, for a becoming multiple of philosophy (that is neither a making multiple, i.e., multiplication; nor a letting be multiple, showing itself as multiple), in order to make trouble for metaphysics. Thus, the interrogation of metaphysics, the application of a polygraph to its skin—but not only to test when it tells the truth (when it lies); rather, to read the multiple senses that write its history, the sensations that are interpreted, reduced, that are read by the machine, in order to yield truth or reveal the lie (in all its paradoxes).

First, however, Aristotle's metaphysics of the *archē*-many, then Kant's critique of the manifold.

The Substance of Many

> Worse could not really happen to a person or to a whole country, as not even to exist.
>
> —*E. T. A. Hoffmann*[10]

From the beginning, Aristotle's *Metaphysics* constitutes a massive attack on Plato and the Pythagoreans: insofar as they fail to think the many, they cannot explain how everything that "has being and is one," is also many. Only by joining many to the universal predicates of being and unity can Aristotle take account of the substance (*ousia*) of things, and thereby avoid the split between Here and There, between Platonism and Neo-Platonism, as well as the aporia of idealism that opens a gap between the thing in itself and knowledge, and the difference of ontological difference between "Being and beings" (Heidegger).[11]

For Aristotle, being (and oneness) is always the being of beings. And as the primary sense of being, substance can neither be simply one (for then all substances would be one, without difference) nor many (for then no substance would be substance, i.e., one). The many of substance, however, is precisely not the category of many; rather, it is that to which the many beings must relate in order for them to be many—and one. Indeed, if beings simply have being and are one, then nothing has being and is one—only the many can prevent the fall back into Platonism.

A series of questions shows itself. On the one hand, how can substances be substantial only with reference or in relation to substance? From the side of the one, how can being be spoken in many ways? On the other hand, how is it possible for beings to be many and not merely one? In other words, from the side of the many, how can substances be substances and not simply substance?

Indeed, for Aristotle, from the very beginning, the question of being qua being (*to on he on*) is tied to the question of the one: "being and one are the same and are one thing [of one nature] in the sense that they are implied in one another as principle and cause."[12] And "there are many senses in which a thing may be said to 'be,' but all that 'is' is related to one central point, one definite kind of thing, and is not said to 'be' by a mere ambiguity."[13] Indeed, of the many senses of being, substance is primary.[14] But what is substance? For substance is also spoken in many ways (beingness, essence, universal, form, genetic, substratum, cause, or sensible perishable, sensible eternal, non-sensible). And even if primarily substance means beingness, that is, what a thing is by its nature, then what is primacy (*prōtos*)? For primacy is also spoken in many ways (in definition, order of knowledge, time).[15] And finally, what is this many (*polla*) through which being, substance, primacy or *archē* are all spoken? What is the being and substance of the many?

In the *Metaphysics,* all of these questions remain unexamined—for being qua being (and one, substance, etc.) is not really Aristotle's question; it is his answer, the answer to the question of the many, the answer to the critique he launches against Plato and the Pythagoreans, namely, that they do not ask the question "How relative terms are many and not one,"[16] that they use "many" without asking what it is, without understanding what it means, how it is spoken, what causes it, what we mean when we say "many." And the aporia of the *Metaphysics* is not how being as substance is one, but far more how being as substance can be many. As Aristotle writes: "the difficulty arising from the facts about substances is rather this, how there are actually many substances and not one."[17] Or again: "the question evidently is, how being, in the sense of 'the *substances,*' is many."[18] The problem of the *Metaphysics* then is not how can there be one if there is many (the search is not for a single foundation or ground, not for the one divine substance, first cause, prime mover, not for the unity of individuals, or *pros hen* equivocals); it is: How can there be many if there is one? And how must substance be thought in order to allow for substances? How can the many be thought as many?

Indeed, if the question is posed categorically, in one way ("What is the many?"), then Aristotle answers that many is the opposite of one, the contrary of unity:

> evidently "many" will have meanings opposite to those of "one": some things are many because they are not continuous, others because their matter—either the proximate [primary] matter or the ultimate—is [formally] divisible in kind, others because the definitions which state their essence are more than one.[19]

First then, the question: What is the "one"? The word is used in two ways: accidental (*sumbebēkos*) or by its own nature (*kath' hauto*). The accidental "one" is either accidentally attributed to one substance, for example, cultured man, or conditions the states or affections of one substance, for example, cultured and just man—here "one" is possible only as produced, possessed, affected by, or related to, some heterogeneous other. The "one" by its own nature is sixfold: continuous (*synechē*), in its substratum (*hypokeimenon*), generic (*genos*), by definition (*logos*), in its substance (*ousia*), eidetic (*eidos*). As continuous, "one" means indivisible with respect to time (*adiairetos de kata chronon*), that whose motion (*kinēsis*) is simultaneous, a continuum—the more natural, essential, and whole the continuity (the less artificial, merely contactual, segmental), the more true the continuity and oneness; for example, the straight line is more truly one than the bent, the shin or thigh more than the leg, the piece of wood more than those bound in a faggot. In its substratum "one" means indistinguishable with respect to primary or final substrate; for example, wine is within itself primarily uniform, all liquids are finally uniform. As generic, "one" means "of a single proximate or final genus" (as substrate despite *differentiae*); for example, horse, human and dog are proximately animals, isosceles and equilateral triangles are finally triangles, one figure (*hen schema*). By definition, "one" means semantically or conceptually (*noesis*) indistinguishable with respect to the meaning that expresses its essence (although the definition itself may be distinguishable into genus and differentiae); it means identical with respect to *logos:* increase and decrease are, in their essence, semantically indistinguishable, have one meaning (despite their distinguished senses); all humans qua human are essentially indistinguishable, one with their *logos* (rational animal); and even humans and oxen are univocal insofar as they are both animals (*zōon*).[20] With respect to substance, "one" means primarily whatness or beingness, that is, continually, formally, or by definition (not genetic, as in that which is one substratum—hence, the difference between substratum and substance), capable of being counted as one, as one being. As eidetic, "one" means quantitatively continuous (continuity alone is insufficient): for example, a shoe, as a whole form, type, kind, is one; a circle, of all lines, is a whole and complete one. Thus, one has many meanings, many ways in which it can be spoken, used (in praxis), defined, many meanings divided into two categories (accidental, by its own nature), categories that are themselves divided: a hierarchy of meanings—many ones, but all one. Yet in all the ways in which the term "one" is spoken, the ways in which it is used, the term is itself employed: the demonstration presupposes the very term it is supposed to explain (e.g., the one is "one" by accident, the one is "one" substance, the one is "one" whole, etc.). Here the one is merely tautological, a hermeneutic circle of ones, a phenomenological empiricism of "one." Praxis must lead out of itself, out of its viciousness to a "one" that does not assume that which it sets out to describe, to the being of the "one"—for this is a sign that the essence, the definition, the substance of one, is not attained in the category or word "one."

If the two genera (and many species) of ones are all one, however, then it is because they are, in their being, essentially, one: "the [being] of what is one is to be some kind of beginning (*archē*) of number."[21] Here the understanding of "one" as *archē* is dependent upon the sixfold meaning of *archē;*[22] but common to all meanings of *archē* are the threefold primary ways of "beginning," namely, the first from which a thing either "is or comes to be or is known."[23] And as first, the "that from which," of being, becoming and knowledge, *archē* means cause, that is, cause of being (*aiti-on*), not an abstract concept, but that which is responsible for that which a being actually is: immanent material or the inner-stuff-beginning-being (*en-up-arch-ontos*), formal (*eidos*), efficient or moving or change-producing (*metabolās*), final (*telos*).[24] Yet as a first, one beginning, one *archē,* the understanding of *archē*'s many meanings is dependent upon the understanding of "one," upon the *pros hen.* Thus, not just a circle of meanings within the definitions of the "one," within one chapter of the *Metaphysics,* but a circulation of meanings in language between chapters and books, between definitions or ways of speaking (techno-logoi, technologies), of interpretations, *logos*-circles or logo-centrisms; and the question, once again, or rather, still, of origin, beginning, cause, of *archē,* and of the one—or rather, of the many.

To return to the *archē* of number then—for Aristotle, the "one" is the beginning of knowledge, the "that from which," cause, origin, of knowledge; it is the first measure as the mark by which a thing and its genus can be made intelligible, brought out of darkness: "the one, then, is the beginning of the knowable regarding each class."[25] Here knowledge begins with the "one" by which natural philosophy numbers, by which physics counts and science quantifies. Yet even as the origin of knowledge, the one is not always identical: as the formally indivisible unit of measure in each class, it is the quarter-tone in music, the vowel or consonant in linguistics, weight or movement in physics. Nevertheless, scientific knowledge is originally quantification of things, a geometry of the one as it shows itself in nature: from the unit (*monas*) as wholly indivisible in dimension (*a-diaireton*) and without position (*a-theton*) to the point (*stigma*) as indivisible in dimension and positioned, the line as divisible in one dimension and positioned, the plane as divisible in two dimensions and positioned, the body as divisible in three dimensions and positioned.[26] Here physics brands a mark of origin on its property (*stigmata stizein tina*), on the runaway slave of knowledge as it appears in the science of being qua being: things must be measured by some sort of divisible unit—be it triangles (cf. *Timaeus*), atoms, or quarks—that has its origin in an indivisible unit. The indivisible unit, however, is not the one; "although everywhere the one, as quantity or kind, is indivisible."[27]

The meaning of "one" then is not "some kind of number," but "some kind of *starting-point* [*or principle*] *of number.*" The beginning of number lies in that which itself, strictly speaking, is no number at all, non-numerical, a-rithmatic, that which has not yet been counted or quantified—"one" is not "one, two, three, and so on"—for "one" is uncountable, unquantifiable. The one does not compute; and if number is a plurality of measures, then the one is no number. And not only with respect to quantification—for the beginning of number lies before qualification as well, prior to the divisibility of beings according to kind, type, form, earlier than the fixing of essence, the limitation of species and frontier of genus—for "one" is that in-divisibility, that negation, privation, or lack of the power of divisibility. Thus, the *archē*-one precedes the numerical one (quantification) and the essential one (qualification); and as that which it is by its own nature, as *archē*-indivisibility, it precedes the abstract numbers and eidetic figures of the sciences of specific beings.[28]

Neither a predicate among predicates, nor a type of substance: "one" is before (but not spatio-temporally) the subject/predicate split, prior to the ontological difference between things and ideas; thereby, it makes number, counting, quantification, formal definition, generic categorization, and subject/object predication, possible—for in its being, the one is (like being) a "universal predicate," that which permits heterogeneous, indivisible elements (A:B::C:D) to come into (homogeneous) contact, to be in an analogous relation.[29] And the universality of "one" lies in its status as an analogical equivocal—for the "one" is the way in which (*methodos*) things are said "to be one" in many ways (*pollachōs legomena*); it is the cause or principle of *pros hen* equivocals, and a *pros hen* equivocal itself.[30] The *archē*-one is a referential-one and the principle of reference itself. Neither the substance of things nor merely ideal, the "one" indicates the analogical equivocity of beings—for the "one" is a sign of the oneness of a thing, just as things are one only with reference to (*pros*) the "one." Indeed, the substance of a thing is no longer just the (Platonic) universal: in fact, since these universals are derived from essences, individuals, particulars—strictly speaking, they do not exist.[31] If beings can be one, therefore, it is because they are one with being, because "to be" means "to be one." The one is the semiotic form through which beings, as essentially indivisible ones, are equivocal; it is the primary instance (the *archē*-one) to which secondary instances (the many ones), that is, words or concepts signifying things themselves, are ones at all—for equivocation itself depends upon the *archē*-one. Things are one with reference to one one, but one is always spoken in many ways.[32]

And being then, like the "one," is spoken in many ways, but all with reference to one principle—for as "the to be" (*to ti einai,* nominalized verb, gerund) of a being, as that which belongs to (*dativus possessivus*) every being, entity or thing, it is neither the universal essence that stands in Platonic contradiction to particular beings, radically different from individual things, nor a conceptual-logical universal or empty word, nor a genus (that is, indifferent—for a genus is, by definition, "difference free"). As Aristotle insists:

> But it is not possible that either unity or being should be a single genus of beings; for the differentiae of any genus must each of them both have being and be one, but it is not possible for the genus taken apart from its species (any more than for the species of the genus) to be predicated of its proper differentia; so that if unity or being is a genus, no differentia will either have being or be one.[33]

If being were a genus, then (like other genera) there would be no difference between being as genus and as species. Being is not a genus because genera must always already "have being and be one." What then are the universals of metaphysics? "These would turn out to be being and one, for if these might most of all be supposed to contain all things that are, and to be most like principles because they are first by nature; for if they perish all other things also are destroyed with them; for everything is and is one."[34] For Aristotle, being and one are even wider, even more universal than Platonic universals—they are equivocal universals.

Universal being, however, that which the science of being qua being investigates in order to find its principles and causes, is not to be found outside the universe; on the contrary, it is to be sought in individuals, in their substance (beingness), in that which simultaneously makes the individual in-divisible and in-dependent, separable—if being is separable from beings, then it is because it is already in (not spatially, but essentially) beings: being is always the being of beings. Being is bound up with, strapped in-to, the individual act of being, an act that is in the being (be-*in*-g). Here beingness or substance is separable from a thing—but only in thought. Like categories, signs cut off from their referents, concepts abstracted from experience, ideas placed over and against the real, images of that which has been lost—like all this, pure being can be thought as such, but only because it is in beings and not in another world, transcendent, merely independent, without qualification. And beingness or substance, as the primary instance of being, is always the substance of beings. Thus, "human" and "human being" and "one human being" can be the "same" (nothing added/nothing subtracted) because substance is distinguishable but not distinct from being and unity, because "one" is the "one" of being, in being, (b-*ein*-g)—"for being and one are the most universal of all predicates."[35]

As the study of beings qua beings then, metaphysics is the study of the "to be" of beings, of "the cause of the 'to be,' "[36] the cause of being (here nominalized infinitive), of what it means for a being to be, and what it means for being to be in beings. Indeed, for Thomas, as the study of being qua being, metaphysics means that *ens est primum notum,* and being has the transcendent character of *unum, verum, bonum* (to which Kant will show himself tied). And the order of being, for Aristotle as well (I would argue against Owens), is prior to the order of knowledge, and certainly prior to the specific sciences: ontology ("is or is not, without further qualification") precedes epistemology and being itself lies before any kind of beings (be they mortal or immortal, separate or not). In this way being is knowable through an existential sort of pre-knowledge.[37] Here metaphysics functions via definition, by ascertaining substance (primary form/definition of a species or genus), the kind of being, an individual's substance, that is, the beingness that can fall under the genus, within a species: for example, by dialectically asking for the being/not-being of a predicate if a human being is two-footed or is not two-footed. And metaphysics moves from the existence of beings to their causes of existence to substance; but a substance that cannot be proved, only defined—for the end of theoretical knowledge, and philosophy, is truth (not action, i.e., the end of practical knowledge).[38]

Regardless, the metaphysical question of the one of being remains the question of substance: one is always one being, one substance.[39] If beings as beings can all be, then it is because they are all equivocally substance (i.e., substance is the equivocal-one, the *pros hen* of heterogeneous substances), through the homogeneity that allows beings to be different (although not merely next to one another, i.e., indifferent) while being connected: substance is the community of differences—for "the causes and the principles of different things are in a sense different, but in a sense, if one speaks universally and analogically, they are the same for all."[40] Substance—neither simple, material substratum as the natural philosophers insisted, nor simply ideal (Platonism)—is that which (without predication, quantification/qualification) underlies all predication; it is that to which all categories are referred, that which allows substances to be and to be separable (ones).

Yet if beings as beings can be one, individuals, then it is also because in being, they are simultaneously mortal and divine. As mortal, beings have their cause in the combination of form and matter (and proximate efficient and final cause); as divine, their (ultimate efficient and final) cause is separable from them, the unmoved mover. Divine being is, strictly speaking, separable from beings because it is an individual, a particular kind of being, but it is one with beings because it is itself a being; and it is one with substances although it is different from substances insofar as it is another kind of substance, namely, it is first substance: unmoved (yet the cause of motion), separable, eternal, actual, and one in definition and number.[41] Each of these predicates, however, is found in substances other than the divine: objects of appetite are unmoved although they are the cause of motion; beings as the combination of form and matter are separable substances; mathematical objects are eternal; activities like seeing and knowing are actual.[42] Only the combination of predicates, therefore, makes this divine substance essentially different from other substances. With respect to the divine's being then, since being is not a genus, but a universal predicate, the divine is one with substances; with respect to its essence, the divine is one, that is, simply one, without parts and indivisible, the one (for there can be only one first) *archē* and cause.[43]

Yet divine substance is not merely divine-substance-itself, it is not merely separate, distinct, alone, isolated—for the divine is a substance, one of three kinds (perishable sensible, eternal sensible, immovable).[44] And as a substance, albeit of another form (*eidos*), essentially of a different species, divine substance is always the divine substance of substances, always in an ontological (equivocal) relation to substances, always in a desiring relation, a causal connection, to substances. Platonic participation or demiurgic creation has become Aristotelian imitation—but the relation between mortals and immortals remains intact. Indeed, for Aristotle, the divine-one cannot simply triumph over the many; it is not merely the totalizing indentification of individuals—as Hegel will later write of Schelling: "philosophy is not an identity system; that is unphilosophic."[45] And divine being is not the universal of beings, divine substance not the genus of substances, not the highest Form of Forms apart, a distinct *ens perfectissimum,* separate, different (and hence, unable to be the ultimate cause of movement/change) from the particular beings—a difference that results in the irresolvable aporia of two worlds, the unbridgable distance between Ideas and things. Hence, Aristotle must answer the hardest and most perplexing question of all: "whether unity and being, as the Pythagoreans and Plato said, are not attributes of something else but the substance of existing things."[46] For as substance, the divine has being and is one. Divine substance is divine precisely because it is in individuals; and it can be an individual itself, that is, divine substance, precisely because it is also substance, because simple, onefold, substance is only one type of substance (no longer merely universal or material).[47] Like being, substance and one, individual is an equivocal. In fact, the individuality of divine substance, the difference in quantity and quality, number and kind, is possible because all substance is and is one, substance of substances, of actual things, substances.

And these equivocal universals cannot lead back to other more universal universals—for they are substances themselves; for example, the beingness of good is one with the good, the beingness of reality with the real, of the beautiful with beauty, of unity with one (thus, infinite regress is avoided); and because every universal and individual has being and is one. What causes a thing to be what it is, is its substance, the cause(s) of beings. Yet the threat of infinite regress (physical, epistemological, political) drives Aristotle to posit the divine as a substance: "for how is there to be order unless there is something eternal and independent and permanent?"[48] In this way, theology, the search for the first principle, ground, *archē*, *archē*-logy, shows itself as the search for another kind of being, for a being that is substance in its primary instance, but a special kind of substance, that is, non-material, non-sensible, independent. If divine substance can stop the infinite regress of substances, of the causes of substances, of the *archē* of individuals, of the origin of the motion of things, then it is because it is essentially a substance, that is, a being. However, since being itself is neither a being nor a genus, ontology is the cause of theology, not in the sense of one of the four causes—for being is not the beginning or end of motion, not the form or the matter of things; it is their unity, all four insofar as they have being. And causality can be spoken in many ways only with reference to the substance and being of cause. Metaphysics, therefore, the study of being qua being, is only identical with theology for theologians. And as equivocal, being as substance must be spoken in many ways.

For Aristotle then, although Plato and Parmenides untied the knot of the "one," they could not answer the aporia of the many because their concept of one (and being, substance) was merely one-itself, being-itself, that is, was not already multiple, not *in* the particular individual things. The problem remains: "but if there *is* to be a being-itself and a unity-itself, there is much difficulty in seeing how there will be anything else besides these—I mean, how things will be more than one in number."[49] It is no wonder, then, that many (*polla*), like the one from which it is derived, is spoken in many ways.[50] As concept or category, it is opposite one—and like one, it is twofold: by accident and by its own nature. By virtue of its own nature, many is by virtue of another, by virtue of its opposition to the one—yet opposition (*anti-keimenos*) is also spoken in many ways: as contradiction (of attributes or constituents), contrariety, relative terms, privation/possession, the extremes of generation/dissolution. As contrary (being-in-opposition—not negation), many is either an attribute that cannot belong to ones without a contradiction or, if the one is an attribute of one thing, then it is the most extremely different attribute predicate or cause of generation/dissolution of the thing from its oneness. As privation of one, many is deprived, poor in unity: it is discontinuous, of divisible substrate or genera (i.e., no primary/first or ultimate/last matter), of no single definition, divisible substance, nonuniform, and without essence or beginning point—here many is opposed to one via its relation to possession of the attributes of the many (e.g., divisibility). Many as other, unlike and unequal is contrary to one as same, like and equal, contrary in number, form, matter, and/or definition. All contraries, however, like substances, presuppose one and being: "'other or the same' can therefore be predicated of everything with regard to everything else—but only if the things are one and are."[51] For Aristotle, the substance and being of the many must be sought elsewhere, prior to the predication of particular contraries.

For its part, the categorial many is dependent upon the one—for contrariety is a kind of difference (*diaphora*): in fact, it is the greatest difference between many and one (e.g., there is no way or bridge between genera, species are incomparable); and this difference is a complete limit. Since the limit is that which is most completely different, every class has one and only one contrary. Differential contrariety is based on identity: "but that which is different is different from some particular thing in some particular respect, so that there must be something identical whereby they differ. And this identical thing is genus or species."[52] Since one category cannot have more than one other, limit, contrariety, difference is always between two: "to put the matter generally, this is clear if contrariety is a difference, and if difference, and therefore also the complete difference, must be between two things."[53] In opposition, the one and the many are both negated/privated: "it cannot be the negation or privation of one of the two; for why of the great rather than of the small? It is, then, the privative negation of both."[54]

Yet between genera, species, definitions, substances, classes, there is, strictly speaking, no difference—for difference implies an intermediate term, a substratum, continuum, or fluidity, between the two categories that permit the difference to differ, for example, between the many and one as opposite (difference of privation, negation, contraries, correlates). The categorial many, insofar as it is not distinct or separate from substance, is many because the substance that becomes or is (or is known in science) is many, because it is "one" with one through difference, enabled through its opposition in the contrary one/many (e.g., if one and many are in relation to one another, then the few or the many must be more or less than each other). The many is predicated of divisible things, of that which has an absolute or relative excess (one is, thus, privation of plurality, of the numerical many). In this way the contrary predicates of substance (one/many) are displaced to all contraries via opposition (quantitative same/different, equal/unequal, or qualitative small/large, few/many, etc.): for example, water is a much (*polu*) but not many (*polla*), since many is always divisible into many ones, but much is indivisible; and much is opposed to few/little in quantity and many is to one in numbers (as measure to thing measured). In other words, quantity is the class (genus) of many (and one) understood as a number, and quality is the class of many (and few) understood as an attribute (absolutely or relatively excessive, deficient, etc.).[55]

The difference between contraries then, their intermediate, is the difference of the contraries themselves. On the one hand, the logic of identity is endemic to things: opposition is possible because of that which is common to different terms, identical or one for different categories. And that which mediates within a given genus is composed out of the contraries, out of the terms that are themselves first principles, self-identical, and then in relation to their other. The genus which mediates between species belongs to both. Aristotle writes: "for by genus I mean one identical thing which is predicated of both and is differentiated in no merely accidental way."[56] Species (specific) difference is a difference from something in something, of an otherness of the genus, "difference in the genus"—and it is this otherness that makes the genus itself other.

On the other hand, the definition of species (and causes of individual beings) is de-limitation of indivisibility according to a logic of difference. Things are only actually that which they are, insofar as they are determined through contrariety via complete difference, that is, that difference that closes off the species from others, determines the form and formal boundary, limit, frontier, horizon, between kinds. Between species or realms there is no movement, connection, exchange, complicity, or bridge, rather, a closure under the name of simple difference, the difference of the many from the one, the difference that is always between two. Like the difference between sign and referent in *pros hen* equivocals, between substance and the many ways in which it is said, between health and the healthy, between medical science and the knife—like all this, the many and the one, the difference of the difference that permits the predication of the many, that orders the ways in which many and one are spoken, and the many deferrals of definitions, an infinity of deferrals contained within, subsumed under, gathered into, difference—all this will determine the horizon of the discourse and philosophy of identity and difference to this day.

Yet what of the many itself, and the many substances? In other words, what of the many that is not a function of identity and/or difference? A many qua many? This many has no name. Certainly, analogies can always be drawn: being and unity could be predicated of the many, the substance of many things could be delimited, opposition could be imposed; the many qua many, however, would remain nameless—which is not to say that it does not exist, that it is nothing, or merely an empty word, that is, not a characteristic of beings and things. Rather, the unnamed remains opposed to metaphysics, and that which is spoken in many ways is many, not just one. As Aristotle writes: "and that which is neither good nor bad is opposed to both, but *unnamed*; for each of these has several meanings and the recipient subject is not one."[57] Yet this does not mean that between good and bad, just or unjust, one and many, there is no intermediate state; rather, the many is in one sense coupled with the one through an intermediate (substance), but in another sense not—although this many can always also be thought within the schema of opposition, within difference, the many qua many. The differential many then is not the substance of many—for it is named. And the many qua many remains an aporia. What then would it mean to think this many with Aristotle?

If substance is the substance of substances, if being is the being of independent and actual things, individual, particular, unified beings, then substance and being cannot only be one; on the contrary, Aristotle's critique of Plato and the Pythagoreans rests upon an understanding of substance and being as many (*polla*). In fact, the many is all over the *Metaphysics;* it marks the text, the thought and things, from the beginning, from the very way in which everything is said in "many" ways. No longer simply universal or material, the being and substance, the beingness of beings, are not only many in number, species or genus—for they are also many in kind (*eidos*), the many of equivocals, many equivocals, many kinds (not poly-morphic, but *poly-eidetic*), of many substances, things, individuals. With Aristotle, the study of being moves from the Forms to the forms, from universals to particulars. And if predication (the equivocal categories and being and unity) is of substance, then the answer to the question of being qua being cannot be simply being, being alone; on the contrary, "being as being" is "being as beings," is many—and it is being only insofar as it is not simply being, and not merely one. Being and one are special predicates insofar as they are necessarily predicated of substances; however, the one, as the universal predicate of indivisibility (*a-diaireton*), is already a privation (*steresis*), opposition, negation, a lack of divisibility (*diaireton*), a privation of the many—and before all things can be deprived, be said to possess being and to be one, they must be said in many ways.

The categorial many, however, can be predicated of beings because substance itself is pre-categorically many—substance is always many, substances, just as being is always beings, and one is always ones. And if beings or substances are many, then it is because they cannot be reduced to one common denominator (e.g., because like taste, sight, touch, etc., are, strictly speaking, irreducible to one another), because their beingness is in-comparable (e.g., human qua human, six qua six). Indeed, for Aristotle, everything is, is one and is many. And the many qua many lies before the identity and difference of number and kind, genus and species, sign and referent, form and matter, beginning and end, here and there. The many is neither a thing nor many things, but it is inseparable from things, from individual substances (like being and unity); and it is not opposed to one (conceptual universal), but one with many (simultaneous—not in time, but essentially) with the equivocal universals, insofar as they unite heterogeneity, make one of the many. In other words, opposition is possible (differential predication) because the substance of things is already one and many; or more precisely, because the many qua many is neither a genus, nor a category, but an equivocal *archē*-many that has no name.

Aristotle's *Metaphysics* then is determined by the many that philosophy refuses: although Plato (and the pre-Socratics) ask and answer the question of the one, of that and how being is one, they should also ask the question of the many—for only then can they think being qua being. As quantitative, the many can be understood as number; as qualitative it can be understood as kind, irreducible difference of species, genus (e.g., the gap between *archē*-one and categorial one): the fruit seller, for example, sells not "fruit," but apples, pears, peaches, and so on; and the history of western metaphysics presents not being, but *logos, idea, energia,* substance, objectivity, subjectivity, will, will to power, and so on.[58] Here, on the one hand, with the identity of things, beings as many can always be thought as one kind, one particular individual—for their essence is endemic to their species or genus alone, their substance, what they are by their own nature, not by accident; what they are in their being, their definition, their *logos,* is determined differentially, through dialectic ("is or is not, without further qualification").[59] On the other hand, beings are many because their substances are different and differ: individual beings are many means that each is itself, by its nature, only one kind of being—the identity of the individual, its particularity (and the entire critique of Plato and the Pythagoreans), is at stake. With the difference of things, although no longer thought as subsumption under a species or genus, the being of each being, its kind, substance, essence, cannot be many—or rather, if a being belongs to a particular species or genus, then is it not because the being with respect to substance is always already many substances, but because each being is simply different from the next? Yet if the question of the meaning of being is only answerable with respect to one (its primary instance in substance), and if substance is always the substance of substances, then the many of the substances of things is essential for answering the question of the meaning of being qua being, and of beings as many. In fact, the study of the being of beings presupposes the study of the many, of a many that can be reduced neither to a categorical contrary of one nor to the identity and/or difference of things; rather, the study of that which is and is one must turn to the study of its many, the many of being, the many of one, and the many of many.

The question of the many, however, remains unasked (or perhaps unaskable) by the *Metaphysics*—for Aristotle has already asked and answered it with *pros hen* equivocity, with the priority of the per se (*kat' hauto*), qua itself, over the *per accidens.* Here the question "What is x?" is only answerable in one way: by refusing the many, in defining x qua x, one essential definition, one *logos,* one specific answer, attains priority over the others. Here the split between *as itself* and *as another,* between primary and secondary instances, between essence and accident, is an essential difference (perhaps the "*oldest difference*").[60] The as itself, the expression of substance, implies pure individuality (i.e., the predication of specific, incomparable, non-convertible particularity of "essence, quantity, quality, relation, place, time, position, state, activity, passivity").[61] Yet this "particular-many" always determines its being, its "thisness," that is, kind, type, species, genus, and so on, its cause as "that by which it is seen and known," in relation to its non-being, itself in relation to another, identity in relation to difference—the reduction of many *pers* to *per se* and *per accidens,* via difference, to identities; beings are reduced to one (albeit their own, particular) essential being because dialectic thinks the many in opposition to the one, or simply as the many, and because thereby it cannot think *polla he polla.*[62] The law of identity and difference implies the exclusion, forgetting, repression, refusal, avoidance of the many.

After Aristotle, that which is left to be thought is the *archē*-many that lies at the core of identity and difference. Categorically, the many is the original opposite of the one as privation of divisibility: by excluding the many from which they are the privation, identities and differences of substances (and beings and ones) cannot be many. As pre-categorical, the many (like being, substance and one) is the many of things. If being and one are inseparable (from each other and from substances), then they cannot be thought under the sign of the ontological difference between being and beings, substance and substances, oneness and one being, manyness and many beings, one meaning and many ways in which it is spoken—for all this, endemic to the separation of quantitative (Pythagorean) or conceptual (Platonic) ideas from things, fails to think the many as many. And if the study of being qua being raises the question of the meaning of the question "What is being?" as asked under the sign of the question "What is substance?" then it must always also ask the question "What is many?" Implicitly, at least, the *Metaphysics* has asked and answered this question with the *archē*-many, the many of substances, the original many that lies prior to predication as the cause(s) of categorial reductions, *re*-presentations, *de*-limitations of things, not as they are, but in terms of identities and differences. Yet if there are many things, and they are spoken in many ways, then it is because the things themselves are many; beings are many because being itself is many, not just identical and different, because substance is many, many-formed, of many materials, moved in many ways, toward many ends, because the one is many—and all of this because the many is many. Against Plato and the Pythagoreans, Aristotle insists that the substance of things has being and is one—and thereby, is many. Metaphysics speaks being and one in many ways—but that which is not explicitly named, the *archē*-many, the many qua many, remains nameless. Questions remain: How is it possible that things are many? That being, substance, cause, is many? What is the many that being must also be? And what if it could be thought as many? Then could this many be called manys?

The Manifold of Critique

> In both cases, natural polygamy and historic monogamy, the place of the man always determines the concept. Monogamy is a man and a woman; polygamy is again a man and many women. The woman is never polygamous, neither in Kantian nature nor in Kantian society. So it appears: in truth the woman always has everything, both in monogamy and in polygamy. In the harem, for example, there is no true multiplicity and man loses every time, with every stroke. The women make war in order to restore the monogamous relationship and so that one among them has the whole man, at least potentially. With the result that they all have him, no one is deprived of him, and one among them also ends by reigning over him. Thus described, the harem belongs neither to nature nor to culture. Polygamy cannot be thought in this opposition. In nature there is no marriage; in true culture, it's monogamy. Kant qualifies as "barbaric" this unclassifiable phenomenon, this society that is no longer natural and not yet moral. One ought to interrogate from this "perversion" the opposition of concepts from which polygamy escapes, that of the man about which Kant speaks, that of the woman about which he says nothing.
>
> —*Derrida*[63]

The *Critique of Pure Reason* is the critique of *polla,* of the many as given under the sign of the manifold. If the manifold appears, then it does not appear; that is, it appears under the condition that it submit to the transcendental law of objectification, the pure forms of intuition, the pure categories of understanding, and ultimately, the principle of the pure, original-synthetic unity of apperception. And if the manifold can submit to the forms of intuition and knowledge, that is, can become a possible object of experience, then it should be because pure reason is itself purely multiple—but this does not even become an issue for Kant, for this is not his goal (i.e., an explanation of how a priori synthetic judgments, and thereby metaphysics as a science, are possible); rather, its denial is precisely the means by which the *Critique* affirms its identity qua critique of pure reason. In the end, Kant cannot perform a critique of *polla* because he "thinks" the manifold as non-manifold.

In the *Critique,* in fact, the analysis of space and time in the Transcendental Aesthetic sets the formal conditions for all possible intuitions of the manifold in intuition: space and time are infinitely limitable (*unendliche einschränkbare*), limit concepts; and are represented as undetermined, unlimited, "infinite *given* magnitude."[64] The multiplicity of spaces and times are only limitations, only parts, of one and the same space and time, of the pure forms of intuition.

In the processes of knowledge, then, the Synthesis of Apprehension in intuition holds the manifold together in time (the form of inner sense), as the sequence of one and only one object, as the impression of one *absolute unity* following another: "every intuition contains in itself a manifold which can be represented as a manifold only in so far as the mind distinguishes the time in the sequence of one impression upon another; for each representation, *in so far as it is contained in a single moment,* can never be anything but absolute unity."[65] Here object means plurality subsumed as unity, "unity of the object and unity of the manifold in the object."[66] And manifold means that which can only be known under the condition that it be unified, that it be ordered in the form of an appearance—the manifold as manifold cannot be given in intuition; it is, strictly speaking, closed to sensibility (and hence, it cannot be thought, but remains unknowable). Intuition then is that "which does indeed offer a manifold, but a manifold which can never be represented as a manifold, and as contained in a single representation, save in virtue of such a synthesis."[67]

If the manifold, however, is only given as a single representation, then how could Kant even claim that intuition contains a manifold, that the manifold even exists? And why could intuition not offer simple (non-manifold) unities to sensibility, represent unities already constructed as unities (e.g., Empiricism) in time, one after another? Why is the synthesis needed? Kant writes:

> Since connection in accordance with universal and necessary laws would be lacking, all relation of knowledge to objects would fall away. The appearances might, indeed, constitute intuition without thought, but not knowledge; and consequently would be for us as good as nothing.[68]

Or again:

> the manifold of the representation can be given in an intuition which is only sensible, that is, nothing but receptivity; and the form of this intuition

> can lie *a priori* in our faculty of representation, without being anything else than the way in which the subject is affected.[69]

Or again:

> [only] in intuition, which is distinct from the "I," can a manifold be given; and only through *combination* in one consciousness can it be thought. An understanding [e.g., God's] in which through self-consciousness all the manifold would *eo ipso* be given, would be *intuitive;* our understanding can only *think,* and for intuition must look to the senses.[70]

In other words, the chaos of appearances (*Gewühle von Erscheinungen*) cannot fill our souls—but it can be intuited; the material (*Stoff*) of intuition, "the inexhaustible multiplicity of appearances," the manifold, enters into experience, is unified as an object of knowledge because it falls under the formal rules of space and time.[71] Thus, the manifold can be intuited as an object because it can be spontaneously received and synthesized—and it can be synthesized, because synthesis means the combination into a unity of that which shares a common ground, the manifold, and because synthesis means the combination of smaller units to form larger.[72]

Further, if the manifold is intuited in space and time, then it is known insofar as it submits to the understanding, namely, the concepts—for metaphysics functions through concepts alone.[73] Here the concepts must be seen within the history of metaphysics (as transcendental philosophy) that stretches from the ancients (*Transzendentalphilosophie der Alten*), through Scholasticism and Cartesianism, to modernity: the primary purpose (*uranfängliche Absicht*), from Aristotle on, remains for Kant the same—although the "manner of execution" and terminology are transformed, translated.[74] In the Schools, metaphysics found its expression in the proposition *quodlibet ens est unum, verum, bonum.* The predicates unity, truth and perfection, however, were originally thought as mere logical requirements of thought, and thus, from the Greeks to Leibniz, falsely taken as empirical, as belonging to the possibility of things themselves. Therefore, they demand a transcendental translation (i.e., critique, a critique of pure reason that reason performs upon itself: *genetivus objectivus* and *subjectivus*), in order to be properly understood, not as experience, but as the condition of the possibility of experience—Kant is no philosopher of experience, no *Erfahrungsphilosoph.* Thought transcendentally (i.e., conceptually) *unum, verum, bonum* mean unity, plurality, totality (transcendental perfection): as such they are "the prerequisites of all knowledge with respect to the understanding, judgment, and reason (the last of which will demand apodictic certainty, i.e., complete truth)."[75] Thus, to think is to think conceptually, is to think categorically: *unum* as qualitative unity, *verum* as qualitative plurality, *bonum* as qualitative totality.[76]

Yet if *unum, verum, bonum,* can be qualitative, then it is because they already have their origin and ground in a priori categories:

> Hence it is evident that these logical criteria of the possibility of knowledge in general are the three categories of quantity, in which the unity in the production of the quantum has to be taken as homogeneous throughout; and that these categories are here being transformed so as also to yield connection of *heterogeneous* knowledge in one consciousness, by means of the quality of the knowledge as the principle of the connection.[77]

Yet how can the three categories of quantity be the logical criteria of the possibility of knowledge and experience in general? For Kant, the categories can be homogeneous throughout transcendental philosophy only if they are grounded in unity, plurality, and totality (*CPR* A 80/B 106): the unity of qualitative unity is a determination of quantitative unity; the plurality of qualitative plurality is grounded in the quantitative category of plurality; the completeness of qualitative completeness, or of any completeness whatsoever, including that of the *Critique*'s systematic completeness, is a translation of quantitative completeness (totality). Indeed, the oneness, truth, and completeness of the Transcendental Aesthetic and the Transcendental Logic (as well as within the Aesthetic, e.g., between the difference between forms of intuition) are the very categories of quantity.[78]

With the transcendental translation of *unum, verum, bonum* as unity, plurality, totality (*Einheit, Vielheit, Allheit*), knowledge and truth (correspondence of concept and object) become possible. Within quantity itself, a circular economy of concepts whereby the understanding moves through the *momenta* of unity, plurality, and totality, and back to unity: "the third category in each class always arises from the combination of the second category with the first. Thus *allness* or *totality* is just plurality considered as unity."[79] The truth of the concepts is the unity (*unum*) of plurality (*verum*) in a totality (*bonum*)—and the object's submission to the categories is the condition of the possibility of knowledge.

Knowledge itself then is categorical, that is, conceptual: as the condition of the possibility of knowledge, the manifold is received and unified through the synthesis of apprehension in intuition; the synthesis of reproduction in the transcendental faculty of imagination makes the reproduction of the objectified manifold possible; and the synthesis of recognition in a concept by pure understanding makes knowledge of the object possible for consciousness (through the categories, rules, laws), that is, for that consciousness that itself generates the representation of the object from the manifold of representations. The unity of the manifold in *one* object (and "the one and the same general experience" of the object) finds its transcendental ground in original transcendental apperception.[80] The unified manifold (the object) finds its a priori ground in the principle of transcendental apperception as the condition of the possibility of all unification, in "the thorough-going identity of the self in all possible representations."[81] Apperception is a unity, an original-synthetic unity (*ursprünglich-synthetische Einheit*), a unity to which the predicates of original and synthetic must be assigned. And apperception means "that highest point, to which we must ascribe all employment of the understanding, even the whole of logic, and conformably therewith, transcendental philosophy; indeed this faculty is the understanding itself."[82] The unity of apperception is characterized as original-synthetic (*ursprünglich-synthetischen*) in at least three senses: (1) insofar as the hyphen (-) is read as connecting and replacing the dative adjective ending "en" in *ursprünglich-en,* the unity is both original and synthetic, both are interdependently predicated; (2) insofar as the unity is double, the two adjectives emphasize "synthetic"; (3) insofar as the synthesis is original, the adverb describes an adjective.[83] And these multiple meanings of the unity of apperception function simultaneously in the *Critique:* transcendental apperception is synthesized-synthesizing.

Apperception then is not original as causal "origin"; rather, as transcendental, purely non-empirical, as responsible for the generation of the representation "I think," it is the condition of the possibility of all knowledge whatsoever, original apperception (*Ursprüngliche Apperzeption*). And apperception is synthetic because it is a priori combined (*determinatio qua conjunctio*): a synthesized apperception is the condition of the possibility of the combined manifold in intuition (and the "identity" of apperception as well)—and this synthetic character cannot be given through objects; rather, "being an act of the self-activity of the subject, it cannot be executed save by the subject itself."[84] As a unity, apperception is explicitly not the category of quantitative unity (nor as one of the other categories), nor is it a simple entity from which a representation of the manifold could be produced (e.g., a substratum, entelechy, or monad); rather, it is the spontaneously original-synthesis of the self-grounding understanding that precedes (and grounds) a priori all logic and all employment of the understanding—the unity of apperception is a peculiarity of our understanding (*Eigentümlichkeit unseres Verstandes*), a unity that is produced solely by means of the categories (the formal rules by which it synthesizes the manifold).[85] Hence, apperception's original-synthetic unity precedes (as ground, is "higher" than), all concepts of combination and all intuitions; it is the unity of unity (and all the other categories): apperception "as the source of all combination, applies to the manifold of intuitions in general, and in the guise of [under the name of] the categories, prior to all sensible intuition, to objects in general."[86] And the categories are, in turn, grounded in the transcendental unity of apperception. Kant concludes:

> Pure concepts of understanding are thus *a priori* possible, and, in relation to experience, are indeed necessary; and this for the reason that our knowledge has to deal solely with appearances, the possibility of which lies in ourselves, and the connection and unity of which (in the representation of an object) are to be met with only in ourselves. Such connection and unity must therefore precede all experience, and are required for the very possibility of it in its formal aspect. From this point of view, the only feasible one, our deduction of the categories has been developed.[87]

In other words, "the understanding does not, therefore, find in inner sense such a combination of the manifold, but *produces* it, in that it *affects* that sense."[88] And the object's manifold is only possible on the ground of unity, on the unity of transcendental apperception as "the form of all knowledge of objects; through [which] the manifold is thought as belonging to a single object."[89] Thus, the understanding can think the manifold as a unity not simply because transcendental apperception is one, but because it is itself always a synthetic manifold. As synthetic, apperception is originally manifold, an Ur-manifold, a transcendental multiplicity, a combined manifold of apperception that cannot be represented except under the condition of unity. Both subject and object are unified, synthesized manifolds.

The entire *Critique* then, as transcendental philosophy (not ontology), as the "that" and the "how" (*daß und wie*),[90] of knowledge, not the "why"—Kant is a transcendental philosopher, not a metaphysician—as the exposition of the possibility of a priori synthetic judgments depends on a certain conception of intuition and understanding as unified, total, complete, perfect. The manifold as such remains outside the realm of possible knowledge; yet it is subject to formal conditions in intuition (given in space/time) and understanding (combined according to the supreme principle of the original-synthetic unity of apperception in one consciousness).[91] In fact, for Kant, the extension of knowledge to the manifold (like the empty extension of concepts beyond intuition) is not only impossible, it would be of no advantage to us: "thoughts without content are empty, intuitions without concepts are blind."[92] Indeed, this also holds for the forms of intuition: time without space is empty, space without time is blind; if reason remains within itself, then it cannot know the world—however, if outer intuitions are not also subject to time, they cannot be objects for us. In fact, thoughts can never be without content, could never be empty; and intuitions can never be without concepts, could never be blind—just as time and space, pure and practical reason, are always simultaneous, coextensive, a priori necessary. Yet this does not mean that time (as the form of inner and outer intuition, as schema) and pure reason (as transcendental ground of practice) do not have priority.

Kant then closes off the possibility of intuiting the manifold qua manifold—for experience is subject to intuition and intuition is subject to the categories.[93] And all knowledge, as knowledge of an object, is "object-ive," knowledge of the manifold united in a concept of the object. Yet sensibility and understanding are unified in pure reason—for the difference between faculties is only formal, only logical, that is, only in the context of a critique of pure reason. And the differences between concept and object, subject and object, empirical and transcendental, are also only logically double, only formally heterogeneous—the critique of pure reason is only pure in the *Critique:* the manifold of appearances as object can be conceptualized, the empirical can correlate with and be grounded in the transcendental, because they are the same. Indeed, for Kant, time is the schema that makes the connection possible: it is that "third thing" that is homogeneous (*gleichartig*) with the category and the appearance, the empirical and the transcendental, it is a "mediating representation" that "must be pure (without anything empirical) and yet, on one side intellectual, on the other side, sensible."[94] And the difference between space and time is possible because of their schematic identity or homogeneity:

> Time, as the formal condition of the manifold of inner sense, and therefore of the connection of all representations, contains an *a priori* manifold in pure intuition. Now a transcendental determination of time is so far homogeneous with the category, which constitutes its unity, in that it is universal and rests upon an *a priori* rule. But, on the other hand, it is so far homogeneous with appearance, in that time is contained in every empirical representation of the manifold. Thus an application of the category to appearances becomes possible by means of

> the transcendental determination of time, which, as the schema of the concepts of understanding, mediates the subsumption of the appearances under the category.[95]

There is no schema of space—the temporal form of intuition has priority:

> Time is the formal *a priori* condition of all appearances whatsoever. Space, as the pure form of all *outer* intuition, is so far limited; it serves as the *a priori* condition only of outer appearances. But since all representations, whether they have for their objects outer things or not, belong, in themselves, as determinations of the mind, to our inner state; and since this inner state stands under the formal condition of inner intuition, and so belongs to time, time is an *a priori* condition of all appearance whatsoever. It is the immediate condition of inner appearances (of our souls), and thereby the mediate condition of outer appearances. Just as I can say *a priori* that all outer appearances are in space, and are determined *a priori* in conformity with the relations of space, I can also say, from the principle of inner sense, that all appearances whatsoever, that is, all objects of the senses, are in time, and necessarily stand in time-relations.[96]

Insofar as time is the homogeneous element of intuition and understanding, it mediates their interrelation—heterogeneity is possible on the basis of homogeneity; transcendental and empirical are, strictly speaking, like time itself, homogeneous, "two sides of the same coin." The difference between transcendental and empirical, the usual subterfuge (*gewöhnlichen Ausflucht*),[97] is merely nominal, perspectival; the heterogeneity is one of direction (*Sinn*), not meaning (*Bedeutung*).

Yet what is time? And how can it mediate if it is, strictly speaking, merely homogeneous? To return to the Aesthetic: time is the formal condition of inner and outer sense—everything (the manifold, objects, the understanding, and so on, empirical and pure, even transcendental apperception) can only appear in time. As neither an empirical nor discursive (general) concept, time is a necessary a priori representation and a pure form of sensible intuition. Like space, time is homogeneous (different times are only parts of one and the same time) and infinitely limitable (not in the metaphysical sense of a maximum or greatest; rather, in the sense of greater-than-every-part). As the form of inner sense, time mediates the pure object/concept relation; as form of inner and outer sense, the empirical/transcendental relation—and it is capable of mediating because it is homogeneous across different realms, homogeneous precisely because it is an (extensive and intensive) magnitude (*quantum*):

> *Proof:* Appearances, in their formal aspect, contain an intuition in space and time, which conditions them, one and all, *a priori*. They cannot be apprehended, that is taken up into empirical consciousness, save through that synthesis of the manifold whereby the representations of a determinate space or time are generated, that is, through combination of the homogeneous manifold and consciousness of its synthetic unity. Consciousness of the synthetic unity of the manifold [and] homogeneous in intuition in general, in so far as the representation of an object first becomes possible by means of it, is, however, the concept of a magnitude (*quantum*). Thus even the perception of an object, as appearance, is only possible through the same synthetic unity of the manifold of the given sensible intuition as that whereby the unity of the combination of the manifold [and] homogenous is thought in the concept of a *magnitude*. In other words, appearances are all without exception *magnitudes*, indeed *extensive magnitudes*. As intuitions in space or time, they must be represented through the same synthesis whereby space and time in general are determined.[98]

If all representations (from outer or inner sources, transcendental or empirical) must, as modifications of the mind, belong to inner sense, then "all our knowledge is thus finally subject to time, the formal condition of inner sense."[99] Indeed, time makes representation first possible. And synthesis (*nexus, Verknüpfung*) of transcendental apperception and of the manifold can only be possible on the basis of time.

The manifold then appears in time; or rather, the manifold as unified, the non-manifold or no-longer-manifold, appears in time insofar as it (the manifold in itself, as such) does not appear—the manifold is the non-appearance of the non-manifold in time. Time is absolutely singular, homogeneous, without difference, that is, non-manifold. Time and the manifold, therefore, are radically incommensurable, heterogeneous; but time mediates through homogeneity. The manifold cannot appear in time—it is non-temporal—because time's homogeneity only mediates that which it is itself. Time refuses the manifold under the condition that it appear as what it is not, that is, that it not appear at all—at precisely the moment when time proposes to make the manifold possible (its appearance, its thought, or their correspondence), it makes it impossible. The entire understanding-process of the *Critique* is inadequate (adequate-inadequate) to the manifold as given. On the one hand, the problem of the manifold remains unsolved, beyond the realm of transcendental philosophy, outside the horizon of human understanding and the truth (*verum*) of the critique of pure reason, problematic: like the regulative ideas, like free will, immortality of the soul, the existence of God, the manifold qua manifold can be neither affirmed nor denied by reason. On the other hand, the problem of the manifold is solved as the unified manifold given in intuition, in time, the homogeneous schema, for pure reason, thought via the categories.

Yet if time is only the formal condition of sense, then it remains empty; rather, it must be filled by the manifold as the material condition (given, stuff) of sense. In fact, the manifold can belong to *one* object (*zu Einem Objekt gehörig*), because as such, it is many, many understood as homogeneous with the forms of intuition, the concepts and the original-synthetic uni-ty (*Ein-heit*), the one representation (*eine Vorstellung*) of apperception.[100] And the homogeneity that allows for the unity of the manifold and time is the real condition of the possibility of the *Critique*. In other words, the manifold is just as necessary as time—although Kant fails to exploit its schematic capacity, its power to connect inner and outer, transcendental and empirical. If time is the formal schema of transcendental philosophy, then the manifold is its material schema.

The *Critique of Pure Reason* then, as the critique of the manifold, no longer thinks multiplicity as a predicate (Aristotle), but as a substantive, *the* manifold, *a* multiplicity. Yet it thinks this multiplicity as non-multiple (even according to its own criteria), as that which disappears in appearing. Heterogeneity is reduced to homogeneity. As the other of time, the given manifold is purely multiple; yet insofar as the manifold as such is not a problem for Kant, it remains problematic. Indeed, transcendental philosophy cannot think the manifold as manifold within a critique of pure reason, and under the names of homogeneity, unity, substantive, multiplicity as such remains nameless.

The Questions of Multiplicity

What begins with Aristotle's questioning of being qua being, then, with the identity of being with itself, the identity of identity, and with its difference to the eidetic many, to qualitative and quantitative multiplicity, the being that is the being of beings; what continues through the Middle Ages and finds its apogee in Kant's metaphysics of quantification (formalization, systematization, normalization, rationalization), of the category of qualitative multiplicity derived from quantity via a reduction of *eidos* and applied to the manifold—comes to completion in Hegel. Conceptual multiplicity means that in a system of sciences, and a phenomenology of the experience of consciousness, qualitative multiplicity, as the determinations of beings, has its truth in mediation with quantitative multiplicity. Conceptual multiplicity, at the end of the German transcendental idealism that stretches from Kant through Fichte and Schelling (as well as Reinhold, Maimon, etc.) means that the speculative solution to multiplicity as such is not a barbaric thinking (*barbarisches Denken*) of dead identity; rather, it is the motion of thought as a living dialectic, and the movements of the moments of multiplicity within the identity and difference of identity and difference.[101] And conceptual multiplicity is not just a dead difference (even at the origin), not the one-sidedness of an understanding caught in the (blood) logic of either/or, neither/nor, not a multiplicity that stands simply over and against unity; rather, it is a difference that raises immanent contradiction to the level of truth—and it is the multiplicity that is itself the multiplicity of its moments. No longer merely qualitative or quantitative, predictive or substantial, multiplicity has become a totality that is multiple, multiple identities, multiple differences, multiple multiplicities that has quality and quantity as moments, identical and differential multiplicity as sides, subjective and substantial multiplicity as perspectives.[102] Being and non-being, quality and quantity, are no longer the fundamental terms, no longer maintain their priority (existence does not precede essence, ontology is not before epistemology); rather, they are moments of the multiplicity of spirit. Multiplicity as conceptual has become absolute.

Questions then for Hegel: What does it mean to do a phenomenology of multiplicity, to let it show itself as itself, in order to complete it in a science of the speculative idea? What is the logic of multiplicity? What does it mean to think multiplicity as neither merely subject nor substance, subjective nor objective; but multiplicity as absolute—or rather, multiplicities as absolute? How do the supersessions of dialectic respond to beings as beings (and to the identity and difference of being and beings), to multiplicity as multiple? What is the multiplicity contained and released in the forgetting/remembering of the concept of multiplicity? What are its truths? Its times and spaces? How are being and beings to *become* multiple? And how can this multiplicity be thought? As Heidegger writes:

> *What is called thinking?* The question sounds definite. It seems univocal. But even a slight reflection shows: the question has *many* meanings. Therefore, no sooner do we ask the question than we begin to vacillate. Indeed, the *many* meanings of the question foils every attempt to push straight toward the answer without some further preparation.
>
> We must, then, clarify the *many* meanings. The *many* meanings of the question, "What is called thinking?", conceals *many* ways of dealing with it.[103]

The question as multiple is the question of its own multiplicity, and the questions of multiplicity become multiple. Ontological multiplicity calls into question the method by which the *logos* (or *logoi*)[104] of Aristotelian substances are established, the onto-theo-logical constitution of metaphysics that culminates in Hegel's system of science, in the living-machine, the logic of material formalism that is just as much formal materialism. Yet a multiplicity of questions remain: What does it mean to call (*heißen*) thought? To be called thought or called to thought, to thinking? How is "calling" akin to a certain sort of crime? What steals thought? And what does thought steal? What could it mean to think the metaphysical *heist* of multiplicity?

Regardless, if Hegel is a key figure in a history of the philosophy of multiplicity, it is not only *because* he thinks multiplicity, but *how* he thinks it (under the dual signs of identity and difference). Here the problem is neither a specific identity (the one, unity, logical identity, essence, the subject, the truth, the object, the world, totality, etc.) nor a specific difference (active/passive, true/false, male/female, presence/absence, transcendental/empirical, *per se/per accidens,* etc.)—rather, it is identity and difference themselves. Here the thought of multiplicity is just as much a non-thought—for the concept means thinking multiplicity as multiple and non-multiple. Multiplicity as such, multiplicity qua multiple, *polla he polla,* the identity of multiplicity, loses its privileged position, its priority, with respect to its own multiplicity—for the difference between multiplicity as such, as itself, as self-identical; and multiplicity as other than itself, as non-multiple, is a difference that is just as much no difference at all. Hegel then makes trouble for metaphysics, irritates, goads, inveigles, seduces, inspires, instigates the ways in which philosophy speaks, acts, writes, and thinks multiplicity.

More questions then: Must the rethinking of multiplicity in philosophy, and of philosophy in multiplicity, fall into the discourse of identity and difference, that is, of the many who take sides, draw borders, frontiers, barriers, of those who are drawn into sides? Does multiplicity as such, of philosophy as such, open up a different world, one essentially incommensurable with the history of western metaphysics, a history of semantic ruses, theories, philosophemes, structures, formulations, processes, practices? Is it possible that at the moment metaphysics returns to itself, to its totality, its completion, it finds that which it cannot complete, that which is, strictly speaking, out of its control, another within itself, but an other that is no other at all? Or is the movement of completion and in-completion not the very motor of metaphysics? Is the question of multiplicity then not that of remaining within or of getting out of, completing or not-completing, metaphysics (for this question is not multiple), but of how multiplicity taken seriously could become the question of the question of multiplicity, and thereby, become multiple itself? Or rather, if it is possible today, with Hegel, with metaphysics, to think *polla he polla,* to take the manifold to its logical conclusion, to complete (in incompletion) the question of multiplicity, to stop questioning, to answer, then is it because the question of multiplicity as such, questions as manys, has never even been asked? And does that mean that philosophy can begin to think manys?

2

Difference of Absolute Particularity

Concept of Philosophy

> *A multitude of men, now one person.* A multitude of men, are made *one* person, when they are by one man, or one person, represented; so that it be done with the consent of every one of that multitude in particular. For it is the *unity* of the representer, not the *unity* of the represented, that maketh the person *one.* And it is the representer that beareth the person, and but one person. And *unity* cannot otherwise be understood in multitude. *Every one is author.* And because the multitude naturally is not *one,* but *many;* they cannot be understood for one; but many authors, of every thing their representative saith, or doth in their name; every man giving their common representer, authority from himself in particular.
>
> —*Hobbes*[1]

Multiplicity as multiplicity is the extermination of thought, the death of philosophy—for it is no multiplicity at all. Like simple identity, A is A, A *he* A, A qua A, A as A, A = A, mere identity, identity with self, sheer multiplicity ends in indifference to difference. For Hegel, if multiplicity is to avoid its own identity (or rather, find it), then it can be understood as neither purely qualitative nor quantitative, predicate nor substantive, identity nor difference, neither simply real nor ideal, itself or another; rather, it must be understood as absolute. What then is the absolute? Neither simply subjective nor objective, the absolute is a totality—but not just. Not simply "totality," that is, "totality qua totality," the absolute is the form of totality, the totality of totalities, that which makes totality total—and not just. And it is with this totality that multiplicity as radical individuality can finally show itself—for here multiplicity means particularity, that is, multiplicity in totality and totality in multiplicity, totalizing multiplicity and multiple totality. In other words, the absolute is the identity and difference of their identity and their difference. Yet how can multiplicity be multiplicity, if it is in fact particular? How can particularity, if it is in fact particular, be multiple?

For Hegel, in the *Differenzschrift*, if philosophy is to be a science, then its totality must be systematic, it must think the multiplicity of individuals in relation to the absolute—not only as merely subjective or objective, knowledge or being, for-itself or in-itself, certainty or truth; but as absolute (as spirit), as the original harmony, the original identity (*ursprüngliche Identität*), that necessarily rips itself apart, that takes on a multiplicity of forms, moments, in order to re-constitute itself as a living whole, as a whole that is just as much non-whole, a totality that is also non-totality. Spirit then reproduces itself through separation, via division in two (*Ent-zwei-ung*); and this "lost unity" is the source of the need of reason (*Vernunft*) for philosophy, a reason that steps out of the flow of moments, abstracts itself from spirit's shapes, in order to attain knowledge of the absolute, that is, the disappearance of the division between the absolute and the totality of its multiple delimitation. And reason thinks the absolute only insofar as it steps out of the movement, the becoming (*Werden*) of the multiplicity of spirit's moments, into being and nothing. Reason's need, however, cannot be satiated by the mere gathering of spirit's forms into a system—for it must sacrifice itself as well, insofar as it is not only the master-gatherer of shapes, the collector of moments into a simple next-to-one-another. Here reason must learn that it is imbricated in its science, that its philosophical assumptions are the expression of its need to re-unite with spirit, with an absolute of which it is itself a moment. Philosophy, therefore, as the need for totality, the unification of multiplicity, has a double source: (1) the absolute itself, as the identity of the beginning and end of philosophy, *archē* and *telos*, as the infinite, assumed unlimited (*vorausgesetzte Unbeschränktheit*), the condition of the possibility of reason's delimitations—and it is from these delimitations that reason must free itself, if it is to attain the absolute, that is, the synthesis of what appears to reason as spirit's division; and (2) consciousness's separation from the absolute, its difference—but a difference that is itself absolute (not merely abstract or complete), absolute difference, the absolute as the difference between itself and consciousness that philosophy must unify.[2]

Reflection is the instrument that philosophical reason employs to think the absolute, to produce totality out of multiplicity for consciousness. Yet reflection is not merely a unidirectional positing (*setzen*) of being as undetermined/determined that infinitely reproduces itself without return, not only a delimitation of unlimited spirit (which is a contradiction); rather, realizing that every positing and determining entails a non-positing and non-determining (neither pure identity nor pure difference, pure subjectivity nor pure objectivity, are possible—everything is contaminated—and pure), reflection returns to self in the totality of supersession (*Aufhebung*), that is, the negation of the negation, absolute (not only abstract) negation that resolves contradiction/opposition and preserves it (negation is two-edged [*zweischneidig*]), the going under (*Untergang*), perishing, that is a going over (*Übergang*), transition, to that which is higher, raised up (*aufgehoben*). What holds for *aufgeben* (to give, pose, set, put, place, and to give up, give in) also holds for *aufheben:* "to give, like to supersede, two-meanings: α) to give *up*—to view it as lost, destroyed; β) [to *give*]—but even therewith simultaneously, to make it into a problem, whose content is not destroy; but which is saved and whose distortion is a difficulty to be solved."[3] Derrida, for example, can therefore translate *Aufhebung* as "nothing any longer, coming from the outside, forbids you from cheating on your wife, but you no longer want to since you love her."[4] And this "vulgar translation" can be modified: you have always already both cheated on your wife and not cheated on her, and you always want to cheat on her and not (and the same for her)—for is the truth of infidelity and its other (fidelity) not desire? And is desire, like *Aufgeben,* not ambiguous? Not precisely that which is renounced in order to be satiated, fulfilled and not-fulfilled? Or have you ever been faithful in the first place? Or unfaithful? For could *Aufhebung* not also be translated by the vulgar question: "Have you stopped cheating/beating on your wife/husband?" Or, for Heidegger: "Are you still a Nazi?"

Yet if, for Hegel, supersession is the totality that takes care of multiplicity with the absolute, then perhaps "taking care of" is a better translation of *Aufhebung* than "supersession," that is, "taking care of" in the many senses of the term, not as worrying (*sorgen*), but marking the inner connection of tenderness and violence, as taking in for the sake of protection and love, giving shelter to being and nothing alike (not simply a "house of Being"), guarding particularity and universality; and as eradicating, getting rid of, wiping out, killing (as in the hit man who "takes care of problems" through murder). In this way the *Phenomenology of Spirit* would be a "Phenomenology of Care," of care as multiple, and the *Science of Logic* would be Hegel's way of taking care of multiplicity. The question of the translation of *Aufhebung* would be: How does the logic of spirit take care of multiplicity? How do we take care of our wives and husbands? Friends and enemies? Or how do we take care of fascists?

In this way, for Hegel, already in the *Differenzschrift,* as understanding (*Verstand*), reason posits (supersedes and takes care of), being and nothing; through negation, they determine each other as well as the multiplicity of beings: for example, the positing of being is the negation of non-being (and vice versa). And when reason realizes that positing of being entails non-being (against Fichte, no pure positing), when it understands that determination of finitude is mediated by infinitude, then it supersedes their differences: "it exterminates both, in that it unites both, since they are only insofar as they are not united. In this unity, both are simultaneously preserved; since the opposition, and therefore the delimited, is hereby in relation to the absolute."[5] Here knowledge (*Wissen*) means the conscious identity of contradictory moments, of the finite and the infinite, of both, that is, the identity that is absolute (*absolute Identität*)—not abstract—insofar as it preserves differences within itself, takes care of the "identity of concept and being, of subject and object."[6] In this way philosophical reflection first negates the understanding's contradictions by demonstrating the interrelation and co-implication of oppositional terms ("through analysis, the terms of unity and multiplicity [as one of its opposites] no longer emerge");[7] second, it brings the moments into a totality—for parts only have sense and meaning (*Sinn und Bedeutung*) through their relation to the whole; finally, it raises its knowledge to the level of the absolute, rather than drag the absolute down to it. When reflective reason comes to realize that not only the relation of conscious understanding and knowledge (but also its being) is in relation to the absolute; then, following the law of self-destruction (*Gesetz der Selbstzerstörung*), it raises itself to the level of speculation, to the concept within which form and matter are ideal and real, subject and substance, are identical and different—and the name of this supersession (taking care qua destruction and preservation) is the absolute.

Yet multiplicity remains the problem of the absolute. Repeating Aristotle's charge against Plato, Hegel claims that philosophy (Fichte, Schelling, and transcendental idealism in general from Kant on) refuses the many, remains indifferent to multiplicity, to the difference of totality and particularity, identity and difference, same and other. Philosophy over-looks (trans-cends) the specificity of a specific age, the polymorphic organizations of "world historical" reason, because multiplicity is understood as completed totality. Indeed, "such a multiplicity is no philosophy":[8]

> The true characteristic of a philosophy is the interesting individuality in which reason, from the building-material of a particular age, has organized a form for itself; the particularly speculative reason finds therein spirit from its spirit, flesh from its flesh, it looks at itself in it as one and the

> same, and as an other living being. Each philosophy is in itself complete and has, like a real artwork, totality in itself.[9]

If philosophy is to finally think (and be) "the same and the other," then it must find a way to think (i.e., reason) not only as absolute totality, but also as radical individuality. History then, and the history of western metaphysics, would not just be the history of spirit; rather, its true character would shows itself as the history of particulars. Multiplicity as particularity is the specificity of spirit in motion, in the totality of historical development (through which it sees itself). And the task of the *Differenzschrift* is to reveal the individuality hidden in identity and in identification, the difference within/between Fichte's and Schelling's systems (in the unrelenting rejection of multiplicity, or rather, in its acceptance—but only under the condition that it remain potential/subjunctive and subjective, or actual but unessential), in order to allow particular multiplicity to show itself. If the history of philosophy as multiple is a history of particularities, then Fichte and Schelling think the same and differently about the same and the different.

The Difference of Dogmatic Subjectivism and an Important Evil

Attempting to think philosophy as science, that is, as system, Fichte begins where Kant left off, namely, with the unfulfilled promise of the identity of subject and object. For the *Critique*, a priori synthetic judgments are only valid for me, for my reason, for the transcendental object = x in my understanding; but not for things in themselves, not for that against which (*dawider*) I judge, the given manifold. Indeed, the conceptual structure of "triplicity," is already here—but only as subjective: "the concept which Kant in the *synthetic a priori judgments* put forward (the concept of something *differentiated* which equally is *inseparable*, of an *identity* which is in its own self an *inseparable difference*) belongs to what is great and imperishable in his philosophy."[10] And, the "infinitely important form of triplicity," showed itself in Kant only as a "formal spark of light."[11] The critique of the thing in itself, however, seems to rest upon a misunderstanding—for the transcendental object is the necessary unity (*Ein-heit*) and correspondence (*Über-ein-stimmung*) of the thing in itself and the thing for us. The thing in itself (and the logic) is not "transcendent"; rather, it appears to us as against (*dawider*) us. And it shows itself to us as it is; and it is known as it shows itself because it is given in space and time (the Aesthetic is already phenomenology), and (spontaneously) thought through the categories. Thus, no dualism and no dogmatism. But if the non-identity of subject and object is made into a *petitio principii* for an absolute a posteriori first philosophy, then transcendental deduction of the categories conceals dogmatism. Strapped to Kantian idealism, Fichte is unable to think particular multiplicity (and its difference from/with totality) because he falls into absolute subjectivism: "the principle, the subject-object, proves to be a subjective subject/object."[12] In other words, stuck in the history of metaphysics as first philosophy, Fichte thinks multiplicity as subjective (human): "the object of the doctrine of science is after all the system of human knowledge."[13]

In fact, Fichte's system breaks down for two reasons: (1) "the pure consciousness, that is presented in the system as absolute identity of subject and object, is a subjective identity of subject and object,"[14] and a subjective-absolute-I is not absolute (the conclusion contradicts the premise); (2) if the "I am I" is absolute in any sense, then it cannot remain on the level of striving (*streben*), a mere "I *should* be I"—an actual identity, and not a potential identity (i.e., non-identity), should ground the system, and the absolute (*schlecthin*) I is a bad infinity (*schlechte Unendlichkeit*).

For Fichte the origin of the system of transcendental idealism is a first, absolute, unconditional principle: namely, the absolute I (*absolute Ich*), I am I, I = I (*Ich* = *Ich*) that expresses itself as the connection (X) between A and A, A is A, in the formula A = A, that posits itself—for positing is self-positing, that is, the "I" posits itself as absolute. "*I am absolutely, i.e. I am absolutely because I am; and I am absolutely what I am; both for the I.*"[15] Then later,

> the absolute I is absolutely identical with itself: everything in it is one and even the same I, and belongs (if it is permitted to express oneself so in-authentically) to one and even the same I; there is there nothing to differentiate, no multiplicity; the I is everything, and is nothing, because it is *for itself* nothing, cannot in itself differentiate positing and posited.[16]

In other words, unlike Descartes's unidirectional *cogito* wherein thinking implies being, whereby the difference between thinking and being, despite their co-implication, signals an original equivocation, Fichte's "absolute I" is simple, undifferentiated identity, unity without anything foreign (*fremd*), pure positing/posited, *sum ergo sum*. Here the I is certain of its own being and can thereby ground the system; it is the one, independent principle that ensures the chain of propositions. And "one does not necessarily think, if one is, but one necessarily is, if one thinks."[17] Descartes, however, in the *Meditations* is careful to avoid the *ergo* between *cogito* and *sum*: "*I am, I exist* is necessarily true whenever it is put forward by me or conceived in my mind.[18] Yet why is the *cogito* expressed as a tautology ("*I am, I exist*")? Does he repeat it merely for emphasis? And where is the "thinking"? And what is thinking? Indeed, on the one hand, if the *cogito* is a logical inference (from thinking to being), then Descartes looks forward to Kant: in *Med II,* thinking is doubting, understanding, affirming, denying, willing, being unwilling, imagining, and sensing; and in the wax example, I know the wax clearly and distinctly, not from its sensible and imaginary qualities, but by removing all its outer forms and perceiving it with the mind alone as the wax is itself. Descartes continues (as in the *Critique*'s transcendental deduction) that my judgment that the wax exists, presupposes that I exist. My thinking presupposes my being (thinking itself presupposes being itself). And thinking is a mode of being (as doubting, understanding, affirming, and so on are modes of thinking). But what is being? And what does it presuppose? For Descartes, being presupposes itself as a self-sufficient, irreducible ground. Just as the wax in its sensible and imaginary qualities can be expressed clearly and distinctly as what it is itself (in its inner form) only without its outer forms, thinking as it is itself (an outer form of being) can be expressed clearly and distinctly only as being itself—the *cogito* expresses the inner form of the inference. On the other hand, Descartes looks back to Parmenides: "thinking and being are the same."[19] Here no logical inference is needed. Being and thought are the same means: only that which *is* can be thought (Empiricism), and thinking allows things (*physis*) to be (Idealism). Thought can think *physis* because it belongs to *physis,* shares in its power, is and is part of nature. Being appears—but in order to appear, it must appear to something or someone. Being, therefore, appears to thought, and it is what it is qua appearing only if and when it appears to thought. Without thought, *physis* cannot appear, cannot be what it is; it remains inert, inactive, dead—and essentially is-not. Being can appear to thought because thought too *is,* is being; and thought can think being because thinking *is* only of that which is, being. Although thought is *physis,* it only becomes what it is, has its being, in its separation, its difference, from being; just as being, for its part, only is, insofar as it takes its distance from thought. Thought and being are co-constituted in their identity and difference, their relation and non-relation—even further, they are determined in the identity and difference of their identity and difference. The certainty of this relation/non-relation, however, remains perhaps the essentially unexamined and unthought (thought as unthought) of the *Meditations*' metaphysics of multiplicity.

Following Descartes then, Fichte thinks the absolute I as pure (transcendental), that is, deduced via abstraction from everything foreign to itself (*von allem Fremdartigen*), everything that it is not (empirical);

and therefore it is only and purely itself, A = A, I = I: "the act of self-consciousness differentiates itself determinately from other consciousnesses because its object is the same as the subject."[20] Thus, the first principle is the only case where form and content are simultaneously posited: I = I determines itself unconditionally with respect to form *and* content; while the second principle (pure positing of a not-I) and third principle (pure unification of the I and not-I) determine themselves conditionally with respect to content or form.

For Hegel, however, if the I were posited unconditionally, then it could not serve as transcendental origin, or if "purity" meant "indifference" (Schelling), then it could not resolve the contradiction of identity and difference; it would have no way to differentiate itself since qualitative multiplicity cannot be derived from quantitative unity and negation. Pure identity then cannot remain one-sided abstract positing: in the A of A = A, a not-A (*omnis determinatio est negatio*) is also posited; in the A = A, an A ≠ A is always also thought. Dragging non-identity, difference, its negation, along with it, pure identity is no longer pure; A is perverted by itself, its own other: "the identity of the pure and empirical consciousness is not an abstraction from their original being-in-opposition; on the contrary, their opposition is an abstraction from their original identity."[21] In other words, the "absolute I" is conditioned (not absolute), and its purity has always already been compromised—but it is conditioned by itself, by its own content (self-negation, not-I) and form (the resolution of identity and difference via divisibility); its impurity is its own:

> to simple reflection, this deduction seems to be a contradictory beginning: to derive multiplicity from unity, duality from pure identity; but the identity of the I = I is not a *pure* identity, i.e. not produced through the abstraction of reflection; if the reflection I = I is conceived as unity, so must it also simultaneously conceive the same as duality; I = I is simultaneously identity and duplicity, it is an opposition in I = I: the I is one time subject, another time object.[22]

The absolute I contains both itself and its other: I = I contains the difference of subject and object (Hegel reads Fichte against Reinhold). The absolute I then, via the second principle (negation of the infinite repetition of A = A in A = not A), should be applied to an empirical object; but when Fichte comes to the unified, absolute identity of I = I, to the identity of a subjective-A and an objective-A that contains their difference, to the third principle, it is too late—for the difference between transcendental and empirical consciousness, the opposition between subjectivity and objectivity, is derived from original subjective identity:

I = I means that the I is equal only to itself. The I's synthesis is the synthesis of the I, a merely subjective act (*Tatigkeit* or more precisely, active deed, *Tathandlung*), a simply "ideal" synthesis: the "I" is subjective subject/object, never objective subject/object—the object has no positive character, never comes to itself; it is sheer negation, radical reduction of the I, posited only *through* the subject, determined only *as* a not-I. The absolute I should unify subject and object, ideal and real—but it can only do so under the condition that the object remains un-objectionable, a subject, that the real remains ideal, that the multiplicity of appearances (and the appearance of multiplicity) remain conditioned "through *our human* discursive *understanding*."[23] With the "absolute I," philosophy as the "science of science in general" should have secured a firm foundation on which it can construct its house (*Gebäude*), and the *Doctrine of Knowledge* should have achieved the absolute totality wherein "one is all and all is one"—unfortunately, it remains an incomplete subjectivism. And if the absolute I's freedom (and reason) is reduced to that of a mere subject, then it constitutes the highest tyranny (*höchste Tyrannei*).[24] Fichte writes: within a system,

> at least one proposition, that joins its certainty with the rest, must be certain; so that if, and to what extent this one should be certain, also a second, and if, and to what extent this second should be certain, also a third, etc., must be certain. And so would many, and as such perhaps quite different propositions (exactly thereby that they *all* have certainty, and *the same* certainty) have only one certainty in common, and thereby will be only one science.[25]

Indeed, the question of science and philosophy (omnipresent today in the political economy of the human genome project, the competition in biotechnologies, cloning, patented body parts, etc.) shows itself here to be simultaneously that of nationalism and language: "the nation that invented [the science of science] would be well worthy to give it a name from its language; and it could then be called simply *science,* or the *doctrine of science.*"[26] Fichte immediately footnotes: "it would also be well worthy to give it the remaining artistic expressions from its language; and the language itself, like the nation that speaks it, would thereby, possess a decisive advantage over other languages and nations."[27]

Yet Fichte's system has a second flaw: in order to think causality as subjective, and subjectivity as practice (positing as "active deed"), it posits the I = I as free striving (*streben*) toward an infinitely receding goal, a permanently unachieved *telos.* As Hegel writes in the *Logic:* "the philosophy of Kant and Fichte sets up the ought as the highest point of the resolution of the contradictions of reason; but the truth is that the *ought* is only the standpoint which clings to finitude and thus to contradiction."[28] The infinity of the "ought," like a straight line or ray, exemplifies a bad infinity (*schlechte Unendlichkeit*), and the strived for identity remains unreachable. The ought,

> held fast as only negative, is even *supposed to be not there,* is supposed to be unattainable. However, to be thus unattainable is not its grandeur but its defect, which is at bottom the result of holding fast to the finite as such as a *merely affirmative being.* It is what is untrue that is unattainable, and such an infinite must be seen as a falsity.[29]

In other words, the I's identity is only postulated, a mere ought (*Sollen*), never to be realized: "absolute identity is, in fact, principle of speculation; but it remains, like its expression I = I, only the rule that postulates infinite fulfillment, but in the system will not be constructed."[30] The absolute I wants to posit a real other—but it ends by translating itself into its desired object, by projecting a posteriori a vision of itself as reality. Here the assumed unity is simply utopic: the "highest demand remains, in the Fichtean system, a demand."[31] The charge of unidirectionality—made against Descartes—returns: the I = I has transformed itself into I should = I because the (=) of subjective subject = object remains (theoretically and practically) outstanding, never resolving their difference. Fichte's system falters not only because totality is subjective, but because totality is no totality at all: the causal difference as the condition of the possibility of striving means that "the principle of identity will not be principle of the system; just as the system begins to construct itself, identity will be given up."[32] As first philosophy, the *Doctrine of Knowledge* ends, before it has begun, in dogmatic idealism: subjectivity, the absolute I, the I = I, from which multiplicity should be deduced, on which the whole system depends, never comes back to itself out of reflection; it never completes its own circle, it remains unfulfilled, a mere "should," an "unending striving," for self-identity: "I should be equal to I."[33] And if the absolute I is pure, a mere striving, then it cannot ground the system (the system that is itself—anyway—merely subjective). Indeed, without an originally reflexive identity, Fichte cannot think absolute contradiction.

Against Fichte then, against mere factual positing (*Tatsache*), simple action (*Handlung*), and their combination in active deed, Hegel thinks reason by unifying "negative" reflection and "positive" intuition (*Anschauung*) in a "transcendental intuition" for a speculative philosophy wherein "concept and being" are superseded (in the destruction that preserves the difference of multiple particulars). Speculative reason is not merely empirical intuition (wherein subject and object, ideal and real, remain separated); rather, it is transcendental consciousness, that is, the totality of knowledge and intuition—for transcendental intuition (not Fichtean "intellectual intuition") is the condition of the possibility of speculation in general: "without transcendental intuition, one could not philosophize."[34] Speculative reason then, bolstered by transcendental intuition, supersedes contradiction (limited/unlimited, finite/infinite, etc.)—not by placing antinomical terms abstractly next to one another (*nebeneinander*); but as the absolute of idea and being that does not forget (but re-collects, re-members, takes care of) their individualities, that thinks and is (and does not think and is not) by relating totality to multiplicity.[35]

A philosophical system then relates particularity, specificity, individuality to totality, as both delimited and completed in the absolute. Here multiplicity frees itself from mere chance, from simple contingency—but not as simple necessity in the causal chain of a formalist-constructivist science; rather, the absolute shows itself in reason as multiplicity in totality, contingency, and necessity. Indeed, reason needs no first principle, no ground; it is its own ground, its own beginning, middle, and end, self-grounding, not only synthesis or analysis, but the supersession that takes care of both. If philosophy therefore is to be systematic, then it cannot be simply mechanistic, cannot provide a merely quantitative totality. For example, as Fichte writes: "the *Doctrine of Science* contains simply what is necessary; if it is necessary in every observation, then it is also the same with respect to quantity, i.e. it is necessarily limited."[36] And here identity and difference (and multiplicity), I and not-I, are quantitative determinations or reductions: the third principle of synthesis and divisibility (*Teilbarkeit*) functions via quantity. If the I is the highest concept, then quantity is the deepest—it is the schema that permits the absolute I to differentiate itself into I and not-I. For Hegel, however, spirit, nature, the state, human beings, and so on must be thought as living organisms—not dead machines. The difference between life and death rests in particularity, and living multiplicity dies in the will to constructivism—it is transformed into mere calculation, numerical multiplication. Conceptual science cannot think its object through dead concepts, through mere formalism: "the formal unit of the concept that should rule, and the multiplicity of nature, contradict one another; and the crush between them soon shows an important evil."[37] If the history of philosophy is to be the history of reason, then it must learn to think the contradiction as contradiction, evil qua evil (and also non-contradiction and good). The history of an unending, polymorphic reason is one of totalizing reason—but a reason that is one, only insofar as it is particular, that is, also many (non-totalizing). And this history must be a philosophy or phenomenology of spirit—for only the totality of spirit as concept can approach a living multiplicity.

The Threat of Identity and the Fundamental Error of All Philosophy

If Fichte is a dogmatic idealist under the guise of transcendental philosophy, then Schelling is a dogmatic pantheist ("Spinoza taken as pattern") masked as a natural philosopher.[38] While the *Doctrine of Knowledge* thinks multiplicity out of subjective subject/object, Schelling thinks Fichte's other as well: objective subject/object, the identity of transcendental and natural philosophy in the continuous whole of science. With Schelling, however, the subjective-objective difference is not superseded, not "taken care of" in the totalizing identity of the concept; rather, it is destroyed in synthesis, in the absolute indifference point (*Indifferenzpunkt*) between subjectivity and objectivity, that is, in an absolute that is no absolute at all: "it conceives not both poles in itself, but in a superficial modification and neighborly unification, the essence of both disappear for it; and it is a stranger to both, as well as to philosophy."[39] Here multiplicity is no multiplicity at all: "on this view of colorless light, rapture keeps a firm hold; a multiplicity is in it only insofar as it combats multiplicity."[40] With Fichte, synthesis is possible because quantitative multiplicity implies identity as quantum (and categorical differentiation, the multiplicity of kinds, as quantitatively posited); with Schelling, however, synthesis is impossible because it has always already happened—the absolute is the only quality (no quantum); it is total indifference. Here "objective totality and subjective totality, the system of nature and the system of intelligence, *is* one and even the same"—yet their indifference point, their turning point, the place where they lose themselves in one another, non-separation, indivisibility, immediacy (*unvermittlt*), their middle-point, is also doubled, twofold: identity and totality.[41] In other words, Schelling may think development (historical becoming) as the expansion and contraction of the absolute from original identity (*ursprünglich Identität*), through subject/object division (that corresponds to the scientific separation of the sciences into natural and intellectual), to negative supersession in synthesis, destruction of difference in totality; and he may think the other of Fichtean subjective totality, the objective totality wherein subject and object are unified "in the intuition of themselves in complete totality of the objective, becoming absolute—in the intuition of the infinite incarnation of God, of the creation of the word from the beginning";[42] but he never thinks the absolute as the movement of the concept.

In fact, from beginning to end, the *System of Transcendental Idealism* is subjectivistic—intellectual intuition is the subject's intuition:

> A system is completed when it is led back to its starting point. But this is precisely the case with our own. The ultimate ground of all harmony between subjective and objective could be exhibited in its original identity only through intellectual intuition; and it is precisely this ground which, by means of the work of art, has been brought forth entirely from the subjective, and rendered wholly objective, in such wise, that we have gradually led our object, the self itself, up to the very point where we ourselves were standing when we began to philosophize.[43]

Hence, Hegel's critique: "the absolute principle, the only real ground and fixed standpoint of philosophy, in Fichte's as well as in Schelling's philosophy, is intellectual intuition;—expressed for the reflection, identity of subject and object."[44] Transcendental philosophy's *subjective* absolute, however (e.g., philosophy as the "progressive history *of self-consciousness*"), its subjective identity of subject and object ("*one* continuity"), starting from consciousness and going over to nature, is *explicitly* only one side of Schelling's system—the other side of idealism is realism (the philosophy of nature): if idealism is the soul of philosophy, then realism is its body, and only the two together constitute a living whole.[45]

The organic totality of Schelling's thought appears in his *Presentation of My System of Philosophy*, in the absolute identity-system (*absolute Identitätssytem*) wherein reason finds the indifference point between transcendental and natural philosophy, idealism and realism, wherein it views absolute identity, that is, the absolute totality (of subjectivity and objectivity), as the condition of the possibility of multiple differentiation. Here "reason is the absolute": neither simply subjective (the thinking of thinkers) nor merely objective (that which is thought), absolute reason is pure reason, *abstraction* from both "to the true *in-itself*," their total indifference-point—it is absolute totality, identity with self, all being, and nothing is aside from it.[46] The infinite law of identity (the A = A of Fichte's *Doctrine of Knowledge*) governs the being and totality that is absolute reason (as well as the relation between thinking and being that occur for it): identity (not particular and independent subjects or predicates) is the only being (*einzige Sein*) that is posited as unconditional, certain, and never superseded (*nie aufgehoben*)—for in this being, thought and being are identical, one (*Eins*), with absolute reason, that is, identity is the identity of absolute reason.[47] Both reason and identity then have being: "*being* belongs as much to the essence of reason as to that of absolute identity."[48] Identity here is not the Spinozistic simple identity of A as subject and A as object; rather, identity means "indifference to A = A as expression of being and A = A as expression of knowledge."[49] And absolute identity is not simply material (Schelling is no natural philosopher)—for matter (*primum Existens*) is only the first relative totality, and *is,* only insofar as it belongs to the being of absolute identity. In other words, the law of reason is totality, and the law of totality is reason; they imply each other like being and one (Aristotle), and absolute reason = absolute identity—for Schelling's reason is the totality of all that is, and all that is, that has being, is one.

If philosophy then thinks reason as absolute reason, as the indifference point of subjectivity and objectivity, it thinks it as absolute identity. As absolute, however, in its totalizing identity, this reason re-inscribes how philosophy can conceive multiplicity: to view beings, things, as various or multiple (*mannigfaltig*), is to see them "not *in-themselves* or from the standpoint of reason."[50] Indeed, for Schelling, multiplicity in-itself (as the emergence of absolute identity from itself) is the "fundamental error of all philosophy."[51] Here the form under which absolute identity can be seen in the multiplicity of beings (predication) does not belong to its "essence"—for absolute identity *is* only under the "form" of an identity of identity (pre-predicative totality, the indifference point of all contradictions, of all difference between subjective and objective, form and essence). And the difference between essence and form, in the being of absolute identity, is an epistemological (not an ontological) issue: formally, multiplicity is subject to the predicative semantics of knowledge; essentially, multiplicity is *in-itself* no multiplicity at all—rather, it *is,* with respect to being, absolute identity. Although human reason thinks via predication, the absolute identity of absolute reason knows itself (*sich selbst erkennen*) as identity with self—yet it can only do so if it posits itself (*sich selbst setzen*) as the difference between subject and object, a difference in the magnitude of being (*Größe des Seins*) that is posited as a predominance of subjectivity (knowledge, *noein*) or objectivity (being, *on*), that is, as a predominance of potency or power (*Potenz*) in subject or object. Insofar as absolute identity, however, is seen in-itself, there is no difference between potencies, between subject/object; there is rather, absolute indifference (as the condition of the possibility of difference)—for "absolute identity is absolute totality."[52] Multiplicity then, the particularization of being, must be thought outside of absolute totality, outside the view of totality as identity (not spatially or temporally, but outside its essence, ex-terior, and outside its form, ex-static, *differentia formalis*). Thus, if philosophy is to view the multiplicity of beings (*physis*), then it must be *as-another,* that is, under the form of different potencies, separate from "the absolute," and not as they are *in-themselves,* not as the pure, clear identity (*reine ungetrübte Identität*) of absolute totality (*universum*), not as the total indifference of knowledge and being, subject and substance, not as the original (*ursprüngliche*) non-differentiation of subjectivity and objectivity, "*the first being,* and the being that has never been produced, but is"—for the difference between the absolute, totality, identity, indifference, and the multiplicity of individual beings, the difference of particular things, is a difference of representation (*Vorstellung*) and not of essence (*Wesen*): "things or appearances that appear to us as different, are not really different, but in reality one."[53]

Multiplicity then, in the identity-system, as the difference of particular beings, of individual entities (a kind of schematism that, like Kant's, permits a type of identity to be maintained across differentiation), is an appearance, an ir-real representation, a way of existing that remains unessential. The totality of each being is, with respect to itself, a totality—albeit a relative totality—however, insofar as it is expressed as potencies, and insofar as determinate potencies are representations of the absolute, individuals are identical with absolute totality. The absolute, therefore, explains all physical processes as material translations via differentiation, modifications in the potency that appears as outer changes in individual entities, in their way of existence (*Art der Existenz*), but not an actual heterogeneity in inner essence (*Wesen*).[54] Light or water, for example (as the original, self-identical substance), are appearances of absolute identity that translate via a shift in predominance from one pole to another: in the identity-system, physical transformations of beings (construction), reproduction, and deconstruction (*Dekonstruktion*) of relative totalities are existential, not essential, changes.[55] The truth is that all beings, with respect to essence, are homogeneous, absolutely identical. Although they may appear as existential transformations, therefore, the nature of physical processes are not to be understood as causal relations; rather, they are translations of identity relations, eidetic shifts in the drive toward unity: "*nature strives, in the dynamic sphere, necessarily towards absolute indifferenz.*"[56] And the drive toward absolute identity, toward unity of being, a kind of absolute pleasure principle, is common to both the human and natural world: "The human being is not alone in the world, there is a plurality of humans, there is a human race, a humanness. Like the multiplicity of things that in nature strives towards a unity, and completes itself and as it were, feels joyous, only in this unity, so too the multiplicity in the human world."[57] The inner identity of all things, the nature of a real-ideal pantheism (Schelling is no simple, dogmatic Spinozist), of all in all (*Alles in Allem*), is insured through the being (*Sein*) of absolute identity—and here nature is "absolute identity in general, insofar as it will be seen not as being, but as ground of its being."[58]

Schelling's solution then, to the problem of multiplicity, is the difference between essence and existence: the absolute is essentially one—and existentially many (differences), it is the absolute identity that shows itself as the existence of beings. The essential difference that Heidegger will later name the "ontological difference," the difference between Being (*Sein*) and beings (*Seiende*), the difference within *ens* "between essence, insofar as it exists, and essence, insofar as it is merely the ground of existence," is translated as the difference between God and all other beings: God has the ground of his existence in himself—and beings are inseparable (*unabtrennliches*), but different (*unterschied[e]nes*) from him.[59] Indeed, Schelling had already insisted upon this difference in order to clarify his conception of absolute identity as it appears in gravity: "in gravity (§54, *Anmerkung*) we must have, in fact, recognized the absolute identity with respect to essence, but not as being [existing], which it is, in that, much more the ground of its being (itself)."[60] And this is the difference that lies, for Hegel, within the "objective logic" (the first two books of the *Science of Logic,* "The Doctrine of Being" and "The Doctrine of Essence," as the displacement of the difference expressed in metaphysics and ontology, a difference superseded in the "Doctrine of the Concept") that investigates the nature of *ens* in general: "*ens* comprises both *being* and *essence,* a distinction for which the German language has fortunately saved different terms."[61]

For Schelling then, absolute identity posits itself as many (entities), wants to know itself as beings, because its nature, its ground (*Grund*) of existence (understood as essence [*Wesen*], not as cause [*Ursache*], as identical with and different from its existence [*Sein*]), is the totality of universal "love"—for love drives the absolute:

> In spirit, that-which-exists is one with the ground of existence; in it, both really are simultaneously, or it is the absolute identity of both. But over spirit is the original non-ground, which is no longer disinterest (indifference), and not even the identity of both principles, but the universal, the unity that is to all the same and yet from none apprehended, the beneficence that is free from all and yet interwoven in all; with a word, the love that is everything in everything.[62]

With the "ontology of love," freedom (of the absolute and all of nature, including the human experience of sensation and intelligence) is explained as will, that is, as the power or potential for good and evil:

> There is, in the last and highest instant, absolutely no other being as willing. Willing is original-being, and to this alone pass all predicates:

> groundlessness [i.e., unconditioned being], eternity, independence from time, self-affirmation. The whole of philosophy only strives to find this highest expression.[63]

And this is the willing (*Wollen*) that Heidegger will name the "Being of beings as a whole"—for within the unthought (*ungedacht*) of modern metaphysics that assumes time as passing-away (*Vergehen*), Schelling thinks the same (*Selbe*) but not identical (*Gleiche*) thought as Nietzsche: "with his thought of the eternal recurrence of the same, Nietzsche thinks what Schelling speaks of when he tells us that all philosophy strives to find the highest expression for [original] being as the will."[64]

For Schelling, however, the "absolute as love" is the "original-being as free willing"—and God, as absolute totality, as everything in everything (*Alles in Allem*), as higher than spirit, is one with love. The absolute identity of love (God) is the ground (essence) of all grounds (causes), a ground that is no ground at all, an original-ground (*Urgrund*) or rather, non-ground (*Ungrund*), pre-predicative indifference (not merely predicative identity) as the condition of the possibility of predication and ontological difference alike: "*without* indifference, i.e. *without* a non-ground, there would be no duality of principles."[65] In fact, indifference, means the place within which difference and identity are the same: following the distinction between *antecedenz* and *consequens,* Schelling thinks the (copula's) identity of difference in "in-difference" (*In-differenz*—precisely not *Ununterschiedenheit*). Thus, the love that is God, is the absolute identity, the absolute indifference of the ontological difference, the one essence in which two ways of functioning (*Wirkungsweisen*) are differentiated: on the one hand, (real) ground of existence, on the other, (ideal) essence—and if the absolute splits itself into being and beings, if it multiplies itself, appears as entities (to which it is essentially identical as totality), then it is because, as original-being, non-ground, its will is absolutely identical with its love.

From Dead Logic to the Bacchanalian Revel in Which No Member Is Not Drunk

> In Hegel, everything is worthless gray.
>
> —*Nietzsche*[66]

> The fury of disappearance lands finally in refuse.
>
> —*Krolow*[67]

Fichte and Schelling are not the only ones to think the absolute as non-absolute. Indeed, classical logic, like the empirical sciences, reduces thinking to quantification. Jealous of pure mathematics, "concept-less scientific method" exterminates the life of the mind. Following Kant, therefore, Hegel proposes the life of thought:

> Kant is chiefly concerned to banish the vulgar mechanistic way of thinking which stops short at the one determination of impenetrability, of *self-determined and self-subsistent puncticity,* and converts into something external the opposite determination, the relation of matter within itself or the relation of a plurality of matters, which in turn are regarded as particular ones—a way of thinking which, as Kant says, will admit no motive forces except pressure and thrust, that is, only action from without.[68]

Ironically, Hegel's charge against the dead bones of a classical, spiritless (*geistlos*) logic reappears today—and this time against Hegel himself.

For Derrida, not only the *Logic,* but the *Phenomenology,* insofar as it employs the *Logic*'s deep structure of the concept, falls into simple, repetitive calculation and becomes machinelike. In other words, following Nietzsche's "there is, in the spiritual, no extermination," dialectical negation is no negation at all: "what would be a 'negative' which did not allow itself to be superseded?"[69] Indeed, there is a moment in which Hegel's reflection on language in the *Encyclopedia* exhibits a twofold hierarchy: first, linguistic systems (*la parole, le voix*) are prioritized over other semiotic systems (*l'écriture*); and second, among semiotic systems, phonetic writing is prioritized over ideographic, hieroglyphic, or mathematical writing. Here Hegel claims that Chinese (like religion in the *Phenomenology*) is tied to representation: regardless of phonetic aspects (e.g., the capacity for tonal reproduction), it remains too empirical, too naturalistic, to serve as a tool for speculative thought insofar as its letters are taken from nature (e.g., from the designs of a tortoise shell). It is not surprising then that since thought is connected to language, the Chinese yin/yang, like numbers, are charged with formalism, with mere abstract thinking that remains inappropriate to concrete concepts. For Derrida this repressed (apparently capricious) logo-phallo-phonocentrism is paradigmatic for western metaphysical interests—and Hegel follows tradition. Yet as the preeminent philosopher of difference, is Derrida's own logic of rupture, substitution, or supplementation (like Bataille's of *dépense*), which seeks to provide a space for abstract negation under the sign of non-return, not simply the latest version of one-sided Hegelianism?[70]

Regardless, for Derrida, supersession as re-appropriation is the denial of abstract negation ("this structural incapacity to think without supersession"—a purely negative negation? Without a remains [*reste*]?).[71]

As he argues in *Glas,* Hegelian circularity, the annulus of *Sa* (*savoir absolute,* absolute spirit) so endemic to a Christian onto-teleo-theological horizon, cannot think the angle (of Bataille, or that which is "bent" in Genet): in *Aufhebung* (*rêleve*), either there are no remains at all (no finitude, individuality, proper name, nothing, non-presence, etc.—God is not really dead; the Phoenix rises), or the nod to abstract negation, within the conceptual moment of the double-mark, is an appearance, a "ruse of reason," ironical mask or "feint" (like the Jewish simulation-economy of castration in circumcision), that is, the logical paradox of the apotropaic that infinitely re-appropriates an opponent's power by doing to oneself (already) that with which one is threatened (castration), thereby also demonstrating the extreme to which one will go.[72] Or as he insists in *Of Grammatology,* for a Hegelian "metaphysics of the proper," both the trace of materiality, of writing, and irreducible difference, fall within the horizon of absolute knowledge under the sign of the Book. Or, thirty years after *Writing and Difference,* maintaining a surprising critical consistency while admitting "a sort of active and organized allergy, even organizing, with respect to the Hegelian dialectic," Derrida still claims that Hegel thinks history, the future (*le futur*), or more precisely, that which is always (like the Messiah) to come (*l'avenir* or *l'à-venir*), as a surprise without surprise (*surprise sans surprise*), as that which is bound to come (*voir venir*), without chance, contingency, accident, invention, as the somehow motivated repression of the radically new or aleatory.[73] And the *Logic* of spirit without negation ends in a dead machine: on the one hand, the concept should be the movement of living, free, speaking thought; on the other hand, its structure is a simple repetition, a rigid, computational system that tolerates variability only within a determined invariable structure. Difference is repressed (in a certain dialectical way), excluded under the sign of identity, unity, similarity: "it is not insignificant that the concept reduces difference to nothing."[74] Or again: "as soon as difference determines itself, it determines itself as opposition; it manifests itself to be sure, but its manifestation is at the same time (that is, the time of the same as the effacement of the time-remain(s) in the self [*Selbst*]) the reduction of difference, of the remain(s), of the gap. That is the thesis."[75] As Nietzsche writes: "spirit wants equality, i.e., a sensible impression subsumed under a present order: just like the body assimilates the inorganic."[76] Thus, for Derrida, the "truth" of Hegel's *Phenomenology* needs to be deconstructed because its absolute does not correspond to the totality it promises, to the completion of thought, insofar as supersession excludes exclusion (abstract negation); and the *Logic* must be deconstructed because its simplifying systematics re-constructs differences as indifferences, re-presents and re-presses free, living thought as that which it is not, that is, enslaved, dead repetition compulsion (*Widerholungszwang*).

Yet the one-sidedness of Derrida's reading is, strictly speaking, non-Hegelian. Avoiding the Charybdis and Scylla of Fichte's (Kantian) formal subjectivism and Schelling's absolute-identity without difference ("the night in which, as the saying goes, all cows are black"), Hegel's absolute, on the one hand, cannot be a mere work of reason (*Werk der Vernunft*), that is, intellectual or transcendental intuition that synthesizes (or transcends) unity and multiplicity; on the other hand, it can be neither simple oneness (unity, identity of nature) nor duality (of infinitely translating forms that hide one and the same, intractable logical structure—since classical logic reduces philosophy to computation); nor absolute non-identity (raised from the dead and passed off as living, that is, the indifference that loses the difference between absolute identity and absolute non-identity—for "unity floats only over death").[77] Rather, the absolute must show itself in its development, self-production, self-restriction, self-construction, in the multiplicity of forms and beings, subjects and substances, that is, as self-organizing totality; it must be (and must be thought as) the supersession of transcendental and natural philosophy, the double-movement that destroys and preserves contradiction by positing and exterminating it as truth, as the truth that is both neither one nor the other, but that is taken care of insofar as it is simultaneously both.[78]

Hegel answers Derrida's first charge: Negation is neither merely abstract nor simply determinate, but both—for the logic of the absolute is already in and for itself (*schon an und für sich*) the concept, that is, the movement that does and does not include and exclude that which is negated, its other. As in the *Phenomenology*, the absolute (as true concept) is the essential subject and substance of philosophy:

> The true is thus the Bacchanalian revel in which no member is not drunk; yet because each member collapses as soon as he drops out, the revel is just as much transparent and simple repose. Judged in the court of this movement [*quid juris* and *quid facti*], the single shapes of spirit do not persist any more than determinate thoughts do, but they are as much positive and necessary moments, as they are negative and evanescent.[79]

Here absolute spirit is totality because the negative is not only absolute—it is also abstract. Hegel writes: "the wounds of spirit heal without leaving scars."[80] If spirit's negations were always only absolute (supersession), then its wounds would leave scars, but this lack marks, the moment in which spirit negates abstractly. In other words, the concept is not only either/or—but either/or and both/and. Yet if the language of the concept in the expression of speculative truth must be both abstract and determinate, then it cannot remain merely predicative (S is P):

> Judgment is an *identical* relation between subject and predicate; in it we abstract from the fact that the subject has a multiplicity of determinatenesses other than that of the predicate, and also that the predicate is more extensive than the subject. Now if the content is speculative, the *non-identical* aspect of subject and predicate is also an essential moment, but in the judgment this is not expressed.[81]

Here the laws of classical logic (identity, non-contradiction, etc.) must be superseded in order to think the concept (wherein S is P and not-P)—for in the *Science of Logic,* the concept is a sign for that which it is not, a name for the nameless, an expression of the unexpressed (but not only) in subject and predicate. Like the beginning of the *Logic* itself which refers to an other, points to some other beginning (*weist auf etwas Anderes hin*), the concept is not yet (*ist noch nicht*)—for it is always on the way to itself, in motion; and it is this "on the way to," this semiotic hint (*Hinweis*), trace (*Spur*), or sign (*Zeichen*) of that which already exceeds expression and transcends language: "Language, as work of the understanding, gives expression only to universals," and the concept is not only (although also) a universal.[82] Thus, the non-predicative concept of the absolute names (and does not name) that which is named (and remains nameless): insofar as the concept is the dialectical movement that negates and does not negate (abstractly and determinately), it is a name-non-name referring to a name-non-name.

If the concept then is non-predicative (or rather, not only predicative), it is understandable why Hegel explicitly attacks ordinary mechanics:

> In judgments and syllogisms the operations are in the main reduced to and founded on the quantitative aspect of the determinations; consequently everything rests on an external difference, on mere comparison and becomes a completely analytical procedure and mechanical calculation. The deduction of the so-called rules and laws, chiefly of inference, is not much better than a manipulation of rods of unequal lengths in order to sort and group them according to size—than a childish game of fitting together the pieces of a colored picture puzzle. Consequently, this thinking has been equated, not incorrectly, with reckoning, and reckoning again with this thinking. In arithmetic, numbers are regarded as devoid of any concrete conceptual content, so that apart from their wholly external relationship they have no meaning, and neither in themselves nor in their interrelationships are thoughts.[83]

By equating the immanent and free movement of Hegel's logic with a machine, Derrida's second charge misses the way in which a particular determination undergoes negation—for negation means not only *that* (*daß*) something is negated, but *how* (*wie*) it is negated, why, wherefrom, whereto, wherein, to what extent, to what end, and so on. Negation as such, superficially taken as negation, reveals absolutely nothing of the quality (*eidos, Art*), of negation—for the concept, not the sheer form of negation, expresses and takes care of the essence of its content.

For Hegel, if pure quantitative determination appears as solely external, superficial to the life of spirit, then it is because its attempt to reduce qualitative differences to quantitative identities, to quantum (abstractly taken), ends in mechanical calculation (*Rechnen*). Thinking is the work of spirit (*Geist*), not of machines—and multi-tasking is not the function of thought. The automaton's perfection is not that of the mind (*Geist*):

> Because calculation is so much an external and therefore mechanical business, it has been possible to construct *machines* which perform arithmetical operations with complete accuracy. A knowledge of just this one fact about the nature of calculation is sufficient for an appraisal of the idea of making calculation the principle means for educating the mind and stretching it on the rack in order to perfect it as a machine.[84]

Calculation then is the torture chamber of spirit. And confusing quantification or mechanical calculation with speculative thought only serves to conceal the work of philosophy and the movement of the concept. For Hegel, as for Benjamin and Heidegger, technology (and technocracy), in the age of mechanical reproduction, is the slaughter of spirit.

Assuming that the *Logic* then is a machine functioning along a thesis/antithesis/synthesis or immediacy/negation/mediation blueprint, divided into "trinities," into three subsections each with the moments, is misleading. In fact, the tripartite structure is continually interrupted; for example, in "Quality," the section entitled "Transition" is a supplement (it is not a third and has no three); in "Quantity," the section entitled "Continuous and Discrete Magnitude" has only two moments and not three; in the "Inverse Ratio," of "Quantity," the second moment has only two sub-moments; the section on "Measure" finishes before the third moment of the chapter entitled "The Becoming of Essence," in order to make the transition from the "Doctrine of Being" to the "Doctrine of Essence" (being becomes essence). And the structure of each new chapter is not a mechanical repetition of previous chapters—for the living movement of thought, the life of spirit, is continuous as well as discontinuous, infinite as well as finite, identical as well as different. And the concept is always two-sided, always already pure/contaminated: on one side, the boring repetition of logical structure, the dialectic of thought (and spirit), is mechanical reproduction; on the other side, it is precisely that which cannot be thought through this repetition—for logic is not only the end or truth of thought, it is also its beginning. Thus, if logic as method is living thought and not only the predictable effect of some automaton, then it is because the concept is historical, because negation means the *way* in which a thing is and is not; and *Phenomenology*, as witness to the *Logic*'s concept, as the record of the moments of its pathway, cannot be mere calculation.

Hegel then needs no deconstruction because (in reaction to Fichte and Schelling) he has already self-deconstructed—and those who find here only worthless gray (*nichtswürdiges Grau*) have not seen the bacchanalian revel of absolute spirit in motion. Nevertheless, by thinking contradiction as contradiction (and as non-contradiction) in the movement of the concept, Hegel prefigures and determines the entire history of the "philosophy of difference" (of which Derrida is only the latest avatar). Conceptual logic means that totality is always already pure/contaminated, that the absolute is tainted by its other and spotless, that negation is and is not, that supersession cannot only mean supersession, and that thought can never be simply reduced to computation. Here the very logic of interior/exterior (*intérieur/extérieur*), upon which deconstruction depends, has always already been superseded in the concept that is/is not inside and outside, the identity and difference of identity and difference. As Derrida himself insists: "that it is submitted to the law of which it is the law, that is what gives to the structure of the Hegelian system a very twisted form so difficult to grasp."[85]

Indeed, if Derrida does have something important to say with respect to "Hegel's law," it very well may be the "law of the may be," that is, a skepticism (or suspension, that perhaps ends in nihilism) about the possibility of distinguishing kinds of negation, types of supersession, ways of taking care of ideas and things. In other words, opposed to the "yes" and/or "no" of philosophy today, of being and non-being, presence and absence, identity and difference, Derrida thinks the "maybe," that which may be and may not be, in order to demonstrate, in a perfectly Socratic fashion, that those who insist on the "logic of war," the binary or double economy of "with us" or "against us," do not even know that they do not know—for under the exigencies of war, that which appears as most necessary is to think and act in a refusal of necessity. Yet just "maybe," by underestimating the flexibility of the concept, deconstruction leaves intact the Hegelian threat, a threat constituted not by the logic of negation or the reduction of life to a machine, but by the way in which the dialectic serves as the horizon of all thought, by the way in which the logic of identity and difference circumscribes all action, history, and so on—precisely by not limiting or circumscribing it, that is, by subsuming the multiple possibilities for thought under the sign and structure of the is/is-not of the concept, and by taking care of the very problem of multiplicity. For can the concept not think the "maybe" as moment? A moment that may be? A may be "maybe"? A maybe that may only be a deconstructive moment that transitions into *différance*? A *différance* that may make no difference at all? For in the end, to paraphrase Derrida, who could really distinguish between a destruction and a deconstruction, between *différence* and *différance*?[86] And is the task at hand far more not to establish distinction, but to multiply that which is distinguished to the point where the very logic of distinction collapses, to the vanishing point of identity and difference? Or even further, to think that which cannot be thought by the economy of yes/no/maybe, that is, to think not just many, but manys?

Regardless, Hegel's absolute responds to the problem of multiplicity in a way that Fichte's and Schelling's could not: as a self-organizing totality, the absolute is neither a simple identity or pure totality, nor a mere difference machine, nor a pure multiplicity, radical plurality without unity; rather, it is essentially conceived as multiple. Indeed, a science of this absolute articulates the logic of multiplicity as multiple. And phenomenology prepares a preliminary image of the truly multiple absolute, and the truth that is absolutely multiple, the truth of the multiple shapes of absolute spirit. Yet how does multiplicity within a moment, and as the many moments, of absolute spirit show itself? If Hegelian multiplicity is particularity, and if phenomenology is supposed to permit this radical individuality to show itself, then how can it accomplish its goal without falling into the fixity of a philosophical system? Or is phenomenology precisely about the breakdown of systematicity, the thinking and being of the machine that both functions and fails? About the breakdown in multiplicity at the very moment that it becomes multiple? And about the breakdown of this breakdown in manys?

3

From Science to Speculation

The Logic of Multiplicity

> It is a common point from which I start; for there again and again I shall return.
>
> —*Parmenides*[1]

> In a circle beginning and end are common.
>
> —*Heraclitus*[2]

From the Greeks to Kant, a certain logic of multiplicity shows itself. Implicit to the pantheistic ontology of both Parmenides and Heraclitus ("listening not to me but to the *logos* it is wise to agree that all things are one"),[3] a circular metaphysics reappears in the structural economy of Kant's thought:

> Everything derived from the one.
> Everything connected in the one.
> The one derived from everything.
> Unity of subject, of ground, and of the whole.
> Possibility reality necessity.
> There are three transcendental criteria of the possibility of things in general. 3-fold formal unity.[4]

Here a circle of pure, primary concepts, of *unum*/unity/the-one, *verum*/truth/*panta*/plurality/everything, and *bonum*/perfection/totality shows itself—and truth is possible only if plurality functions with unity to form totality: "essence is unity, the essential parts are truth, all attributes together are totality."[5] Plurality (multiplicity, manifold, *Mannigfaltigkeit*) falls under the sign of unity—and unity is only possible out of multiplicity: "1. unity out of plurality, 2. unity of plurality under one another,

3. plurality out of unity."[6] The object of knowledge and knowledge of the object ("unity of the object and unity of the manifold in the object"),[7] as well as the structure of logic, the rules of subsumption, the understanding of truth as the relation of a representation to an object, and so on—all this is only possible in terms of the circular movement (*Kreisbewegung*) of the threefold concept of unity, plurality, totality. Yet how does the "logic of the circle" think multiplicity? What is the logic of this multiplicity? To what extent is it multiple? And what are multiple logics? Philosophical logics? For how does the concept enable (and disable) philosophy to think this multiplicity?

Hegel takes up the form of Kant's thought as the essence of the logic of the concept—an "in itself return-turning circular line" that permits philosophy to think before philosophy, prior to itself, to that which is (essentially, not necessarily temporally) "always already," to jump behind its own shadow: "the foundational-and motivational-tendency, to philosophize before philosophy, was finally conscious to completely articulate itself; it found exactly what was to be done, namely, the transformation of philosophy into the formula of knowledge, in logic."[8] Yet although Hegel takes much from Kant, his critique of transcendental logic, "pure reason," the categories, the thing in itself, and so on ends in a harsh judgment: "the Kantian philosophy thus serves as a cushion for intellectual indolence which soothes itself with the conviction that everything is already proved and settled."[9] Philosophy, therefore, is logic only insofar as it thinks the absolute as totality, as the unconditioned proposition that conditions all others, as that which is prior to (and the ground of) all identity and difference, the whole that is its determinations, the totality that is conditioning/conditioned (*bedingend/bedingt*) that is itself origin and result (thereby avoiding a bad infinity [*schlechte Unendlichkeit*]), that is, the absolute that supersedes the simple appearance (*Schein*) of beginning, middle, and end. And philosophy thinks absolute multiplicity insofar as it "includes essentially only one idea"—for it is absolute knowledge (*absolutes Erkennen/Wissen*), that is, the knowledge that multiplicity is a moment of that which is, from the other side, all-encompassingly the same, the identity and difference of identity and difference, the knowledge that shows itself to itself, and demonstrates "that its last is just as much its first."[10] Here philosophical division (*Trennung*) is absolutized in the concept, and multiplicity is superseded: in the relation of the one to the many, their contradiction is taken care of, resolved, and preserved, in the absolute one (*schlechthin Eins*). The movement of one and many subject(s) and substance(s), from abstraction through contradiction to universality, is the movement of the concept itself as the unification of opposites (*Vereinigung Entgegengesetzter*): the abstract identity that, through a determinate (particular) form of difference which is simultaneously an inseparable element in the identity, shows itself to be "the determination of a difference in which the differences are inseparably conjoined."[11] If logical investigation is to serve philosophy (and not the reverse), by taking the forms of thought, the categories, as its subject, as the pure thought (*reine Gedanke*) of the thing itself (*die Sache selbst*), and not as a mere thing (*Ding*), object (*Gegenstand*), pure thought or thoughts for themselves in complete abstraction from things; then philosophy must supersede formal logic, free itself from empty abstraction and indifference to content. Yet how can the logic of the concept (in the living sense of *logos*) become the logic of multiplicity?

With classical logic, freedom is slavery; liberation means limitation, delimitation, that is, the drawing of boundaries, frontiers, that permits it to show itself as itself, as determinate. In other words, logic frees thought from things, in the fixed forms of thought (*Denkformen*) that appear in language as super-natural (*übernaturlich*), as that whereby humans transcend empirical nature, things, objects, and simultaneously differentiate themselves from animals. Here, grounded upon the law of identity (A = A) and the principle of non-contradiction, logic functions with the full power of abstraction, through the separation of form and content, truth and certainty; it takes the rules of thought (*Regeln des Denkens*) as its object, organizes them into a finite system without infinity, produces half-truths (not the agreement or correspondence of thought and thing)—but this logic cannot think things in themselves (*Dinge an sich*) precisely because, by definition, "what is essential in truth, its content, lies outside of it."[12]

In the western philosophical tradition then, Hegel's name stands for the first loosening of the strictures of classical logic. Kant accepted the laws of logic as those of thought:

> That *logic* has already, from the earliest times, proceeded upon this sure path [i.e., of science] is evidenced by the fact that since *Aristotle* it has not required to retrace a single step, unless, indeed, we care to count as improvements the removal of certain needless subtleties or the clearer exposition of its recognized teaching, features which concern the elegance rather than the certainty of the science. It is remarkable also that to the present day this logic has not been able to advance a single step, and is thus to all appearance a closed and completed body of doctrine. . . . We do not enlarge but disfigure sciences, if we allow them to trespass upon one another's territory. The sphere of logic is quite precisely delimited; its sole concern is to give an exhaustive exposition and a strict proof of the formal rules of all thought, whether it be *a priori* or empirical, whatever

> be its origin or its object, and whatever hindrances, accidental or natural, it may encounter in our minds.[13]

For Hegel, however, "if logic has not suffered any change since Aristotle—and in fact, judging by modern compendiums of logic the changes frequently consist mainly in omissions—then the conclusion which rather should be drawn is that it is all the more in need of a total reworking."[14] Out of Kant's psychologism, a merely subjective critique that never comes to the object in itself, that never attains the very certainty it asks of itself, a new logic emerges—for Hegel's logic of the concept is both subjective and objective, his phenomenology of the absolute is both subject and substance, and his phenomeno-logic of the absolute concept is as ideal as it is real. And this frees logic from mere abstraction, mere form, revivifies it: the dead bones of classical logic find new life in the concept, that is, each concept is simultaneously determinate (in its content) and universal (in its form)—for here *a* concept (*ein Begriff*) is a moment of *the* concept (*der Begriff*). And the concept's truth is not merely subjective, not simply doxalogical, figments (*Hirngespinste*) of the rational subject (as in the metaphysical arch from Descartes through Schelling) that turn philosophy into a formalistic fear of objects; rather, as it emerges in absolute knowing as the identity and difference of truth and certainty (*Wahrheit* and *Gewißheit*), it is a spiritual or living (*lebendige*) unity, an absolute-concrete (*absolut-konkrete*) concept.

For Hegel then "logic is, accordingly, to be understood as the system of pure reason, as the realm of pure thought. *This realm is truth as it is without veil in and for itself.*"[15] Yet logic is not the realm of unveiled truth, but the realm of truth "as it is without veil," that is, the realm of truth unveiled (like God in religious representations)—for unveiled truth is not truth; it is a result, and the originally impure truth of the concept shows itself, appears phenomenally as veiled, a moment in the system of pure reason. Indeed, if conceptual truth is pure, then its purity cannot consist in non-mixture or indifference (Schelling); rather, purity implies impurity, that is, the concept as the supersession of opposites, as the absolute qua identity and difference of identity and difference—this dialectic is no longer logical abstraction since logic shows itself to be the element of thought, element that is, not in the sense of "material element," e.g., "smallest part" or "point"; but as a fish in water is "in its element"—for fish live and breathe by virtue of water; and they are not simply "in" water, as water is in a jug, but water is always also in fish. In other words, the element of thought, as the logic of the moving, differentiated/unified concept (neither as material/empirical, nor as simply ideal/transcendental, nor as subjective and/or objective) that permits (like Kant's schematism—although no longer via transcendental projection) the transition between moments. The concept as element essentially precedes (and teleologically determines) differentiation; it is the inseparability of that which is separated, that is, that which is prior to logic, that true impurity of purity. And as its unveiled truth, the conceptual element is the life blood of logic. Thus, as the "science of pure thought, the principle of which is pure knowing," logic means that its unity is not simply one, undifferentiated unity; on the contrary, the concept has two essentially different moments; it is the inseparability of two different types of beings (a subjective being for itself [*für sich Seiend*] and an objective being for another)—and difference makes an elemental difference: "it is solely because they are simultaneously known as different (yet not with an independent being) that their unity is not abstract, dead, unmoving, but concrete."[16]

As the living supersession of its moments, Hegel's logic has the double-concept as its element. The movement of supersession, however, even supersedes itself, that is, itself as its other, natural philosophy (cf. *Enzy,* "Philosophy of Spirit")—for even an "absolute logic" cannot remain one-sided, cannot only be the identity of identity and difference, a logic of identity; nor of the difference or division between the two; and nor of their identity or difference. Rather, from the very first system fragment in the *Jena Logic* (1804–5), before the *Phenomenology of Spirit,* through the first chapter of the *Encyclopedia* (1830), to the *Science of Logic* (1812–32), Hegel's logic is the logic of the movements of the moments of the absolute concept—a movement through which the circle is both broken and whole, incomplete and complete. As temporally and methodologically prior, as a propedeutic and precursor to the living conceptual multiplicity of the *Phenomenology,* the *Logic* provides the beginning, base, structure, form, the lifeless bones of a skeleton (*leblose Knochen eines Skelettes*) upon which spirit fleshes itself out in its totality, in the totality that is just as much non-total—and since the beginning is the end, the *Logic* is the absolute knowledge, the "pure science," to which the *Phenomenology* drives.[17] Indeed, taken together, in their identity and difference, the *Phenomenology* and the *Logic* are conceptual; they form a single proposition, the one idea of speculative philosophy, that is just as much double.

Logic then is "the form of the inner self-movement of the content," the form of the negative as positive, self-negation in motion, self-realization in process.[18] And the "logic of logic" may be expressed in one sentence:

> the negative is just as much positive, or what is self-contradictory does not resolve itself into a nullity, into abstract nothingness, but essentially

> only into the negation of its *particular* content, in other words, that such a negation is not all and every negation but *the negation of a determinate thing* which resolves itself, and consequently is a determinate negation, and therefore the result essentially contains that from which it results.[19]

Here the concept is result, the negation or opposition, the unity of itself and its opposite, the product of the process, that which takes care of itself and its other. And if the negation can include its opposite in itself, then it is because its opposite is *its* opposite; that is, it belongs to it. In classical logic "negation" and "negation of negation" remain indifferent forms, mechanical functions, applied to interchangeable contents—but here negation is not just any negation; it is content specific, dependent, negation in a particular way of a particular moment.

As the form of particularity then, logic is no longer purely form: the multiplicity of moments means that in spite of their abstract form, they maintain their multiple differences, their individuality, their own negative—and this is the *Logic*'s multiplicity. On the one hand, insofar as no two moments are identical, logic is multiple; on the other hand, however, insofar as the moments can be systematized, can also be thought in conformity with the concept, the logic is non-multiple. In other words, Hegel's concept follows the logic of multiplicity and non-multiplicity.

Beginning at the beginning of the *Science of Logic,* however, logic qua science appears as purely non-multiple; it takes on the narrative form of a systematic re-presentation of the concept in its philosophical development from the form of immediate-unconditional being, through essence, to its concept. As always two-sided, a double-entendre, the concept determines itself by superseding its constitutive moments, by both preserving and destroying them in their relation. In every moment, however, the concept is not just the same, identical, nor is it merely different; rather, it is the identity and difference of identity and difference. Indeed, for the *Logic,* being is identical and different from essence (and vice versa), and the concept of both is the identity and difference of both. The logic of the identity and difference of identity and difference is that of contradiction, of contradiction as contradiction and as non-contradiction, the logic of the concept that is just as much the logic of the multiplicity of its moments, the logic of multiplicity itself, of the concept of multiplicity and the multiplicity of the concept. Indeed, the logic of multiplicity is that of the concept; the question remains, however: What is the multiplicity of the concept? In other words, if the concept is a contradiction (and not just), a contradiction that contradicts itself, a multiplicity that is not just multiple, then what is the logic of contradiction and the logic of multiplicity?

The Multiplicity of Logic

> [W]e are not inclined to concede that our human logic is logic as such or the only kind of logic (we would rather persuade ourselves that it is merely a special case and perhaps one of the oddest and most stupid cases).
>
> —*Nietzsche*[20]

For Hegel the content of logic belongs to a formal unity, to a dialectical system of reflective-determinations (*Reflexionsbestimmungen*). The system is a "science" insofar as its method (in which it is one with its object, contains no difference [*nichts Unterschiedenes*]) is dialectical—but not *a* dialectic that is applied from outside as an isolated instrument or means of investigation; rather, *the* dialectic that is the content's own, that belongs to it, that is its own moving rhythm, the course of the thing itself (*Gang der Sache selbst*) wherein differences have their own inner connectedness, their own immanent, coming-to-be with their particular other. The scientific system, therefore, moving itself forward through (*durch, dia-lectic*), by way of, the conceptual negative, via the element of thought that it has in itself, the positive (inner) negation that is "the principle of all natural and spiritual life in general," is speculative; and the concept is the "soul of the structure, the method that dwells in dialectic."[21] Thus, the forms of logic are no longer merely next to or alongside (*neben*) their contents, nor are they (dead) abstract universals; rather, insofar as they embrace the wealth of the particular (*Reichtum des Besonderen*), they are speculative-dialectical concepts, the essence of all contents—and logic is no longer "a particular alongside other particulars," but the essence of particularity, the absolute-true (*Absolut-Wahre*).[22]

If the science of logic then is to determine its object (and itself) as its own, as particular to the moments, to the many moments in their own difference, that is, as multiple, then it must itself, from the very beginning (and in the end), be multiple. First, multiplicity falls onto one side (particularity) of the speculative dialectic; and the multiplicity of multiplicity shows itself as one of two moments, the many of the ones that are many. Yet second, multiplicity must serve as that through which unity determines itself, the other (element and way)—but not only, for universality must be multiple, universal multiplicity. Third, the logical concept must multiply itself, determine itself in terms of (by superseding) particular and universal multiplicity—and not just once, but a multiplicity of times in a multiplicity of ways—and not just, but also as supersession of the supersession, multiple supersessions. Thus, if the concept follows the logic of multiplicity, the concrete way in which multiplicity can show itself as multiple and as non-multiple, if there is *a* logic, then it must be just as much not *a* logic, but logics.

On the one hand, Hegel thinks the multiplicity of logics in their intimate (conceptual) relations to their contents: for example, the logic of being multiple, of not-being multiple, of becoming multiple. Yet on the other hand, becoming becomes the multiple/non-multiple logic for the multiple beings, essences, and concepts, for the being, essence, and concept of multiplicity. If the logic of multiplicity is multiple, then it is because it is also non-multiple, that of the two- (and only two) sided concept.

The multiplicity of logics then is just as much subject to the non-multiple logic of conceptual contradiction. And movement is Hegel's way of thinking the logic of contradiction, the two-sided concept. Scientific systematicity implies that the "inner necessity" of the account (*logos*) of the movement of the moments is neither dogmatic, historical, nor merely formal: for instance, computational or logical in the classical sense, nor predicative in the sense of simply analytic. Scientific judgments express the movement of science itself, namely, of conceptual thought. The necessity here lies in the movement from implicit to explicit: from body to extension, from being to nothing, and vice versa—in the same way that extension belongs to the concept of body, nothing belongs to being, universal to real, difference to identity, and so on.

Being, for instance, can only determine itself via that which it is not, through negation—and its negation is nothing (not just any-thing, any other or accident) because nothing belongs to being. Nothing is as implicit in being as extension is in body, and its explication is not the will of a subject (however pure), but the "synthetic" movement of dialectic, of the things themselves. Substance then is not to be understood as a real predicate of a subject; rather, as substance, it is its essential explication, that is, scientific explication expressed as the movement of the concept. And if subject melts away, dissolves, or disappears (*zerfließt, vergeht, verschwindet*) in substance, it is because *its* substance is its own.[23] Speculative thought, wherein the concept (the end) is the beginning, thinks the truth of subject and substance as determinations not because (like body and extension) they define it; rather, since it is the identity and difference of the identity and difference of both, the subject and substance of subject and substance. Similarly, becoming is the essence (substance) and the being (subject) of being and nothing; it is the name of their own movement, of that which becomes and explicates itself (via negation, i.e., diremption into its moments) in them. Becoming disappears in being and nothing, just as they disappear in each other, because they belong together (as identically different and differently identical). In Kantian terms, the dialectic's necessity is analytic; but for

Hegel, the movement of analysis shows itself as synthetic: the analytic synthesis and synthetic analysis is the movement of the science of the concept in the logical moments of subject and substance.

Yet although the narrative (time and space) of science is linear, that of speculative thought is circular. Here being and nothing have already gone over into one another when they submit to the diachronic laws of scientific re-presentation; they show themselves as the beginning of science, but they are always already results, abstractions, from becoming, from the concept that is their truth. Speculative philosophy sees through scientific method to the deep, logical structure, to the movements of things in themselves, to the presentation of moments as moments. In other words, to paraphrase Heidegger, for Hegel: science does not think "speculatively"—for speculative thought approaches the logic of multiplicity as both double (i.e., not multiple) and non-double (multiple). Yet can Hegel think multiplicity as multiple if determination always means negation? Is even the most multiple of logics not subsumed under yet another non-multiple logic, however contradictory? Is the metaphysical horizon of conceptual logic not the logic of multiplicity or the multiplicity of logics, but rather its dependence upon a Spinozist understanding of determination qua negation—both for its way of thinking that which it determines as the identity and difference of form and content in its particular multiplicity (and in its non-multiplicity), and that which determines it as a logic or logics? What would it mean to think multiple determination? And what is the multiplicity of multiple logics? Is it quality? Quantity? Relation? Is multiple determination multiple if it is always multiple negation? Does the knot of Hegel's attempt to think the logic of multiplicity and the multiplicity of logics lie in the "not"?

The Beginning Is the End

> In my beginning is my end. In succession
> Houses rise and fall, crumble, are extended,
> Are removed, destroyed, restored, or in their place
> Is an open field, or a factory, or a by-pass.
> Old stone to new building, old timber to new fires,
> Old fires to ashes, and ashes to the earth
> Which is already flesh, fur and faeces,
> Bone of man and beast, cornstalk and leaf.
>
> —*T. S. Eliot*[24]

The identity of the concept is already set at the beginning (that is the end), but its truth is only determined in the process. The *Science of Logic* begins with being, with pure being as unconditional, undifferentiated, simple, original immediacy: "*being,* and nothing else, without further specification and filling."[25] This purity however, is not only original, but also a result of abstraction; it is the concept as both origin and result. In one sense, the beginning of logic has already occurred when the science begins—for everything is always already impure, a combination or mixture: "there *is* nothing, nothing in heaven or in nature or in mind or anywhere else which does not equally contain both immediacy and mediation, so that these two determinations reveal themselves to be *unseparated* and *inseparable* and the opposition between them to be a nullity."[26] And similarly, in the *Phenomenology*: consciousness has raised itself to the level of the absolute, and insofar as it is no longer merely subjective or objective, subject or substance, it is result, that is, the concept—for the logic of beginning is result in the sense of end (*telos* and result of abstraction). But in another sense, the "science" of logic, of pure thought, begins with the unmediated, what seems to be a pure, abstract beginning that presupposes nothing (and thus grounds the scientific result): pure-immediate being is accepted as the beginning of logic, taken in its one-sidedness (*Einseitigkeit*), because the science qua science must have a beginning, "precisely *because* here it is the beginning."[27] The identity of science is determined by its ability to begin with a mediated concept, to start with what appears as pure, one-sided—and this is its limitation or horizon. Philosophy, however, cannot really start with pure being—for then nothing can proceed from it, difference cannot be derived from simple identity; rather, the beginning of pure being is just as much the beginning with pure nothing, with the nothing that always already contains being—that is, the beginning "is" and "is not"; it is the "unity of being and nothing; or is non-being which is at the same time being, and being which is at the same time nothing."[28] And the unity (identity and difference) of being and nothing is the beginning as both undifferentiated and differentiated: the beginning itself (*der Anfang selbst*), the absolute beginning of logic, is the concept, the absolute, the end, the "unity of differentiatedness and non-differentiatedness."[29] Here Hegel follows the course of the history of philosophy: he seems to accept Parmenides' assertion that the beginning must be with being because non-being is not—if the beginning is nothing (*Nichts*), then it cannot be pure nothing (*reine Nichts*); rather, it must be non-being, the nothing that is (*Nichtsein*). However, although the *Science of Logic* begins with being, its ground, the beginning that has always already begun, that is the end (*telos*), is the absolute concept, the identity and difference of identity and difference, the becoming of being and nothing. Logic, therefore, progresses from this one-sided purity to its supersession in the concept that appears as result of dialectic—however, this "advance is actually a retreat into the ground, to what is primary and true, on which depends and, in fact, from which originates, that with which the beginning is made."[30] Likewise, in the *Phenomenology*, the end is the beginning, the result, the ground:

> consciousness on its onward path from the immediacy with which it began is led back to absolute knowledge as its innermost *truth* . . . this is true in still greater measure of absolute spirit reveals itself as the concrete and final supreme truth of all being, and which is at the *end* of the development is known as freely externalizing itself.[31]

In other words, the temporally (causally, narratively) first is essentially last (result), and that which appears latter is truly prior (ground). Although the science of logic fulfills its demand for a beginning with being, with indeterminate immediacy (*unbestimmte Unmittelbare*), speculative philosophy's circular structure, "wherein the first is also the last and the last is also the first," means that the beginning, middle, and end, prior to the logical beginning, are superseded in the concept, are taken care of in the true ground.[32]

The concept as circle then *appears as* "infinite," that is, the supersession of the relation and non-relation of the finite and the infinite; it *appears as* the identity of their identity and their difference that resolves and preserves their contradiction, that is and is not self-contradictory, and therefore can and cannot persist as a result, in its stable/unstable unity—the dialectic is driven by being and nothing, by the self-contradiction and the non-self-contradiction (or rather, by the self-contradiction of the self-contradiction and the non-self-contradiction) of the concept. Yet is this not a bad infinity (Kant/Fichte) once again? Is the dialectic not doomed to unending progress? The solution to the problem of conceptual infinity lies in the circle's finitude (Parmenides/Heraclitus)—for if the beginning is the end, then the finite and the infinite (and their double in/through their other) are only moments of finitized infinity: "the image of true infinity, bent back into itself, becomes the *circle*, the line which has reached itself, which is closed and wholly present, without *beginning* and *end*."[33] The concept is neither finite nor infinite, but absolute, an infinite finitude, finite infinity; it is both finite and the infinite. For Kant, this absolute would constitute a fallacious cosmology, wherein reason could only be in contradiction with itself, a "bedazzling but false illusoriness."[34] Yet insofar as the purity of finitude and infinity are abstractions, the superseding concept solves the problem of their contradiction by thinking them qua contradiction. Here speculative philosophy takes care of different moments as differentiated and brought together (*zusammengebracht*), thinks opposition as determined and resolved, the infinite relation of contradiction and reconciliation—and "this inseparability is their concept," that is, the absolute that is the logical form of the concept, that is always already (*ewig schon*) as finite as it is infinite, as identical as it is differentiated, ideal as it is real, subject as much as substance, attraction as repulsion, one as many, and so on.[35] Thus, the *Logic* is the systematic exposition of circular (speculative) thought—and therein, it must think the concept that is the means, method, the forms, for thinking the particular multiplicity of its object (and not just the multiplicity of objects), it must be a multiple logic, multiple within each moment and across moments, the multiplicity of multiplicity that *appears to* have its solution in the circle, in contradiction and reconciliation, the identical difference and differential identity of identity and difference, the one of many, the many ones. Yet does the "and-structure" (however interior, immanent) not imply a reduction of multiplicity to the double? How can the logic of infinite and finite, of finite infinity and infinite finitude, become multiple?

4

Being Multiple

The Being of Multiplicity

For Hegel the logic of multiplicity begins as a science of being. Yet being is neither simply a particular predicate ascribed to a substantive, nor that substance that makes a thing what it is, nor a consequence or effect; rather, it is that quality through which a being is in the first place, that is, the very ground of each being that allows it to be, before it is some kind of being, some-thing or ob-ject. To be means to be qualified, to have the quality of being. A being is not first, and then it is qualified; on the contrary, if a being is, then it is always already qualified. The problem of being then is not to find some original unqualified or pure being that could serve as the ground of beings—for being will always show itself as an abstraction—rather, it is to let being show itself as concrete, as a quality, quantity, relation, and so on. In other words, to let being show itself as multiple, thereby allowing the multiplicity of being to become a problem.

The problem of being multiple then is one of multiple qualification and of the quality of being multiple. The science of logic, however, in beginning with the beginning that has already begun, in seeking its beginning, its ground, essence, begins with that which *immediately* shows itself, with existence itself, pure being as indeterminate, without difference or diversity (within or without itself), empty self-identity (without any relation to an other), that is, lacking all qualities, being qua being, not yet here or there, then or now, present or absent, and so on. Yet this "pure being" as non-determinate, non-immediate, non-qualified, is *nothing.* Being (not nothing) is the beginning of logic because it is an indeterminate immediate (*unbestimmte Unmittelbare*). But if Hegel follows Parmenides here (only being is, nothing is not), then it is because science follows history: "what is the *first* in the *science* had of necessity to show itself *historically* as the *first.* And we must regard the Eleatic *One* or being as the first step in the knowledge of thought."[1] Although science is temporal, corresponds to history, that which is first, the beginning (origin in the sense of ground/essence) appears latter (in the narration or in thought): becoming follows being and nothing in the *Logic;* absolute spirit only appears at the end of the *Phenomenology*. In the narrative beginning of the science of logic, pure (abstract) being shows itself to be nothing; but nothing, the other of being (*to heteron* [Plato, *Parmenides*]), like being, is pure nothing, indeterminate, complete emptiness, without content, lacking all qualities—but this nothing is, that is, is being: "the said reality in all realities, the being in all determinate being, which is supposed to express the concept of God, is nothing else than abstract being, which is the same as nothing."[2] The difference between being and beings, essence and existence, exemplifies a not yet superseded moment in the dialectic and the history of philosophy. Here being is still reality (*Realität, Wirklichkeit*), and God is determined as the sum-total of all realities (*Inbegriff aller Realitäten*); yet being is far more a moment, only one side, of becoming; it is a determination that must take its place alongside other determinations as one of many (however multiple it may itself be)—any priority (*Vorrang*) of being (e.g., Heidegger's in *Being and Time*) is the impropriety of being. The *Logic* then could just as well begin with nothing: for nothing is an "indeterminate immediacy" as well—and, as the absence of being, nothing is. Indeed, "nothing, it is said, is only the absence of being, darkness thus only the absence of light."[3] And again: "nothing is not yet posited in being, although being is essentially nothing, and vice versa."[4] Thus, in every movement of the logical dialectic, it is immaterial (*gleichgültig*) whether the first moment is named first and the second moment, second: what appears as immediacy, as immediately true, is a function of contingent history, but the speculative necessity of history does not consist in the narrative or temporal order of its moments. Absolute spirit wears no watch.

In fact, if being and nothing can equally function as beginnings, then it is because they are precisely not the beginning; rather, they are results of abstraction (*Resultate der Abstraktion*) from the concept of becoming, from the identity and difference of being and nothing.[5] That which appears as given has already been "given"; the facticity of the fact has always already been constructed, reduced, produced. The hint to the true beginning of logic is to be found in the apparent purity of being or nothing—for it is becoming wherein their contradiction is taken care of, simultaneously maintained and resolved, that is, the transition (*Übergehen*) from being to nothing and vice versa, the being that is not and the nothing that is, the becoming that unifies being and nothing, in neither just being nor just nothing, the concept wherein their difference is superseded.[6] The truth of being and nothing is the movement (*Bewegung*) of becoming in its dialectical moments: from coming-to-be and ceasing-to-be (*Entstehen und Vergehen*) as the determinate unities of being and nothing wherein each is differentiated from the other, each is the unity that contains them both (on the one hand, starting from nothing and going over to being; on the other hand, starting from being and going over to nothing)—although not yet as superseded in determinate-being (*Dasein*). Becoming allows being and nothing to show themselves as inseparable (*untrennbar*), simultaneously different and non-separated (*ungetrennt*); and it is here that they appear in the form of the concept, as the supersession of an absolute (not merely abstract) difference. Hegel's grammar is quite precise here: "what is the truth is neither being nor nothing, but that being—does not pass over but has passed over—into nothing, and nothing into being."[7] Yet becoming is here not to be understood as mere synthesis (and Hegel's dialectic cannot be reduced to the mechanical motions of thesis/antithesis/synthesis): "because synthesis suggests more than anything else the sense of an external bringing together of mutually external things already there, the name synthesis, synthetic unity, has rightly been dropped."[8] Nevertheless, although it is still concealed (*verborgen*), the transition has already happened: being has already become nothing and nothing has become being—for this becoming is their truth, their between (*Zwischen*), and they are and are not only insofar as they become (and do not become) one another, insofar as they take care of each other.

Becoming then, the identity and difference of being and nothing, is the first truth (*erste Wahrheit*) that forms (literally) "once and for all the basis and element of all that follows."[9] As basis, becoming is the paradigm for all further logical determinations: determinate-being, being-for-self, measure, and so on (all philosophical concepts) are translations of this first concept; yet as concepts, their relation to becoming must be conceptual, they must be both the same as and different from becoming. And as element, becoming is characterized by the unrest (*Unruhe*) that remains in the unified difference of incompatible moments, that causes movement, the movement within which thought moves, *a movement inside a movement,* the contradiction and non-contradiction of the identity and difference that is and is not, the concept in which being and nothing is dissolved and remains. Indeed, becoming is not an abstract/one-sided unity of being and nothing; it is the true result (*wahre Resultat*) as original lack (*Mangel*), the end that is always already beginning (however latent, or rather, unexpressed, implicit, in being and nothing)—and this concept shall determine (absolutely, conceptually) "all that follows," shall act as the living form of the *Logic*'s many moments, as the concept of the concept of the particular differences of multiplicity.

Multiplicity then emerges at the precise moment in which the concept shows itself to be, strictly speaking, outside of language, inexpressible, nameless—or at least a problem for the logic of language and thought. The language of becoming is no language at all: "*pure being and pure nothing is thus the same.*"[10] Here grammar marks the breakdown of language as expression (*Ausdruck*) of the concept (the sentence does not read "being and nothing *are* the same")—that which has remained nameless can only be named in superseding the rules, forms, the grammar, and logic of language.[11] Predicative structures in the form of judgments (S is P) are profoundly inadequate for the expression of speculative truth: "language, as work of the understanding, gives expression only to universals"; and the concept is not only (although also) a universal, for instance, becoming is not only an individual (i.e., proper) name—for then it would not express its universality and would simultaneously appear arbitrary, forget the "multiple determinatenesses" concealed in subjects and predicates.[12] Against the critique of pure reason that yields a conceptual structure of abstract unity (e.g., Kant's a priori synthesis of self-consciousness, transcendental apperception) that excludes all multiplicity and manifoldness (*Vielheit und Mannigfaltigkeit*), confines itself to the difference-less and the indeterminate (*Unterschiedslosen und Unbestimmten*), falls into the ideal/real, transcendent/immanent, subject/object, subjective/objective dualisms (and their preferences, hierarchies, polemics), shuts out all that is differentiated and determinate (*Unterschieden und Bestimmten*)—against all this, the *Logic* thinks multiplicity because it thinks dialectically, that is, the inner movement and transitions of speculative thought in conceptual supersession.[13] Thus, the concept is the logic of naming the nameless, a non-name that refers to a non-name, to the multiplicity that has no name—and the logic of the concept is the logic of multiplicity.

To Be One

The question then is no longer if the *Logic* thinks multiplicity, but what does it mean to be multiple? It is not *having* a plurality of parts, perspectives, aspects, dimensions, sides, and so on; rather, it is a particular quality, a kind or type of being. Multiplicity means a way of being many, many ones. Being many does not mean "having many predicates" or "having many as a predicate"; rather, as a concept, being many is the "ways" in which being both is and is not many, is one and is many. To be many as many is to be without one, wholeness, unity, to be pure dissemination, indeterminate dispersion, simple deterritorialization; but as such, being many is not just many—for it is also its negation, that is, one. Being then means being-determinate (and indeterminate) as many—and as not-many. Being many does not mean "being present as many," because it means just as much "being absent as many," and "being present/absent as not many," being the movement of presencing/absencing—the being present/absent (always already) *as* many/not many. The "to be," from which being as indeterminate and immediate (or as present/absent) is abstracted in thought, is what it is, is at all, insofar as it always also is a particular quality: to be means to be of a certain quality. The quality of being multiple is not a predicate of things, beings, entities; rather, it is the condition of the possibility of multiple predication: a being can be multiple insofar as it is already determined via the quality of multiplicity. The multiplicity of beings is their quality, their way of being what they are. Multiplicity is not pluralization because a single being is in a multiplicity of ways—and the way it can be multiple is its quality. In other words, multiplicity is a determination, a quality in the sense of being, that which being is.

In the *Logic* then, multiplicity shows itself explicitly (for the first time at the end of "Section One," of the "Doctrine of Being") as a determination or quality of being. Previously, being showed itself purely with respect to itself as such, in itself (*an sich*), as indeterminate, alone, without any determination whatsoever, lacking identity, not even different from an "other." And when being becomes determined as multiple, it has already developed to the point of relating to an other; it has shown itself as the movement of itself in relation to that through which it is, namely, nothing—and in this movement, it is not only being as such, in itself; it *is* just as much another for another, an other for nothing. More concretely, being is both a being-in-itself and a being-for-another—and that is its being-for-self (*Fürsichsein*). True being is being-for-self, and the truth of the concept of being-for-self is the movement of being and nothing qua movement, namely, becoming.

As immediate, however, being is one (*Eins*)—and multiplicity is the immediate other of one. But as the negation of being one, multiplicity is a way of being. And multiplicity is itself, insofar as it is *not* multiplicities; rather, its being is its negation in the otherness (*Anderssein*) of a multiplicity of ones (*Vielheit der Eins*), not only in the "negation of one." In other words, being multiple means not being non-multiple, not being one, not being in relation to those beings that are ones. Being multiple is what and how it is as repelled from the multiplicity of ones which are not multiple. The truth of being-multiple then lies in being-one; or rather, the truth is the concept of being-for-self that supersedes both, that takes care of both by relativizing their relation to each other, that is, their relation of repulsion (and its other, attraction) in alternating, qualitative determinations (*Wechselbestimmungen*), under the form of mediation that is everywhere, in every moment to come, in every concept (*in jedem Begriff*). Like pure and determinate-being before it, being-for-self first takes the form of immediacy; yet it quickly shows itself to be (for-itself) insofar as it excludes an other, a being-for-another (*Sein-für-Anderes*). In this determination being as being-for-self is, first of all, being-for-one (*Sein-für-Eines*) as abstract non-difference, non-differentiation (*Ununterschiedenheit*). Being-for-self is the same as that other (being-for-another) from which it is indistinguishable, namely, being-for-one: "to-be-for-self and to-be-for-one are therefore not different meanings of ideality, but are essential, inseparable moments of it."[14] And here Hegel's term being-for-one (*Sein-für-Eines*) is explicitly ambiguous: the indeterminate article (*ein*) means both "a" and "one"—for in the moment of quality, being-for-one means not the abstract number "1," but the pre-quantitative ground, the condition of the possibility of number: "what for a/one thing" means "what kind of a thing," asks for the thing's determination, its quality (not yet quantity), the identity that constitutes its ideality (*eidos*) as one with its reality.[15] As for Aristotle, the beginning of number lies in that which is not yet numbered, *archē*. Thus, the concept of being-for-self, via its other, as that particular other for which it is, being-for-one, and its other (namely, being-multiple), shows itself to be one (*Eins*). From this one-sided perspective, the very possibility of the multiplicity of being multiple remains unexpressed, not yet real or explicit, merely ideal. The possibility of multiplicity is an impossibility—for "to be" means "to be one," not "to be many."

Ideally Multiple

For Hegel the quality of being-for-one in the history of idealism (from the Greeks through Spinoza) climaxes in Leibnizian pantheism, in the *Monadology:* all is *ideally* one (*hen panta*), and *real* multiplicity is represented in the monad. Insofar as monadic multiplicity (*Mannigfaltigkeit*), however, remains merely one-sided, that is, non-conceptual, it cannot supersede the system's contradictions between monadic unity (qualitative identity) and multiplicity (qualitative difference), ideality and reality, monadic independence or indifference to the multiplicity of otherness and interdependence or dependence on the other (monads and the monad of monads, i.e., God). Yet this is no coarse materialism (Democritus or Epicurus)—for "*Atomistic* philosophy does not have the concept of ideality; it does not grasp the one as containing *within itself* the two moments of being-for-self and being-for-it (thus, as ideal being) but only as a simple, dry real being-for-self."[16] Nevertheless, although the *Monadology* does not assume a two-world view (so determinative for metaphysics), Leibniz's multiplicity cannot be Hegel's insofar as it fails to resolve the real/ideal difference, lacks the logic of the concept: the multiplicity of this idealism is no multiplicity at all—for here the many disappears in the one (as in the concept of being-for-self), and the one in the many; ideally, but not really.

For Leibniz, on the one hand, multiplicity must be a *real* determination: monadic identities and (connected/connectable, hence detachable) differences must be in-and-for-themselves (*Anundfürsichsein*) since only then can multiplicity belong to individual monads; their absolute multiplicity (*absolute Vielheit*)—not *one* substance from which all multiplicity emanates (Spinozistic pantheism)—must form the parts from which complex wholes are constructed (via addition or multiplication), the building blocks of metaphysics. Real matter is then a multiplicity (and bodies are aggregates) of monads. On the other hand, multiplicity must be an *ideal* determination, that is, monadic multiplicity is abstract, and they are not-in-and-for-themselves (*Nichtanundfürsichsein*): "the multiplicity is only ideal and inner and in it the monad remains related only to itself; the alterations develop within the monad and are not relations of it to others."[17] All monadic movement (activity, desire, *appetitus*) is represented/reflected inside the monads themselves—for every monad is universal representation, in itself totality (*an sich Totalität*), reproduces the entire world within itself: each monad is, simultaneously, a representation of the universe and a determination of this representation in a multiplicity of particular situations, in its specificity. The real multiplicity of relations between determinate existing monads shows itself to be only ideal, "an independent, only simultaneous becoming, enclosed within the being-for-self of each of them."[18] And here one-sided abstract, ideal monadic multiplicity excludes precisely that which it is supposed to include as well as that through which it determines itself, that by which monads are multiple. The relation between real multiplicity and the ideal monad that contains all externality within itself, as abstraction from reality, is dependent upon and connected to that which it negates. Transition from the ideal monad (God, the monad of monads) to reality remains abstract—between unity and plurality, connectionless identity and connected multiplicity, there is no transition or history: "Leibnizian idealism takes up the multiplicity immediately as a given and does not grasp it as a repulsion of the monads; consequently, it has multiplicity only on the side of its abstract externality."[19] If Leibniz thinks the movement of real multiplicity in unity, thinks monads as concepts, then it is only ideally, only within monads: the contradiction between real and ideal multiplicity cannot be resolved because as always already resolved, it never even becomes a contradiction. Beginning with a "pure" abstraction, not a result, the *Monadology* cannot think multiplicity's other (the identity and difference of repulsive relations), cannot supersede real/ideal multiplicity in the concept.

And the ideal/real split leads to other problems: if multiplicity as a fundamental determination (*Grundbestimmung*) of monads remains merely abstract, if monads are radically discontinuous, independent, closed (*abgeschlossen*) from one another (not in causal relations), if monadic being-for-an-other (*Für-ein-Anderes-Sein*) is supposed to be only a representation, an appearance (*Schein*), and if monads are simultaneously supposed to coordinate their activities (like synchronized watches), then it is understandable why Leibniz needs pre-established harmony (*l'harmonie préétablie*) (*Mond,* §78); and like Descartes's God (*Med VI*), this law of relations is supposed to make monadic connectionism possible (a kind of "parallel distributed processes"), to resolve the contradictory difference between ideal and real, interior and exterior, to make the transition between monadic unity and multiplicity. Yet if this harmony is "pre"-established, the "usual subterfuge," that is, prior to monadic multiplicity in time, space, or essence, then it is brought in from without, applied, a means or instrument—the harmony of monads is not their own, not monadic harmony, not immanent to their multiplicity itself. The transition problem (real/ideal) is displaced, pushed further back to some transcendent realm; it is not even simply resolved (which would create a second transition problem, that is, between God and the real/ideal monads, an infinite regress of transitions that contradicts God's status as ultimate ground). And if God were understood as absolute substance, then the substantiality of individual monads, their multiplicity, is impossible: one substantial monad (as ground and cause of many) contradicts monadic independence and individuality. Thus, the unified schema that is supposed to resolve the difference between monads is arbitrary (*willkürlich*) and ends in the dualism from which it started—formal independence and essential interdependence remain the *Monadology*'s unrealized concept.[20]

Even further, Leibniz's qualitative multiplicity, the difference between monadic types (organic, inorganic, conscious), is only formal: all monads, in their independence, insofar as they include all others within themselves, are identical, that is, the unity wherein nothing is to be differentiated (A = A)—multiple differences are grounded (resolved, destroyed) in the monad, in the abstract identity of difference.

Every monad falls into boring, one-sided abstraction without opposition, contradiction, multiplicity: for example, God as universal, the absolute monad of monads (*Monas monadum*), is the cause of monadic harmony, but only as an abstract unity, a non-conceptual (*begrifflose*) identity of possibility and actuality. Here the total coordination of God's law (absolute unity of pre-established harmony) precedes monadic multiplicity; the origin of absolute multiplicity, abstract individuality. In this way Leibniz thinks multiplicity as unity, the monad as excluding its other; or as such, as multiplicity, as monads in a bad infinity, as infinite multiplicity (*unendliche Vielheit*)—and fails to think it as concept, as the supersession of unity and multiplicity, reality and ideality, dependence and independence, as the circular totality that takes care of separation because it is just as much non-separation in non-totality.

The contradiction of ideal/real multiplicity then reappears (unresolved, unthought) in the monads themselves. On the one hand, a monad is supposed to be a unity, the refusal of multiplicity (no parts, the non-difference of abstract negation), a multiplicity that is non-multiple: "all multiplicity is included in the unity."[21] Each monad as a pure being-for-self is indifferent to its other, to others in general: "that there is a multiplicity of monads, that therefore they are also determined as other, does not concern the monads themselves; this is the reflection, external to them, of a third; they are not in themselves others to one another; the being-for-self is kept pure, and is free from the accompaniment of any real being."[22] Indeed, for Hegel the dialectic is here the movement of (material and spiritual) clarity and confusion: monads, as pure being-for-self, lack accompaniment (*das Daneben*), but this "next to," "in addition to," this "supplement," is a mark of confusion—for to be completely confused, crazy, mixed-up is to be "beside one's self," to be *daneben*. Change and development then are merely interior: "the monads are only *in themselves,* or *in God* as the monad of monads, or even *in the system.*"[23] The monad's unity is its multiplicity—a multiplicity that is excluded insofar as it is included, is real only if it is ideal. Multiple relations between monads are non-relations; thought-of-an-other is always only thought-of-self. In Leibniz's multiplicity as such (*Vielheit als solcher*), each monad is a unity for itself, a one that is indifferent to the others, to its other—external multiplicity is internalized: monads have no windows because they need none, because everything, the entire world, is always already reflected in every monad. As Deleuze argues, monads must be windowless in order that they, like baroque-style houses or echo chambers, may record the world; and monads can translate or communicate reality into ideality precisely because they are not bodies but folds, folds between folds, a "structural" infinity of folds in a labyrinth of folds, single folds that harmonize with their multi-*pli*-city, that belongs (*appartien*) to every fold: monads are an allegory, a negative image of the world, "blind and closed, but on the other hand resonating, like a music room."[24] In other words, if the *Monadology* solves the ontological difference, the ideal/real contradiction, then it is via a theory of belonging (*théorie de l'appartenance*) wherein the "to have" (*l'Avoir*) is substituted for the "to be" (*l'Etre*), wherein predication as the possession of perceptions, as property, is the effect of other monads, the expression of the power of another: each monad, as an absolute interiority (*intériorité absolue*) has every other monad via projection (not action), is a symptom of the force of the other as presence (*présence*). Or, as Heidegger maintains, monads need no windows, not because the world is immanent in them, not because they encapsulate all reality, but because they are always already (originally), transcending, outside their unity, in multiplicity, ex-isting; they are (like *Dasein*) being-in-the-world, among other beings, that is, beings-in-multiplicity.[25] But Leibniz could not think the monads as being-in-multiplicity because he remained dependent upon the Cartesian/Spinozistic version of substance. Yet perhaps monads have no windows not only because they need no panes through which the world may pass, but because they need no frames: For are monads not already framed, self-framed and self-framing? Or frame-less (*ohne Gestell*—Leibniz contra Heidegger)?[26]

Nevertheless, monads are, on the other hand, supposed to be multiple; their multiplicity should be real and qualitative: "otherwise they would not even be beings."[27] If multiplicity were merely interior, then monadic multiplicity would be indifferent multiplicity, indifferent to the real/exterior source of it own/ideal multiplicity, of the otherness through which it contains otherness within itself. Multiplicity means qualitative difference: "for in nature there are never two beings which are perfectly like one another, and between which it would not be possible to find an internal difference, that is, a difference founded on an intrinsic denomination."[28] Each monad is a different perspective on totality, reflects the whole with a particular clarity/cloudiness—for the multitude of monads creates the appearance of many worlds and relations, a variety of points of view as the qualitative difference through which monadic multiplicity is determined. Monads then are really multiple insofar as the real world is represented in them: every monad expresses every other, expresses real totality; they are mirrors of nature, of the real universe (*Mond,* §§56–57). If monads are unities, and if simple unities are to be capable of change, then they must be multiple, comprehend (*enveloppent*) multiplicity: "there must be in the simple substance a plurality of affections and relations, though it has no parts."[29] Monadic unity is multiple: "We ourselves experience a multitude in the simple substance, when we observe that the least thought which we apperceive in ourselves comprehends a variety in its object. Thus, all those who recognize that the soul is a simple substance must recognize this multitude in the Monad."[30] In other words, the monad's multiplicity, its qualitative difference from other monads, consists precisely in the way in which it ideally represents the multiplicity of other monads—but in the monads themselves, the contradiction of unity and multiplicity remains unsuperseded.

Leibniz's ubiquitous solution, however, to the ideal/real and unity/multiplicity contradictions is God. In reality, the world is a living plenum, the interconnected unfolding of the totality that is already infinitely folded and mirrored in monads—for multiplicity and unity are one and many; in one monad is every monad and all monads are every one. The monad then is neither only ideal nor simply real, neither only unity nor multiplicity; rather, it is entelechy and body in one, mind and matter, living machine, natural automaton. Multiplicity is not only interior (nor exterior)—for the inside is the outside: everything is interconnected, networked together into the totality of nature qua machine, through the ultimate reason of all things, the substance of substances, Supreme Substance, monad of monads. And without God, there is only half the truth (*la moitié de la vérité*) (*Mond,* §76). God's pre-established harmony, the perfection of pure love (*pur amor*), is the schema that permits body and soul, two different substances (and formally differentiated monads), to meet—for they are only different perspectives on one and the same whole: "the soul follows its own laws, and so does the body; and they meet by virtue of the pre-established harmony prevailing among all substances, since they all are representations of one and the same universe."[31]

For Hegel, however, if Leibniz's God can harmonize monadic multiplicity, the totality of nature, then it is only through compromising monadic unity and independence. Monads become absorbed in God, in the unity wherein their reality is merely ideal: "the word God is thus the assistance that itself leads only to unity, which is only one in name; but the coming-out of the many from this unity will not be demonstrated."[32] In other words, the *Monadology* thinks the unity of the concept (the unit [*monas*] of the Pythagoreans as opposed to the one [*hen*]), but it falls into one-sided abstraction, idealism: the unity of qualitatively differentiated monads, as solution to the problem of multiplicity, cannot think the movement of its other; rather, it always unites in totality, a dead totality that refuses to accept its own self-negation.

Becoming Many Ones

For Hegel, insofar as qualitative multiplicity is a moment of the concept, a moment that can only be what it is insofar as it is not what it is, that is, in relation to its other, in relation to the one, the multiplicity of the *Logic* cannot remain merely ideal. Previously, the one (*Eins*) was posited as immediate (once again in the form of being), without its other, pure self-relationality—and here the one is not yet exclusion of the many, but pure being-for-self as abstract undifferentiatedness (*Unterschiedslosigkeit*), the one qua one. Like being then, the one (as self-negating) is determined as supersession of its moments, as relation of itself to itself and to its previous forms, its historical others. In fact, the one is this relation itself, the relation as the truth of multiplicity, the unifying connection that (ironically) excludes the very multiplicity from itself that it seeks to make possible; it is a negative unity that posits itself by negating the other that is itself, by excluding the one as other. Here the one is in its own self (*Eins an ihm selbst*), abstractly posited as the being-in-itself (*Insichsein*) wherein all difference and multiplicity (*Verschiedenheit und Mannigfaltigkeit*) have disappeared (*verschwunden*). But the "one in its own self" is nothing; however, since the one has superseded its previous moments, since it has a history, is historical (in its being, and its nothing), since it is more determinate than nothing, its quality justly deserves a different name, a sign of that which takes care of its past determinations, of that to which it always also refers: "the void is thus, the *quality* of the one in its immediacy."[33] At this moment, multiplicity means that which is voided (excluded immediately or mediately) in order that a particular quality of being (one) and/or not being (nothing, the void), a way a thing is or is not (is a no-thing); it is the necessary sacrifice, that which must be disappeared, a-voided, in the name of the one.

The difference then between the "one in its own self" and the void lies in their interior (immediately posited) relation; but the void is simultaneously different (*verschieden*) from and exterior to the "one in its own self." For the Atomists, the qualitative determination of the void is one side of the paired contradiction from which the infinite multiplicity of the world can be derived—but as that space (or non-space) "in which" the many exists, or as that "from which," source or origin, assumption or condition of the many's movement; the void remains exterior, next to, the many; that is, it does not realize the interior connection, the interdependence of the two, and does not think the ground of both in the concept. Atomistic multiplicity is merely the effect of matter, of atoms in combination/permutation, as product of a nature-machine functioning according to a differential or fractal grammar, according to a metaphysics or, rather, a physics (and is this not the essence of metaphysics?).[34] Externally the multiplicity that disappears in the "one in its own self" as abstract totality, in immediacy, finds here no place in the non-place, the non-space of the void—for the void is completely different from the "one in its own self," not insofar as it recognizes the multiplicity that is denied, but insofar as it recognizes its own difference from its other, its own particular way of denying multiplicity, its particular quality of negating the many. Internally, however, the other (negation) of the "one in its own self" is the void, and the negation of the void is the "one in its own self"; they are both negations of negations, self-relation, return, reflection into self, self-negation—but they are negation in different ways (with different qualities): the "one in its own self" (as being) negates non-being, and the void as non-being negates being. Further, this negation is just as much an affirmation, a positing of determinate being—but in different ways (qualities): the "one in its own self" as being-for-self as such (*Fürsichsein als solches*), and the void as indeterminate determinate-being in general (*unbestimmtes Dasein überhaupt*). Thus, with the internal/external relations between the "one in its own self" and the void, multiplicity is still (albeit differently) denied, refused, is still merely a product or effect of a unified origin—even if that origin is negative, the negation of the one-in-its-own-self, a type or quality (*Art, eidos*) of nothing, of a nothing that insofar as it contains its moments within itself, insofar as it has its particular history, is the void and not nothing.[35]

Between the "one in its own self" and the void then, the relation of otherness shows itself as the negation of the negation, wherein each is not only in relation to its other, but also (or rather, essentially) in relation to itself. And the relation of these relations is their mediation (like becoming) insofar as it takes on the quality of multiplicity determined as many one (*viele Eins*). Here, once again, the grammatical failure is the failure of grammar: the concept breaks the laws of language, but in a conceptual way (i.e., the negation of grammar supersedes the correct/incorrect, proper/improper, right/wrong, difference)—the text precisely does not read: many ones/units (*viele Einheiten,* or *Einser*)—for the ones are not yet quantifiable, not subject to the law of number, not many of number ones (*die Zahl Eins*); rather, each one is in relation to itself, and its determination remains qualitative, particular to itself—but also each is (insofar as it is a being, exists as an entity) in a negative relation (i.e., repulsion) to itself, to the many others as not itself. Thus, the ones are only conceptual for-themselves and not yet for the others through which they are determined—and the many is not yet many others. Multiplicity is only one-sided, only from/of the ones themselves.

For the ones then, repulsion is only a negative relation, pushing away from self, that is, the positing of itself, of "many one," as self-repulsion, the "one's own coming-out-from-itself" (*eigene Außersichkommen des Eins*). Here repulsion is the infinite creating, fathering/mothering, begetting, engendering, giving rise to (*zeugen*), manufacturing, producing, generating (*erzeugen*), of multiplicity, of "many one" from "one one"; and multiplicity testifies (*zeugt*) to it own creation, points back to, refers to, its origin, shows its source, bears witness to its parentage, gives evidence (*Zeugnis*) to the material or stuff (*Zeug*), to the one from whence it comes. This multiplicity is repulsive, a bastard creation, monstrous; and accusative, pointing the finger at the one.

Then, inversely, the "many one" are posited as the origin, as already present (*schon vorhanden*)—the one is not original; it too is the result of repulsion, of a reduction or abstraction from a presupposed multiplicity. Yet these "many one" (like monads—and Leibniz already thinks this concept, albeit ideally), insofar as they are each themselves one, do not relate to the others qua others, do not concern themselves with the others; rather, each is in relation to itself, only a negative being-for-self, to the exclusion of an affirmative being-for-one-another. Each falls back into the moments of the one (wherein the relationality of the one to itself is no relationality, non-relationality) and the void—and this is the outer limit/frontier (*äußerliche Grenze*) of multiplicity as "many one," the horizon or threshold through which multiplicity determines itself as such, by which it is multiple as negation of its other, is many in relation to the one as void. The becoming many of the one, however, the becoming of "many one," becoming of many (*Werden zu Vielen*), is already (*ist schon*) implicitly conceptualized—for the becoming and being of multiplicity *are* the one, the coming out of itself (*außer sich*) of the one in itself (*an sich*) from the side of the one, the supersession of one in multiplicity.[36]

For Hegel, however, multiplicity, the many one, means multiplicity of beings, of many beings, entities—the many one are beings (*die vielen Eins sind Seiende*). As multiple, the "many one" negates the one; yet they are relative to (reduced by) that through which they determine their multiplicity, through which they posit themselves as that in which the ones are not (*worin die Eins nicht sind*), as exclusion of the one (*ausschließen des Eins*)—and in this negation, this non-one or void, their common relation is mutual repulsion (*gegenseitige Repulsion*). They do not yet, however, posit their repulsion as that which binds them together; rather, repulsion is (although no longer merely abstract) the way they are in their being, their determinate quality insofar as they supersede the others as being-for-ones, or rather, being-for-each-other. First, the "many one" are all ones: they posit themselves as beings-in-themselves (like being); they all are, and they are, with respect to their being, therefore, identical—in their difference from one another (and from the one), they exclude their difference; they are the same, each is a being-in-itself. Second, the "many one" are all negating: they mutually repel one another and posit themselves as that which repels. In this way, with respect to their being and their determination as negating (repelling), the ones that are supposed to be many are (ironically) one, the same, identical—they cannot be what they are without being what they are not. In other words, their multiplicity is their identity.[37]

The identity of the "many one" then, in mutual repulsion, the multiplicity that is only multiple, multiple multiplicity, is attraction. Sheer multiplicity is no multiplicity at all (and this can only be a moment on the way to the multiplicity of logic). Multiplicity here is not only multiple, not only the multiplicity of all against all, the many of the "many one" (repulsion); rather, it is also their identity, the one of the "many one" (attraction). At first, attraction appears to be derivative or latter in time, an a posteriori interpretation of the "many one" in repulsion—yet attraction is repulsion. The mutual repulsion that separated the "many one" now connects them: attraction mediates through the moment of repulsion, contains repulsion within itself (not as abstract, but as its determination). In other words, as the completion of repulsion, attraction is the oneness of multiple multiplicity.[38]

The qualitative difference then, between the one and the many, is concretely determined as the difference between relations, between repulsion and attraction. Initially repulsion as the fundamental determination of the one insofar as it generates the many, produces multiplicity, or, rather, reproduces itself, takes the form of immediacy (like being) and has attraction as its other, negation (like nothing)—but this repulsion is itself a negation, namely, the negation of the relation of the "many one" to each other, the negation of relation as relationlessness (*Beziehungslosigkeit*). Here repulsion is not the same as the void: the latter is simple, abstract negation of the one; the former is negation and affirmation—more precisely, it is the connection of the many disconnected ones, the inclusion of the excluded—yet this moment of connection is the attraction at the core of repulsion. The connection or inseparability of attraction and repulsion underlines their disconnection, brings out their disjunction, their separability; identity implies difference, and vice versa; determination and relationality are relative to one another. Repulsion is positing of the many (and negation/disappearance of the one); attraction is positing of the one (and negation of the many): each is posited for itself, as itself, and for another, as other; each assumes itself, its position, its positing, to be absolutely real and the other's to be merely ideal—but each is only relative, manifests and maintains itself via negation of its other, to which it is indebted for its very being. And repulsion is the mutual repelling of the "many one" that assumes that which it negates, that is, their attraction—and vice versa. As relative, as the already assumed other, that which is to be negated, repulsion and attraction are the same: each is the determination of the one, albeit differently, and they are not the same. Thus, for Hegel, the relations of repulsion and attraction of the one and the many are related in one (the same) mutual mediation, in the infinite negating of the negations, the co-superseding; yet since this supersession is only relative, not absolute, the *Logic* must continue—and the dialectical result of quality, that which takes care of the one and the many, bears the name of quantity.[39]

The moments of quality then have found a kind of completion. From immediate being and nothing that determined themselves as becoming, through immediate determinate-being developed via finitude into infinity, to immediate being-for-self in relation to the one/many and the relative relations of repulsion and attraction—through all these moments, the fundamental determination of quality is being and immediacy (*das Sein und die Unmittelbarkeit*). For quality, the difference through which it determines itself vanishes, falls outside immediate unity; yet this vanishing is itself only a moment: quality's other qua disappeared is implicitly present within it, a possibility for explication. Thus, quality can become (not just be or not-be, that is, be nothing; not just be one or many, or their non-relation or their relation) the genuine unity of its moments insofar as it takes the form of the concept, the true concept that is no longer immediate but is posited as corresponding (*über-einstimmend*) to itself, that is true to itself because it has raised itself above the level of un-true, one-sided opinion, that necessarily remains within the logic of contradiction, debate, argument, of war, the two-sided logic of blood, blood logic, because it realizes that its unity takes care of its differential moments, the identity and difference of (*genetivus objectivus* and *subjectivus*) identity and difference.

Quality of Being Multiple

The quality of the multiplicity of logic then means (1) abstract multiplicity, not even excluded, not even considered as resulting from the concept that posits the one (like abstract being before it) as immediate being-for-self, as given or fact, as that which is; (2) excluded multiplicity that is posited as unexpressed, that is, an undifferentiated one, that is multiple insofar as it denies its real multiplicity, that remains merely ideal or potential; (3) multiplicity a-void-ed, originating in a non-multiple void (like nothing), as a product, effect, expression, symptom, sign, allegory, metaphor of something else—or rather, a multiplicity that has its source in a something else that, strictly speaking, is not a thing, a no-thing, a pure signifier without referent; (4) multiplicity that is not just one many, but "many one" (from an original one or void), a multiplicity of beings—but, as repelled from the one itself, as a product, effect, creation, a multiplicity that remains one-sided; (5) original multiplicity that is no longer only one (a multiplicity as that one being or nothing from which many could be produced), but a multiplicity that is originally multiplicities, pure multiplicity without unity; (6) qualitative multiplicity in the logical form of the concept that supersedes the other kinds (qualities) of multiplicities, that is their truth insofar as it posits them in relation to their others, that is the becoming multiple of many, that is, repulsion (multiple multiplicity), relative to its other (the becoming one), that is, attraction (unification of multiple multiplicity, non-multiple multiplicity), in alternating determinations, but that also (from its side) is the result of its moments, dependent upon the other ones and multiplicities from whence it came.

The qualitative multiplicity of the concept, however, is not a static solution to the problem of multiplicity—for it refers to something else: the moments that it has superseded and the moments that will supersede it, that which it has taken care of and that which is to be done. If the concept is the *Logic*'s basis and element, then it is because it is one and many, because the circular movement destroys and preserves the multiplicity of one and the one of multiplicity: the dialectic is the pathway and method (*hodos*) of speculative thought. The truth of multiplicity is multiple (moments) and non-multiple (a moment)—for it is the form of thought that moves between both, the movement that reveals a circular reciprocity among moments. And multiplicity in the concept remains expressed and unexpressed, named and nameless. Qualitative multiplicity is multiple—but not just, for it is also (but not only) one side of the concept wherein multiplicity is one. In other words, qualitative multiplicity is a multiplicity of determinations, the being and non-being (nothing) of one and many, the dialectic that takes care of its other: each moment has a particular form, each abstraction is from a particular other in its own way, negation is of a particular content—and the multiplicity of quality means that the concept and the moments *is* the same.

The many kinds or types of multiplicity, therefore, are the many ways in which they are and are thought, but the dialectic's qualitative multiplicity is itself only one-sided, only one moment that must find its other in quantitative multiplicity, in the quantification of the forms of thought, the ways of negating, the movements of supersession. Qualitative multiplicity is not forgotten, destroyed, exterminated in the logical forms of quantity; rather, it is superseded as a form of thought that is only *a* form of thought—for from the side of quality, quantity is simply another way (a quality) of thinking multiplicity, quantification as abstraction. Thus, before returning to the question of the logic of multiplicity as multiple (and the question of manys), the following questions: In what does the logic of quantitative multiplicity consist? What is multiplicity on the side of quantity? And how can it relate to or take care of quality?

5

Quality of Quantity

The Evil Demon of Quantity

> The order of things, in which they place themselves as natural realities, rests on the assumption that all the multiplicity of their characteristics will be carried by a unity of essence: equality before the law of nature, the persistent sum of material and energy, the convertibility of the most various types of appearances with one another, reconciling the distances (as first seen) in a thoroughgoing relationality, in an equality of rights for all.
>
> —*Simmel*[1]

For Heidegger quantification is the emasculation of spirit, a misinterpretation of quality; and its translation from the ontological to the historical is the will of the (then superpowers) United States and the (former) Soviet Union. Obviously dependent upon Nietzschean metaphors, Heidegger writes to oppose the Cartesian project of a *mathesis universalis* that seeks to become the master and possessor of nature via technological innovation, that claims to function in the name of spirit's empowerment and human emancipation:

> All things sank to the same level, a surface resembling a blind mirror that no longer reflects, that casts nothing back. The prevailing dimension became that of extension and number. Intelligence no longer meant a wealth of talent, lavishly spent, and the command of energies, but only what could be learned by everyone, the practice of a routine, always associated with a certain amount of sweat and a certain amount of show. In America and in Russia this development grew into a boundless et-ce-tera of indifference and always-the-sameness—so much so that the quantity took on a quality of its own. Since then the domination there of a cross section of the indifferent mass has become something more than a dreary

> accident. It has become an active onslaught that destroys all rank and every world-creating impulse of spirit, and calls it a lie. This is the onslaught of what we call the demonic (in the sense of destructive evil). There are many indications of the emergence of this demonism, identical with the increasing helplessness and uncertainty of Europe against it and within itself.[2]

The multiplicity of signs for the evil demon of quantitative hegemony, for the multiple misinterpretations of spirit, shows itself in the "metaphysical arch of indifference to spirit's qualities" that stretches from Descartes to Schelling. Yet if signs of quantity are multiple—however demonic—then the question of multiplicity is already in question.

For Hegel, however, if spirit can receive the mark of quantification, then it is because quantity is not just misinterpretation. For its part, quality is the expression of essence, of the irreducible character of a being in relation to an other: the determining limit (*Grenze*) between oranges and apples lies in the taste; an acre of land is a farm, wood, clearing; two individuals cannot be exchanged for one another; red is not blue is not yellow. Yet quality also implies the pure interchangeability of beings: if hunger can be satisfied by many fruits, then choice is inconsequent—stronger or weaker, cinnabar or rose, red remains red. As radically (qualitatively) incomparable, beings are completely (quantitatively) convertible—precisely because of the possibility of translation to quantitative determinateness. Here the other of quality shows itself as quantity: the truth of qualitative determination lies on its quantitative side. Quality's repulsion and attraction sink into equilibrium, mutuality, into the one-sided identity, that posits itself, like being, as pure—but this time, as pure quantity. In this way Hegel's *Logic* of quantity is not merely the violence of misinterpretation, the "extermination of particularities," the reduction of all quality to numbers (numbers are not simply numbers), the abstraction of all determinations in terms of amount or units, the death of thought in mechanism, in the homogeneity of calculation and computational codes; rather, it is the movement of the moments of pure quantity (*reine Quantität*), quantum (*Quantum*), that is, determinate quantity and quantitative ratio (*quantitative Verhältnis*). In other words, the particular quality of quantification, the reproduction/restoration, is taken care of in the dialectic of the qualitative-quantitative concept—and here multiplicity means the quantification of quality and the qualification of quantity, a multiplicity of the double-entendre, of the inevitable double-meaning (*Doppelsinn*).[3]

Now, in the moment of pure quantity, as the mediation of oneness and multiplicity, the many are one (*Vielen sind eins*): as with pure being, quantity means that being and its determinateness fall into an immediate self-relationality—they are the same. Pure quantity means indifference to that which it quantifies, to the thing (cf. *Enzy*, §§99–100). Here quantitative multiplicity is, first, posited as continuity (*Kontinuität*): individual beings (for-themselves) are contained in a self-same univocity without negation, a non-differentiated, uninterrupted self-movement of a quantity, many identical ones. Second, multiplicity breaks up as discreteness (*Diskretion*), the negation of continuity, the flowing-together of a quantity of differentiated ones. Unlike the moment of quality, wherein the creative, generative, productive repulsion of "many one" means becoming via the negation of the others in the "void" that connects them; quantitative repulsion is the relation wherein the many ones negate themselves (not their others) in the repulsive "self-connection" of multiplicity as discrete. Pure quantitative multiplicity is the continuous discreteness that contains (*enthält*) the totality of its prior moments within itself. In this way quantitative purity has the possibility and necessity of self-production "without further determination": for example, space and time as the perpetual self-creation of multiple units; space as *being*-out-of-itself (*Außersichsein*) in points, lines, planes; time as *coming*-out-of-itself (*Außersichkommen*) in pasts, presents, futures. Pure quantitative multiplicity then is discrete continuity, "multiplicity without qualities," the many seen as quantity in-and-for-itself (*an-und-für-sich*), the simple unity wherein each is what the other is (Leibniz), namely, "one among many." Thus, the concept of pure quantity is the uni-ty of (uni-nterrupted) continuity and discrete multiplicity (a quantitative multiplicity that, in its self-negation, remains multiple).[4]

The identity and difference then of continuous and discrete quantity is superseded in the double-edged limit (*zweischneidige Grenze*) of both and of neither, the limitation (*Begrenzung*) of pure quantity in general. Continuity and discreteness are simultaneously in relation to themselves (via negation of the other, each contains the other) and to each other: each is the limit of the other, the frontier, border, horizon, threshold, that marks a determination (not a quality, type, *Art*) of quantitative multiplicity, that allows each to be itself (identity) insofar as it is not the other (difference). And each is itself delimited: discrete and continuous quantity are determinate magnitudes of beings; that is, they are quanta—quantity is always a quantity of some-thing. In other words, pure quantity as discrete continuity (and continuous discreteness) is multiple (and unified) only insofar as it is limited—and this concept of limitation, the limit that is and is not a limit, is called quantum.[5]

For Hegel then, Heidegger's lament of quantification as mis-interpretation is a missed-interpretation—for quantification shows itself to be just as important for the life of spirit as qualification. The demonization of quantity, the fear of technology and those who embrace it, conceals the real threat to spirit, thought, humankind, philosophy, and so on, namely, the will to one-sidedness, the dogmatic refusal of the concept, of conceptuality and its complexity, the failure to think and act as both one and multiple. Indeed, for Hegel, the inability to read history as two-sided, as both continuous and discrete, to see beings as double, as both quantitative and qualitative, is the road to the destruction of spirit. Yet what does it mean to think multiplicity as two-sided, as subject to the process or movement of double-edged de-limitation, to the logic of the concept and its relational borders, frontiers, horizons, thresholds? What are the implications for thought, philosophy, history, and so on? And what does it mean to think multiplicity as both quality and quantity?

One, Unit, Quantum

> ½ + ½ not = 1, but = 2.
>
> —*Nietzsche*[6]

The Pythagoreans, for Hegel, in representing the concept as purely abstract thought, in taking numerical certainty as their model, are paradigmatic for the thought-less quantification of philosophemes. Here number means abstraction from the sensible manifold (*sinnlichen Mannigfaltigkeit*) to the realm of *pure thought.* Yet if spirit seeks an expression of itself in the element of "pure" number, then it will find only external, empty forms—for its own (spiritual) element is logic (*logos*), that is, the movement of the (spiritual) concept. Speculative philosophy needs not the help of symbols:

> if numbers, powers, the mathematical infinite, and such-like are to be used not as symbols but as forms for philosophical determinations and hence themselves as philosophical forms, then it would be necessary first of all to demonstrate their philosophical meaning, that is, the specific nature of their concept. If this is done, then they themselves are superfluous designations; the determinateness of the concept specifies its own self and its specification alone is the correct and fitting designation. The use of those forms is, therefore, nothing more than a convenient means of evading the task of grasping the determinations of the concept, of specifying and of justifying them.[7]

Although they differentiate between unity (*monas*) as thought and the one (*hen*) as number, the Pythagoreans take number as the transition between empirical and ideal worlds; they thereby transform the moments of concrete, living, moving spirit into a merely "symbolic" logic of dead determinations—their thoughts swim in the non-conceptual element of relationlessness, their business is the work of madness (*Arbeit der Verrücktheit*), and their concepts (a numerical nominalism) are contemptuous of speculative thought. Here, as abstract number, multiplicity means quantity without qualification. The critique of Pythagoreanism at the origin of mathematics, however, is not a mere diatribe—Hegel is quite emphatic: this analytic science is of great, although one-sided, importance (*große, jedoch einseitige Wichtigkeit*); it is that side wherein the activities of thought (unification/differentiation), of the subject, remain separated from and merely external to their other, the object. If logic, however, is to think not only the difference between "unity" and "one," but also their identity (and not only quantity, but also quality), then it must think the immanent development of the concept as both the purity of numerical abstraction and the dirt of empirical things.[8]

As a number or quantum then, a quantity is non-qualitative; it has the "one" as its principle (*archē*) and element. Here multiplicity is unified—like continuity—in amount (*Anzahl*); it is the excluding (not yet superseding) limit, the delimitation of multiplicity as one amount (e.g., one *hundred* is *one* hundred). Yet a quantum is a determinate aggregate (*Menge*) of units (*Einheiten*)—like discreteness—*one* hundred is always also one *hundred*, a multiplicity of ones. Quantum then is the supersession of amount and unit in number (*Zahl*), their unity (*Einheit*) and not their identity (*Gleichheit*) in a numerical one (*ein numerisches Eins*), wherein a quantum as one and only one (number) is simultaneously a determinate multiplicity: "*one*, as a *number*, possesses determinateness (insofar as this *is a relation to other*), as the moments of itself contained within it, in its *difference of unit and amount;* and amount is itself a multiplicity of ones."[9] Indeed, Hegel (the former math teacher) indicates three positive (and three negative) types (qualities) of calculation: addition (subtraction), multiplication (division), raising to a power (extraction of the root)—and their difference is one of velocity: addition is fast numbering, multiplication is fast addition, raising to a power is fast multiplication. The quantitative concept, however, is most evident in squaring (*potenzieren*): amount and unit are identical, that is, the number is multiplied with itself; the many numbers are the same, a multiplicity of units (e.g., 3^2 is 3×3, 4^3 is $4 \times 4 \times 4$).[10] As a determinate number, therefore, quantum exercises a limiting function: it delimits a multiplicity in relation to itself, encloses or includes it, excludes other numbers, unities and multiplicities. Thus, according to the "principle of one," number is a quantum of ones (or many ones), the delimitation (determination) of a quantity of ones that are many and ones.[11]

The concept of quantum, however, is not merely quantitative. Indeed, if number can show itself as qualitative, then it is because every quantitative difference (numerical e-quality and ine-quality, arithmetic and geometry) is always also a qualitative difference (*qualitative Unterschied*). In fact, quality reappears insofar as it has already appeared and disappeared: the double-meaning and ambiguity (*Zwei-deutigkeit*) of the term "one" contains the qualitative one, the "a" (*ein*), and the quantitative "one" (*ein*); every "being-for-one" is a "being-for-a." The to-be and the to-be-one are in a conceptual relation. In other words, not only is number always the number of something, of some being; the number itself always is, that is, has being. And a being does not have a quantity of being—for being is a qualitative determination. If becoming was the negation of being in nothing and vice versa, then from being (*on*) on, all determinations are qualities (*omnis determinatio est qualificatio*). Even when determination is explicitly quantification, it remains always also (however implicitly, forgotten, concealed) qualification. The difference of the concept, the qualitative difference between amount and unit within quantity itself—for they are different kinds of things—means that quantitative multiplicity is simultaneously a question of qualitative determination.[12]

The concept of number then, like pure quantity's continuous and discrete magnitudes, as the supersession of unit and amount, takes two forms (extensive and intensive quantum)—and this is precisely not a mechanical reproduction, simple repetition, of the dialectic of previous moments: on the one hand, "extensive and intensive magnitudes are determinatenesses of the quantitative *limit* itself, but quantum is identical with its limit; continuous and discrete magnitudes, on the other hand, are determinations of *magnitude in itself,* that is, of quantity as such, insofar as in quantum abstraction is made from the limit."[13] The qualitative difference of the moments is decisive—and that is why the other of extensive magnitude is its own, why intensive magnitude as its opposite is particular to it: both continuous/discrete and extensive/intensive magnitudes are determinations of limit; however, the former determines magnitude as abstract limit and the latter as non-abstract limit. In quantum, oneness (as limit) is negation/limitation of the continuous many (as limit)—the limit of a limit. Pure quantity is self-limiting, but only one-sided, without reference to its others (i.e., continuity is only the "abstract" limit of discreteness and vice versa); but quantum is limited by itself and its others (extensive and intensive quantum are self/other determinations). Although pure quantity is a determinate magnitude, a unity of many, a composite, compound, assembly, putting-together (*Zusammensetzung*), a combination, holding-together (*Zusammenfassung*), as un-numbered, it remains accidental: for example, ideas or reflections are more/less clear/turbid along a continuum, colors are more/less distinct from one another. Quantum (intensive/extensive), however, has the determination of number; its units and amounts, its ones, can be counted, calculated, measured, fixed, recorded. If quantitative limit is infinitely repeatable, an unlimited edition, then it is because numerical quantification acts as the condition of the possibility of mechanical reproduction.[14]

The difference between pure quantity and quantum is a question of quality, the difference of "how" unity/multiplicity is determined, a difference in the way in which limit functions—for limit is the qualitative-quantitative concept. On the one hand, as qualitative, limit is the negation/determination that constitutes, that makes out and takes care of, a composition's quality. A quality is what it is within its limits, insofar as it is not another—it *has* a limit and its other *is* its limit; yet, a quality's other also *has* a limit, namely, the limit that it *is* for another. Each of the two qualities, therefore, *is* and *has* the limit of the other: "*through the limit something is what it is, and in the limit it has its quality.*"[15] The difference between being and having (predication) a limit is superseded in the concept of limit, in the movement and mediation through which something and its other both are able to be and not to be, to have and to have not. On the other hand, as quantitative, limit is the internal other of a quantum (that is, an other quantum), and the limit of limit, the unlimited, that is, the external other of both. The extensive limit of a quantum (as a multiplicity expressed in one determinate number) supersedes the identity and difference of amount and unit, contains its other within itself, multiplicity within unity as a "relation-to-other *within its self*."[16] The intensive limit, on the contrary, has its other outside of it—and as such quantum is degree (*Grad*), that is, only *a* (universal) multiplicity (*Mehrheit*) wherein the (particular) aggregate/amount has disappeared; it is only *a* degree.

Multiplicity then is interior to extensive quantum (but superseded as a particular number) and exterior to intensive quantum (and thereby determined as merely universal). Here number reveals the quality of quantum: determinate *indifference* (*Gleichgültigkeit*) to its own multiplicity (within or without), to the other quanta from which each is inseparable, through which each is delimited (and also, of course, indifference to content, to that which is numbered—although this is not yet number's determination). Although extensive and intensive quanta are differentiated according to the ways in which they express the multiplicity that forms their other, they are identical insofar as they both are characterized by qualitative indifference. The quality of quantity as quantum is indifferent to multiplicity.[17]

Intensive and extensive quanta, however, are not only qualitative, but also specifically quantitative: degree is one of many (*Eins der Mehreren*), a one that is determined in relation to the others, in the identity of one and multiplicity (*Mehrheit*), the double-identity from within (containing many ones in a degree) and without (as negation of the many that it is not), the double-identity constituted by the before and the to come (e.g., the present degree along a continuum that contains those discrete degrees that it was [past] and that it will be [future]). Here continuous/discrete magnitude is not yet fully determined as spatiotemporal. Quantitatively then, extensive and intensive magnitude are essentially one and the same determinateness of quantum: "they are only distinguished by the one having amount within itself and the other having amount outside itself."[18] In the *Phenomenology*, for example, force and its expression function like intensive/extensive quantum: consciousness explains the expression of force, its quality as repulsion/attraction and its quantity as positive/negative, according to a law (to which force is identical and different); yet in this subjectivistic explanation, the understanding only enjoys itself (*nur sich selbst genießt*), experiences only onanistic satisfaction (*Selbstbefriedigung*)—one-sided subjectivism (ideal or material) is mere masturbation.[19] In the *Logic*, however, every determinate numerical magnitude is double: as amount it is extensive, a multiplicity; as unit it is intensive, an identity (e.g., *one* ten, *one* hundred)—and each number is within a system of numbers. Here degree shows itself as simultaneously the measure of that which is contained within it, a particular quantity of force, an in-tensity, and the measure of its effect, its ex-pression or capacity for ex-tension—however, like the "now" (present, and the priority of presence) of time, degree is only a moment of the concept. With the intensive-extensive concept, quanta *is* one and the same. Thus, the qualitative something (not just a being—for it is just as much no-thing, i.e., it is the process and movement of becoming) is submitted to the law of quantification: through negation of particularly qualitative differences, something (*Etwas*) is a quantum, but this indifference to quantification means that quality remains in a negative relation to quantity.[20]

Quantum then is indifferent to extensive/intensive determinations and to its quality; it is the limit of both and neither, or more precisely, it is their alteration (*Veränderung*), their limit in becoming, their becoming limit (*werdende Grenze*). Strictly speaking, quantum "is" (being) not only a limit. As one quantum, a quantum is infinite self-negation, production, creation, self-repulsion, a coming-out of itself as increase/decrease, that is, the moving, growing, living limit (like the concept) that determines quantity insofar as it infinitely supersedes, determines and takes care of itself. Each quantum has a double-identity (*doppelte Identität*), its own determinate quantum and its other limit—each quantum ceases in the next and is/has a specific quantum as itself and not another; each limitation is interior (the immanent unrest, self-contradiction, self-transcendence, spontaneous movement through a conceptual dialectic of a quantum out of itself) and exterior (a quantum moved by another quantum). In this way as numerical limit, as the extensive/intensive alteration of the identity and difference, quantum raises the question of the unlimited, the negation of their finitude in their other, the infinite.[21]

Infinite Multiplicity

> The enigmatic model of the *line* is thus the very thing that philosophy could not see when it had its eyes open on the interior of its own history. This night begins to lighten a little at the moment when linearity—which is not loss or absence but the repression of pluri-dimensional symbolic thought—relaxes its oppression.
>
> —*Derrida*[22]

With infinity, the question of multiplicity reaches its quantitative logical conclusion—for if multiplicity is determined as infinitely multiple, a multiplicity that is never attained, always outstanding, waiting, lacking, a multiplicity to come, a should (like a Fichtean *Sollen*) be multiple, a to-be-determined; then how can it simultaneously be multiple, that is, delimited, finite, a multiple multiplicity? Indeed, with respect to quantity, the other of a determinate finite quantum is also finite (its negation); yet each also takes on the role of infinity, the unlimited, forever continuous as negation of that which is limited, the going-out-of-itself (transcendence) that has an infinite return-to-self (immanence) as its other. Here finitude and infinity are doubly opposed: within themselves and to each other. Previously, with respect to quality, infinity meant the opposition between qualities (particular somethings, determinate beings, etc.) wherein the transition between infinite and finite remained merely interior (and not yet immanent): its other was only as such (*an sich*) and its finitude (the other of infinity) was not an other for it, not in it. Now, however, with quantity, infinity means finitude is in relation to its own infinity, to that infinity as the other that is "in it." In other words, the concept of quantitative infinity thinks the process through which the finite finds its other (the infinite) in itself—and infinite multiplicity, the multiple forms of infinity, therefore, is what it should become.[23]

Infinite progress then is the expression (although not yet the supersession) of the contradiction of quantitative infinity, of the problem of perpetual generation: on the one hand, infinity is transcendent, metaphysical, to come, that ever-receding beyond, other-side (*Jenseits*) which should be reached but, *by definition,* never is (an infinitely big/small); an ir-real progress, the desire for mastery that always/infinitely strives, but never can; the longing for the power to measure immeasurable space or time, the pathetic will to number the innumerable stars—like bad, qualitative infinity before, it is the expression of "bad *quantitative* infinity," the boredom of repetition (*Langeweile der Wiederholung*), one and the same positing and superseding and positing and superseding, and so on. On the other hand, infinity is, it is an immanent this-side (*Dieseits*), a determination of self-repulsion, the other of one and the limit of multiplicity—for an infinity (that no longer follows the logic of "bad quantitative infinity") is a quantum that continues in its non-being, infinitely. The contradiction reveals that quantitative infinity is not only quantitative: "the increase of quantum brings it no *nearer* to the infinite; for the difference between quantum and its infinity has essentially the *moment* of being a non-quantitative difference. The expression 'the infinitely great' only throws the contradiction into sharper relief; it is supposed to be great, that is, a quantum, and *infinite,* that is, not a quantum."[24] Infinity is a qualitative determination, and if infinite progress is indifferent to its own already superseded qualitative infinity, its other, to the difference between potential and actual infinity, between infinite infinity and finite infinity, then it cannot think absolute infinity, the particular quality that precisely is not grasped in the concept of quantitative infinity, that is forgotten if all oppositions receive quantitative determinations—for the absolute must be the identity and difference of qualitative and quantitative infinity and finitude.[25]

Quality then shows itself at the core of quantitative infinity: infinity is a quality of quantity (*genetivus objectivus* and *subjectivus*)—and qualitative multiplicity is the limit of quantitative multiplicity. Yet with the concept of infinity, quantum is no longer simply immediate; rather, it determines itself (via the negation of its negation, the return of already superseded qualitative infinity) as good and bad, achieved and unachieved, qualitative and quantitative infinity—and its infinity is immanent to its self. Here, as limit, quality makes quantum into quantum; yet quantitative infinity is not only qualitative—as quantum it has its particular quantitative determination, that is, numerical/mathematical infinity. At the quantitative limit of multiplicity, infinity reveals its qualitative side: the concept of quantum is the supersession of the supersession, that is, the supersession of qualitative infinity (wherein the finite/infinite contradiction is superseded) and quantitative infinity (wherein the contradiction between qualitative and quantitative infinity is superseded)—yet quantum is itself only one moment of quantity, it is a quantum that is no quantum at all (although it remains quantitatively determined), and quantity will show itself as only one side of the concept of measure (*Maß*).[26]

No wonder then that for Hegel the task of thinking the concept of infinity, of taking multiplicity to its quantitative logical conclusion, cannot be accomplished by calculation. Abstract quantification cannot think the qualitative-quantitative infinite precisely because it is numerical, because it remains within itself, does not think its negation, and its supersession—and "quantum, insofar as it is infinite, is required to be thought as superseded, as something which is not a quantum but yet retains its quantitative character."[27] Yet (perhaps ironically), in seeking to remain purely quantitative, quantity reveals its connection to qualitative infinity and its dependence on that which it denies, refuses, abstractly negates. In this way the implicit, unthought, ground and other of quantitative exactitude (*Genauigkeit*), the basis for its "correct results," is not simple probability (*Wahr-schein-lichkeit*), not merely the appearance (*Schein*) of truth, but rather, the speculative truth that shows itself in the concept of infinity as qualitative-quantitative limit.[28]

Indeed, for quantification, magnitude means that which can be increased or diminished, an indifferent limit (*gleichgültige Grenze*); and infinity means that magnitude "*above which there is no greater* (when it is defined as the infinitely great) *or no smaller* (when it is defined as the infinitely small), or in the former case is greater than, in the latter case smaller than, any given magnitude."[29] Infinity then, by definition, since it cannot be increased or decreased (however infinitely small or great), is neither magnitude (a maximum or minimum of finite quantum) nor quantitative relation (between a whole and a part that is greater or smaller than any magnitude)—and larger or smaller infinity is simply inconsistent.[30] The qualitative difference of terms (e.g., in the mechanics of velocity, accelerating force, resistance, etc.) can never be reduced to quantity—just because their difference is infinitely small or great it will never be non-existent. In this way quantification fails to reflect upon the very infinity that it employs. At the limit of mathematical method, however, quantitative infinity is no quantum at all; rather, it is a qualitative determination as well, the philosophical concept of true infinity (*warhafte Unendlichkeit*).

The qualitative character of infinity, however, never even becomes an issue for quantification. Infinity appears (like "bad" metaphysical infinity, arithmetical summation, or the "infinity of the imagination") as an external negation, incomplete synthesis, lack, non-being: each quantum in a ratio seems indifferent to its other, can be taken alone as specific amount/unit; and each is only a moment of the ratio, of a ratio that is indifferent to them—for abstract quantity is indifference to quality, and quantitative infinity means infinite substitutability. Yet quantification must also (implicitly) employ the concept of infinity (like Spinoza's *infinitum actu,* the infinity of immanent negation)—albeit without reflection, without explicit reference to its extra-numerical, that is, philosophical, origin: infinity as non-indifferent limit (e.g., ratio as a finite expression) contains bad infinity within itself, has infinite succession as a moment (like the *Phenomenology*'s law under which the expression of forces falls).[31] Quantitative infinity then is also qualitative (although not in-and-for-itself): relations between quanta are not themselves quanta (sums, quantitative determinations), but qualitative determinations, that is, limits that give quanta meaning by instituting a qualitative difference between quantities.

With respect to the limit of the ratio (*Grenze des Verhältnisses*), for example, Hegel invokes calculus in order to argue for the implicit quality of quantity, the qualitative relations of quantitative ratios, and of the qualitative character of quantitative infinity. Here inseparability (like Heidegger's belonging-together [*Zusammengehörigkeit*]) marks the quality of the quantitative ratio—for the ratio (dy/dx) means that dx is relative to dy (not to the quantum x):

> dx, dy, are no longer quanta, nor are they supposed to signify quanta; it is solely in their relation to each other that they have any meaning, *a meaning merely as moments.* They are no longer *something* (something taken as a quantum), not finite differences; but neither are they *nothing;* not empty nullities. Apart from their relation they are pure nullities, but they are intended to be taken only as moments of the relation, as *determinations* of the differential co-efficient dx/dy.[32]

In other words, the qualitative aspect of quantity means qualitative opposition, that is, having determinateness in another, by means of its non-being, having its being by virtue of its nothing: "the qualitative is what it is only in its distinction from an other."[33] Terms then are related to one another. Variation is indissociable, and quanta can no longer be (or not-be) independent (or rather, states [*Zustände*] of being or nothing), but rather moments of their (becoming) concept: "infinite magnitudes, therefore, are not merely comparable, but they exist only as moments of comparison, i.e., of the ratio."[34] Infinity is not a whole made up of parts, increments, sums, quanta; it is a limit, a qualitative limit. As not merely quantitative, quantitative infinity functions as a limit (not a quanta or sum)—and as such, it only is insofar as it has something to limit, an other without which it dis-appears.

The qualitative aspect of conceptual infinity appears most clearly in ratios—in fact, the logical concept of the moments of pure quantity and quantum are superseded in a relation, namely, the quantitative ratio (*quantitative Verhältnis*). For speculative thought, the quality of quantitative infinity means that ratios are not determinate parts, sums, ratios, but the "*limits* (*limites*) of *sums* and *ratio*"; that magnitudes are not determinate quanta, but dis-appearing moments—and in the dis-appearing of the individual quanta (the sides of the ratio), the ratio itself, insofar as it is a quantum, also dis-appears: "the limit of the quantitative ratio is that in which it both is and is not; or, more precisely, in which the quantum has dis-appeared, with the result that the ratio and its sides are preserved, the former only as a qualitative relation of quantity and the latter similarly as qualitative moments of quantity."[35] Qualitative infinity then is superseded in quantitative infinity, in the concept; and vice versa, quanta are qualitatively determined in a ratio—if they were torn out of the relation, they would be nothing (not even have being). And infinity is the supersession of quanta in a qualitative relation that retains its quantitative determinateness as "element" of the principle of the quanta.

Quantification then fails to think the concept of infinity for two reasons. First, although conceptual infinity is implicit (in itself) in numerical infinity, its specific nature and qualitative side (e.g., in ratios, or as a limit) is not explicated, not brought out and grasped (*herausgehoben und gefaßt*). Contrary to Badiou's wish to make it into ontology, that is, metaphysics as the science of being qua being, quantification both refuses qualification and the logic of the concept—and therein lies both its limit and its force.[36] Second, in the cleanliness of its formulations, the exactitude of its results, the perfection of abstraction, quantification forgets (conceals, excludes) that its propositions are bound to their origin, to the dirt of experience (*Erfahrung*), the identity and difference of quality and quantity:

> mathematics is altogether incapable of proving quantitative determinations of the physical world insofar as they are laws based on the *qualitative nature* of the moments [of the subject matter]; and for this reason, that this science is not philosophy, does *not start from the concept,* and therefore the qualitative element, insofar as it is not taken lemmatically from experience, lies outside its sphere.[37]

The (positive and negative) limit of pure mathematics then shows itself: insofar as it does not think its own qualitative-quantitative infinity, it cannot satisfy the "need of philosophy" to think the concept.[38] In using infinity as a limit-concept (*Grenzbegriff*), mathematics forgets its own limits, forgets that limit is a "between," as well as an "end." Furthermore, heterogeneous forms, figures, functions, ratios, cannot be equated without exterminating their differences—and insofar as mathematics seeks to rid itself of all traces of experience, of all empiricism or immanence, it cannot think the qualities of which it is supposed to take account. As an abstraction or functional description, a mere metaphor for the life of thought, mathematics can neither consider what is true in itself, nor can it approach the real world.[39]

The question of infinity then is the question of the concept qua determinate limit; yet this is also the question of its negation, of delimitation. And it is the possibility of the concept as the transgression (and non-transgression) of the limit, that is, the transition that limitation makes possible (and necessary). The quantitative solution to the problem of transition, however, is as inadequate as its response to the problem of infinity. For quantity, transition between sums or quanta is guarantied by abstraction, by the schema that assumes the translation of qualitative multiplicity into quantitative identities (without a loss of essential meaning). Yet the transition between qualitative moments within quantity itself does not even become an issue.

Hegel names the need for the "moment of qualitative transition" within quantification as *the* source of *the* "greatest difficulty." Transition (*Übergang*) here is between types, ratios, kinds (the trans-form-ation between arithmetic and geometrical determination); and it is qualitatively inter-dimensional (e.g., between lines and planes). The demand is no longer to let the qualitative moment of quantification show itself; rather, it is to solve the problem of qualitative transition itself, to explain how allegedly pure quantitative transition *already* contains qualitative transition (within itself)—and this is the problem of infinite multiplicity, the "greatest difficulty," that is, the relation between qualitative and quantitative multiplicity.[40]

And Hegel's response to the problem of transition, of infinity and infinite multiplicity, lies in becoming, in becoming multiple, that is, multiplication. Two senses of multiplication must be disengaged. First, computational multiplication is accelerated summation. Here like kinds (discrete quanta, units, numbers, magnitudes) are multiplied by like kinds in a homogeneous alteration of subject matter to yield like kinds: multiplication remains a purely mechanical transformation of quantum, and number is the limit of thought. Yet multiplication can also be understood as heterogeneous alteration, as the multiplication of like kinds in the generation of unlike kinds: the change is no longer simply quantitative, but also qualitative—it is essentially self-externalization (*Außersichkommen*), conceptual alteration, change via negation and supersession.[41] Indeed, dimensional transition cannot be reduced to numerical multiplication:

> the arithmetical multiplication of magnitudes spatially determined as *lines* also produces, from the linear, a *plane-determination;* 3 times 4 linear feet gives 12 linear feet, but 3 linear feet times 4 linear feet gives 12 plane-feet and, in fact, square-feet, since the unit in both as discrete quantities is the same. The *multiplication* of *lines* by *lines* at first sight appears meaningless insofar as multiplication concerns simply numbers, that is, is an alteration of that which is *perfectly homogeneous* with what it passes over into, with the *product,* only the *magnitude* being altered. However, what was called multiplication of a line as such by a line—it has been called *ductus lineae in lineam,* like *plani in planum,* and is also *ductus puncti in lineam*—is an alteration not merely of magnitude, but of magnitude as a *qualitative determination of spatiality,* of a dimension; the transition of the line into a plane must be grasped as the *self-externalization* of the line, like the self-externalization of the point is a line, and of the plane a whole space.[42]

The difference then between temporal (arithmetical) and spatial (geometrical) determination is also qualitative (insofar as the latter has a three-dimensional, the former a one-dimensional, concrete limit). Motion appears as continuous across homogeneous time, as a mere external alteration (*äußerliche Veränderung*); yet it also includes a qualitative multiplication because of the difference between states of rest and motion, that is, between states of becoming. And time seems one-dimensional (past, present, future), appears as pure addition of discrete units, moments, as quantitatively homogeneous; but when it is considered as history (e.g., the history of the education, *or rather,* transition, of consciousness from the standpoint of sense-certainty to that of absolute knowledge in the *Phenomenology*), then its qualitative character shows itself to include a multiplication (and a qualitative relation to other dimensions). Space and time are multi-dimensional because they are qualitatively as well as quantitatively determined (although their scientific multiplication runs up against the concrete wall of experience, against the empirical conditions that are immaterial to pure mathematics and theoretical physics). Yet if self-multiplication produces qualitative difference out of quantitative identity, inter-dimensional transition, change of state, then it is because original identity is no origin at all, but a result—in its self-relatedness, quantity has its truth in the concept, that is, in the becoming of quality and quantity, of identity and difference.[43]

The process of multiplication as qualitative transition is implicit in the translations of quantity (for example, the transformation of discrete quanta into a continuum). Yet the alleged pure summation, quantitative multiplication, must include (and simultaneously exclude, conceal, deny, resolve; i.e., precisely not supersede) a qualitative multiplication, a transition from, for example, linear to planar dimensions: "the analytic procedure itself which appears as a mere *summation*, in fact already contains a *multiplication*."[44] As Heidegger insists in reading Heraclitus's Frag. 10 ("out of everything, one; and out of one, everything [ἐκ πάντων ἓν καὶ ἐξ ἑνὸς πάντα]; *aus Allem Eins und aus Einem Alles*"): "how long does it remain a library, if we take out one book after another? But we see already that all the individual books together do not make up a library. 'All,' understood as summative, is quite different from allness in the sense of the unity of the peculiar sort that is at first not so easy to specify."[45] Constitution as qualitative multiplication denies computational summation its claim to purity. In other words, if the sum of an infinite number (quanta) of discrete lines constitute a continuous plane, then a plane will never exist (Zeno's paradox, like Badiou's pure and incoherent/inconsistent multiplicity, assumes bad infinity);[46] rather, constitution must mean philosophical multiplication, qualitative determination, the moment of transformation from one type, kind, *eidos,* to an other. A plane is an infinite number of lines because infinity constitutes a conceptual limit (a supersession of quantitative summation and qualitative multiplication, i.e., the transitions between points, lines, etc.). Just as the totality of whole numbers is not a whole number (Russell), the set of all sets is not simply a set, but exceeds set theory itself (Cantor)—as "too big" to be "big" at all, the biggest set is not big enough to be the concept. The objectivity of objects is nothing objective. Even making being into a variable (Quine), rather than a thing, and making every variable multiple (Zermelo/Fraenkel), every element or being into a relation, in an attempt to eliminate the ruinous excess of the multiple, does not solve the problem of multiplicity—it far more returns it to identity: if every set is a multiplicity of variables, then there exists at least one variable that is not multiple, namely, multiplicity itself. And the multiplicity of multiplicities is nothing multiple. Indeed, for Hegel, the concept of concepts does not merely gather the totality of concepts together into a still bigger, more totalizing concept; rather, it supersedes and takes care of its moments—for it is not simply quantitative, but simultaneously the qualitative (multiplicative) limit in which it both is and is not qualitative and quantitative. Conceptual infinity cannot be reduced to a question of consistent or inconstant, coherent or incoherent, pure or impure, rational or irrational, limited or unlimited, one or non-one, multiple or non-multiple, as such or as another, self-identical or self-differential; rather, it is the point where the double itself must be superseded.

The seamlessness of quantification then, the unquestionableness of its transitions, belies its qualitative moment, obscures the essential quality of determinations. Like quantitative infinity, quantitative summation is already qualitative multiplication. The identity of spatial figures, their coincidence and continuousness, is the forgetting of their discreteness—for it is the identity of sense perception and the pleasure of picture-thinking that conceal the differences, the differences of differences, the quality of multiplication. In other words, an incommensurability marks the moment of qualitative difference, signifies the irreducibility to simple quantity; and their supersession in the concept that computation cannot think. Qualitative and quantitative infinity, the moments of numerical and philosophical multiplication, analytic and synthetic cognition, cannot only be held apart, as if they were not also already mediated; although within the discourse of quantification, enumeration functions flawlessly, transition operates as summation, and infinity is qualitative limitation. For speculative thought, in every quantification, a negative determination comes into play—and this is the greatest difficulty: to think that which has already taken place in infinite summation, that is, to think the concept of philosophical multiplication.

The solution to the problem of infinity then, for Hegel, lies in relationality—for the concept of infinity is neither simply bad (infinite infinity that is that which it should be, namely, infinite) nor good (finite infinity that in being, is no longer that which it should be, infinite); rather, it is the qualitative-quantitative concept that takes care of finite infinity as well as infinite finitude. And here infinite multiplicity must be thought conceptually: no longer infinitely multiple (pure or inconsistent multiplicity, the multiplicity of multiplicities, multiple multiplicities) nor finite multiplicity (impure but consistent multiplicity), infinite multiplicity is the contradictory relation of both. Yet what is a relation? The concept of relation? And how does it think multiplicity? That is, how is multiplicity a relation, or relations? And how are relations multiple? Or even further, how can the relation between multiplicity and the multiple be thought multiply?

The Concept of Relation

After the moment of quantum, after the numerical equation (*Gleichung*), the comparison (*Vergleichung*) of the incomparable (*unvergleichbare*), of qualitatively different determinations—after all this, the quantitative relation (*quantitative Verhältnis*) shows itself as the concept of quality and quantity, the this-side (immanence) and that-side (transcendence) of limit within which each determination is in relation to the other. Here, as its beyond that belongs to it, the quality of *quantum* is superseded—and their relation is itself (at first, now, for the quantitative moment, provisionally) a quantity. The quantitative relation shows itself as ratio: first, as direct ratio, as a closed totality (*geschlossene Totalität*), as the indifferent limit of immediate quanta without any reference to quality (the gain of one is the proportional gain of the other); second, as indirect ratio (the gain of one is the loss/negation of the other); third, in the concept of the power ratio (*Potenzenverhältnis*), the identity and difference of self-creating quantity and quality posited as measure.[47] In all the ratios, however, identity is determined by the particular movements of the moments of unit and amount, that is, of the exponent (in the direct and indirect/inverse ratios) or power (in the power ratio). The multiplicity that was expressed as a dissociable part of a ratio in abstraction, "pure" quanta without connection, many ones, now shows itself as both an indissociable part of a relation, a quantum in qualitative connection with the other quanta in a ratio, and indicative of the types or qualities of ratios. And if the raising to a power is the multiplication of a quantum by itself (or rather, by its other), then it is because this raising is the quantitative operation of qualitative transition.[48]

The concept of quantity then finally shows itself as (implicit and explicit) qualitative-quantitative determination in the logic of the relation: two sides of a ratio must (but cannot simply) be maintained in isolation from one another, as if they were not related, as if they were not also functions of each other. In direct and indirect ratios, however, quanta are determined by the exponent and its double-identity. Quantitatively the exponent is a fixed quantum or real number, directly related to its other; it is a magnitude in a quantitative relation wherein quanta "are" (as also self-related), simply posit themselves over and against one another in their quantitative difference, *that is,* indifference—as such, the ratio is completely dependent upon the quantum that has raised it, slave to the magnitude that determines its self; and the exponent is strictly speaking, no number at all, merely a sign or numerical shorthand, a name that the quantity gives itself. Qualitatively, however, the exponent functions as limit, as "law," "command," or "operation," whereby it determines the amount of times the unit shall be multiplied—and as such it is the determiner, the fixer of meaning, the master legislator who orders the quantum to replicate a given number of times, to multiply, to produce and reproduce itself. The exponent, in other words, is the difference of the quantum in itself, but it is a difference that is no difference at all—for taken alone, the exponent and the quantum are incomplete, only dis-appearing moments, insofar as they constitute *one* quantum.[49]

The difference then, between direct and indirect ratios, lies not only in the particular way in which quanta relate to one another, but in the exponent's role: in the former, it is simply quantitative; in the latter, "the exponent as the determining quantum is posited as negative toward itself as a quantum of the ratio, and hence as qualitative, as a limit—with the result that the qualitative for itself manifests itself in contrast to the quantitative."[50] While in the direct ratio, the exponent was negated as "*one* alteration of the quantum," in the indirect ratio, it is also affirmed—the ratio contains the difference within itself; it is its own internal, qualitative-quantitative limit, the affirmative-negative identity-difference, the within-without of its self-other, of its quanta and their reciprocal limiting. In this way in this contradiction—which is that of the concept of infinity in a new form—the exponent and its quantum are negative moments and continuations of each other in each other. As Hegel insists: "the magnitude of the other is an indispensable factor in the value of each and is therefore inseparable from it."[51]

Although it appears then, as the transcendent other-side (*Jenseits*) of the quantum, in truth, the exponent is the quantum's negation, its immanent and affirmative this-side (*affirmatives Diesseits*), and the negation of the negation of quanta. Here the exponent is the expression of the law by which a ratio functions, the determination to which the ratio's quanta must submit: ($y : x^2$) means that y has a relation to the square of x (not to x itself). In the direct ratio, the exponent means that x increases in direct proportion to y—but "squared" as fast. In the indirect ratio, however, the exponent determines the "speed" of the negation, the degree of the difference, between terms: ($y : x^{-2}$) means that as y increases, x decreases. The exponent is the "truth" of the ratio insofar as it fixes its sides, determines its quanta—for the ratio's identity and difference are limited by their quantitative-qualitative other. Yet each quantum is also, implicitly, in itself (*an sich*), the exponent; in other words, each can determine the whole ratio, can also function as its truth, as the law of the ratio (e.g., if y is determined, then x^2 is a determined quantum), and each is simultaneously quantum, that is, determined by the ratio as the exponent's self-externality (*Außersichsein*), its self-*ex*-pression. In this way the negation of the exponent shows that the direct and indirect ratios are negations of one another—as such, the ratio is the ratio of powers.[52]

In the power ratio, however, powers are no longer *ex*-ponents, no longer *ex*-terior to the direct or indirect ratio, and no longer immediate; rather, "the power is an aggregate of units, each of which is this same aggregate."[53] In raising to a power, the qualitative transition that remained merely implicit for quantitative summation becomes explicit—for in the power ratio, the law of the ratio is the ratio's law: the difference between quanta and exponent is superseded in the identity and difference that characterizes the relation between quanta and their powers, the ratio in which the other-side is this-side; transcendence is immanence. The power ratio takes care of being-in-itself and being-for-self. And it is in the ratio of these powers that quantum presents its quality, reveals that which was in itself already known: quanta only have meaning (qualitative determination) insofar as they belong to a ratio as functions of one another, thought in their conceptual identity and difference. The non-relationality of quantum means that quanta are completely indifferent determinations, perfectly convertible, interchangeable; yet this indifference is precisely the quality of quantity, the quality that, as superseded, returns to quantity as its truth, as the truth expressed via the ratio. The power ratio explicitly posits the concept of magnitude as it is in itself, and quantum is the difference of quantum, of its own difference from itself. In other words, the qualitative-quantitative concept can explicitly show itself in the ratio of powers because the powers as quantitative-qualitative self-multiplication find themselves in relation to an other power and to their other: the transition of quality is the transition of quantity, and vice versa.

And if the quantity of the power ratio is not disengaged from its other, then it is because the language of quantification is always also in relation to that of quality. Hegel's terminology here is quite precise: power means not only the quantum, but also potency (*potentia, dynamis*), the power to move and create (*schöpferische Potenz*), to produce, beget, generate (*genita*), engender (*erzeugen*) (as opposed to the im-potent or disempowered progress of bad infinity). Ratio is not only a quantitative connection, not only a kinship between numbers, a matter of quanta, but also a type of relation, a *liaison* of qualities, a corporal kinship, an affair of mind and body (*Liebesverhältnis*).[54] The power ratio here is the ratio of *powers,* and the potency-relation is the relation of *potencies*—they are already multiple, a multiplicity that finds its ground, its reason (*ratio,* i.e., *logos*) and truth, in the concept. In other words, quantity is impleached with quality, and quality is stained with quantity: they are strapped together, and their intimacy is that of lovers. The mathematician cannot help but speak (always) the words of the philosopher and the sexologist; the decent, respectable power ratio is (also) the indecent language of fornication, the multiple obscenities of the polygamist.

The (mathematical-linguistic) relation of the ratio then, the potency of the power, means that quality and quantity (always also) belong together. In the moment that quantity determines itself as ratio, it is simultaneously determined as relation: what was only in itself, in principle, implicitly (for pure quantification), is now also for itself, in reality, explicitly; determination is determinateness (being-in-and-for-itself). Quantity reveals qualitative meaning, or rather, a multiplicity of meanings within a finite determination. And the multiplicity of senses cannot be controlled, but it can be contained—in reducing this multiplicity to a double-bind, a double-entendre, to a logic of self and other, to bifurcation or binomial quantification, this multiplicity is forgotten-remembered, concealed-revealed, is becoming-multiple (being) and becoming-non-multiple (nothing). If power indicates a mathematical intrusion (*Einmischung*) into the realm of speculative thought, then the science of logic follows a "policy of containment"—but a qualitative (as determination, essence) and quantitative (as magnitude, size) containment, that is, one that deploys the philosophical concept, that functions via its opposite, its other, and that is just as much a "non-containment," "release," or "dissemination," for a relational-unrelatedness and an unrelated-relationality. Hegel's language reveals that a semiotic multiplicity lies at the core of every determination, is contained in every qualitative and quantitative limitation; this multiplicity, however, can show itself only insofar as it submits to the law of the concept, the identity and difference of identity and difference, an identification-differentiation that is itself infinite and finite. The power of ratios, the potency of relations, the power of relations, and the potency of ratios form the logical framework within which multiplicity becomes what it is and is not in response to infinity, to an infinity that is both infinite and finite.

Multiplicity of Quantity

Having made the double-transition (*doppelte Übergang*)—from itself as in itself, to its other (quality) and return (*Rückgang, Rückkehr*) to self, a becoming self-related, a quantitative being-and-nothing-in-and-for-itself—Hegel thinks the concept of quantity. Yet having found its true mediation and lost its alleged immediacy, quantity is no longer a quantum over and against, opposed to quality; rather, quantity has a quality, a determination that is itself determined in negation to its other, insofar as it is not quality, a negation that is contained in it. And quality, realized through the moments of quantity, has found its other, its particular negation that is its own: for quality, quantity is not simply any quality, not just one among many; rather, it is *the* quantity of quality. Here the qualitative-quantitative concept means that quality is *a* quantity, that is, one quantity; yet as such, it is still only a one-sided determination—for, inversely, "quantity is itself *a* quality," that is, it is a determination. In other words, the truth of quality and quantity is that they have gone over into one another; their truth is the movement of their becoming, their identity and difference—and this will show itself as measure.[55]

The multiplicity of quantity then means (1) a multiplicity of ones as pure quantity, as discrete magnitudes, of somethings (beings), that constitute a continuum, that is, a continuously discrete and discretely continuous concept; (2) a multiplicity as finite, a limited quantum, a quantum that has a limit expressed as a counted amount of an aggregate via the exclusion of other aggregates (hence, a multiplicity that is a limit for another multiplicity), or determined as a number of units (of beings, materials, ideas, components, smallest parts, lowest common denominators, building blocks, concepts, etc.), a number of ones, many ones, or as a unity, one unit, composition, construction, combination, that can be produced, infinitely re-produced, exchanged, distributed, consumed, and so on; that is, a multiplicity that *has* and *is* a limit (i.e., being, nothing, or more precisely, the concept of becoming, a limited multiplicity in itself and for another); (3) an infinite, quantitative multiplicity, that is, unlimited, purely numerical, symbolic, ideal abstraction or simply one-sided transcendent concept that expresses itself as the negation of limit, a bad multiplicity that progresses toward an infinity which it never achieves; (4) an infinite, quantitative multiplicity that has finitude as its truth, a quantitative (and/or qualitative) semiotic infinity contained within the concept of finite-infinite multiplicity as limitation of the unlimited; (5) a non-relational, indifferent quantitative multiplicity, that is, a determinate limit that has its other (to which it remains qualitatively indifferent) within/without itself, that is, that maintains a double-identity (one/many, intensive/extensive, etc.); yet an indifference that makes a difference, that is also not indifferent its other, to the qualitative multiplicity within itself; (6) a quantitative-qualitative multiplicity of the ratio-relation that is simultaneously incommensurable with (and inseparable from) quantitative-qualitative unity, a multiplicity as exponential lawgiver and victim, as submissive to its own law (and therefore, free multiplicity), a multiple multiplicity within a doubled multiplicity within the concept, the identity and difference of qualitative-quantitative multiplicity, the *poly-entendre* that can be "heard" because it is contained within the double-entendre.

A multiplicity of multiplicities then, but a multiplicity that will be superseded in the concept of measure, and in a multiplicity of moments to come—for this multiplicity will show itself as once again multiple, a multiplicity within a multiplicity. Yet if measure is supposed to supersede the quality and quantity of multiplicity, then it must also take care of their qualitative-quantitative transition, their becoming, the movement of both. The questions remain: How is this transition possible? The multiple transitions and transition as multiple? Through some kind of uniformity? A lowest common denominator? The fundamental identity of variables? Or some mechanism of difference? A gap, space, deferral? Or is the transgression or violation of boundaries, frontiers, horizons, thresholds, far more a question of the concept of transition? Or, even further, is the question of transition a question of multiplicity? Of a multiplicity that would call the very question of transition into question? A question of manys?

The Problem of Transition

How then is the change of state from quality to quality, from type to type, from quantity to quantity, possible? If the multiplicity of quantity (and quality) is neither pluralization nor multiplication, then the transition from multiplicity to multiplicity must be explained in other terms. Qualitative transition (becoming) is negation (determination functions via the negation of the negation); but quantitative transition is also qualitative translation. For quantity, qualitative determination is not an effect or appearance of alterations in magnitude, nor is it a symptom of an always already performed reductive quantification or conversion to quantitative difference (that is, to quantitative identity); and it is not a mask strapped onto the face of quanta, not a concealment of qualitative truth—rather, it is a moment of quantity, a moment as the limit of an other, of qualification. If limit is and has a between (as well as an end), if infinity is finite as well, then quantitative transition is delimitation via qualification.

Indeed, for Hegel, the concept is the solution to the problem of quantitative transition. The truth of quantitative multiplicity is qualitative transformation, a transformation that is possible because the moments have already gone over into one another, because it has already happened (and because it is always happening and will happen). And delimitation of sides, boundaries, frontiers, drawing of horizons, that is, qualitative determination, occurs because limit as incomplete-complete follows the logical structure of the concept, the double-entendre as the truth of the identity and difference of becoming-moments.

Conceptual transition then, as quantity's answer to the problem of its relation to quality, as the answer to the problem of qualitative-quantitative infinity itself, of the transition from the infinite to the finite, is perhaps *the* answer to what Schelling called "the problem of *all* philosophy."[56] If the question of quantitative transition (multiplication) reveals the qualitative aspect of quantity by taking numerical multiplicity to its logical conclusion, to the point where quantity reveals that it is itself not only quantitative, that it presupposes (and employs) qualitative determinations, then every quantification is and is not a qualification. And if qualitative transition is qualitative only insofar as it determines itself via negation of its other, of quantitative infinity; then every qualification is and is not a quantification. Qualitative determinations can find quantitative expression because their other (quantification) does not only stand over and against it as an indifferent other, but because they also belong to one another as others, as the moments of quality and quantity in a conceptual relation. The difference between determinate existence (*Dasein*), consciousness, finitude, and things—and the difference between infinite spirit and finite consciousness (that is not only a thing)—is a difference that is and is not a difference, that is an identity and a difference. For this reason, in the moment of magnitude, for example, the solution to the problem of qualitative-quantitative transition is that it has already happened (and not happened). In other words, the logic of the concept's transition, the movement that is and is not, that has and has not occurred, as the identity and difference of determinations, a homogeneous-heterogeneity (and a heterogeneous-homogeneity), is that which makes transition (becoming) possible.

And the question of infinite transition, as the question of (qualitative and quantitative) infinity, is also answered by the concept:

> The essence of philosophy is often, by those who are already entrusted with thinking, posited as the task of answering: how does the infinite go forth from itself and become finite? This, one believes, cannot be made *comprehensible*. The infinite, which we have reached in the concept, will in the course of this exposition *further determine* itself and will show in all its multiple forms what is demanded, that is, *how* (if one wants to express it so) *the infinite becomes finite*.[57]

In other words, the infinite shows itself in a multiplicity (*Mannigfaltigkeit*) of finite forms because transition is multiple, the multiplicity of infinity in transition. Yet what is this transitional multiplicity? For Hegel conceptual transition means that multiplicity is and is not infinite, that it is a qualitative-quantitative finite infinity. Transition itself is two-sided, a unity and a multiplicity, one and many, *hen* and *panta,* infinite and finite, qualitative and quantitative. Yet how can the becoming of transition remain multiple, if it is submitted to the logic of the speculative dialectic, if it is superseded in the two-sided and only two-sided (i.e., not even many-sided, except under the condition that it is two-sided) concept? For Hegel transition is infinite only as finite, and finite only as infinite, multiple only insofar as it is always also non-multiple. In other words, the concept is the logical solution to the problem of infinity and finitude, as well as that of limit and transition. Yet what is the limit of transition? The limit of the logical concept? And how is this limit itself a transition? Or, even further, how is the logic of transition itself a limit of the *Logic?* A limiting transition and a transitional limit?

The Logics of Limit

The quantitative multiplicity of the concept is not the end of multiplicity—for insofar as it has a limit, it refers to something else, transitions into its other, has its truth in another, in quality (and its superseded moments) and in the measure (that will supersede it). Quantitative multiplicity is multiple (moments) and non-multiple (a moment), quanta and a quantum—for it is the concept as the form of thought that moves between both, the circular movement among moments. The multiplicity of quality showed itself within the moment of quantity as excluded by pure quantification; and then, at the core of an already inquinated quantification, as the other of a magnitude that cannot maintain its purity—for the concept is neither pure nor contaminated, and both pure and contaminated, pure contamination, contaminated purity. In this way the moments of quantity are multiple in number (quantitatively), in kind (qualitatively)—and these multiplicities are themselves multiple, that is, the multiplicity of connotations. For each moment has a singular type of quantum, each quantification is from a particular other in its own way, limitation is of "this" content—and as in quality, the multiplicity of quantity means that the concept and its moments *is* the same.

Yet the quantity of quantitative multiplicity, of the many kinds or types of quantifications, is itself only one-sided, only one moment that finds its truth in qualitative multiplicity—for the concept is the identity and difference of quantity and quality, "the concept of a *difference* which equally is *inseparable,* of an *identity* which is in its own self an *inseparable difference.*"[58] The concept is a qualitative-quantitative unlimited-limit, finite-infinity—and the identity and difference between quality and quantity is (from the side of quality) qualitative and (from the side of quantity) quantitative. In this way qualitative-quantitative determination posits a limit between itself and others, but this limit is not fixed-unfixed—for determinations have meaning only insofar as they are through (the element of) and by one another, in a relation wherein the moments develop a meaning within the relation. Not only must quantitative quality and qualitative quality be identified, they must be differentiated: the former is limitation of *quantity* (determination of magnitude); the later is limitation of *quality* (the moments of being, nothing, becoming, etc.)—but both are limits of limits, transitional limits and limiting transitions, the *limit* of quantity and the *limit* of quality. And the science of logic is the science of the limit between (and at the end of) quality and quantity, the science of the purity and impurity of purity and impurity, of impure purity and pure impurity, the science of hearing the double-entendre of the concept of speculative thought.

At the end of the moment of quantity then, multiplicity is no longer considered as a predicate or substantive, but as both qualification and quantification. Being and not being (nothing) multiple showed themselves as possible because becoming is already multiple—and its moments are constitutive for its own multiplicity. The logic of qualitative-quantitative multiplicity, however, only becomes explicit in the concept of measure—for here what it means to be multiple, to not be multiple, or rather, to become multiple, becomes both measurable and "the measure of all things." Being both returns to itself and does not return. And becoming shows itself not to have multiplicity, multiple moments, but to *be* multiple. In this way, the logic of limit is that of measure, of the ways in which limits become multiple. Yet what is the measure of this multiplicity? The multiplicity of measure? How can its concept supersede and take care of the qualification of quantity and the quantification of quality? And how does multiplicity make pluralization and the other multiplicities possible?

6

Measure of Multiplicity

The Measure of All Things

> Don't do it! responded the captain, who unhappily crossed-out the convictions of others with his own while he from experience had learned that the views of men are much too multiple for them to be able to be gathered, even through the most rational representations, to *one* point.
>
> —*Goethe*[1]

With measure (*Maß*) the first book of the *Logic,* the "Doctrine of Being," comes to an end. The science that began with being returns to being—yet this being no longer has its original immediacy; rather, insofar as it has superseded the difference of its other from itself within itself, it is self-related, that is, mediated being. Mediation here means that a particular unified concept disperses itself in its other and returns to itself; but through its experience of self-dissemination, it does not simply fall back into its previous mode of determination—for that would be "far more spiritlessness, not spirit."[2] In measure then, being's return is not a re-identification with itself, but union (*Einigkeit*) with self, a re-union that concretely preserves/destroys its own history, as the history of its multiple moments, insofar as it simultaneously takes care of the difference between itself as measure and as being. In fact, the "Doctrine of Being" is the science of the history within which immediate being becomes the concept of being, becomes (and does not become) that which it always already was and will be—the beginning is the end, the return of being to itself as not-itself, as the other of itself that is being.

Measure is being; however, since everything depends on the kind and manner (*Art und Weise*) of determination, measure is not identical to the way of being in the moments of quality and quantity. As the end of the movement by which qualitative difference and quantitative indifference are thought in their identity and difference, measure is quality and quantity, the qualitative-quantitative and quantitative-qualitative concept; it is the truth of quantity as the truth of quality—but it is just as much its non-truth. For truth lies neither in the realm of quality nor in that of quantity, neither in being nor in nothing; rather, the truth of both is their movement, their becoming one another. And measure is the concept of quality and quantity, the identity and difference of both, their other and truth; however, it is also a concept in itself.

Indeed, for a science of logic, if measure is the meaning of being, if "to be" means "to be measured," then it is because the concept is still burdened with being, with that determination of being that has not yet found its other in essence (although it is already implicitly essence insofar as it determines itself only in relation to its other), that essence with which it will enter into mediation. Here the dialectical movement by which the implicit truth of measure becomes explicit takes three forms: first, as specific quantity (*spezifische Quantität*), measure *is* a specific quantity of a/one (*ein*) quantum and *has* a particular qualitative meaning; second, as real measure (*reale Maß*), qualitative and quantitative measure are separate from one another and quantified—they show themselves as self-subsistent members of a ratio, as independent participants in a relation, but in a relation wherein their identities rest upon a mere difference in magnitude, that is, upon a difference that is no difference at all, but far more the indifference of measurelessness; third, as the becoming of essence (*Werden des Wesens*), measure's quantitative indifference is inverted, becomes conceptual, the immeasurable essence of absolute indifference that supersedes all previous determinations of being. In this way measure takes care of being by positing the identity and difference of qualitative and quantitative determination. Scientifically, on the one hand, with the concept of measure, quality and quantity *is* the same as being, just as measure "is"; and the concept of *being* as measure is the *concept* of being, but not yet essence. Speculatively, on the other hand, being is a result of measurement; that is, "to be" means "to already have a measure"—for being is merely an abstraction from concrete measurement, or a reduction and fixing of immeasurable singularity.[3]

Like quality and quantity before it then, the moment of measure has its own way of thinking multiplicity. Yet what is the multiplicity of the logic of the measures of measure? How does a measure function to regulate beings? How does a standardization or normalization of measures serve to limit, delimit, control multiplicity? Through what processes and to what ends is measure determined? If being as measure is what it is only in relation to essence as its other, then what does it mean that measure is the measure of beings? Or that being is a result of measure? And to what extent does measure think multiplicity?

For Protagoras, human being is the measure (*metron*) of all things (*pantōn chrāmatōn*). In the *Theatetus* Plato writes: "the account you give of the nature of knowledge is not, by any means, to be despised. It is the same that was given by Protagoras, though he stated it in a somewhat different way. He says, you will remember, that 'the measure of all things' is man, 'alike of the being of things that are and of the non-being of things that are not.' No doubt you have read that?"[4] For Hegel, however, the "human" alone, like the one-sided subject, cannot serve as the measure of all things—for measure is always also the measure of objects, of nature (*physis*), or more precisely, of substance. The science of logic is the science of both these measures (*Wissenschaft der Maße*), objective and subjective, and speculative thought thinks the concept of measure as subject just as much as substance. It is possible then to re-write Protagoras after Hegel: the becoming concept is the measure of all things—alike of the being of things that are and of the not-being of things that are not; or rather: "*everything, that is there, has a measure.*"[5] Yet what is this "everything" that is measured? For Protagoras, like Parmenides, all things, all matters and affairs, are twofold: that which is and that which is not. And measure is, therefore, double as well: of being and of non-being (nothing). Protagoras and Hegel agree that everything is twofold; however, they disagree as to what there is to be measured and how these things are to be measured: for the former, all things are subject to the meter, rhythm and time, of the human being; for the latter, all beings (thoughts and things) are subject to the concept, to the science of measure.

The questions for multiplicity then: Is the initial assumption, namely, that all things to be measured are twofold, not already problematic? Does the difference between beings and non-beings, thoughts and things, not already refuse multiplicity? Can the twofold measure do justice to all things? If all things are plural, then must their measure not also be pluralized? Or is pluralization itself, in fact, radically inadequate for taking account of multiplicity? And of manys? Must there not be measures for those beings which are to be measured? And how is the multiplicity of measure possible?

For the science of logic, the multiplicity of all things is measured by the concept, and the concept of measure is the multiple measure of all things. Here measure is political, physical, chemical, biological, social, economic, musical, aesthetic, and so on. Hegel's use of language is precise: measure is to be taken in its full polyvalence, in the multiplicity of its meanings in order for it to play the role of the concept. Indeed, measure means unit (*monas*), a quantity to be counted, to be numbered as a determinate amount or quantum; rule or ruler in the sense of scale or standard (foot, meter, etc.), mark of the norm, but also as "rules of the game," that is, law and lawgiver, sovereign legislator, the master (*Herr*) meting out punishment or praise in appropriate (or not) mass—for rule is also to be taken in a multiplicity of senses: balance, equilibrium, fairness, proportion, measurements; the virtue of *sophrosyne,* temperance, prudence, moderation; comparison of many, masses, abundance, riches, plenty; extent or degree, that is, as comparison of greater or lesser; measure of volume, and so on. Yet what is the multiplicity of measures that are themselves multiple? How is this multiplicity characteristic of the measuring concept? And how does multiplicity show itself as multiple in the concept of measure?

Specifics of Measure

First, as specific quantum (*spezifische Quantum*), measure is an indifferent quantitative determination of a particular quantity and immediately related to beings, to the determinate being of a "something." Since every "thing" has a size, quantity, it is a unit to be counted, a quantum to be numbered as a determinate amount, an "artificial" standard that permits exterior comparison (and it is "foolish to speak of a natural *standard* of things").[6] If it belongs to the nature of a being to have a specific magnitude, then its measure is not indifferent to its being: alteration in quality corresponds to change in quantity—for a being is what it is only insofar as it is determined as a specific quantum, only insofar as it falls within a certain definite standard: "everything that exists has a size which makes it what it is, and in general enables it to have determinate being."[7] As specific quantum, measure has a double-identity: on the one hand, it is that fixed quantity to which quality is strapped, the size that a being must attain in order to claim its identity, the magnitude that a thing must reach in order to fulfill its function; on the other hand, it is the quantity that can be altered without losing qualitative determination, that range of sizes within which a being retains its definition (*logos*), a magnitude that is flexible enough, tolerant enough, generous enough to permit difference, to include variety, but that is sufficiently rigid to exclude others, strangers, foreigners, aliens, to refuse beings that belong to other categories, species, kinds (*eidos*). In this way, the multiplicity of a specific quantum is a multiplicity of units, a quantity expressed as a unity to which a being must accord, the quantities of qualities that permit the identification and differentiation of beings.

It is in the quantification of nature then that measure as specific quantum is exploited for the explication of all things via mechanical laws. For Hegel, however, insofar as quantitative determination remains nonconceptual, it simply cannot take account of the multiplicity (*Mehrheit*) of conflicting qualities. The proportions of the human body, for example, can be quantitatively determined, their ratios can be measured, fixed, and compared, abnormalities and anomalies can be described and classified, categories can be established upon which normative judgments can be grounded; yet the range of differences between capacities and the multiplicity of types themselves cannot be grasped by biological essentialism, mechanistic physiognomy, or the pseudo-science of phrenology:

> when, therefore, a human being is told, you (your inside) is this because your bone is so constituted; this means nothing else than, I regard a bone as *your reality*. To reply to such a judgment with a box on the ear, as in the case of a similar judgment in physiognomy mentioned above, at first takes away from the *soft* parts their importance and position, and proves only that these are no true *in-itself*, are not the reality of spirit; the retort here would actually have to go the length of beating in the skull of anyone making such a judgment, in order to demonstrate in a manner just as palpable as his wisdom, that for the human being, a bone is nothing *in itself*, much less *its* true reality.[8]

Ideal qualities, in other words, cannot be reduced to material expression. The physical body may express mental characteristics, thoughts and things *may* be connected, but they cannot be identified. Spirit is not a thing, and its movement is not mechanical; and if measure is specific quantum, then spirit cannot be measured. Attempting to tie spirit to physical (or corporal) laws, the quantification of nature remains one-sided, the dead-side, because it fails to account for the multiplicity of qualities and the living movement of the concept.

Nevertheless, if quantitative determination is seductive, then it is because it claims to provide the ruler's rule, seems to give the law of the law by which judgments can be made, transgressions identified, because it appears to produce the method by which beings can be classified, grouped, ordered, controlled, by which they can be limited and delimited—but for Hegel it is massively insufficient insofar as it ignores the way that quantitative determination as limitation is what it is only in relation to other quantities (i.e., the way in which a determination continues in its other), and because it forgets its other, qualitative determination. As limit, measure is the quantitative difference between qualitatively different beings; yet the determination of beings via negation is not pure—the size whereby a species is what it is can never be fixed. For example, a rational animal (*vernuftige Tier*) is an existing being (*exis*-tier-*ende*) only insofar as it not only accords to a certain size and proportion (quantity), but also insofar as it falls within a certain type of animal (*Tier*), species or genus (quality). The differences within a type are never pure, or rather, they are pure and impure; and the line, frontier, border between types can never be completely fixed, never perfectly sealed. In the moment of totalization, of standardization, normalization, legalization, lies the impossibility of that totality—and that is the way that determination works, the way that identity is fixed. Here measure is a quantitative as well as qualitative limit, and multiplicity is that which is delimited, that which is cataloged, grouped, measured, controlled; it is that measure which must be simultaneously excluded in the determination of a species, of a type, brand, band, or group, and included within the continuum of possible members.

Change then, along a quantitative continuum, is possible without an alteration of quality. The destruction (*Untergehen*) of a determinate measured being, however, the negation of a specific quantum (and its double-identity), appears as sudden, unexpected, or even impossible. If qualitative determination were simply a question of more or less, of quantity, then the disappearance of a quantity, the transition between having and not having a quantity, the difference between zero and one, or any other amount, remains unexplained. Abstract quantitative determination cannot account for qualitative transition because it takes measure as an indifferent limit, that is, as non-conceptual. Multiplicity is the unexpected quality that appears unexplainable in terms of a specific quantity—for at what point along a continuum does multiplicity begin and non-multiplicity end? In other words, taking the difference between quality and quantity as immediate, specific measure cannot explain the sudden quality of transition at the core of quantitative determination and cannot account for the sudden shift to qualitative multiplicity.[9]

The determination of the measure of beings then, of a class or species, can function via abstraction or deduction from the multiplicity of beings to a specific quantum. Inversely, however, beings can be specified by measure, by a specifying measure (*spezifizierendes Maß*). Here the assumed rule as a fixed magnitude, a number of units, determines via external (transcendent) comparison whether or not a given example measures up to the standard. A particular something has the right to be called what it claims to be, to enter into one category or another, if and only if it submits to the normative force of law. And the measured being has a self-determined measure in itself, has an immanent magnitude that it alters according to its way of being, only insofar as it accepts the other's external specification as its own. Yet since both the external and internal measures of a being are alterable quanta, they are related to one another and may be expressed as a ratio with a specific exponent. The specifying measures of types appears as the difference between incommensurable ratios: for example, materials of varying qualities (shape, structure, construction, etc.) exhibit variable susceptibility to changes in water temperature—the relation between a body and its element is neither direct nor indirect; rather, it is determined by the exponential law of their power ratio insofar as it quantitatively expresses the relative relation of the element's to the body's qualities (qualities that are themselves measures). The external quantitative measure then specifies a quality only insofar as it supersedes its externality, that is, does not accept to remain merely outside a specified being; rather, the quantum must be (conceptually) both inside and outside that which it measures. The difference and the relation, however, between the measure and its quantity is itself qualitative, that is, one of immediate being insofar as both are determined as qualities. If specific quantity is always the specific quantity of a quality, then it is because quantum is already doubled as a twofold quantity (external/internal), as two types of quantity that are themselves in a qualitative relation to one another, namely, they are a measure, the measure that is "the *immanent* quantitative relationship of *two* qualities to each other."[10] In other words, quality is a function of quantity, of the ratio of quantities within a specific measure and between the internal measure and the external measure that specifies it. And multiplicity is both the source or origin of measure (i.e., that from which abstraction or deduction must be made in order to fix a measure for a class, species, genus of beings, to determine a rule of inclusion and exclusion) and also that which is ruled, determined, measured, submits to the very measure from which it was abstracted. In this way qualitative specification is determined by quantitative measure: the measure of a being is the relation between the ways in which its quantity, as specified from within and without, presents itself as qualities.[11]

Real Measures

In specified/specifying measure, quality is a function of quantity. Yet if quantity itself functions as measure, then it becomes real insofar as it is realized as a measure, as realized measure (*realisierte Maß*)—for this measure is really the identity and difference of a multiplicity of qualities and quantities. The measure of the qualitative difference, for instance, not only between the element and the bodies within it, but also between bodies themselves, is their quantity—and vice versa, their quantitative difference is their quality. Indeed, as quantitative, measure is a qualitative determination: for example, space and time, in the ratio that expresses the law of the revolution of planets, are simultaneously determined as quantitative (measured/measuring quanta) and qualitative (different types of movement, sides of the concept of motion, that is, the identity and difference of the moments of traversed space and elapsed time). Here quantities and qualities are inseparable within their determinations and from one another. Yet if measure is realized, then it is because it is the result of a qualitative determination of quantity—for what is realized as a measure is that a multiplicity of measures (*Mehrheit von Maßen*) lies at the core of specified/specifying measure, a multiplicity of qualities and quantities determined as a quantum, as a ratio, but a ratio that is the quantification of multiple qualities, a ratio that is really the ratio between qualities. In this way realized measure reveals the qualitative difference within quantitative determination.[12]

Behind the realized quantum of measures in a ratio then, quantity has concealed itself—not as itself, but as another, as a specifying determination of magnitude; yet quanta themselves are fundamentally different qualifications, each of which is itself two-sided (measures of quantity and of quality). Here measure expresses itself as a relation between two quantitative measures, sides or moments, of *one* self-subsistent determination of measure wherein quantity and quality are immediately identified. The difference of the ratio of measures dis-appears (change in measure is simple arithmetic progression along a seamless continuum); and the self-subsistence of the ratio of measures is negated by the immediate quantum of the ratio's exponent, by the law to which the measures must submit in order to be in relation to one another. For example, the realized measure of a body is the specific ratio (quantity) that, according to fixed physical laws, expresses its type of motion, its way (quality) of moving in the abstract qualities of space and time; however, as previously in quantity, the law of the exponent determines the ratio's quanta, and the measures of the body as well—in the moment of real being-for-self (*reales Fürsichsein*), the negation by which a body achieves (incomplete) self-subsistence, that is, submits itself to a ratio of measures, appears as a mere function or product of the ratio, that is, is itself negated: via the negation of the negation, the negation of multiple qualities and their submission to the ratio of measures, a body becomes a something, achieves complete self-subsistence. And multiplicity here appears as dis-appeared, as present insofar as it is not-present as itself, but as another, as a multiplicity that is no multiplicity at all—for the ratio of measure shows itself as a double-identity: on the one hand, measures are dependent, sides of the ratio; on the other hand, repelling from the ratio, measures are independent, that is, differentiated self-sufficient somethings.[13]

When the body then—that which was only some-thing (*Etwas*), only a function of the ratio of abstract or ideal measures of space and time—is materially determined, it shows itself as a self-sufficient thing (*Ding*). Here measures are measures of things, and science is the science of measures. Chemistry and music, for example, are the study of the real measure (*reale Maß*) of existing things. And as measure of a thing, measure becomes concrete, as real as it is ideal; just as multiplicity is as real as it is ideal—for it is the qualitative-quantitative measure of a self-sufficient thing. In this sense, science is the study of the relations of existing things, of that which is related and of how it is related; it is the study of the multiplicity of things themselves, their immanent multiplicity and that multiplicity of multiple relations between multiplicities. Self-subsistent measures appear as a multiplicity of materials united in a relation: first, a relation of merely external combination; second, a relation of differences that culminates in their indifferent membership in one series; third, an exclusive relation of elective affinities.[14]

In the form of an external relation then, the combination of physical things is the combination of two measures with different immanent measures (quantity) and different properties (quality). Each member of the composite is itself a combination of quantitatively determined qualities: for example, specific determinations of weight to volume by the direct ratio ($x : y^2$). And each member qua combination of qualities is quantitatively expressed by measure as a number (2) of units (y) of a quantity. In the composite, although the comparison of the exponents that determine the ratios of particular things and the inner measure of their qualities connects them (externally) to one another, their combination (e.g., of two metals with different masses) brings them into an internal relation expressed by the exponent of the ratio of their relation. The result of external relation is that two multiplicities combine to form a third. And here multiplicity means the qualitative-quantitative measure of that which is contained within a thing that combines with another thing to form another multiplicity; but it is also the multiplicity that disappears in the combination, in the new thing as some-one-thing. Yet here combination is merely summation—the exponent of each thing (and of their result) fails to express the change, the supersession, that occurs to each in their combination. In the form of external relation, the specific measures of components are forgotten, dis-appeared, abstractly negated in the combination.[15]

Serial Multiplicity

In a series the measures of things are related by neutralizing multiplicity. Particular qualities do not disappear as in abstract negation; they mask themselves in the thing's new relation of measures (quantity). Here the connection of many (*mehrere*) measures with one another are expressed as different ratios with different exponents and different amounts of different materials. Each component is identical with itself in comparison with the others, but each can make this comparison, be self-identical, self-sufficient, only insofar as it is in relation with the others—identity is based on difference, difference is grounded in identity, and multiplicity means that which is summarily constructed from differences, the row of measures, more of the same. Serial particularity lies in the relation of the measures of its members. The quantitative exponents in a series are the expression of quality, of the way in which it maintains its self-sufficiency, and the self-sufficiency of its self-sufficiencies. Although a series explicitly appears as sheer quantity (a row of exponents, relations of quanta, time or number line, color spectrum, temperature gauge), it is implicitly a qualitative relation: the quantity of the relation (*Verhältnis*) is the way in which its exponents conduct themselves, the specificity of the behavior (*Verhalten*) of quanta. In this way the series fixes its self-sufficiency, its identity (momentarily), insofar as its ratios take the form of a constant—their becoming recedes, fades into the background, their differences are concealed, their multiple relations to one another (through which they are what they are) mask themselves in a common cause, their identities via comparison are determined via negation.

The particularity of measure as series then is that each number, amount, each exponent of each series is simultaneously itself in its own series, and in relation to its other, to the series of units. In the series itself, however, differences are neutralized insofar as the qualitative side of quantity remains merely implicit: the series shows itself as one series, indifferent to the quality of quanta. The relation of magnetic poles or electricity, for example, is such that one is the negative of the other, wherein the two are quantitatively differentiated, but cannot be indifferent to one another because they are not explicit about their qualitative difference, about that which makes up their self-sufficiency. Nevertheless, the serial relation of measures is not conceptual: each side of the ratios "goes over" into the other but has not "gone over" into the other; each conducts itself negatively to the others, but its negation is indifferent to the other that it negates, to the other that is its own negation. Multiplicity is here qualitatively neutralized in the series—and then reappears as boring repetition, or, under the mask of repetition with a difference, as serial displacement, functioning as an ever more sophisticated means for neutralizing, containing, controlling, ordering multiplicity. Concealment of quality in quantity then means that the affinity of serial measures shows themselves as indifference to qualitative multiplicity (as well as the truth of quantity), as neutralization of differences.[16]

The Chemistry of Measures

> Need I insist that the only enemy of the mature marriage is monogamy? That anything less than sexual multiplicity (bodies upon bodies, voice on voice) is naive? That our sexual selves are merely idlers in a vast wood?
>
> What is marriage if not a vast and neutral forest in which our own sexual selves and those of our first partners wander until momentarily stopped in the clear actuality of encounter? Yes, the best of marriages are simply particular stands of pale trees sensuously stitched into the yet larger tapestry, which is not to say that our entire troop of sexual partners (other than wives or husbands) need necessarily be composed of women or men who are themselves in turn already committed to their own matrimonial partners. There are exceptions. Not every finger is ringed. But why voice what simply runs in the blood and fills the mind of any considerate man who has sat with another man's wife on his lap or of any woman who has cast off prudery and tugged at cloth and moved out among the trees?
>
> —*Hawkes*[17]

In the relation of elective affinity (*Wahl-verwandtschaft*) then, multiplicity is negated by choice (*Wahl*): the desire for an other to the exclusion of all others. Previously measures were neutralized via their affinity (*Verwandschaft*) for one another in a series; this was the multiplicity of indifference wherein substantial differences were neutralized, wherein the instability of multiplicity was regulated—seriality was the law of stability. With elective affinity the relation of the couple via the logic of exclusivity takes on the function of the law—multiple (*vielfach*) connections are permitted, but only between two. Chemical bonding, for example, is the identity of different kinds of substances (qualities) in determinate amounts (in a quantitative ratio according to saturation laws)—and not every substance can bind with every other; rather, certain materials exhibit an inclination and choice for one another. Or, if musical tones in a composition have a meaning only within a context, only insofar as they are connected with particular other tones of other pitches, then it is because not every note can combine harmoniously/dis-harmoniously with every other; rather, the measure of music is the choice that certain notes have for one another to the exclusion of others. Previously measures were structured or organized as members of a series wherein each was related "indifferently" to every other member via quantitative neutralization; here they are related "differently" as qualities: an acid, for instance, finds its neutralization by a particular base—and when the choice of an "other" is made, the possibility of satisfaction or saturation (*Sättigung*) with any "other" is closed off. Even the exponents of elective affinities are qualitative: they are determinations of measures that express a priority or preference (*Vorzug*) that a member or part be more or less, greater or smaller. The measure of the exclusion of others (the multiplicity of other connections, encounters, couplings, relations, etc.), however, is just as much the inclusion of a preferred other, a fixed holding-together. Thus, in the elective affinity of measure, the multiplicity of indifferent quantitative connections in the series has been replaced by the exclusion of multiplicity, discrimination against those others that are not *the* other, preference for the chosen.[18]

The discourse of the other then is not the neutralization, but the refusal of multiplicity. And in the chapter on "Elective Affinity" Hegel plays on the multiple meanings contained within the twofold sense of chemistry's double-entendre, its double-meaning (*Doppelsinn*). On the one hand, explicitly scientific, elective affinity is the relation between substances that are self-sufficient only in relation to a particular, chosen other: chemistry's double process (unification/separation) means that acid and base saturation points stand in a quantitative ratio with a particular (qualitative) other, and that new unions are built through division, parting, splitting of old.[19] On the other hand, following the logic of "interpersonal chemistry," elective affinity is inter-subjective, sexual, intimate, corporal: the term for member or part (*Glied*) is also that for the male reproductive/sexual organ. Yet if Hegel's language is doubled, then it is because nature itself has a double-nature (*duo-physis*)—and the terms of logic can think this duplicity only insofar as they are double themselves. The penis and vagina embody nature's double-meaning:

> the *depth* which spirit brings forth from within—but only as far as its *picture-thinking consciousness* where it lets it remain—and the *ignorance* of this consciousness about what it really is saying, are the same conjunction of the high and the low which, in the living being, nature naively expresses when it combines the organ of its highest fulfillment, the organ of generation, with the organ of urination. The infinite judgment,

> *qua* infinite, would be the fulfillment of life that comprehends itself; the consciousness of the infinite judgment that remains at the level of picture-thinking behaves as urination.[20]

Natural science then must make use of a double-language; it must be bilingual. The two languages exhibit an affinity for one another: chemistry resorts to the metaphors of copulation just as much as sexuality employs the discourse of elective affinity. The semiotic slippage is uncontrollable because the materiality of language (to which philosophy must also resort), is always already (at least) double. For Hegel the concept's two-sided logic of equivocation is designed to account for both meanings of measure—the antanaclasis is explicit: terms of natural science and mathematical measure are displaced, repeated with a difference, in the shift between analogic realms of politics and morals, a shift that is possible because each realm is itself already equivocal, not only itself, has an other as its truth, is identical and different from every other.[21] Logic is precisely not the exclusion of ambiguity: shallowness in science and superficiality in philosophy mean omitting the difference of different terms, and then taking them as identical.

The doubled-multiplicity of language then is and is not that of natural science (of *physis*)—for the concept is designed to think both sides as included-excluded, to hear and understand the double-sense of terms, to see and think the language of sexuality as in-side/out-side the discourse of science. Yet is language only double? Is it not a question of poly- rather than bi-linguism? Of multiple realms and relations far more than the identity and difference of the analogy between two discourses? Is ana-logic not insufficient for the multiple relations of spheres? And is the double-entendre all that nature offers? On the most superficial level, does the penis not have more functions than pissing and procreation? Is the penis not an organ among organs, one of a multiplicity of parts? And is it not also in relation to a multiplicity of organs that do not explicitly belong to one body? Must the body be subject to a twofold logic? Or can it also be heard in its polymorphous perversity? Is the discourse of sex and gender (*Geschlecht*) not spurious (*schlecht*) if it remains subject to binary assumptions? And can multiplicity be named without leaving out (or in) multiplicity?

The Exclusive Economy of Desire

The exclusionary economy of elected affinities, implicit in Hegel's *Logic,* becomes explicit in Goethe's novel of the same name. In *The Elective*

Affinities, a married (i.e., exclusionary, *mono-gamia*) couple splits and finds new partners. Neither the urge for coupling with the "one and only one other half of a whole," nor the Platonic nostalgia for a lost unity,[22] Goethe's characters are signs, representations of the "chemistry" of serial polygamy:

> Yes sir! retorted the captain: these cases are certainly the most meaningful and curious, where one really can present the attraction, the relationship, this desertion, this uniting as it were, cross over; where four, hitherto only two to two connected essences, brought into contact, desert their previous union and connect themselves to something new. In this abandoning and grasping, in this fleeing and seeking, one really believes that one sees a higher purpose; one entrusts to such essences a type of wanting and choosing and holds the artificial word "elective-affinities" for completely legitimate. . . .
>
> If you believe that it does not look pedantic, retorted the captain, I can very well quickly summarize in the language of signs. Think on an A that is immanently connected with a B, that is through many mediums and through some violence not to be separated from him; think on a C that relates just the same to a D; bring now the two pairs into contact: A will throw itself to D, C to B, without that one can say who first deserted the other, who first connected again with the other.
>
> Now then! it occurred to Eduard: until we all see this with our eyes, we want to view this formula as a parable from which we take a doctrine for immediate use. You represent the A, Charlotte, and I, your B: because actually, I am only dependent upon and follow you, like the A to the B. The C is quite clearly the captain who this time extracts you somewhat. Now it is easy, if you should not escape into indeterminacy, that for you a D will be acquired, and that is quite without question the lovely young madam Ottilie against whose approach you may no longer defend.[23]

In other words, legitimated by natural science, corporal lust finds its "higher purpose" (*Bestimmung*) in God's will. The determination (*Bestimmung*) of individual desire is the work of religious truth manifesting itself as scientific fact. Yet for the victims of the economy of elective affinities, science is merely an anthropomorphic explanation of nature's necessity (or chaos), an interpretation of God's ways and means—the election is more the chemist's than the chemical's:

> excuse me, said Charlotte, as I excuse the natural scientist; but I would here never see a choice, rather a necessity of nature, and this hardly: for it is, in the end, perhaps really only a matter of opportunity. Opportunity

> makes relations, as it makes thieves; and if the talk is about its natural bodies, it seems to me that the choice lies simply in the hands of the chemist who brings these essences together.[24]

For others, however, as the chemist of nature, God determines the elective affinities of acids and alkalis, as well as men and women. If the plan is clever (*geschickt*), then it is because it legitimates desire as manifest destiny or fate (*Schicksal*), as the fulfillment of scientific necessity, that is, a higher purpose. In Goethe's text, however, religious truth (behind scientific laws and sexual intrigue) remains hidden, merely implicit, that is, exclusive, not for public consumption—and this is the law of the parable.

Benjamin, for example, reads *The Elective Affinities* as a "classic" (modern) novel: its true meaning must remain secret, disguised in an economy of symbols or signs, and exclusively accessible for those with the code.[25] The key to deciphering Goethe's text is the metaphysics of morals that stretches from Kant through Hegel and places monogamous marriage (and the family) as the fundament and culmination of all culture and society. Here, as Kant insists, "sexual commerce (*commercium sexuale*) is the mutual use that one human being makes of another's sexual organ and capacity (*usus membrorum et facultatum sexualium alterius*), and either a natural (by which the same kind of being can be generated) or unnatural use, and this either of a person of the same sex or an animal of another as that of the human species."[26] Marriage then is defined as:

> the connection of two persons of different sexes to the life-long mutual possession of their sexual properties.—The goal of generating and raising children may always be a goal of nature which implants the tendency of the sexes towards one another; but that the human being who marries, would have to put this goal before, will not be required for the legitimation of this connection; because otherwise marriage would simultaneously dissolve from itself when the generation of children ceased.[27]

Benjamin's judgment is short: "so much for Kant."[28] And this would hold for Hegel as well—for the ethical order is conceptual insofar as it is grounded upon the family, that is, on monogamy, on the exclusivity of elective affinities:

> the difference of the natural sexes appears as well, as both a difference of intellectual and ethical determination. These personalities connect themselves according to their excluding details, to *One person;* the subjective intimacy, determined as substantial unity, makes this union into an *ethical* relation,—into *marriage.* The substantial intimacy makes

> marriage into a indivisible bond of the persons,—into *monogamous* marriage; the corporal unification is the consequence of the ethically tied bond. The further consequence is the mutuality of personal and particular interests.[29]

Explicitly then a moral tale wherein the concept of choice is secured for ethical thought in order to be annihilated by the excluding law of fidelity, Goethe's work is implicitly (latently) determined by religious truth and constituted by the original phenomena that can only show themselves as veiled. Yet if the truth buried in the work of art—in its images and oracles, and not as such, not in its nakedness—can be unearthed, then it is only as it reveals itself in its concealment, as concealed. Essence presents itself (*sich darstellt*) but does not appear (*erscheint nicht*) in a "beautiful" work of art—for art is the truth made visible, the non-visible truth that appears precisely not as such, as truth in itself; but rather, as non-truth, the non-truth (not the lie) wherein the truth appears, wherein the ideal presences itself as non-presencing. And the truth of the work remains self-identical under the condition that it does not appear. In this way the work of art is the appearance of truth, that is, its non-appearance—and critique is the business of viewing the beautiful as concealed, seeing the secret as secret, according to an economy of the secret. Indeed, the work of art is a unity of cover and covered, mask and masked, and not the simple state of naked or clothed truth. In other words, for Benjamin, the work of art is religion's (and philosophy's) virtual space, that is, the place in which the problem of the ideal appears as non-appearing, where truth presences as absent, an absence that is necessary—for the beautiful truth (like Plato's sun) cannot be viewed without the protection and medium of a veil, of that veil which in revealing, necessarily metamorphoses the origin.

If *The Elective Affinities* then is a work of art, it must function as the site of the ideal's presencing as non-presencing. The ideal is itself, however, as essentially multiple. The work of art is the appearance of multiplicity as the non-existent unity of philosophy's (religion's) ideal. As Benjamin writes:

> there is no question that encompasses the inquiry into the unity of philosophy. For the concept of this non-existent question that inquires into the unity of philosophy is signified in philosophy as the ideal of the problem. If however, the system is also in no sense subject to inquiry, there are still images which, without being questions, have the deepest affinity to the ideal of the problem. They are works of art. The work of art does not compete with philosophy; it merely comes to it in the most exact ratio through its affinity with the ideal of the problem. And in fact can,

> according to a legitimacy grounded in the essence of the ideal in general, present this only in a multiplicity.[30]

In this sense, the work of art is a philosophical allegory: the ideal truth of philosophy is one with that of art because they seek to represent the ideal as non-present, and to think multiplicity as non-multiple. And the (elective) affinity or analogical relation between art and philosophy is thought by Hegel under the name of the concept, that is, the identity and difference of disciplines.

In *The Elective Affinities* then, the relations between human beings, the economy of desire, is determined by natural (chemical) laws, that is, ultimately by God. According to Benjamin, Goethe's representation of God's work functions as an aesthetic ideal—for it makes real that which essentially belongs to another sphere, re-presents the (onto-theological) truth under the condition that it remains non-present, revealed as concealed: unity presents itself as multiplicity, the problem of ideal unity as multiple problems. Yet the question of questions, the question of the unity of philosophy does not exist: If the ideal of the problem does not appear, then is it because it too does not exist? Because the essence of the ideal is already multiple? And does the assumption that philosophy's unity presences, comes into presence, imply that it cannot represent multiplicity adequately, that it cannot do it justice? Or is it, rather, that the very economy of unity and multiplicity, of veiling and unveiling, sets the limit or horizon of the multiplicity that can be thought? If the work of art is already determined as following the law of revealing and concealing, of the variation of double-determinations, binary terms, words, positions, of their identity and difference, then can it ever think the multiplicity that it is supposed to reveal and/or conceal? Are these not the presuppositions of the ways in which the history of western metaphysics has solved the problem of multiplicity, namely, by insisting that it submit to the law of the double-entendre, that it fall under the two and only two-sided knife?

For the *Science of Logic* the answer to these questions (as well as that of elective affinities) lies in the concept, that is, that logic by which the particular difference of human and chemical relations shows itself. Hegel's self-sufficient measures, unlike Goethe's, are not the manifestation of some higher purpose or ideal (and here philosophy does not correspond to Benjamin's definition of a work of art) because they are already ideal, as well as real, insofar as the concept is the identity and difference of real and ideal. Art is not the presencing of a non-present ideal; rather, it is both the presencing and non-presencing of the present and the non-present of the real in the ideal and the ideal in the real—for only then, when both sides are both present and non-present, can the work of art as living individuality (*lebendige Individualität*) be said to stand in the middle-point between inner and outer, ideal and real, thought and thing.[31] For Hegel philosophy is not an allegory for truth—it is truth itself (and also not, always also not truth, the thought of the non-truth in relation to truth, the logic of the movement of their becoming one another). The "logic of revelation," however, is not that of speculation since science is not a mask or veil to be (or not to be) removed, not a concealing or non-presencing; rather, the *Logic* thinks the truth of measure because it always also does not think it. In this way the exclusionary relation of elective affinities, the desiring logic of monogamous coupling, which shows itself in both the natural and human sciences, is that of the concept, and the systematic relations between sciences is conceptual as well. Yet if philosophy fails to present this "in a multiplicity," then is it perhaps because the problem of philosophy is the concept itself, the identity and difference of presence and absence, revealing and concealing, ideal and real?

Including Knots

If "exclusion" marks the elective affinities of self-sufficient measures, then "inclusion" marks them when they take on the form of a knotted line (*Knotenlinie*). Here the movement is a translation from (identical to/different from) that of quantitative discreteness/continuity; that is, measure (as end/limit) shows itself as the between of that which it seeks to exclude. The indifference of a particular measure against a multiplicity of possible others is its own indifference; and it suffers therefrom, is imprisoned by its own imprisoning—for the excluded others are the very multiplicities through which a measure determines itself, is self-related, produces and maintains its identity via difference. In other words, the determination continues out of itself and into its other; as excluded, they are included.

In this way the relation between the "elective affinities" and the "knotted line" is conceptual: that is, they are the same and not the same. On the one hand, both show that a material substrate, that which is measured, is constitutive for measure—a way of measuring (quality) needs something to measure (quantity)—and both insist that measures are qualitatively-quantitatively related. On the other hand, while in elective affinities saturation rights are granted via indifference to other possible connections, to the exclusion of multiplicity, in the knotted line others are included insofar as they are excluded. And not surprisingly, multiplicity, too, is included as excluded; it is that necessary exclusion through which a line determines its identity in spite of knots, imperfections, disturbances, disruptions, to which identity is no longer indifferent. In other words, immediate exclusion becomes mediated: that which is negated reveals itself as negated, as an other to which a given measure maintains its relation precisely by not coming into contact with it, insofar as their difference (no longer indifference) constitutes their interrelation.[32]

In the image of "knots in a line," like a knot of toads, the concept of measure appears to be qualitatively identical and only quantitatively distinguished—for discrete measures are only "more" or "less" on a continuous scale. Yet qualitative alteration (as in qualitative-quantitative multiplication, i.e., the dimensional shift between point, line and plane) along a knotted line is not the smooth transition from one quantity to the next, not the continuous motion of a seamless polymorphism; rather, qualitative change means the radical shift from one form to a completely foreign, strange other, to another being and a new, surprising, unforeseeable world. Between kinds there is only an infinitely deep cleft—and their connection is no connection at all. Here transition is a leap (*Sprung*) over the chasm, break, pit or shaft (*Schacht*) that opens up between determinations. No bridge spans the gap between the multiplicity of species, genera, types, between solid, liquid, and gas, between the states of life and death; no continuum between one note on the musical scale and the next, no contact between one *eidos* and another. A relation between types appears to be that of elective affinity; however, their radical difference from one another is their identity—causal contact is *actio in distans* and disconnection is connection: like knots on a line, they are continuously (quantitatively) discontinuous and discontinuously (qualitatively) continuous. The difference that forms the non-relation between kinds opens up as their relation, constitutes their specific ratio via the leap. The experience of hearing a harmony, for example, its appearance, the event of its happening, is the connection between radically disconnected tones, their play and relation to one another. Multiplicity shows itself as an effect of difference, of the discontinuity that opens up the possibility of radically disconnected multiplicity. The connectionism of analogy is refused by the infinite difference between realms, and multiplicity is that which can never be unified. The knotted line of measures, in other words, shows that qualitative difference cannot be explained by quantitative determination, and that only a leap between realms makes transition possible: solid wax will never become liquid (contrary to Descartes's experiment) if their difference is simply one of extension or degrees; life is not merely more death, and good is not less evil.[33]

Yet the knots on a knotted line are all tied together; they constitute *one* line, and their unity is the determination of the quantitative fluctuating ratios of measures on a scale of infinite qualities and quantities. If the alteration of magnitudes that could determine a being's identity remain in flux, then the determinate quantity of something measured is thereby simultaneously infinitely indeterminable. In this way the knotted line implies that between differences a leap is possible, that is, necessary—and impossible, always outstanding, lacking, a mere "should be made." The discourse of difference is possible-impossible. At this moment an infinity opens up between knots that renders the leap infinitely wide (like bad infinity, un-bridgeable, even by the longest stride) and the scale itself, against which a given magnitude is to be measured, infinitely flexible. Here multiplicity is reduced to identity: the *knots* on a line show themselves as knots on *a line.* The problem of these qualitative-quantitative infinities, however, is not the problem of measure (for they have already been solved by the concept of finite infinity and infinite finitude); rather, the entire determination of real measure is always already in relation to that which lies beyond it, namely, the measureless (*das Maßlose*).

Measureless Measure

With the measureless then, measure finally finds its negation, that is, the immeasurable other through which the quality and quantity of a measure determines itself. The measurelessness of measure is infinite: a quality has a measure insofar as it does not have an infinity of other measures and a quantity is a measuring of the immeasurable, a limiting of the unlimited, the finitude determined from an infinity. Yet as the negative beyond of measure, the measureless is that through which a measure is determined—and thereby it is the truth of measure: "the qualitative-finite *becomes* the infinite; the quantitative-finite is in its own self its beyond and *points beyond itself.*"[34] And as negation of this negation, of measureless's negation, measure *is* the measureless: a being is radically immeasurable insofar as it never corresponds to a measure of quality or quantity; the things themselves never submit to categorization, standardization; insofar as its qualities and quantities can never be adequately measured, they are beyond measure, transcendent, measureless. Qualitatively then, infinity erupts at the core of finitude: at the very moment that a being is determined as a particular measure, it un-fixes itself—within its determination, a being is always beyond its determination, always signifies that which transcends determination. Quantitatively, infinity is that beyond into which a finite measure continues, that unlimited through which limitation occurs.

Yet in the concept of the measureless, qualitative and quantitative infinity are superseded (have gone over into one another): qualitative transition is quantitative alteration and vice versa. And multiplicity as measureless is the other, the beyond, of non-multiplicity; it is that immeasurable multiplicity that as such, as immeasurable, is no multiplicity at all. Like nothing, the measureless multiplicity is multiple only insofar as it is always also non-multiple, and therefore measured—for the measureless shows itself to be the negative moment of the concept of measure.[35]

The dialectical movement of measure and measureless then becomes concrete in the thing: measure is always the measure of a thing (*Sache*), of a persistent, self-sufficient material—for the thing is determined as the continual alteration of the identity and difference of qualitative-quantitative measures. First, the thing itself (*die Sache selbst*) is posited immediately as a self-identical substrate of its differences, that is, that measure that is in itself already the unity of its qualitative and quantitative determinations (each of which constitutes the limit and beyond of the other). Second, qualitative differences are posited as dependent upon quantitative changes. Third, quantitative alterations are themselves posited as negating that quality to which they refer—the difference between the two has become complete, and the quality of a thing (from the side of quantity) is a function of quantitative measure relations. Yet if a thing can be determined qualitatively as well as quantitatively, then it is because the thing itself is that substrate that serves as the unified ground of their transition, of the process by which the thing shows itself as itself, the self-positing through which the thing gives itself a qualitative or quantitative meaning, sense, interpretation. The (ideal) leap on the knotted line, so necessary for any change of state, shows itself materially as a change of one and the same (real) substrate: from ice through liquid to vapor—the differences are those of one and the same self-identical water. And multiplicity here is a qualitative-quantitative measure grounded in the thing itself. In this way the truth of measure, as the supersession of immediate measure and the measureless, of the ideal and the real, is that the *measure* of a thing is the measure of the *thing*, that is, it is itself conceptual, the identity and difference of qualitative and quantitative determinations.[36]

Measure then comes to completion, as always (*wie immer*), in a concept, in the supersession of a multiplicity of moments, in the movement (becoming) that takes care of their identity and difference. Yet the concept is also not always (*nicht immer*) the identity and difference of its moments; rather, in the moment when measure posits itself as material substrate, as the particularity of this measure, "here and now," it shows itself as abstract identity, as indifference to difference. At this moment measure returns to being: as immediately self-identical, it is the same as being; insofar as it has a history, it is not identical with being. The self-identity of indifference is its non-identity with being. And multiplicity disappears in the simple, immediate unity of measure. In this way the moment of measure ends in indifference, in the abstract identification of measure and measured, of quality and quantity, ideal and real, without difference.

The Measure of Nothing

Indifference, however, the loss of difference, is not only abstract—for it is also absolute, and as such it will drive being out of itself to its particular other, will constitute the loss that marks the *becoming* of essence that is the becoming of *essence* (Werden *des* Wesens). Absolute indifference is double, a circle within a circle: the end of measure and the return to being, the end of being and the beginning of essence (that in the concept of the concept, the absolute idea, will return to being). First, absolute indifference, as the final determination of being (measure), is return to being—but it is not the simple return to the origin, the same place, because its dialectical history puts it in a different time, and thereby in a different space. Immediately, like being, measure is abstractly, simply indifferent to the multiplicity of its own previous moments, the moments that make out its difference from being, its particular history—it is the measure of nothing. The truth of measure is, however, its history, that is, the multiplicity that it has superseded, those moments that make it what it is and what it is not—that is, the moments of its becoming. In other words, the beginning and the end of the "Doctrine of Being" are conceptually related: measure and being are identical and different.[37]

Second, absolute indifference is the transition (becoming) from the "Doctrine of Being" to the "Doctrine of Essence." Quantitative measure goes back to and through the moments of quality (being, determinate being, being-for-self); it makes them its own by thinking them again, by re-thinking, re-presenting them as the same but not identical, by repeating them with a difference, via the analogic of displacement—"and everything turns on how these are posited in it."[38] Measure as being means immediate indifference to the difference of its indifference, to its own determination via negation/mediation of its qualitative-quantitative moments, to the disappearance of its other; and this measure posits itself as indifferent substrate, as indifferent to all possible determination, capable of every qualitative and quantitative alteration—as absolute indifference, measure does not think its indifference as result, as product of an abstraction (but as true, original, absolute). Measure as determinate being (in–but not yet for–itself) means negation of immediate *indifference* to difference as the *difference* of indifference. And qualities show themselves as factors of the indirect ratio that serves as their indifferent substrate wherein they are more or less preponderant through their quanta. Nevertheless, the difference between the *one* unifying ratio (identity) and its *two* factors (difference) is an indifference, the relation of two merely self-sufficient, simply self-determining measures that have not yet realized their interconnection, their conceptual interdependence, that is, their identity and their difference as their own. Measure as being-for-self means negation of the negation in an indifferent difference that is a differentiated indifference—the ratio of factors (that was supposed to be purely quantitative) shows its qualitative nature in the totality of factors and ratio as the indifference of their identity and difference, as the self-superseding concept of the contradiction of dependence and independence, being-in-itself and being-for-itself. Yet measure as being-for-self remains within the science of being insofar as indifference (however differentiated) *is* absolute—the little word "is" betrays the indifference of measure as a moment of the "Doctrine of Being." At the end of the movement of being lies the absolute indifference to the totality of determinations, the immediacy (no longer being) of the totality of qualitative and quantitative measures, the disappearance of the difference between thought and being, idea and extension. Indeed, the solution to the problem of the multiplicity of measures is the dissolution of measure altogether in the immediacy wherein difference is posited as one, that is, the indifferent identity of essence. The transition between doctrines, therefore, is possible because indifference too is absolute; and it takes on the form of the concept—not simply an end, but also a beginning; not merely a limit, but also "going over into another." The identity and difference of measure and being, which shows itself as the indifference of measure to being, to its very own history, is not identical to the immediacy of being (because of its history, however dis-appeared), but as such it is the immediacy of essence. In other words, being and essence *is* the same.[39]

Being then is the same as but not identical to essence: the absolute indifference of measure is the absolute indifference of being; however, its *difference* is not yet *its* difference; that is, it remains merely external (and quantitative). Being is not yet essence because its specific differences are indifferently differentiated: that is, they are one, identical difference. If difference is thought as one-sided identity and not also as difference, then it is because being is not yet absolute, because its logic is simply that of the identity of identity and difference, and not yet that of the difference of identity and difference as well. In other words, indifference to the difference of differences marks being, constrains it: being cannot be essence because it does not realize that the other, through which it determines itself, is its own—its negation remains abstract, and indifference to the other is just as much indifference to self.

The transition from being to essence, however, in the *Science of Logic* is made; and if it is made, then it is because it has already been made. Being and essence have already gone over to one another, their concept has already been given, they are themselves results from their absolute concept. Just as being and nothing were the results of becoming, the "Doctrine of Being" and the "Doctrine of Essence" result from the "Doctrine of the Concept"—and their relation is conceptual as well; they are the same but not identical, that is, the identity and difference of identity and difference. Being is only a one-sided determination of the two-sided concept, only in-itself and not yet for-itself as well, merely a negative totality and not yet positive as well. Thus, although being has superseded the one-sidedness of its moments, it has not yet superseded its own one-sidedness—this shall *be* the work of essence, namely, to be the other-side of being.[40]

The Multiplicity of Measures

At the end of the "Doctrine of Being" then, measure shows itself as multiple. And the multiplicity of measure means (1) a specific quantity of units that serve as a measure or rule of determination, a standard for defining the quantity of a being; (2) a quantity that is measured, ruled, cataloged, limited, and delimited, the original multiplicity that is controlled by both fitting and not-fitting a mold, by being both included and excluded from a category, species, genus, type (*eidos*); (3) a determinate measure in its qualitative difference that appears suddenly, unexpectedly, and that cannot be explained as a function of quantitative alteration along a continuum; (4) a quantity of qualitative measures expressed in a ratio of qualitative-quantitative measures; (5) an abstractly negated measure, a multiplicity that appears insofar as it does not appear, insofar as it appears as an other, as unity without multiplicity; (6) a measure of a thing, that is, the ideal multiplicity made real, the multiplicity contained within a thing; (7) the measures of the external relations between things, wherein multiplicity disappears in the moment when their relation is determined qua quantitative ratio; (8) the measures of the relations between things determined by a series, wherein a neutralized multiplicity reappears masked as a product of repetition (with or without a difference); (9) the measures of the relations between things determined by the economy of elective affinities, wherein multiplicity is expressed by a series of choices, of preferences, to the exclusion of all others; (10) the measures of relations between things determined by the form of the knotted line, wherein multiplicity is excluded via the mediation of its inclusion, that is, is expressed as an effect of the infinite gap between discontinuous/non-analogous differences, and simultaneously as belonging to the continuity of one line; (11) the multiplicity of the measureless, that is, the other of multiple measures, the infinity that is immeasurably multiple, and (12) the non-multiplicity of the measureless insofar as its multiplicity cannot even be measured, that is, determined; (13) the measures unified in a material substrate, the multiplicity grounded in a thing; (14) the measures thought in abstract indifference to multiplicity; (15) the measures thought as absolute indifference, that is, as the supersession of real and ideal, thought and thing, of qualitative and quantitative multiplicity in the concept of measure, the identity and difference of measure and measures. Yet still, the concept of measure, insofar as it remains indifferent to its own difference, is driven out beyond itself and must seek its truth in an other, in essence.

The multiplicity of measure then is the multiplicity of being; or rather, it is and is not the multiplicity of being. The multiplicity of being means the multiple determinations of quality, quantity, and measure—for in the "Doctrine of Being" multiplicity is itself multiple. Qualitative multiplicity is particular ways of thinking multiplicity. Quantitative multiplicity is a number of ways of thinking multiplicity. Measured multiplicity is supersession of qualitative and quantitative multiplicity, the product of their relativity, that which takes care of their identity and difference, the movement by which quality goes over into quantity and quantity goes over into quality; however, it is also their truth—for quality and quantity have already gone over into one another, and they are the products of measure's self-division, of its dissemination into a multiplicity of moments (cf. *Enzy*, §111). Measure means that multiplicity is never simply a matter of quality or quantity—for they belong together in the concept, in the relation of identity and difference of their identities and differences. And the multiplicity of being is the multiplicity of qualitative-quantitative measure, the multiplicity of multiplicities.

Yet is the thinking of multiplicities as moments of a determination of being not the refusal of the very multiplicity to be thought? Is the concept, insofar as it unites differences, not the forgetting of the multiplicity it contains? For Hegel the concept means taking care to remember the multiplicity within quality, quantity, and measure, the multiple multiplicities as the identities and differences of the multiple moments—this is the multiplicity of the *Logic.* Here the role of memory is crucial for conceptual thought: "it is one of the until now completely unobserved and, in fact, the most difficult point in the doctrine of spirit, in the systematization of intelligence, to grasp the position and meaning of memory and to conceive of its organic connection with thinking."[41] In fact, multiplicity is only multiple insofar as it agrees to be re-membered in the two-sided concept's unification. On the one hand, carried by a unity that functions as substrate, multiplicity is not multiple insofar as it is not unified; it is first multiple only in belonging to the implicit unity, to the unity of being-in-itself (*ansichseienden Einheit*). Moments are first self-sufficient, independent, when they become moments of being, interdependent, relative to one another, in a relation of belonging-together, as unified. On the other hand, moments are multiple in their repulsion from this unity, as non-unified, as that multiple other through which unity determines itself, as those determinations that unity negates that are immanent in the explicated unity, in the unity of being-for-itself (*fürsichseienden Einheit*). In essence, multiplicity will no longer simply be, no longer be the multiplicity of beings; rather, it will be posited as the essence of being, the truth of existence—and not only the end, but far more the beginning of being. At the end of the "Doctrine of Being," however, the multiplicity of determinations disappear in an immediate unity, an abstract totality of moments. In this way multiplicity is superseded in the being that is indifferent to difference, that is simply being, alone, only with itself.[42]

In the simple, self-identification of being, however, being itself disappears. Without difference, the identity of multiplicity of beings is no identity at all. Totality as immediate, that is, without non-totality, is not total. The logical concept must, therefore, think the totality and non-totality of totality and non-totality, both identity and difference. Yet at the conclusion to the "Doctrine of Being," the concept fails to differentiate: the concept shows itself as self-related, as negating an other that is merely itself, as mediated through the immediacy that it has assumed. The beginning of the *Logic,* that assumed original being, however, is itself a result, the result of the concept as it splits (difference) and returns (identity), the movement of the absolute "out from" and "back to" itself. In other words, being is determined as essence by superseding itself, by returning to immediacy (albeit of another sort with a different history and truth), to the being that in being only with itself refers to something else, to another which lies at its core, to an other that is its essence.

And like being, the beginning of multiplicity is the end; or more precisely, the end is the beginning. The end of the *Logic,* the absolute idea, is the beginning of being and the origin of the multiplicity of the logic, the source of the logic of multiplicity. In the *Science of Logic* transition between doctrines occurs according to an historical progression, the temporality of narrative, from beginning to end—but this end circles back and returns to the beginning. Just as historical experience is the law of the education of consciousness to the point of absolute knowledge in the *Phenomenology*, the uni-directional movement of science drives the circle of determinations in the *Logic* toward the "Doctrine of the Concept." Hegel, however, also thinks teleologically: the end is the beginning. Although the origin (*Ur-sprung*) appears later in space and time, the transitional leap (*Sprung*) has already happened: the historically last is speculatively first. And even further, speculative philosophy also thinks the ahistorical circularity of the historical-teleological circle. In this way the history (not just the time) of logic is multiple, a multiplicity of histories, that is just as much the history of multiplicity. And this history comes to a certain end. The question of the multiplicity of the logic, however, and of the logic of multiplicity, remains outstanding until the end, that is, the beginning, the beginning that is both the end and the beginning of multiplicity, of the future of multiplicity. Indeed, it still remains to be asked: Can a science of logic think manys?

7

Conceptual Subjectivity

The Concept of Truth

> In this way Hegel showed that the concept has nothing whatever to do with a general or abstract idea, any more than with an uncreated Wisdom that does not depend on philosophy itself.
>
> —*Deleuze and Guattari*[1]

With the "Doctrine of the Concept" Hegel's *Science of Logic* comes to an end: essence is the negation of being, and the concept is the negation of the negation, return to being. Here being and essence are no longer simply being and essence; rather, in the concept, they have their independence in their relation: each is in-and-for-itself-and-another because the concept is itself identical with and differentiated from itself. Yet this end is only "an" end (not "the" end)—for being and essence are just as much ends, end products, or results of abstraction from the concept. And the "Doctrine of the Concept" is also the beginning, that is, the speculative origin of abstraction and the historically first moment of the system of subjective logic. Philosophy, however, is not history (*historie*)—neither simply the representation of thought as it appears in space and time nor story-telling; rather, it is the recognition of that which is true in history, the knowledge of truth. The order of experience (of *physis* and the education of consciousness) is not the order of philosophy, and the "Doctrine of the Concept" is not only the true end of the *Logic,* but also its beginning.

Indeed, the end of the *Logic* is the *end* of the *Logic,* that is, the attaining of philosophical truth. For theology, truth (identified with God) remains transcendent, unattainable by philosophy. For science, the recognition of *truth* itself (*die* Wahrheit *selbst*) is the goal (*Ziel*)—although it understands truth as an object (*Gegenstand*). Speculative thought, however, has the concept as true goal (*wahrhafte Ziel*), that is, both object and subject, and objective/subjective.[2] Yet what is the truth of the concept and the concept of truth? Is it the concept of concepts? Just another concept? Or that which makes the difference between concept and concepts possible? To what extent can philosophy be essentially conceptual? And what is the concept of multiplicity and the multiplicity of the concept?

In fact, like all concepts before it, like pure being, the concept in the "Doctrine of the Concept" is first immediately given in the form of an abstract, non-derivative, fundamental axiom. As abstracted, however, this concept has always already been derived. Here the concept is substance, that is, the result of the (objective) *Logic*'s genetic exposition, of the dialectic of being and essence: it is "their *foundation* and *truth* as the identity in which they are submerged and contained."[3] Yet substance is neither Spinozistic "matter," nor merely "essential thought"—rather, it is the positedness (*Gesetztsein*) of subject. And as Hegel writes in the *Phenomenology*: "in my view, which can be justified only by the exposition of the system itself, everything turns on grasping and expressing the true, not as *substance*, but equally as *subject*. At the same time, it is to be observed that substantiality embraces equally the universal or the *immediacy of knowledge* itself, and that which is *being* or immediacy *for* knowledge."[4] The genesis of the concept, therefore, is the revealing (*Enthüllung*) of substance in its absolute relation to subject: on the one hand, they are two totalities insofar as each concept contains its other; on the other hand, they are one insofar as their difference as complete opposition is "their" way of appearing. In other words, subject shows itself to be substance (no longer a possible predicate, but essence), and substance is just as much subject (no longer the passive, non-differentiating, self-identity of that which is or simply has being); their truth is the movement of both—for only a movement can expresses both the conflict and the resolution of the conflict, the destruction and preservation, the identity and difference, of the relation between expression and thought. In fact, for Hegel, the concept of the identity and difference of substance and subject will show itself as the "concept of the concept."[5]

Immediately, however, the concept shows itself as the property of self-consciousness, as belonging to the subject: "I" have concepts—and concepts are only determinate as concretely mine. Kant stops here, namely, with an empirical logic of concepts as the formal determinations of human understanding, as universal representations: "Kantian philosophy commits here, a further inconsequence: it *borrows* the categories, as so-called root-concepts, for the *transcendental logic*, from the subjective logic in which they were adopted empirically. Since it admits the latter fact, it is hard to see why transcendental logic resolves to borrow from such a science instead of directly resorting to experience."[6] And, for Hegel, Kant's transcendental unity of apperception thinks subject as a simple thing (*einfache Ding*), as a simple "object" of study for a psychology of feeling. The *Critique*'s one-sided subjectivism, its psychological idealism, maintains that self-consciousness "has no other moment or determination than the I itself."[7] The work of reason, however, that Kant took for merely dialectical (not analytic) comes to completion in Hegel. The synthesis of Kantian a priori synthetic judgments, insofar as they remain abstract universals, that is, the mere connection, external unity or simple identity of different/disconnected concepts, are not those of speculative thought. The *Critique* is self-contradictory: on the one hand, truth means the identity of concept and thing, that is, the objective validity of thought; on the other hand, insofar as concepts remain subjective, they can say nothing of reality.[8]

For Hegel, however, insofar as consciousness has its truth in absolute spirit, substance is a function of universal subject—and the *Phenomenology,* in fact, results in this truth. The concept will show itself as incomplete, as merely one side of the idea. And although initially conceptual knowledge yields only abstract truth, it must also become real. Here conceptual becoming is no longer the "going over" (*Übergehen*) of being nor the "appearance in an other"[9] of essence; rather, it is scientific development (*Entwicklung*). In this way the *Science of Logic* is not science as a whole; rather, it is the development of the science of absolute form (*Wissenschaft der absoluten Form*), that is, the formal part of philosophy, of the sciences of nature and spirit. Yet as absolute, logic is not simply abstract—it also has a concrete content, namely, the determinations of the idea of truth. The *Logic,* thereby, is "already *for itself the truth.*"[10]

Hegel then is able to make good on transcendental philosophy's demand for truth—for here, finally, truth means "agreement of knowledge with its object."[11] The manifold (i.e., multiplicity) of intuition was too powerful for Kant's brand of psychological-anthropomorphic-subjective idealism: only speculative thought can achieve the sought-after identity of idea and thing-in-itself in a synthesis yet higher than a priori judgments, that is, in the concept that thinks difference. And the *Logic* is able to think and express pure truth: to think it not only via scientific method, but also in the pure form and content of speculation's concept; to express it not only in the form of a positive judgment (wherein subject and abstract predicate do not agree, e.g., "the particular is a universal"), or in the subjective words of self-consciousness, but also in the absolute language and living dialectic of spirit itself. The transcendental problem of logic is that of truth, is that of multiplicity—and the concept is the solution to them all.[12]

Hegel's concept of truth then, on the one hand, in accepting "agreement" as its criterion, remains faithful to the metaphysical tradition; on the other hand, by taking *a*-greement seriously, by thinking the relation between knowledge and object as conceptual, as more-than-uni-vocal, more than one voice (*über-ein-stimmen*), more than a *feeling*, more than *a* feeling, and more than feeling *oneness* (*Über-ein-stimmung*), the truth of the concept is "more" than identity, that is, it has become the double movement of identity and difference. In sum, conceptual truth—the true goal of the *Logic*—means the agreement of disagreement and the disagreement of agreement, the agreeing disagreement and the disagreeing agreement of knowledge and object.

Yet what has become of multiplicity? Of the object's manifold and the manifold's objectivity? In truth, as "agreement," the manifold is superseded: multiplicity no longer means simple unity, the many qua one, but another unity, a twofold unity, or rather, the unity and disunity of unity and disunity. The metaphysical agreement, the two-thousand-year-old "philosophical pact," has been honored. Logic takes care of multiplicity—but this multiplicity is no multiplicity at all.

What would become of truth, however, if the manifold object were thought as manifold? Would knowledge itself not have to become manifold? Would subject and substance not become far more subjects and substances? And would the truth of their "agreement" not lie in identities and differences, in agreements? Or rather, must agreement itself, the relation between object and knowledge, become multiple? For is truth as a matter of *mere* subjects and objects not already a reduction? A reduction of the reduction? Is agreement and disagreement not already a result or construct? The questions for multiplicity then remain: What is the truth of the concept of multiplicity? A multiplicity of truths? Of truths that are not just truths, that are not simply true, and a multiplicity that is not only multiplicity, that is not just multiple—but is "manys"?

Subjectivity of the Subject

For the *Science of Logic* subjectivity is not the subject, nor is it the universal concept of the particular subject, the subject of subjects; it is not the psychological "I," the soul, the human mind, and nor is it their a priori condition of possibility (Kant)—for it is as empirical as it is transcendental. And subjectivity is not the existence, reality, or being of a subject, not its being present or absent, there or here, or somewhere in between, nowhere, a "no-man's-land" subject, or some combination/permutation of both, nor neither, that is, a maybe subject, indeterminate, undecidable, a subject that may or may not be. Nor is subjectivity the subject's essence, that which it is in itself, that which shows itself to itself, the reflection of itself, for example, self-consciousness. Rather, for Hegel, subjectivity is a *concept,* that is, the relation of subject and subjects, and of the subject's being and its essence. Yet the *concept* of subjectivity is just as much the *subjectivity* of the concept. And subjectivity no longer belongs to us, is no longer a function of the human subject; rather, we belong far more to subjectivity.

Nevertheless, the subjectivity of the concept is immediately the concept's identity and inner essence. Here truth means the agreement of understanding and the being-[thing]-in-and-for-itself in the concept's subjectivity. However, since the concept is always the concept of something, some object—or rather, as will become apparent, of some objectivity, the truth of subjectivity is far more objectivity. Yet the identification of the concept with its objectivity will show itself as the forgetting of difference; and this drives the dialectic of the concept—for like being and nothing, subjectivity and objectivity have already gone over into one another. The identity of subjectivity and objectivity is the *adequate concept,* that is, the idea. Subjectivity, however, is not yet objectivity; and the idea is not yet the absolute idea, not yet both adequate and inadequate, both the identity and difference of subjectivity and objectivity.[13]

First, then, subjectivity shows itself as a formal, immediate concept: in subjectivity's identity, difference is an appearance. Here the concept of subjectivity is posited as belonging to the subject. This subjectivity, however, is identified by negating an other, that is, that which is not identical to it, but different from it, that is, its difference—and this negation, the movement of determination via negation, means that subjectivity's identity is the negation of its difference. Subjectivity is then, second, the movement that negates that which it is not, its difference—and this movement is itself only possible on the basis of another difference, namely, the difference between the identity and difference of subjectivity. In this way subjectivity's difference is its identity. And this difference, this self-division, original auto-partitioning, Hegel calls judgment (*Urteil*). Third, then, subjectivity as a judgment shows itself as a syllogism, with its conclusion, end (*Schluß*), that unites independent extremes. Thus, the completed concept of subjectivity is the identity and difference of its identity and difference—no longer as merely subjective, but rather, as essentially objective, as a syllogistic judgment of conceptual objectivity.[14]

Indeed, within this broad sketch of the moments of subjectivity, the concept is determined (as universality, particularity, individuality), "so each of these moments is as much the *whole* concept as *determinate concept* and as *one determination* of the concept."[15] As Hegel wrote, with a remarkable consistency that spanned thirty years, from the *Differenzschrift* (1801) through the *Logic* (1832):

> the true characteristic of a philosophy is the interesting individuality in which reason, from the building-material of a particular age, has organized a form for itself; the particularly speculative reason finds therein spirit from its spirit, flesh from its flesh, it looks at itself in it as one and the same, and as an other living being. Each philosophy is in itself complete and has, like a real artwork, totality in itself.[16]

Or again:

> In the concept, identity has developed into universality, difference into particularity, contraposition, which withdraws into the ground, into individuality. In these forms, those determinations-of-reflection are present as they are in the concept. The universal has proved itself to be not only the identical, but at the same time the diverse or *contrary* as against the particular and individual, and in addition, also to be contraposed to them or *contradictory;* in this contraposition, however, it is identical with them and is their true ground in which they are superseded. The same holds for particularity and individuality which are likewise the totality of the determinations-of-reflection.[17]

In other words, Hegel translates the moments of the "Doctrine of Essence" to those of the "Doctrine of the Concept," with an important difference: opposition (*Gegensatz*) becomes contraposition (*Entgegensetzung*) in order to become individuality. Previously the self-contraposed contrapositions (*Entgegengesetzten*) or opposed moments, which withdrew into their essential ground, showed themselves as contradiction (*Widerspruch*)—now contraposition (no longer contradiction) becomes individuality. The determinations of the *Subjective Logic* are/are-not essentially those of the *Objective Logic.*

Thus, the subjectivity of the subject is, for Hegel, a subjective concept. And this concept is the subject of the "Doctrine of the Concept" that shows itself in its identity and difference from being and essence, or rather, as a multiplicity of determinations, each with its own logic of multiplicity. Yet before the subjective concept of multiplicity, or the concept of subjective multiplicity, the questions of the multiplicity of the subjective concept: What constitutes the multiplicity of universality, particularity, and individuality? What is the conceptual logic of identity and difference? How does the *Subjective Logic* think the logic of multiplicity and the multiplicity of logics? And what of concepts? And subjectivities? Of universalities, particularities, and individualities? In other words, what is a concept? Is it not a universal?

The Universality of the Universal

> Her sexuality, always at least double, goes even further: it is *plural*. . . . Indeed, woman's pleasure does not have to choose between clitoral activity and vaginal passivity, for example. The pleasure of the vaginal caress does not have to be substituted for that of the clitoral caress. They each contribute, irreplaceably, to woman's pleasure. Among other caresses. . . . Fondling the breasts, touching the vulva, spreading the lips, stroking the posterior wall of the vagina, brushing against the mouth of the uterus, and so on.
>
> —*Irigaray*[18]

For Hegel, following a logic of identity, like being before it (although no longer simply immediate), a concept is, first of all, posited as an indeterminate, infinite, pure self-relation, abstract universal. As a mere universal, however, this concept would be empty, and unable to be universal, that is, to predicate its object or relate to a particular. A universal cannot be just universal—for its truth lies in its relation to its other, to a particular: the chair is only universal as chairs, the essence of the good is in the good act. An abstract universal, determining itself precisely through the operation of leaving-behind (*Operation des Weglassens*) concrete particulars, is universal only insofar as it is not abstract, negates itself as abstraction, and negates this negation, that is, returns to its positive self-identity. The universal can no longer be merely relative to the particular; rather, "it is the *soul* of the concrete which it indwells, unimpeded and equal to itself in the manifoldness and diversity of the concrete."[19] Nevertheless, the universal must still be universal, must behave as determinate for the particular, taking it not as a limitation of itself, but on the contrary, as an opportunity to embody or instantiate itself, to exercise power, to cause that which is identical to itself, like from like, good acts from the good, to produce. In this sense, the concept as universal is a free power (*freie Macht*) qua free love (*freie Liebe*)—not as the pure violence acted out by an abstract power, but as the doing to others as it does to itself, that is, identical (Christian) treatment: the particular of the universal and the universal of the particular, the particular as particular and the universal as universal.[20]

The universal, however, is not universality—just as subjectivity was not the subject. Certainly from Platonism to Kant, the universal (*Allgemeine*) is already thought as concrete: the chairness of chairs, goodness of goods, beingness of beings (*Seiendheit des Seienden*)—this was no naive idealism, no pure separation or perfect difference between universal and particular; nor was it their simple oneness or abstract identity. Yet if the metaphysical tradition remembers the universal (and its ontological difference from/with particulars), then it is at the price of forgetting universality (*Allgemeinheit*). The concept as universal results from the concept of universality, an abstraction or reduction from that which is not merely "more universal" than the universal, not simply genera of genera, higher genera of higher species, but that which is of an-other species and genus, an-other quality and quantity. Universality is essentially the relation of the universal and particular—and as such, it does not produce, make, find, or invent them; rather, as their concept, it conceives them, creates, begets, bears, gives birth to them, brings them forth, and receives, holds, grasps, cradles them together, takes them in, and takes care of them. In this way, the concept (as *conceptus*) is the double-movement of expression and comprehension, extrication and concentration, detainment or confinement and release, dissemination and gathering, bearing and harvesting (*concipere*). Against (*con*) universality, the universal and the particular are able to see (*conce-voir*) as they are in truth. No longer a Socratic midwife tied to the metaphysics of Plato's receptacle (the *chōra* of the *Timaeus* 52b), Hegel thinks the logic of what Ponge will latter call the conceptacle, that is, the external cavity (itself a *contradictio in adjecto*) containing the reproductive cells of algae. The *Logic* of the concept is an algae-logic, the logic of seaweed, stoneworts, and pond scum, not an algebra (*al-jabr*, reduction)—for *Allgemeinheit* means *Alge-meinheit.*

The concept of universality then is no an longer empty form; rather, it has its positive content, without which it would remain an incomplete, one-sided (albeit universal) moment, simply self-identical and indifferent to its other. And universality not only universalizes the universal and the particular—for it determines itself in relation to particularity (*Besonderheit*), not the particular, as that which takes care of individuality (*Einzelheit*), not merely the individual (*Einzelne*). The concept's creativity, therefore, means self-negation, the power to posit the difference of particularity as *its* difference. Universality is-essentially-conceived (being-essence-concept) as particularity—for "difference, which is an essential moment of the concept though not yet posited as such in the pure universal, receives its due in the determinate concept."[21]

Universality then, if it is to be found in the manifoldness of the concrete, must itself be manifold: the concept must be always also essentially multiple in order to conceive the particular. And the universality of multiplicity can no longer be thought as the double-relation of multiplicity qua universal and the multiple qua particular—for it must itself be multiple. The power then of multiple universality is no longer either abstract and uni-directional, or reciprocal and bi-directional; rather, it is multi-directional, and not just.

The Particularity of the Particular

If the logic of identity governed the concept of universality, then it is with particularity that the concept shows itself as a logic of difference. Yet neither the force of understanding to separate and observe universals as fixed, or to present (*darstellen*) the concrete as abstract, nor the sensible intuition of real stuff, of being as concretely given, of *physis* as immediately there in space and time, as the pure non-unified manifold, are able to think the concept. Only subjective reason as intellectual intuition (*intellektuelle Anschauung*)—itself a contradiction in terms—is able to approach the living contradiction of the concept, to posit through (*dia*) determination and abstraction as the moving logic (*logos*) of dia-lectic.[22] In this moment the *Subjective Logic* has as its goal the thought of the truth of the identity and difference of universality and particularity (and of universals and particulars)—and the individuality of subjective reason will show itself as its fulfillment.

Initially the particular (understood as particularness, and not yet particularity) is posited as identical to the universal—for everything is particular; it includes it within itself: for example, a genus is identical, not different, in its species. Particulars, however, differentiate themselves over and against other particulars—and the particular is always the particular of particular particulars; it has its difference in relation to another particular, its difference in relation to difference. Like simple diversity before it, the particular is essentially non-unified difference (*einheitslose Unterschied*)—but here, unlike the "external" reflection of essential diversity, conceptual diversity means the "immanent" relation of diversities: on the one hand, the particular of particulars is particular, and the universal of particulars is universal; on the other hand, the particular of the universal is particular, and the universal of the universal is universal. The "two" stand over and against one another, but their relation is more intimate than simply being together (*zusammen*), more tightly bound than contraposition (*Entgegensetzung*)—for they determine themselves as "one" particular/universal determination of the concept, namely, as the principle of the determinateness of particularity.[23]

Particularity as particular then first masks as an abstract universal. Here the particular repeats (with a difference) the moments of the universal: the particular continues to determine itself by excluding an other, by superseding other particulars in an albeit immediate identity without difference—it "is thereby, in fact, the *concept,* but as *conceptless,* as concept that is not posited as such."[24] Or, as Hegel writes in the *Phenomenology:*

> the beginning, the principle, or the absolute, as at first immediately enunciated, is only the universal. Just as when I say "*all* animals," this expression cannot pass for a zoology, so it is equally plain that the words "the divine," "the absolute," "the eternal," and so on do not express what is contained in them; and only such words, in fact, do express the intuition as something immediate.[25]

Second then, the particular falls into the same problems as that of the universal: I cannot say what I mean and mean what I say—the concept remains empty if the particular only expresses universals. In this sense I cannot account for particularity at all, for the very difference it is designed to think. At this moment singularity becomes generality, and those, for example, who assert the truth of sense-certainty are confronted with a language that reverses the meaning of what they say, that never lets them get what is meant into words: "they mean *this* bit of paper on which I am writing, or rather have written; but what they mean, they do not say. If they actually *wanted to say* this bit of paper which they mean, and if they wanted *to say* it; then this is impossible, because the sensuous this that is meant, is unreachable by language, which belongs to the consciousness that is inherently universal."[26] In other words, pure particularity cannot think speculatively, cannot approach the absoluteness of the absolute, the expressivity of expression, the discursivity of discourse. Third, therefore, the particular shows itself as non-particular; and its loss of self will not find itself until the concept becomes individual—or rather, becomes individuality. Thus, while universality means the identity of universal and particular, particularity means the difference of universal and particular.

Particularity then, like every concept, can never be just one-sided, not only differences in a logic of difference; rather, it is always both identical and different from itself: the difference of particularity is essentially conceived as its identity. Here, particularity is a double-entendre: real and ideal, subject and substance. Yet is there not an example of that which does not submit to the concept of particularity? A counter-example that resists, refuses the discourse of difference? That negates the logic of identity and difference? In the other of the concept, in the philosophy of nature (*Naturphilosophie*), two problems of particularity show themselves: difference and multiplicity.

First, the problem of particular difference, of radical particularity, is the problem of deviance, of order, homogeneity, identity, law, and transgression, heterogeneity:

> in the impotence of nature to stick to the concept in its execution, lies the difficulty, and in many circles the impossibility, of finding fixed differences for classes and orders from the empirical perspective. Nature blends everywhere the essential limits through intermediate and bad constructions which always deliver instances contrary to every fixed differentiation, even within determinate genera (e.g., human beings) through deviants that, on the one hand, one must count to this genus, but on the other hand, which lack determinations that would be seen as essential property of the genus.—In order to be able to observe such constructions as inadequate, bad, deformed, a fixed typos would be presupposed which, however, could not be created from experience, for precisely this also obviously provides those so-called deviants, deformations, intermediate-things, etc.: it far more presupposes the independence and dignity of conceptual-determinations.[27]

If it is "impossible," in the moment of scientific classification or conceptual determination, to impose order on experience, on *physis* as given, on the radically illogical chaos of appearances, then have the freaks of nature, the disfigured and dispossessed, the abnormal and abject, eluded the *Science of Logic?* Have the maimed and misshapen beat the devil of the concept? Are cripples and pariahs outside the discourse of identity and difference? Is teratogenisis, by definition, non-conceptual? Can Hegel think the inbred-hunchbacked-clubfooted-hairlipped-cleft-palated-Calibans of the human race? Account for the very norm by which they are, are essentially determined, judged, by which they are conceived? And if the limit, frontier or border of a species, secures identity, preserves purity and protects from perversion, from (accidental or deliberate) contamination by difference, then when does a human being become inhuman? Or was a human being ever human at all? And is nature here to blame for its impotence? Or the concept for its impertinence?

For metaphysics, types must be fixed via a logic of identity and difference. Here genera and species are either abstracted from empirical reality or a priori concepts to be found, that is, presupposed, transcendental categories. Deviance, therefore, can be observed, identified, and "properly" excluded as different, abnormal. A determination of nature, however, remains somehow motivated or arbitrary; and the construction of frontiers, borders, distinctions, genres, differences, are always subject to a possible deconstruction. On the one hand, a permeable limit is no limit at all, that is, cannot be used to scientifically fix a type, objectively determine a species; on the other hand, an impermeable limit cannot give an account of a nature that does not "stick to the concept." In other words, if nature, not just often, but always provides a hybrid specimen, a mixed, half-bred, immediate thing—then the exception is the rule. The inhuman always threatens to un-fix the human—or, not only threatening, impurity always contaminates purity. If empirical reality is posited as the origin and beginning of thought, and science is dependent upon the materiality of the nature it hopes to know, then the fixing of categories, types, and the determination of deviance are an act of power—and displacement or projection to a transcendental realm of concepts cannot conceal the violence of the master. Deviance un-fixes determination: bad constructions deconstruct construction in general. The determination of deviance is itself based on fixed types that are themselves never fixed: the frontier is porous—and this holds even if the very difference that is supposed to provide the criterion for classification, particular determination within a norm, subsumption under a genus or species, is itself first provided by the class, norm, genus, species, and so on. In order to fix types, deviation (and its contradiction) must have been always already refused. The logic of identity and difference is the fix of science—and for science (and metaphysics as a science), nature is always impotent. The unfixed genus, the porous limit or indeterminate determination, is no determination at all: it can never be that which it should be, it remains an always on the way to, a debt to be paid, a limit to be delimited, a secret or not yet specified species to come.

For Hegel, however, if the fixing of types is inherently contradictory, then that itself is the truth; that is, genera and species are essentially conceptual. As both fixed and unfixed, limitation means continuation in another, transition. The truth of a determination lies in its relation to another determination, in the difference that it negates in order to fix its identity. The transgression of types, deterritorialization, movement across borders, between spheres (transcendental and empirical, human and inhuman) is the rule—and it is possible because genera and species are not indifferent, impenetrable fixed barriers, but moving, becoming limits. In this sense a species's limit is that place wherein the species both is and is not—for limit is a "between" as well as an "end," the limit of a genus itself and of another, a living limit. Here human being is that which excludes the inhuman: the human *has* a limit and the inhuman *is* its limit, and vice versa. For speculative thought, the limit is neither the condition of the possibility of the identity and difference of species and genus, nor of deviance from or transition between types; on the contrary, the concept of transition first makes possible limitation, identification, differentiation, normalization, legitmation, deviation (and therefore law, transgression, punishment), and the sciences in general. The independence and dignity of conceptual determinations lie precisely in their relation to one another—more specifically, in the movement between them that is their movement, the movement that is their concept, the transition by which they are essentially conceived.

Nature's impotence then is far more its potency. First, nature shows itself, makes itself present as *physis,* that is, on the one hand, as (being) both arbitrary power, chaotic production, unpredictable creation, as negating all rational determination; and on the other hand, as necessary, that is, acting according to physical laws. Second, nature is a limit, a limit for reason, that is, that which (essentially) refuses to stick to the concept, continually transgresses the order of genus and species, produces deviant constructions. Here nature is the fall of reason into unconsciousness, the downfall of thought: spirit becomes weak, pales, and faints (*in Ohnmacht fallen*); but the faint of nature is a feint, a simulacrum of impotence—for negation drives the dialectic, determines the concept: the failure of nature to stick to the concept is its success; non-execution is execution; passivity is activity, and truth is far more to be found in a philosophy of nature than in a philosophy (or phenomenology) of spirit. Yet, third, if reason and nature can be identified as belonging to different genera and species, then it is because their truth is also the concept of their transition, their becoming one another as the absolute idea through which they conceive each other, others, and through which they are (conceived). In this way Hegel thinks natural deviance as the other of species/genera determination: the law preserves/destroys its identity in its relation to difference, transgression, crime—they belong together, transition into one another, are co-constitutive as the living limits of each other. If deviance takes on particular forms, then it is because nature embodies the concept of radical singularity, of the specimen sui generis, the bearers of proper names, pure individuals, and of always also radical universality—we are all deviants and normal, inhuman and human.

Limitation, however, is always only the difference between two genera; transition is only the conceptual relation of two identities. The first problem of difference has been addressed, but the second problem of particularity is that nature is multiple:

> in nature, of course, there are to be found in a genus more than two species, just as these many species also cannot have the relation we have just indicated. It is this impotence of nature that cannot adhere to and present the rigor of the concept, and runs wild in this conceptless, blind multiplicity. We can *wonder* at the multiplicity of genera and species and the infinite diversity of its formations in nature, for wonderment is *without concept,* and its object is the irrational. Nature, because it is the self-externality of the concept, is free to indulge itself in this diversity, just as spirit, too, even though it has the concept in the shape of the concept, engages in representation and runs riot in its infinite multiplicity. The multiple natural-genera or species must not be esteemed as anything higher than the capricious fancies of spirit in its representations. Both indeed show traces and inklings of the concept on all sides, but do not present a faithful copy of it because they are the side of its free self-externality. The concept is absolute power just because it can freely abandon its difference to the shape of self-subsistent diversity, outer necessity, contingency, caprice, opinion, which however must not be taken for more than the abstract side of *nothingness.*[28]

Is the multiplicity of nature then an exception to the conceptual law? Illogical? Outside the range of the concept? Can philosophy only wonder at the infinite diversity of *physis?* Is multiplicity the horizon or end of philosophy? Or is it far more the beginning, the start of an abandonment to the multiple?

Here Hegel thinks against Plato—as Socrates remarks to Theaetetus: "this sense of wonder is the mark of the philosopher. Philosophy indeed has no other origin, and he was a good genealogist who made Iris the daughter of Thaumas."[29] Yet for Hegel, too, science begins in wonder (*ta thaumata*): the *Science of Logic* begins with being, with the study of being qua being (*to on he on*), with nature as it appears in all its diversity, *physis* as a gift or present from the gods, that which gives itself as present, presents itself as there. Speculative thought, however, has its origin (*archē*) elsewhere, namely, in the "Doctrine of the Concept," in the absolute idea—the end is the beginning. Taken ironically then, Socratic wonder shows itself as the inverted world or flip side of Hegelian speculation, its other and brother (sibling or twin), and "wonder" is appropriate for this kind of abstraction.

Once again then, on the one hand, nature confounds the concept: as the being-other, abstract negation, radical contingency, or chance (*Zufälligkeit*), like Kant's concept-less intuitions, the multiplicity of species is blind to reason—the madness of (bad) infinite diversity cannot be thought; it is (for the moment) incommensurable with the logic of identity and difference. Here nature is the negative, non-being (*non-ens*), nothing, the garbage, debris, refuse, the waste product of the idea (*Abfall der Idee*), the break with reason. The sensible intuition or experience of nature (*Natur-Erfahrung*) in consciousness, the accidents of representation, fantasy, analogy, metaphorical displacement of nature's being, can only "externally" agree with conceptual determinations. On the other hand, nature's multiplicity is radical necessity (*Notwendigkeit*): empirical laws of natural science and the regularity of eco-systems are not merely external, not simply a function of the subject or the order of the human mind. Nature's contingency and necessity, its necessary contingency and contingent necessity, are in "internal" contradiction—and their supersession is taken care of by the concept of freedom, the relation of nature and spirit in the absolute.[30]

Indeed, for the *Science of Logic,* nature is the self-externality of the concept, the other of the idea as internal, that is, the way in which spirit shows itself to itself, its own capriciousness: as the other and essence of reason, the irrational is our shadow, what Derrida might call our secret qua trace, but that through which reason determines itself. The presentation and re-presentation of nature's multiplicity is the other side of reason, that is, the infinite and abstract nothingness to which, in its Bacchanalian revel, spirit abandons itself; but it is not the truth of nature—for the infinite has shown itself to be just as finite, diversity is also identity, externality is the other and determinate negation of internality. Nature is both concept-less and conceptual, and reason conceives itself in relation to its irrationality.

The absolute power of spirit then consists precisely in this: that it is both itself and its other, itself as self and non-self, its other as other and non-other, as multiplicity and non-multiplicity, as multiple and non-multiple. On the one hand, nature is spirit means that natural multiplicity has the logical form of identity and difference, wherein diversity belongs to reason, a particular species is determined and fixed insofar as it is not another species. If speculative physics posits "the identical differently and the different identically," then it is because the total individual in nature shows itself in the form of the concept.[31] On the other hand, nature shows itself as itself, as irrational, incoherent, inconsistent, pure multiplicity, non-one, anti-identity, and anti-difference, as the heterogeneous paroxysm of *physis,* the self-abandonment, the going-out-of-itself, being-beside-itself, the fall of spirit into non-spirit. But spirit can only be what it is, if it both takes this fall into madness, and returns to its senses.

If nature then is given as multiple, the multiplicity of species, it is because it is essentially, always also, conceptual. With the concept, wonder gives way to (speculative) thought. Yet in what does the multiplicity of natural multiplicity consist? What does the multiplicity of species mean if not quality and quantity, multiple in kind and number, or rather, conceptually (qualitatively-quantitatively) multiple? Can the always only two-sided concept think the multiplicity of nature as multiple if it only thinks multiplicity/non-multiplicity? Is the impotence of nature (*Ohnmacht der Natur*) in the face of the problem of multiplicity not far more that of the double-concept? What could it mean for the concept itself to become multiple? What would it mean for philosophy to not only limit itself to the dialectic of reason and madness, being and nothingness, finitude and infinity, nature and spirit? And not just conceptualization—but, rather, for abandonment itself to become multiple? Would truth not have to become something other than double, other than the agreement of concept and reality, or the movement of their agreement/non-agreement? Would philosophy itself not have to find another language? A language of multiplicity, a multiplicity of languages? And not just?

Regardless, with nature, reason once again finds its other, horizon, the living limit through which it determines itself: the "impotence of nature posits the limits of philosophy."[32] The multiplicity of nature is commensurable/incommensurable with the doubled concept: the capriciousness of spirit in nature is just as much that of nature in spirit—for both show traces of the concept on all sides. Yet insofar as it is unable to grasp the relation between itself and thought, to think the concept to which it belongs, to become self-conscious, return to itself, know itself, nature remains ignorant of itself, non-reflective—it can only be or exhibit itself, present or show itself, passively express its multiplicity, allow itself to be grasped, held, tied up, bound, allow its essence to be conceived by reason. Here self-conscious reason and unconscious nature follow an absolute logic of identity and difference: on the one side, im-potence, negation; on the other side, potency, affirmation. And in this sense the concept's absolute power in reason is limited by nature—for the truth of both is their transition (i.e., the absolute idea). Yet is the impotence of nature not far more the impotence of the concept to think the many species as many, that is, without reducing them to just two? And is the potency of reason not far more the potency of nature to both submit to the movements of the concept and to permit spirit to satisfy its fancy for caprice, contingency, opinion, nothingness?

In fact, for Hegel the multiplicity of nature is multiple precisely as not multiple: it can be wondered at as multiple, or thought qua the other of reason, that is, as one side of the two-sided concept; but it cannot be wondered at as double nor thought as multiple—for then it would no longer be multiple. Yet conceptualization without wonder is empty, wonderment without the concept is blind—and the absolute idea is the relation of both. Here multiplicity is either irrational (abstract negative of reason, multiplicity as multiple) or rational (the other of reason, representations of spirit, multiplicity as non-multiple, as one side of the concept), and as such, as irrational/rational, multiplicity is (once again) no longer multiple. Hegel thinks multiplicity as double (multiple/non-multiple) because "all conception is negation." Multiplicity is a moment of the double-entendre. There are only two possibilities (and permutations/combinations thereof): the bad multiplicity of nature or the good multiplicity of the concept. Yet what if the double-entendre were far more a moment of multi-entendre? What if philosophy was not only reduced to wondering at the irrational and thinking the rational? For is the double itself not a result? Is conception of the individual, normal or deformed, not far more abstraction? Is origin not always also far more a multiple riddle (and the riddle of multiplicity), than the double origin or descent (*doppelte Herkunft*) of which Nietzsche riddles in *Ecce Homo:*

> the good fortune of my existence, its uniqueness perhaps, lies in its fatality: I am, to express it in the form of a riddle, already dead as my father, while as my mother I am still living and becoming old. This dual descent, as it were, both from the highest and the lowest rung on the ladder of life, at the same time a *decadent* and a *beginning*—this, if anything, explains that neutrality, that freedom from all partiality in relation to the total problem of life, that perhaps distinguishes me. I have a subtler sense of smell for the signs of ascent and decline than any other human being before me; I am the teacher par excellence for this—I know both, I am both.[33]

In other words, is the multiplicity of conception not the becoming multiple of thought? And what would it mean to think conception as being essentially multiple? Or rather, not just as multiple/non-multiple—but as multiple, and not just? That is, as manys?

Multiplicity of Individuality

Nevertheless, for Hegel, the problems of particularity are superseded or "taken care of" in the concept of individuality. Via negation, the concept produces itself as both particular and universal, a particular universality and universal particularity. Individuality is first determined as a *particular* individual—yet this is a double-appearance (*Doppelschein*): on the one hand, if the individual's particularity is merely universal, then it implies an infinite progress to a yet higher universal (abstraction to the genus); on the other hand, if it is simply particular, then it implies an infinite regress, always demands yet another particularity whereby difference can be determined. Individuality therefore is, second, far more the individual as universal—but as a product of abstraction, the individual as "concrete content" remains separate and merely different from its form, conceptless, devoid of individuality and personality (*Personalität*). Here the difference between/of universal and particular means that the individual *may* always be represented as abstract, isolated, quantifiable (threefold), but only at the price of forgetting that the concept conceives its moments as that which has "gone-together" (*Zusammengegangensein*). Even further, the determinate moments themselves (like Leibnizian monads) are each the totality of the concept, and each is no less true than the other. Third, the movement from universal to particular and vice versa shows itself as the "becoming of individuality" itself: the conceptual determinations of universality and particularity (no longer universal and particular) are separate and inseparable—and this is the way of the concept (*Weg des Begriffs*), this is where the height of universality and the profundity of particularity *is* the same, this is what Parmenides called the "way of truth" and, all hylozoism aside, what Heraclitus meant by "the way up [and] down is one and the same."[34]

On the one hand then, individuality means identity: the concept receives itself—"to conceive" means "to return," to reflect oneself to oneself, to be identical with oneself (*sich selbst Gleiches*). Here the other of individuality is *its* other; it is its own profit within the economy of self-investment, the speaker of its own destiny in the middle voice, self-determination. If the creator conceives the created, then it is because the created is the creator. On the other hand, the gain is just as much a loss (*Verlust*). If individuality is simply one-sided, merely conceptual, then it loses its reality (*Wirklichkeit*); it must pay the price of being not-itself, out-of-itself, a no-longer-just-the-concept, non-concept, nothing. Conceptual individuality, therefore, is differentiation as such (*Unterscheiden als solches*), determinate determination, posited abstraction.[35] And if individuality conceives universality and particularity, then they are and are not individuality: they *is* the same.

Individuality (in itself, *in sich selbst*), however, is not merely a concept (for-itself)—for it must also become real, concrete, actual, must go out of itself (*außer sich*). In the *Objective Logic* being was the immediate identity of an individual with itself, a qualitative one or "this," a being-for-self (*Fürsichseiendes*) as self-repulsion, exclusion of others and being together with others, that is, the positing of different individuals as independent.[36] There individuality meant merely existence, shared being; and through the pointing out of "this is [*Dieses ist*]," of "this is an individual," the concept showed itself as the element and ground of beings, the least common denominator of entities. In the *Subjective Logic,* however, individuals are not just entities, presences, immediate beings standing over and against one another; rather, they are essentially their self-relation, that is, the concept of individuality—we are our reflexivity.

Being then has become individuality. Here the difference between individuals, between individuals and the individual, is *their* (conceptual) difference. Being is no longer singular, the "indeterminate immediacy" of the "Doctrine of Being"—for "multiplicity belongs to being."[37] Or, as Heidegger repeats: "multiplicity belongs to Being itself."[38] And in this sense the multiplicity of beings is no longer grounded on being's multiplicity—for the difference between being and beings is neither external to them (an accidental predicate) nor one-sided (i.e., either being's or beings', or nothing's); rather, it is *their* difference, the determinate division (*Teilung*) and difference of their concept (*Begriffsunterschied*). The conceptual difference belongs to the concept of individuality, to that which is both excluded from (like the universal individual) and immanent to the individual. Just as being is not being-ness, or beings, the concept is not a mere universal concept, conceptness, or particular concepts—rather, the concept is the relating/non-relating of both, the identity and difference of the identity and difference of individual and individuals. Thus, just as being is always the being of beings, individuality is always the individuality of individuals—and the concept is their relation of belonging (*angehören*).[39]

With the concept then, the multiplicity of being has become the multiplicity of individuality. And if individuality is always the individuality of individuals, then multiplicity belongs to the concept itself. Indeed, individuals are essentially multiple because individuality conceives them as such; and individuality conceives individuals because without them, individuality is merely the individual, simply abstract, one-sided self-identical, indifferent. Here multiplicity means the individual is far more individuals—and individuals are multiple because individuality is multiple as well. And the relation of individuality and individuals is also multiple. Yet insofar as it conceives the individual and individuals, and the multiplicity of individuals themselves, can individuality ever conceive individuals (and their relation to their individuality) as multiple, that is, not simply subject to the logic of identity and difference?

Regardless, for Hegel the identity of the individuality of individuals is essentially conceived as partition, "absolute, original *division of itself.*"[40] The concept can divide itself because it is always already divided in its being: "to be" means "to conceive," that is, "to become multiple," to multiply, self-dissemination, dispersion, differentiation, and multiplicity means multiplication. Being then becomes partitioned because identity "is" in itself difference, a "one that is self-divided"—if the individual "is," then it has already been conceived from (and as) a divided individual or split subject; the concept conceives being, and individuals multiply. The individual can divide itself, because it is already divided, and the result of division. In this way, the individual is double: divided in itself (*in-divid*-ual), as well as, from other individuals (indivi-*dual*). Here individual multiplication means many differences, many divisions, the repetition of original division. Yet is division not dependent upon a logic of difference? And do differences, the production of doubles, twofold determination, as the origin of multiplicity, not preclude a multiplicity as multiple? Can a logic of dissemination ever even approach the question of multiplicity? And can multiplication even raise the problem of manys?

For Hegel the answer to these questions lies in self-multiplication as bi-directional (original and primordial). On the one hand, scientifically, being qua original division or bifurcation is the source of beings, things, entities, and essences, judgments—as well as the concept. Multiplication (self-production and re-production) occurs not because there are many things, a quantum of beings; but rather, there are beings because being is original self-multiplication, because multiplicity already belongs to being. In other words, because being "is" split, it can "become" beings. On the other hand, however, for speculative thought, being's original division is a result of the concept's primordial division. And the multiplicity of concepts is the product of the concept's primordial multiplication. Being's original division is always already produced, conceived, derived. If the beginning is the end, then the "origin" is result. Speculatively the concept precedes being—it is the "origin" before the origin. The primordial self-split of the concept, difference at the "origin," *Ur*-difference, the "one that is divided in itself" (*hen diapheromenon heauto*), conceives being (and all the concepts). Thus, to being belongs original division (and self-multiplication)—but primordially the concept *conceives* concepts.

The subjective concept then is essentially conceived as multiple, that is, as universality, particularity, individuality. First, multiplicity means (1) abstract or universal multiplicity; (2) particular multiplicity, this multiplicity "there"; (3) the identity and difference of the identity and difference of both, that is, the universality that conceives the double-relation (*qua concipere*) of universal and particular multiplicity, the multiplicity of multiplicity. Second, multiplicity means (1) particular multiplicity posited as an abstract universal, no longer as particular; (2) an abstract particular as either the impertinence of deviance or the impotence of *physis,* which remains (however worthy of wonder), radically non-conceptual; (3) particularity as transition concept, that is, as multiplicity conceived under the double-sign of conceptual/non-conceptual, particular/universal, multiple/non-multiple. Third, multiplicity means (1) the particular individual as supersession of universal and particular multiplicity, of multiplicity as universality and particularity; (2) the individual qua universal; (3) individuality as the concept of the individual and individuals; (4) the original division of individuality, the multiplicity that belongs to being as multiplication; (5) the concept's primordial dissemination, the "original" multiplicity before the "origin." In other words, the concept of multiplicity is the multiplicity of the concept, the multiplicity of multiplicities and multiplicities.

Questions for the concept, however, remain: How can the concept be essentially conceived as multiple, if it only supersedes the difference between universal and universals, beingness and beings? Do concepts (universality, individuality, being, becoming, etc.) not remain tied to a logic of identity and difference? And is this logic not itself already a result? Or how can the *Logic* conceive multiplicity if it presupposes being as original difference? Or the concept as primordial difference? How could the multiplication of differences (or identities) ever hope to reach multiplicity as multiple? How could the concept conceive multiply, if it remains a merely double-sign, multiple/non-multiple? Or is conception itself not already an abstraction? And if multiplicity is neither multiplicity nor non-multiplicity, coherent or incoherent, consistent or inconsistent, pure or impure—nor their concept (i.e., the supersession of both in their identity and difference)—then does it not perhaps lie elsewhere? And does it not perhaps bear the name of that which would be "too much" or "too many" for the concept to take care of? Yet how could philosophy perhaps speak of this many? Would it not maybe have to speak not only many languages, but abandoning itself to the awkwardness of a "foreign tongue," to swim in the current of "another" semiotic tide, to learn to speak manys languages? Would the singularity of speech not have to be not simply singular (*singulus*), but always, like a singular of boars, extraordinarily multiple (*singularis*)? And would we not, therefore, have to cut our gills on a kind of strange and terrifying linguistic improvisation?

Conceptual Language

> The diverse languages, placed next to one another, show that words never arrive at truth, nor at an adequate expression: for otherwise, there would not be so many languages.
>
> —*Nietzsche*[41]

Indeed, the problem of multiplicity is the problem of the language of multiplicity and the word "multiplicity," and of the multiplicity of words, of language as a multiplicity of words, many too many words. What then is language? And how can it become multiple? The language of multiplicity and the multiplicity of language, and of languages—and not just?

For metaphysics, language is the inert tool of human communication. Created by human understanding, speaking and writing are double (impressive-expressive): on the one hand, they are impressions of being, that is, the process of stepping-back from immediate intuition, from "that which is," of deriving or deducing from sensation (seeing, hearing, tasting, feeling, etc.); on the other hand, they are expressions of will, that is, the production of representations of intuitions in picture or letter form, as hieroglyphics or words, the coming into presence of thought. Abstracting from empirical utterances, metaphysics determines language as a machine: letters, syllables, parts of speech, calculated and functioning according to the formal logic of grammar. Yet here philosophy becomes psychology (a logic of the soul, *psychē-logos*): impression is inscription of intuitions on the "magic writing pad" of the "human mind" (which, in submitting to signification, makes the thing or referent disappear); expression as the products of "human" thoughts and memories is supposed to represent things, entities, events, beings—but they can only be signs of signs. In other words, the language of metaphysics always implies subjective psychologism: *I* can only hear what *I* hear, think what *I* think, say what *I* mean.[42]

For Hegel, however, language is not simply subjective (nor is it merely objective, i.e., a show and tell of *physis*); rather, it is conceptual, that is, the truth and self-externalization of the concept—for the concept, too, must be named. Like substance and subject, being and naming are in a conceptual relation; and they become concrete in the element of the concept of language: "to be" means "to be named," and vice versa. And in this sense "the name exists as *language*"[43]—for it is language that first makes designation, signification, meaning, expression, and impression possible; it is the multiplicity of names (*Mannigfaltigkeit von Namen*) that allows reason to speak of things, and things speak to reason. Yet this language is neither simply real speech (the making of tones, with or without meaning), nor merely ideal thinking—for a name is always also the name of a thing, the thing always that which is named. If the concept can only be grasped by spirit, then it can only be externalized in language—and the concept without externalization is empty, language without spirit is blind. And even further, language itself is a concept, the concept of language: not merely a matter of letters, words, sentences, or concepts put together (*zusammengesetzt*) in external juxtaposition, of supplementing quality with quantity, or the addition of qualities to quantities—language is the universal element or living system of names. Yet what is a "name"? And what is the concept of language? The language of the concept? And how can Hegel think the language of multiplicity? The multiplicity of language? Or languages?

First of all, signs are not names. A sign (*Zeichen*) is an immediate intuition (*unmittelbare Anschauung*) of that which is given in space and time, and shows itself as being there, now, that is, standing for an external referent. As an intuition, the sign is a drawing, record or picture (*Bild*) of a meaning (*Bedeutung*), and it depends not on itself, but on a subject (*I* must know what *I* mean): "the meaning of a sign is only in relation to the subject."[44] Like the pyramid that houses a "foreign" soul (or the Platonic *chōra*), the sign takes in, preserves, impresses upon itself and re-presents a content to which it is "indifferent"; it is the double of a thing, and by definition abstract meaningless in itself. Names, however, are far from indifferent; rather, as particular to human reason, they are the essence of humanity and the mark of the conceptual transition between species. On the one hand, to the question "What is it?" comes the response, "It is an ass"—that is, we assign the name "as such," the name "ass," to this entity, this object; on the other hand, humans give things their names, via capricious (or historical) invention, in an immediate act of desire wherein the name is our name, that which the subject assigns—the ass is ours. We are the ass, and the bestowing of names is the mark of mastery, the power (*Potenz*) of the will (or will to power?) to supersede the mere re-presentation or signification of entities. As arbitrary, however, the name "as such" (*als solche*) is meaningless: for abstract nominalism, the "ass" could equally be "rose." Nevertheless, naming "as such," in its independence from physicality, already differentiates humans from animals—although voice can be either animal sounds or human speech. For Hegel, strictly speaking, only the latter has meaning: "first in names is *intuition*, animality, and time and space, actually overcome."[45] And language as naming is the mark of humanity, although all humans do not speak the same language.

Under the guise of a critique of Leibniz then, Hegel attacks tonal languages and hieroglyphic writing in (perhaps) the most eurocentric, racist, and ignorant of ways: in Chinese, many words have a multiplicity of meanings, differentiated (according to the *Encyclopedia*) by an "absurd subtlety of accentuation"; in hieroglyphics, spatial figures are signs for representations, the pictures of picture-thinking, products of abstraction from things.[46] In German, however, writing belongs to speech as a product of intelligence: letters as words are signs for signs (tones) for names, for the intellectual connection of an intuition and its meaning—and the supplemental step here is not a uni-directional (analytic) abstraction, not a mechanical reproduction, but an internal determination. Signifying representations, hieroglyphics remain one-sided, tied to concrete sensibility, signs for things—intelligence is the origin of names and entities are the origin of signs. Both Chinese and German are spoken languages, but the former speaks from beings to meaning; the latter, from meaning to beings. Indeed, for Hegel, the hieroglyph is dead writing, mechanical *mnemosyne,* meaningless.

The name, however, is alive, living spirit. And meaning is produced by the spirit of human thought; it is the remembering of the relation, of the copula (being), between intellect and thing, in actual names (*eigentliche Namen*)—and in this way, it is a "secured sign; maintained relation."[47] Actual naming is always an act performed by intelligence, by spirit. Here names are always names of thoughts—and thoughts are always thoughts of names: for "it is in names that we think."[48] That which has no name cannot be thought; that which cannot be thought has no name. Names without thoughts are blind, and thoughts without names are empty. The naming of objects, empirical entities, beings, is the processes of creating meaning, of thinking the relation of ideal and real—and the act of expressing this relation is actual naming, that is, the "fundamental need for language in general."[49] In other words, names are concepts.

With actual naming then, language becomes "the existing concept of consciousness," the name-giving-creative-force, the power to determine being.[50] First, the actual name expresses itself as immediate universal. Yet here, failing to speak the unspeakable (*Unsagbare*), failing to express the universality of the universal and the individuality of the individual, names are inevitably one-sided, incapable of being that which they should: they are the "I, this, here, and so on." Second, actual names expresses the particular: "me, my proper name, and so on." Third, the actual name (*logos*) as double, as tone (sense-certainty, physiognomy of the glottis) and meaning, as free act of will and expression of essence, is neither the thing nor the intuition of the thing; rather, it is creation, by consciousness, of the connection between thought and being, between meaning and sign, thought and thing, ideal and real—as a relation, the n-ame has a soul (*âme*) of its own. And nature is no longer a picture-world drawn by the imagination, the mere signs of somnambulistic spirit; it is a world with actual names. With the conceptual relation of the name—Hegel and Parmenides agree: "for the same thing is there both to be thought of and to be."[51]

As a system of names then, language is not just a power of consciousness, not only the property (*Eigentum*) of consciousness, our means of expression, the tool and product (*Werk*) of thought, and the mode of designating peculiar (*eigentümlich*) to reason—for consciousness has its being, "exists," as language: the *language* of consciousness is just as much the language of *consciousness*. And consciousness does not just have reason; on the contrary, reason has human consciousness as one shape (among many) of spirit—for reason is always also a moment of spirit, and logic cannot be reduced to anthropomorphic representations, psychologism, or one-sided empiricism. Indeed, if language belongs to reason, then it is unnecessary to torture oneself searching for another (supposed more perfect) mode of presentation (*Darstellungsweise*); rather, philosophy must re-articulate language as "ex-ternalization," that is, the movement proper to speculative thought, corresponding to the dialectic of truth, to the ex-perience of consciousness, the ex-cursion of spirit and the ex-istence of being, to ex-termination by abstract negation and ex-tollment by determinate negation, the ex-cesses of nature's multiplicity, the ex-hibition of essence, and the ex-plication through which the concept shows itself as both the end and the beginning of the *Logic*. And philosophy must show how language is always also incompetent for speculative thought, not only for the articulation of the inarticulable, but also for the non-articulation of the inarticulable, the inarticulability of the inarticulable, the inarticulable qua inarticulable; and therewith the in-cipiance with being, the in-calculability of quantity, the in-commensurability of the concept with a certain multiplicity, the in-corporation of humans in reason, the in-clusion of reason in in-effable spirit—for "the concept as such, essentially, can be comprehended only with the spirit, which is not merely the property of spirit, but spirit's pure self."[52] Yet simultaneously language can show itself as no longer simply one-sided ex-ternalization, but as in-dexical, self-referential, as spirit in-dicating itself as itself, as pointing to that which is not merely outside or inside itself, but rather, its very self; and this (speculative) language is also the in-existence of being in nothing, the in-finity in finitude, the cross-in-semination of objective and subjective logics, the in-dependence of identity and difference, the in-divisibility of quality and quantity, the in-dividuality of particularity and universality, the in-dulgence of reason in madness, the in-stantiation of multiplicity in nature—for here language means the self-in-stitution of spirit (as both ex-ternalization and in-dication). And although the creation of symbols or signs may be only aids for the external eye (*äußerliche Auge*), merely mechanical crutches for fixing the movement of concepts, "if concepts now are so taken that they correspond to such signs, they cease to be concepts. Their determinations are not dead entities like numbers and lines whose relation does not itself belong to them; they are living movements."[53] In this way being, essence, concept, freedom, infinity are not signs but names, the movement that marks the identity and difference of that which is named and that which cannot be named (and remains unnamable): in the moment when infinity is determined as "this" infinity, it is no longer infinity. Thus, the truth of language lies not in its expressive potency or impotency, but in its motion, in its ability to correspond to the concept, to line up and synchronize with the dialectical movements of spirit.[54]

Language, then, in Hegel's *Logic,* is spirit's most complete externalization; and in the *Phenomenology* it is alienation (*Entfremdung*), the self-alienation of spirit. Yet language is not only descriptive; it has performative power—speaking is doing: the monarch's word is law, as Hobbes knew, the enactment of a single will; a marriage, for instance, is consecrated by the words "I now pronounce you man and wife." And with language, the "I" speaks itself out, ex-ternalizes itself and makes itself concrete; self-consciousness makes explicit that it has already gone over into the world, that it is always already in the world. Indeed, self-knowledge is not enough—state power is impotent if it is not used; spirit is incomplete if it is not externalized, in-deed. Here language is the middle term (*Mitte*) or medium by which state power applies force and thereby actualizes itself, becomes real power. As externalization, therefore, language is not simply language, not merely abstract speaking as such; rather, it is concrete, a particular way of speaking—and language is always the language of languages: not simply a question of German or Chinese, French or English, Greek or Latin, language is the language of flattery, of the monarch, the state, of money, power, of ethical spirit, conscience, self-consciousness, or of difference, contradiction, opposition, revolution, and so on. Appropriately in culture, the complete language or the full speech (*vollkommne Sprache*) of spirit is the language of disruption (*Zerrissenheit*): the rip or tear is always between two sides—for speech is far more speeches, talk far more ways of talking: the universal speech of spirit; the inverted speech of spirit's self-deception; the speech of a simple consciousness of the abstract true and good; the self-conscious speech that, rich in spirit, knows that disjuncture belongs to the nature of all relations, the self-consciousness that (as a relation) knows that it is both its disruption and supersession of disruption. In other words, between speaker and spoken, a reciprocal economy shows itself: the monarchy, for example, externalizes itself in language, produces speech; and language produces the monarch, incorporates, instantiates monarchical power, begets the monarch's identity, grants the monarch a proper name (*eigene Name*) and an individuality.[55]

Language then is the determinate-being (*Dasein*) of spirit. In language self-consciousness becomes a self-consciousness; it is present-at-hand (*vorhanden*) for-itself by separating itself from itself, tearing itself away from its self. And self-consciousness "presences" for-another: "to be" means "to be recognized" (*anerkant*). Self-consciousness (as abstract, pure, Fichtean I = I) becomes objective, a thing, entity, or being, in language, in the speech that destroys and preserves its connection with the speaker: the *language* of self-consciousness that is the language of *self-consciousness.* And in this sense language is the self-supersession of spirit: in speech, the speaker is both present and absent, ideal and real, a spiritual concretization and a concrete spirit—for language is the immediate presencing and mediate absencing of self-consciousness; it is both the identity of speakers, and their difference: one hears one's self and is heard by others. Here the copula (being) means being spoken, externalized, and questioned: "to be" means "to be heard"; and that which is spoken is heard, perceived, asked, interrogated (*vernommen*) identically by all, and differently by each.[56]

In language, however, self-consciousness does not only externalize and concretize itself, spirit does not only realize its self; rather, it has already become concrete, ex-ternal, insofar as it is always already in language. For speculative thought, the non-speaking speaker, the non-questioned question, unheard hearing, and so on—all this is the result of abstraction from the concept of language, reduction or translation (and translation of the translation) from the identity and difference of speaker and spoken, of speaker and hearer. The concept of language is prior to consciousness, and the recognition of independent self-consciousnesses as well. And here a living logic is the only appropriate way to think language. In this way the *Logic* is neither merely (true or false) etymology, nor simply the record or representation of the invention and development of language, but the movement of speculative thought itself.

The *Science of Logic* then, on the one hand, no longer thinks language as a machine for communication (impression/expression), but as the self-externalization and concretization of spirit through self-conscious reason, the creation of names as the conceptual relation of ideal and real, subject and substance, subjective will as the mark of (performative) mastery and nature as its other. Here humans speak language as much as language speaks humans. On the other hand, for speculative thought, language is the element and living system of the multiplicity of names, that which a priori divides itself into speaker and spoken, name and named, thought and being—for language is not simply a universal or particular language, nor a mere collection of languages, a sum of dialects; but a concept, the concept of language, the identities and differences of language. Even further, if language conceives determination, signification, symbolization, and so on, then it is because language is always the language of languages.

Yet what if language as multiplicity is not merely a question of names? For is it not also verbs, adjectives, participles, prepositions? Is language not also commas, semicolons, periods, and question marks? Is naming not one way in which language speaks humans, and humans speak language? Is language not far more reading, writing, speaking, and so on? And if so, then could it be possible to put into language the multiplicity of the concept? In other words, if the concept of language is essentially conceived as multiple, then how can it be spoken as multiple and non-multiple? Or rather, must the multiplicity of language not itself conceive the language of multiplicity, and of languages, of sentences, words, letters, and so on, that are themselves multiple—and not just?

In this case the multiplicity of language would mean not only that each language is composed or constructed of a number of different kinds of elements, and that each element is made up of elements, not only that each word contains many characters, each character many lines, each line many points, and so on—for this is the bad multiplicity that always implies its other, and the whole of language is never equal to the sum total of its parts. Nor does it mean that there are simply many languages—the "tower of Babel" is not the answer to the multiplicity of language; it is far more the question. Nor is the multiplicity of language essentially conceived as multiple and/or non-multiple—for multiplicity does not conceive itself as the identity of the difference of being or non-being, presence/absence, essence/non-essence, and so on. And the language of multiplicity is not a new language—for language itself is new every day, and always already also multiple. Nor does multiplicity require a new grammar, a grammar of tomorrow (universal as mathematics or particular as my feelings here and now)—for the grammatical law precisely functions via transgression, and language is not multiple because there are a multiplicity of languages; on the contrary, there are a multiplicity of languages because language is multiple. Nor can the multiplicity of language be derived or deduced from some original multiplicity as its source, an *ur*-language (or *ur*-languages) from which it is constituted via reduction, subsumption, inherence, coherence, distillation, translation, or the necessities of communication, the exigencies of war or intergalactic contact: historiography, etymology, genealogy, natural science, and so on assumes a linear concept of time/space, place, causality, a living/dead-machine of production (or teleological generation, becoming, conception)—for not only is the *archē*-tele-ology of language futile (a bad infinite regress), but the multiplication of differences, translation of the difference between origin and offspring (a bad infinite progress), remain faithful to a logic of identity and difference. If the beginning is the end, then the o-*rig*-in is rigged. Original and derived, copy of the copy, simulation, show themselves as dependent upon metaphysics. With Hegel, no longer tied to a belief in the law of uni-directionality, language (along with thought) becomes double, bi-directional, linear and circular, straight and bent, angular and curved, and so on—for each is a moment, in-itself and for-another. Yet here the double-concept of the multiplicity of language remains doubly duplicitous: multiplicity is no multiplicity at all, and language is not languages.

The multiplicity of language then must far more be the language of multiplicity. First, the *multiplicity* of language is multiple, that is, a quality, quantity, measure, essence, identity, difference, ground, concept, and so on. Second, the *language* of multiplicity is multiple, that is, qualitative, quantitative, and so on. Third, if language is no longer the relation of thought and being, subject and substance, self-consciousness and spirit, then it is because language is far more relations, the multiplicity of relations. And language is relations, because thought is far more thoughts, being far more beings. Even further, fourth, language is the multiple relations of (not just thought and being—for they are results, or relations of relations) multiplicities, the multiplicity of multiplicities. Here, language is no longer just language (however multiple, i.e., speaking, reading, writing, etc., the being of language), nor that which remains outside of language (inexpressible, non-representational, absent, nothing), nor both; rather, language/non-language becomes languages, that is, the multiplicity of languages. And at this moment language shows itself as always threatened with its own multiplicity, with the possibility of becoming languages.

With language as languages then, giving-meaning and making-sense do not simply become meaninglessness, nonsense; rather, "giving" and "making" themselves become multiple. "Languages" means giving multiply, making multiplicities. Here the noun becomes a thing, gift, product, creation, and so on, but always also (multiply performative) cutting into the ear, incision, smack, digging into the brain, wrapping around the body, hugging it close, encompassing and suffocating, caressing—for language is not merely ideal or material; rather, both have become multiple. Here the question becomes a multiple mark of indecision, ignorance, ineptitude, honesty, irony, a rhetorical strategy, tactic, an appeal, a call, a cry. The verb becomes multiple—but "to become" means "to be, not be, identify, differentiate, express, internalize, give, take, think, have, feel, make, and so on." And the multiplicity of language as languages is neither an infinite nor a finite multiplicity—for it is itself multiple, a multiple multiplicity, multiplicities. In other words, language has become multiple, many languages as the language of many—but it is not yet manys, not yet the language of manys or the manys of language.

Multiplicity of Judgments

Nevertheless, it is with the logic of the judgment that Hegel thinks the multiplicity of language under the sign of predication: the multiplicity of predication and the predication of multiplicity—for judgment is far more judgments, and subject and predicate are themselves already multiple, a multiplicity of subjects and predicates. That which remained merely implicit in a concept's original self-division (*Ur-teilen*) becomes explicit in judgment (*Urteil*). Here the judgment of multiplicity shows itself as the multiplicity of judgment. And predication, as the logic of sense, is far more multiple determination.

Indeed, for the *Science of Logic* the language of judgments and the judgments of language can be explained by neither nominalism, psychologism, nor formalism. For abstract nominalism, judgment fills up empty names with content: to the question "what is it?" comes the answer "a pipe," that is, the historically fixed name of a particular subject, individual object, or thing (*Sache*) that is (*existentia*) determined only by a predicate expressing its essence (*essentia*) or concept. For an anthropological psychologism, judgment is ours, that is, the connection in one representation (*Vorstellung*), in a human head (subject), of a real thing in the world (object qua external subject), and an idea or concept (internal predicate).[57] For classical grammar and logic, judgment is formalistic, meta-linguistic (A is B, A = B). All of these judgments, however, insofar as they separate form from content, or remain merely one-sided (objective or subjective, situate truth in the subject or predicate), cannot think the transitions of predication, cannot approach the movements of the concept of judgment.

For Hegel then a judgment far more expresses the identity and difference of the identity and difference of subject and predicate. Here the copula (verb) connects or relates subject (noun) and predicate in four forms for four contents: the judgments of determinate-being, reflection, necessity, and those of the concept (*Dasein, Reflexion, Notwendigkeit, Begriff*). On the one hand, the predicate is the universal: if the "rose is red," then the flower is a particular individual, and the color is a universal predicate of many subjects—the predicate subsumes (or is applied to) the subject: the subject is the predicate. On the other hand, the subject is the universal: the rose is not only red; rather, the color is only a particular determination, only one individual characteristic, of the rose among many, and the rose is the concrete totality of qualities—the subject inheres in the predicate: the predicate is the subject. A judgment, in other words, first expresses the identity of subject and predicate—in fact, strictly speaking, outside of the judgment, subject and predicate do not exist. Yet, second, the predicate is supposed to be different from the subject, not identical. The relation of these extremes is, however, third, the totality of judgment, or the "reality of the concept" of judgment.[58]

Judgment then is precisely not a function of us, not just a product of human fantasy; nor is it the condition of the possibility of judging, some kind of schema within which a subject judges. Judgment does not belong to the subject; on the contrary, the subject belongs to judgment qua subjective. Thought must go through speech, writing, action, and so on, must realize itself in concrete form. And language is not the tool of judgment, but its horizon or limit (*horos, Grenze*)—and their relation is conceptual. Here mere expression (*logos, Aussage*) of a fact (e.g., Aristotle died at age seventy-three), of certainty, reality, of the indubitable news or the actual time of day, of (scientific) truth as agreement of intuition and reality, is not a judgment, but a mere sentence (*Satz*), that is, the result of an abstraction from a judgment by a subject, a reduction that has its possibility elsewhere, namely, in the concept.

For Hegel, however, since possibility precedes actuality, speculative thought is not logocentric but horosmic, and philosophical truth is not just correspondence: "whoever gives the name of *truth* to the *correctness* of an *intuition* or *perception*, or to the agreement of the *representation* with the object, at any rate has no expression left for that which is the object and aim of philosophy."[59] The truth of really dead (*wirklich tot*) and apparently dead (*scheintot*), for example, lies in the original division of the concept of judgment, in its double-possibility. Furthermore, predication can no longer be taken as value-free; all forms of judgment (classifications, subsumptions, determinations) must be particular to their content (human and animal cannot be judged identically)—hence, Hegel's insistence upon a multiplicity of judgments.

What then is the multiplicity of judgment? And the judgment of multiplicity? What would it mean to think judgment's division as multiple? A multiplicity of possibilities and possibility as multiple? And can the split between possibility and actuality ever approach multiplicity itself? What would happen if possibility/actuality became multiple? If logic were no longer just subjective and/or objective? Is this not the thinking, writing, speaking, and so on of manys?

Regardless, in judgments, the particular, universal, and individual—that is, the true contents of logic—show themselves in a multiplicity of ways, a multiplicity of truths. Here all judgments are concepts, and no longer either transcendental concepts or empirical entities; they are the relation of both. Yet if different judgments are all judgments, identical, then it is because their difference lies in their concrete meaning (*Bedeutung*): "the rose is red" and "humans are mortal" mean different things. In this way judgment is far more judgments, multiple judgments, because the copula's meaning is multiple, and because being is far more beings, because in order "to be" an entity must always already have been reduced, abstracted, distilled, a result, originally divided, determined, judged, because "*all things are a judgment.*"[60] In other words, the identity of being is judgment, "to be" means "to be judged"—and judgment is always multiple. But what is a judgment?

First, for Hegel, in the positive judgment (*positive Urteil*) of determinate-being, "*the individual is universal.*"[61] The predicate (understood as a quality) inheres (positively) in the subject: "the rose is good smelling" means "the good smell inheres in the rose." Yet here the predicate is "wider than" the subject; they do not correspond because the scent inheres in an infinity of other flowers: the universal (predicate) is individual. The "smell" is only one moment or quality of the "rose"—but the subject is "wider than" the predicate; an infinity of characteristics inhere in the rose: the individual (subject) is universal. In this way multiplicity means bad infinity (the predicate has infinite subjects, the subject has infinite predicates). As in the "Doctrine of Being," however, this multiplicity is no multiplicity at all—for if it is merely infinite, then it can never be that which it should be, never determine itself as infinite; and if it is simply not infinite, if it is finite, then it is not infinite. Hence, subject and predicate are both universal and individual: universal = individual. And the positive judgment shows itself as an empty tautology of formal logic, that is, the law of identity wherein the difference between subject and predicate is merely one of form: the universal is universal, the individual is individual—but the universal should be universal, not simply individual; the subject should be subject, not merely predicate; and the individual should be individual, the predicate, predicate.[62]

The positive judgment then must be expressed negatively: "the individual is, however, also *not* a universal"; subject is not predicate; the rose is not the scent, and vice versa—rather, subject and predicate, individual and universal, are particular: this rose is like no other.[63] Here the negative judgment (*negativ Urteil*) negates the predicate's "abstract" quality: if the rose is not good smelling and the scent does not inhere in the rose, then it is because the rose is always "this" rose, the scent always "this" scent. The subject is "this" particular individual, that is, more particular than a universal predicate like "good smelling"; and the predicate is "this" particular individual's, that is, too particular to inhere in an infinity of other subjects—"*the individual is a particular.*"[64] In other words, the individual as a concrete "this," is singular, one-of-a-kind, original subject, that which bears its own proper name, that has no equal whatsoever, an experience that remains strictly incomparable—this rose smells only like itself, or for Celan: "no one bears witness for the witness."[65] In this sense, if the individual is purely individual, if it predicates only itself, its "this-ness," then the universal is purely universal, apotropaic, cut off, castrated, relegated to the transcendent sphere of (Platonic) abstract ideas. But is "this" individual itself, not also a universal? Are both subject and predicate, rose and scent, not always also "wider than" the individual? Indeed, that which is particular in the individual is always "wider than" the individual itself: the individual is not only individual; the rose's particular scent is always also a universal (non-particular) scent. And the negative judgment, as the simple non-relation of subject and predicate, cannot maintain the purity of the particular individual.[66]

A judgment of determinate-being then is posited as an infinite judgment (*unendliches Urteil*) as the expression of the identity or difference of subject and predicate. Negatively expressed: a particular individual is not an infinity of universals (a rose is not an elephant, pencil, philosopher, etc.)—but here the difference between subject and predicate is "too big"; that is, they are not related at all, and predication as such is meaningless. The negative infinite judgment (abstractly) negates judgment as judgment, sense as sense—yet it is not simply non-sense, negation of a particular meaning, but also the denial of the very possibility of sense itself, of the whole sphere of communication.[67] Positively: "*the universal is universal,*" the predicate is in fact universal; but it is universal only insofar as it inheres in the individual, insofar as it is also individual: subject and predicate continue in one another; being is always the being of beings—they are identical.[68] Here subject and predicate are particular/universal, but their difference is itself an in-difference, "too small," simply identical: the rose *is* the scent.

With the copula of being then, the (universal/particular) predicate in-heres in the subject—it is, strictly speaking, "in here" (*in hier*), but in a judgment of determinate-being (*Da-sein*), the predicate must also be out there (*da*). The judgment of determinate-being expresses the multiplicity of beings and the being that is multiple; however, in a logic of pure identity and difference, although inherence can explain the identity between subject and predicate, it cannot account for their difference.[69] The judgment of determinate-being is indifferent to difference.

While in the judgment of determinate-being, the predicate *inheres* in the subject; second, in the judgment of reflection, the subject *subsumes* the predicate. The predicate is no longer a determination of being, but the essence that shines through the multiplicity of appearance: for example, humans are essentially mortal; mortality is the essence of the human. Here the copula means judgment of essence. And the judgment of reflection is the relation that holds subject and predicate together—for here there are a multiplicity of essences, and essence is multiple.

A judgment of reflection then is a singular judgment expressing the subject's essence as universal: "*this* [*individual*] *is an essential universal*"; that is, the subject's determination as a "this" is universal.[70] The predicate subsumes the subject: this individual human is essentially mortal; mortality is the essence of the single human being; "to be human" means "to be judged mortal." Yet this judgment is supposed to express the individual as particular, not as universal—and mortality is, once again, a universal: strictly speaking, "this" human is not mortal; the essence of "this" individual cannot be a universal. In other words, not a single individual, but a greater number or particular quantity are the universal: "*some individuals are a universal*"; some animals are human.[71] And "this" is expanded to "these"—for the particular judgment of essence means subsumption under a genus (*Gattung*).

The judgment of reflection, however, is universal: all are individuals; every-one is in-comparable in a community of ones. Here quantitative multiplicity means simple progression, bad infinity: just as the pantanomial is the logical conclusion of the polynomial, not only "this" or "these," but "all" individuals are essentially universal. However, the method or rule of the universal judgment is simple repetition, "so that it gains nothing in universality through the increased number of terms."[72] Yet addition or multiplication, the repetition of individuals, the iteration of identity or difference, never yields allness (or multiplicity). On the one hand, the judgment expresses allness and isolation, that is, the genus (as predicate, universal) subsumes the individual (as subject): *mortal* is all and every human being; but on the other hand, the genus expresses the inner nature (essence) of being human: *the human being* is mortal. Predicate determines subject and subject, predicate; and the copula expresses their identity: "*what belongs to all the individuals of a genus belongs to the genus by its nature.*"[73]

Third, then, with the judgment of necessity, subject and predicate necessarily belong to one another. Here the predicate is neither material substance (Aristotle's *hypokaimenon* or Spinoza's material) nor the antithesis of accident; rather, it is the copulaic identity of subject and predicate. The categorical judgment, therefore, identifies an individual's genus and differentiates it from other species—not only by classifying it as a single quality (character trait) or particular quantity of individuals; but rather, by expressing it as the inner/substantial identity of subject and predicate. The difference of genus and species, however, is identical *in* the individual; and this difference is no longer one of simple being—for here being means ground, cause and effect, condition and conditioned: the subject is the predicate means that the predicate causes the subject to be that which it is, for example, the human *is* human be*cause* it is mortal. Indeed, in a hypothetical judgment (if A then B), "to be" means "to be caused"; and causality's necessary connection implies dependence: the subject's being is not its own, but depends upon the predicate. Hence, identity is grounded upon the necessary identity of genus and species *in* the individual: if the human is human, then it *must* be mortal. Cause and effect, however, subject and predicate, individual and universal, are not merely the same: the particular human is not identical with its humanity, mortals are not mortality—and the judgment must express the difference of subject and predicate as well. The disjunctive judgment (A is either B or C, D, E, etc.), therefore, expresses that the universal subject and the particular predicate are identical and different: on the one hand, the genus contains different species (both/and); on the other hand, species exclude one another (either/or) as contrary (simply different) or contradictory (necessarily exclusionary). Here the truth of "barbaric" multiplicity is identity and difference: for example, violet, indigo, orange, green, and red, yellow, blue are grounded in the original principles of light and dark (as in Goethe's *Farbenlehre*). In other words, the predicate expresses the disjunction of genus (identity) and particular species (difference)—but this disjunctive judgment is disjoined from the individual it is supposed to judge.[74]

Fourth, then, the judgment of the concept expresses the identity and difference of the identity and difference of individual and universal: subject and predicate are related via their concept. With Hegel the subjective judgment (which remained for Kant a function of the thinking subject, the application or subsumption under modal categories, the constitution of a purely external "object = x" for me, that is, an object without objectivity, cut off from the thing-in-itself) becomes objective. And the judgment of the concept means that reality is judged by how well it corresponds to its concept, that is, if it is that which it should be—the "ought to be" precedes the "is."[75]

In an assertoric conceptual judgment, for example, the particular subject should be its predicate—this deed is good, this particular deed should be universalizable. Here the act is external to the actor, that is, the act-in-and-of-itself, action "out there." The copula means that the act-in-itself is "asserted" to be good-in-itself; subject and predicate are strictly identical, and the assurance of the action's goodness as universal, of the connection between act (subject) and good/bad (predicate), is the one-sided subject's—my categorical imperative: "act so that the maxim of your will, at every moment and simultaneously, could be valid as principle of a universal legislation."[76] Judgment, however, is not mere assertion: the power to judge (*Urteilskraft*) is not the power to assert (*logos*); and an actual truth-claim is already abstracted from the possibility that a claim is true or false.

Conceptual judgment, therefore, is far more a problem. The asserted good is first problematic—the problem precedes the answer just as essence precedes being. Here the particular constitution of the subject is at issue: an action itself is neither good-in-itself nor good because I say that it is good; rather, an action is judged to be essentially good according to how, when, where, and so on it is performed. And the act-in-itself is also neither good nor bad—for it can only be particularly judged. Yet as in the assertoric judgment, both the constituted act (subject) and the concept (predicate) remain a function of the subject—even if the subject is double (subjective subject and subjective predicate), the predicate is no predicate at all. The essence of the judgment of the concept is problematic, the power of difference at the origin (*ursprüngliche Ur-Teilen*); but insofar as the problem is only potentially good or bad, the judgment can only possibly be made, the identity of subject and predicate remains outstanding, a could-or-should-be-judgment, a conceptual debt, a not-yet or future concept.[77]

The judgment of the concept then comes to completion in apodeictic judgment: the individual action (subject), in its particularity as constituted so and so, is universally good (predicate). Here, if the copula signifies apodeictic connection, it is because subject and predicate are each the totality of the judgment of the concept. On the one hand, the subject is, can, and ought to be the predicate because, as a "judgment on all reality," it is the original difference, that which is broken into "is" (*Sein*) and "ought to be" (*Sollen*), the condition for the possibility of predication in general. On the other hand, the predicate signifies that which the subject is, can and ought to be, because as a "judgment on all reality" it is the original identity, the condition for the possibility of predication as well. And in this way, the copula, the abstract and empty is (*leere Ist*), is the circular transition from subject to predicate, and vice versa: the former determines the latter, the latter fills the former—for they have gone over into one another. In other words, the copula expresses the identity and difference of subject and predicate, the *subject* of the predicate and the subject of the *predicate:* this action constituted in a particular way is good—because "to be" (*sein*) means "to be right in the middle of something," in the processes, in the movement of becoming, the motion of the concept (*im Begriff sein*). And thus, the judgment of the concept is the process of determining and filling reality.[78]

The concept of judgment then is multiple—and the multiplicity of judgment makes explicit "that and how" subject, predicate, and copula are multiple. First, the subject has a multiplicity of predicates: the rose is red, soft, living, smelling, a reproductive organ, a sign of affection, and so on. Second, the predicate has a multiplicity of subjects, and a multiplicity of senses in which it predicates: inherence, subsumption, expression of essence, of concept, belonging, and so on. Third, the relation of subject and predicate, the copula, is no longer "being"—for being is abstracted from a multiplicity of relations: quality, quantity, essence, concept, and so on. Fourth, the predicative relation is conceptual (identity and difference of identity and difference)—but identity and difference have different senses depending on their concrete contents, depending on the specifics of their copulation: factual, correct, logocentric, concordant, horosmic, speculative, and so on.

Even further, judgment qua predication itself is a reduction—for the multiplicity of judgment is the judgment of multiplicity. In a judgment of determinate-being, multiplicity as particular, universal, and individual means (1) a quality of the subject, being a multiplicity of things, having many predicates inhere; (2) a quality of the predicate, its power to inhere in a multiplicity of subjects; (3) a bad multiplicity taken to infinity, that is, the infinite predicates of a subject and the infinite subjects of a predicate; (4) a quality particular to an individual, "this" multiplicity "there" predicated of "this" subject, and "this" multiplicity "here" wherein "this" predicate shows itself; (5) a radically pure multiplicity without non-multiplicity, for example, a particular multiplicity that is never universal, an individual multiplicity without equal or comparison; (6) nothingness, a negative multiplicity, an infinity of predicates that do not belong to the subject, the nonsense that is excluded in a determination of sense, that which multiplicity is not, multiplicity's non-being; (7) determinate content, that is, that which is contained within an individual, that multiplicity inherent to particular subjects, the multiplicity that belongs in being, the measure of what *is* in here and not out there. But in a judgment of reflection, multiplicity means (1) essence subsumed in one individual, that is, a single essence as essences; (2) a particular quantity of individuals subsumed under a species, subsumed under a genus; (3) a quantity of individuals produced through multiplication of identity (many ones) or difference (many differences); (4) the particular and universal essence of all individuals. And in a judgment of necessity, multiplicity means (1) the identity of an individual by which it can be categorized, through which it belongs to a class as a multiplicity of multiplicities; (2) the ground or cause of being—if multiplicity is multiplicity, then it is be-cause it is multiple; (3) an effect of identity and difference, of identities and differences of species and genera. Then finally, in the judgment of the concept, multiplicity means (1) a should-be or not-yet multiplicity, that promise or future to which subject, object and copula ought to correspond; (2) the subject's assertion of multiplicity—my "multiple imperative" raised to the level of a universal maxim: all individuals should be multiple, all actions should be universally multipliable; (3) the multiplicity of possible thoughts from which an actual thought is reduced, constructed, created, abstracted, fixed, or sharpened, that is, the potential actions through which the act is constituted; (4) a problem, *the* "problem of multiplicity" that appears after its solution shows itself as no solution at all, that remains problematic; (5) the multiplicity asserted to be in-itself, in the subject, predicate, and copula themselves; (6) the multiplicity that is multiple only under certain circumstances, only within particular contexts (the multiplicity of hows, whens, wheres, whos, etc.), that becomes multiple only if judgment becomes far more judgments; (7) the multiplicity conceived by the original division of judgment, determined through original difference, the choice between different identities, between is and is, ought and ought, is and ought to be multiple; (8) the multiple movements of subject, predicate, and copula. Indeed, multiplicity shows itself to be and be thought in the multiple movements between ideal and real, the unity of subject and substance, the difference of intelligible and sensible, affirmation and negation, "yes" and "no" and everything that "may be" in between, the identity and difference of infinite and finite, is and ought, the logic of sense and nonsense, the language and discourse of thought and being, the metaphysical relations of one and many, and so on—yet all this (however multiple) is only the preparation for manys, a lapse in judgment, a multiplication that break down not simply relations (human or otherwise), but relationality itself—and not just.

8

Conceptual Objectivity

Objective Relations

> I am always moving. I am forever transporting myself somewhere else. I am never exactly where I am. Tonight, for instance, we are traveling one road but also many, as if we cannot take a single step without discovering five of our own footprints already ahead of us.
>
> —*Hawkes*[1]

The truth of multiplicity then has shown itself as neither the subject nor subjectness, but as the concept of subjectivity. Appropriately the language of assertion (*logos*), the abstract statement of fact, the account of *physis* (e.g., fire goes up) as *energia* (the actualization of potential), has developed into judgments of substance (the stone is warmed because the Sun shines on it) and the various types of conceptual syllogism. Once again, the beginning is the end: subjective truth belongs to language before it can be abstracted and reformulated as a proposition. The truth of subjectivity, however, is also supposed to be objective: a concept that never corresponds to its object, to the thing-in-itself, is no concept at all—subjectivity without reality is like a god without existence. Yet objectivity cannot mean being (as real predicate, pure position, logical copula or indeterminate immediacy) or existence (*Dasein*), or a mode of existence (*Wirklichkeit*), or essence; rather, it is the concept of the thing itself.

The thing (*Sache*), however, first presents itself to subjectivity as a being. In this way judgment is no mere application of formal logic to some indifferent content; it is a determination of beings, of things. And if knowledge is real, of real entities, then it is because beings show themselves to subjectivity as they are in themselves. The thought of causality, for example, in the representation of things, is the way in which things are present—otherwise, there would be no knowledge whatsoever.

Yet as a being, the thing is already a result: the determination "in and for itself" indicates that a process of abstraction, distillation, fixation, reduction, has already taken place. The being of a being, however, is itself no being (just as time is nothing temporal); it is neither the idea (*eidos*) nor the essence (*essentia*) of being (e.g., presence). But if the being of beings, the thingness of things, is not to be found in the experience of beings, then it is not because it is a pure concept for a transcendental subject, objectness (*Objektheit*), but because it is the conceptual relation of beingness and beings, thingness and things, that is, objectivity.

The objectivity of the object then is not "that" it is, or "that it is there," nor is it simply "how" it is, "how it is an object"—for like subjectivity before it, objectivity is the double concept of both: on the one hand, the difference between the self-identical object as in-itself (free from all subjective reflection) and for-another (a function of the subject); on the other hand, the relation from which they are abstracted and that supersedes or takes care of both. In this sense the objectivity of the object is, for Hegel, neither its existence nor its essence, neither its being nor its substance, but the identity and difference of the identity and difference of the concept.

In objectivity, therefore, the "thing (in itself)" is superseded by the "object." Yet before the question of objectivity, before the multiplicity of its moments, a multiplicity of questions: What is a "thing"? And what is an "object"? What are their multiplicities? And how is it possible to think them multiply? What is the multiplicity of objectivity? And objective multiplicity? Or, even further, what is the multiplicity of this multiplicity?

Mechanical Objects

> Therefore, we must all ask and ask again, in order to know, or also only to know why and to what extent we cannot know it. Is the human being, are the peoples, only stuffed into this universe in order to be spun out once again, or is it otherwise? We must ask. Yet something still more preliminary holds over the long term: we must first *learn* to question again. That happens alone insofar as that which is asked, is surely not just any question. We chose the question, "What is a thing?" It shows itself now: the things stand in *various* truths.
>
> —*Heidegger*[2]

For Kant the thing in itself must be thought as unconditioned (*Unbedingte*) in order for it to underlie the object and ground our experience of the world (for example, causality): that which makes experience possible can be nothing experiential; if things as appearances are given, then there must be a giver for the gift, a presenter of the present—in order to avoid an infinite regress of conditions, things in themselves must be the unconditioned conditions of objects.[3] For Heidegger, through a destructive step back from/out of metaphysics as a science, the possibility of the thing in the opening and closing of the world's annulus comes into unconcealment—for the ground of the thing, the ground that is just as much a non-ground (*Ungrund*), lies in truth as *a-letheia.* For Hegel, however, the concept of objectivity needs neither critique nor destruction—for objectivity is (in truth and not only in meaning) conditioned and unconditioned, empirical and transcendental. If the object shows itself as thing in itself and as object of experience, then it is not because a particular concept of truth as revealing/concealing has been found, but because truth itself is conceptual. And the givenness of the manifold in intuition, the purity of the thing in itself, objective reality and transcendental ideality—all this is merely moments of abstraction or reduction from the double-object; the multiple movements of these moments, however, is the logic of the concept of objectivity. In other words, the multiplicity of objectivity is neither transcendental nor empirical, neither the condition of the possibility nor the possibility of the condition—for as essentially conceptual, it is nothing multiple just as much as something multiple.

More specifically then: against Kant, Hegel thinks metaphysics as a science of the object as thing in itself. Universal and necessary truth is possible in a priori synthetic judgments not because objects as they appear in experience conform to us—that would be a "Copernican revolution in reverse," an anti-scientific geocentricism, the subject-centered knowledge of what we put into the world. In fact, if metaphysics is to raise itself to the status of a science, then human beings cannot be the center of the universe. An "actual Copernican revolution in thought," on the contrary, would mean that knowledge conforms to things in themselves—this is, however, no return to Humean skepticism (wherein truth is mere convention, *habitus*) or Cartesian/Leibnizian dualism (wherein truth is possible only through the intervention of the other "usual subterfuge" of a "third thing" that connects thought and being); rather, a priori knowledge of objects in themselves is possible because of the concept. In other words, the thing in itself and the object as appearance for us (for another) are only abstractions from the object as "in itself and for another." The relation of both is prior to their a posteriori separation or derivation, and this relation is essentially conceptual: not a "third thing," but the objectivity of the object, the identity and difference of the identity and difference of the object qua thing in itself and qua object of experience for another. Here an object is no immediate indeterminacy, no mere being or unconditioned entity—for thereby, everything and nothing would be a thing; that is, like all shifters (then, now, this, that), thingness would be meaningless—or more precisely, a moment. And if the objectivity of the object (that "transcendental chemistry" splits into "object of experience" and "thing in itself") can be for us, "thought" and "known" by a subject, then it is because the subject's subjectivity is always already in a conceptual relation with the object's objectivity, because the subject is essentially (in and for itself) the object. In this way the concept as objectivity/subjectivity (i.e., as the absolute idea) makes a priori synthetic judgments possible. And metaphysics as a science is only possible as the *Science of Logic.*

Yet questions remain for multiplicity: If scientific knowledge, for Kant, is grounded upon the two-sided object, then why stop there? Why must the object only have two sides and not many? For as Kant himself insists: pure speculative reason has the particular characteristic or faculty in itself that it can chose to think its object in "various" ways.[4] Is the variety (*Verschiedenheit*) of thought appropriate for the object of experience because the object has various sides? Not just in itself and for us? But rather, a multiplicity of facets for a cubist imagination and faculty of judgment? And what would it mean to think this thing as multiple? To encounter the thing as multi-dimensional? Or as Heidegger insists: the truth of things are "various."[5] With what right then can the *Critique* ground its metaphysics on a two-sided object? Or must the object of metaphysics become far more "various" if it is to raise itself to the level of a science?

As Hegel argues: the object is not just a thing in itself or an appearance for us, nor is it simply the unification of four things; rather, it shows itself in various ways (mechanical, chemical, teleological, and so on). By thinking the object's multiplicity, Hegel does not think that which makes the difference of thing in itself and object of experience possible, but that which shows itself as various because it is various in itself—Kant's "object" and Heidegger's "thing" result (for speculative thought) from conceptual objectivity. And its objectivity is far more the objectivities (*Objektivitäten*) of mechanism, chemism, and teleology.[6] In this way Hegel thinks not just the object's double-sided objectivity (as in itself and for another)—but its multiplicity as well.

Objectivity then first shows itself in the multiplicity of mechanics, in mechanism and its mechanical objects. Here an object is initially material; it stands over and against its form. Yet these objects as such are estranged from one another, indifferent to each other (immediate indeterminate identities or a relationless multiplicity); and if they are connected, then it is the work of some outside force, some external actor or subject—for they are neither free to decide upon their own movements, nor to determine the principle or order under which they fall. Each object is itself a multiplicity (in itself), and there are multiple multiplicities; however, each can be determined as "a" multiplicity only in relation to others—the relationless shows itself as essentially relational. As multiple, therefore, each object is a totality, a put-together aggregation of self-identical parts (e.g., atoms, quarks, the building blocks of matter). Through a gathering of parts, however, like a gathering of clans, no whole is ever reached—for totality does not belong to the abstracted or sliced-out object. Even a "world" is not totality, but a "universe," cut off from that which makes its "worlding" possible, from its conceptual relation to that "other" through which it determines itself in the first place.[7]

The objectivity of mechanical objects then shows itself as mechanistic. Yet if this is simply determinism, then it is only a subjective and tautological conclusion—as Kant knew, determinism always implies some beginning that is itself not determined.[8] For Hegel, however, mechanism is not determinism; it is a process, the (mechanical) relation of objects, the internal connection of computational machines—for merely self-identical and exclusionary objects could never hope to affect one another. Deterministic causality, therefore, is not originary; it is the result of an abstraction from the relation that objects share. Cause is only an effect. The community of mechanical objects is the condition of the possibility of their communication—no call without telephones—however, this community is itself nothing mechanical, but the continuation (not a thing that continues) or transition (not a message that is transferred) of objects, their medium or element, through which a multiplicity of contents are processed.[9]

Indeed, as a mechanical process, community is formalistic, that is, subject to the (physical) order or (conventional) standard of communication by which a multiplicity of objects (as the supersession that takes care of their individual forms and contents) interact. Here, communication and reception are exchangeable: a given action can just as well be taken as a reaction. With formal mechanism, a mechanical object is a product torn out of the process, the effect of action that appears inactive. In other words, mechanical production brings processes to a standstill (*Ruhe*), constructs an ob-ject (*Gegen-stand*), fixes formally diverse objects.[10]

In a real mechanical processes, however, objects are not simply diverse, but related to one another (like weaker and stronger forces, plus and minus, 1 and 0). Real process relations are those of power (*Macht*) or violence (*Gewalt*): in the former, an object acts upon itself (subject and predicate are identical); in the latter, it acts upon another, a stranger (*etwas Fremdes*). And the negation of violence, resistance (*Widerstand*), must be violent by definition. Resistance to power, however, is impossible—the power to resist oneself is itself an act of power, self-determination. The real mechanical process, therefore, is always a process of power: objects determine themselves by negating the violence of another, and exercising power over themselves—an exercise that is itself a negation. Freedom is never, as Kant thought, pure auto-legislation—for it is always also in relation to an other (its own as well as the violence of a negated other). And the organization by which a mechanical process functions, the means of production by which a community of objects legislates (itself or another community), is essentially the exercise of power or violence. Yet insofar as real objects remain indifferent to their order, insofar as products are estranged from their means of production, power is inevitably violent—the determination of objects in mechanism is arbitrary, the blind fate of a (natural or political) community.[11]

Whereas formal mechanism only produces formal objects, real mechanism can only produce real products. The objectivity of an object, however, must be both formal and real, formally real and really formal; it must be a true individuality, the independent totality. With absolute mechanism, therefore, the multiplicity of an object is initially gathered into a middle point, and the community of objects is a collection of middle points. In the material world, for example, the real medium of middle points is the central-body (the being of the human being is centered in its body)—Newtonian physics is the law of bodies, the order of individual centers bound to each other, sharing a common medium, that is, another center. The centrality of bodies, however, is their decentrality: the middle term of middle terms is itself the middle term of no middle term; rather, it is an extreme. Each centered body, therefore, has another center, a de-center, as the means by which it centers itself and others; and this centrality of objects is the law of bodies themselves, the middle of middles. In absolute mechanism, in other words, the external (formal or real) order of objects shows itself as a free mechanism, as the free submission of bodies to an internal law (*Gesetz*) of bodies, not an external law (the other's law or violence is negated, or more precisely, determinately negated, superseded, taken care of)—determination has become self-determination, their *law* is *their* law, and each is a middle for the other, each an extreme for each, all a means for all, another for another.[12]

Law then is the soul and identity of absolute mechanism, the supersession (the concept of law) that takes care of an object's inner (subjective) individuality and its exterior (objective) objectivity; it is real insofar as it belongs to objects in themselves, and ideal insofar as it is neither an object (entity, being, body, or individual) nor a subjective (psychological, anthropological) concept—for it is the difference of both, the law of difference as the self-movement and self-determination of objects in relation to their other, the inner freedom of their own necessity, the free necessity of necessary freedom (control is always already more effective as self-control, auto-discipline rather than the rule of a sovereign or foreign power). In this way, the objectivity of the object means independence through law and recognition of another's individual difference. And absolute mechanism's law of difference (of objects in a system) is the source and soul of the movement of objects. At this moment, however, this difference is only ideal; it is not yet real, not yet the difference of the body itself.[13]

Indeed, with mechanism, the objectivity of the object posits a free/ necessary law as the difference and independence of objects. Objectivity, however, is always the objectivity of objects. And the concept must be essentially immanent to the multiplicity of an object; it must be the transition of objects over into their objectivity and of objectivity into objects—for objectification (and the memorial to its objectification, as well as the promise of objectifications to come) is only possible under the condition that the transition has already taken place. Hegel thinks against Kant: the condition of the possibility of transition is that transition has already happened—and law (as well as freedom) must show itself in relation to another. The multiplicity of the object implies a multiplicity of objectivity, and a multiplicity of this multiplicity, that is, multiplicities and objectivities. The law of the difference of objectivities, however, is no longer the object of mechanism; it is the multiplicity of chemism.[14]

Chemical Processes

After the object of mechanism, the chemical object makes no pretense to immediate independence and self-determining difference; rather, it determines itself, as essentially "what" and "how" it is, in relation to an other and drives no longer to physical, but chemical equilibrium. Here the objectivity of the object means that objects in themselves are objects for each other; they have their identity only in their difference. Relations between living beings, for example, the interconnections of sex, gender, love, friendship, care, desire, and so on, can only be reduced to an economy of free mechanism at the price of abstracting differences and forgetting that entities are always also more than self-identical: a monadic account of care, a computational simulation of friendship, a desiring machine, an erotic drive in mechanical motion cannot approach the chemism of lovers—for the chemicals of the concept are never simple units (*monas*), never merely alone (neither in bed, nor in the grave), never just chemicals. There is no smallest common denominator of chemical objects; rather, they have particular properties that cannot be reduced to simple building blocks of matter. Like the *dx/dy* of calculus, the chemical relation falls with the removal of one partner (e.g., elective affinities). And in this way, chemism supersedes mechanism because it thinks not the independence of objects in their conceptual relation, but the inter-dependence of ingredients.[15]

Chemistry, however, is not chemism, not the science of the form of chemical elements—for as conceptual, chemism is also the science of its matter. In chemism the object initially shows itself as subject to external violence: the forced mixing of chemicals results in a stable product; objects are made to be immediately identical with their objectivity. Here, just as language is the element of signs, nature is the medium wherein chemical processes "neutralize" the real differences of ingredients, wherein tension is violently resolved in an indifferent, peaceful unity. The chemical product is the dissolution of the identities and differences of its ingredients; yet since they have only been mixed, they can be unmixed. The periodic table, however (like Kant's "Table of Judgments" or "Categories"), in unmixing chemical relations, in determining the "original" elements of chemistry, forgets that "the beginning is the end": analysis breaks the original-synthetic unity of nature apart, tears ingredients out of their conceptual relation to one another—the table is a product. And if a chemical process is to be thought speculatively, it must supersede the chemist's external violence and take care of the disjunctive procedure that splits the object into abstract elements; in other words, it must allow the chemical objects to show themselves in their internal relation to one another.[16]

Chemism then thinks the assumption under which chemical analysis and synthesis, the syllogisms and conclusions of chemistry, are possible, namely, the original relation of chemical objects, the objectivity that identifies and differentiates the object. Here, the mechanism is superseded: the formal neutralization of objects as a centered object of act/element presupposes the chemical process—raw materials must be extricated from nature before they can be indifferently and externally combined in a mechanical object (or chemical product). The chemical process itself, however, is the conceptual relation of objects themselves; and therein their internal relation is their goal (*Zweck*). The objectivity of chemism thinks the process in which chemical objects strive toward each other, seek out their partners to the exclusion of all others, elect their affinities: their determination is self-determination; their neutralization, self-neutralization—the freedoms and necessities of nature are its own;

and here, at this moment, the other belongs to nature. The internal processes of chemism supersede the external laws of mechanism by thinking the inter-dependence of objects that is their own. In other words, the objectivity of the object in itself lies no longer in itself, but in its relation to other objects, in the process from which it has been abstracted.[17]

Indeed, with chemism, an object strives purposively toward a goal not from some external violence, but from itself, under its own power, for its own reasons. The force that drives the chemical process originates in objects themselves. In this way, the object, like a subject (although not yet a subject), has its own kind of understanding (*Verstand*) and reason (*Vernunft*): nature manifests its own rationality. The lawfulness, transgression, chaos, deviance, and so on of objects are not subjective projections, not our fantasies; they are the self-determining actions of an other: the purpose and ends of the natural object are its own; it is itself its *telos*.

The Ends of Reason

The teleological object then (determinately) negates its mechanistic and chemical objectivity: the object's purposiveness (*Zweckmäßigkeit*) has a purpose, and physical mechanics and chemical processes must be superseded in a concept that is the identity and difference of efficient and final cause, of mechanism and chemism. Hegel's question here is not which cause is true; rather, it is what is the truth (in and for itself) of both causes. And Hegel's answer is teleology, the *telos* of *logos,* "the end of reason" that neither originates in some outer-worldly understanding or transcendent finality, nor in a thing in itself that never shows itself as itself to a subject—on the contrary, the originality of the origin must end in the object itself. In this way, teleology is no longer chemism, not while (like the interdependence of elective-affinities or chemical processes) it is self-determination for the sake of its relation, but because the object's *telos* lies not in another, but in itself, in its own *logos.*[18]

The drive of chemism has become the purposiveness of teleology and the object—as rational—has become subjective, or more precisely, teleological. The objectivity of the object is the teleology of the *telos.* As teleological, however, an object takes itself simply as another object, as something present (*Vorhandenes*) over and against itself—it is out of itself. In order to become teleological, the object determined itself as mechanical-chemical (in all its particularity, universality, and individuality); however, the difference between teleological and objective objects undermines the very self-determination that it presupposed: the purposiveness of the objective object is not identical with that of the teleological object; on the contrary, the object is split, doubled, divided, and separated from itself. And in order to determine itself as a *telos,* the teleological object posits a means to its end. The difference of teleological object and its end, the teleological end and its object, shows itself as a means (*Mittel*).[19]

In order to fulfill its goal, in other words, the purposive object needs an external means—for the object's goal comes not at the end, but at the beginning: the positing (*Setzen*) of the goal is far more a presupposing (*Voraus-setzen*). The teleological and objective objects have teleological and objective goals, and teleological and objective means. In fulfilling its goal, the object posits its means as objective (although in truth, the means belong as much to the objective as to the teleological object), as an immediate other to be used (violently)—for the means have no force with which they could (perhaps) offer resistance. The object's goal, thereby, becomes other: its *goal* is no longer *its* goal. The teleological object that was supposed to determine the means to its end finds itself determined by the end and its means—the determining has become the determined. The object as *telos* is subject to its end; it is the powerless servant of its own goals.

In the ends/means relation then, the means is not simply dependent upon the end, nor the end on the means; rather, each must traverse the other in order to determine themselves—the teleological object's free action is bound. And here the objectivity of the object means mediation (*Vermittlung*) of means and ends. At this moment teleological action is no longer mechanical violence, production's one-sided determination. The argument, for example, that humans have priority over nature based on the mechanical exploitation of real resources proves its opposite: the end uses of tools are precisely those of nature, for example, the act of plowing in order to plant in order to eat, and so on—culture is natural. As teleological, human action is conceptual: the process of ends/means self-determination means that the objective power of the end is identical with and different from that of the means. In this sense the goal has become the teleology (and soul) of the object—and this goal is its activity (*Tätigkeit*).[20]

The ends and means then are realized in activity; the goal becomes the fulfilled goal (*ausgeführte Zweck*)—for fulfillment is neither simple end, mortality, one-sided finitude, abstract death, nor mere immortality, one-sided infinity; rather, as supersession, it means translation (*Überset-zung*). In setting the end over into action, in bringing the concept of (the objectivity of) the object into concrete existence, the means and the end are taken care of in their identity. And here, like the immediacy of being, teleology shows itself as one-sided: the end and beginning, consequent and ground, effect and cause, are only identical, and difference is forgotten—for only that which already exists or comes into existence, only that which has already become becomes. The realization of the end shows that teleology is a logic of means and means to means to means—as end, it is a bad infinity of means; and as activity, it is the end of the end. At the moment that a teleological object is determined as means or end, it is no longer means or end; and if it remains indeterminate, then it is likewise neither means nor end—and in truth, both are essentially only in and for their relation. Teleological purposiveness, in other words, can never reach an actual end, but must always remain a means. In this sense, nature's own ends are not the ends of nature; the *telos* of the *object* is never the object's *telos*. And the objectivity of the object is neither means to an end nor ends to a means; it is the relation of both: the means is the means of the end and vice versa. In the identity of teleology, no external violence is necessary in order to use an object as a means—for the *telos* is the object's own, and action is self-determination, self-use, the resolution or decisiveness to conceive of oneself as a means to one's own ends, but at the price of difference and the loss of otherness.[21]

As self-determining then, the object's means are no longer simply exterior to its end; rather, they are mediated by one another: the fulfilled goal is the realization of means. Insofar as the objectivity of the object is teleological, the object acts subjectively, according to its own ends, for its own reasons. More specifically, as conceptual, the object supersedes us, takes care of the subject—for the object's objectivity in itself returns it to its subjectivity for itself. Objectivity has repeated subjectivity with a difference: that which was merely internal shows itself as external; the truth of both, however, is their concept that will show itself as the external/internal totality of the idea.[22]

For Hegel, therefore, the objectivity of the "Subjective Logic" is far more objectivities. The object in itself shows itself as three moments and their moments. Here natural science—a priori synthetic judgments on the whole—is possible neither because of the simple identity of thing in itself and object of appearance, nor because of their pure difference, but because of both, because the object is (in itself) essentially conceptual, the identity and difference of its identity and difference. The objectivity of the object makes metaphysics as a science possible—as the *Science of Logic*. And only through the conceptualization of subject and object, subjectivity and objectivity, can the truth of both show itself as itself.

Yet if objects and objectivities can posit themselves as empirical and transcendental, as the machines of mechanism, the chemicals of chemism, the ends of reason, then is it not because they are already multiple? Because this multiplicity is itself multiple? And if this multiplicity can be neither empirical nor transcendental, neither mechanical, nor chemical nor teleological, if it can be neither simply objective nor subjective; then is it not necessary for metaphysics to think yet more multiply? Not to philosophize before philosophy, but to philosophize multiply? To break down the breakdown at the core of mechanism? To analyze the analysis of chemistic conclusions? To finish off the teleology of teleology? To think, write, speak, and so on the multiplicity of "manys"? And not just?

9

Idea of Totality

Concept of the Concept

> Les langues imparfaites en cela que plusiers, manque la suprême: penser étant écrire sans accessoires, ni chuchotement mais tacite encore l'immortelle parole, la diversité, sur terre, des idiomes empêche personne de proférer les mots qui, sinon se trouveraient, par une frappe unique, elle-même matériellement la vérité.
>
> —*Mallarmé*[1]

With the idea the *Science of Logic* comes to a certain kind of end—for the idea finishes off objectivity and subjectivity and marks the return of the concept to itself. In previous moments the concept was always the concept of or for another: the concept of being, of essence, of universality or individuality, and so on. Now, the concept is the concept of and for itself—the concept of the concept. Yet this concept is neither an abstract universal (the concept of concepts) nor a particular concept among concepts; rather, as conceptual itself, it is essentially not simply itself, not just the concept. And Hegel names the "concept of the concept" the idea—for the concept is true through its idea. Yet what is the idea?

Initially, as the identity of subjectivity and objectivity, the idea is an adequate concept (*adäquate Begriff*). Here "adequacy" means correspondence, congruence, agreement of object and subject. The idea is unconditional—for the end of reason is not merely to represent, but to know the truth. In this sense reason shows itself as the immediate idea, the totality of its concept and the objectivity (of the object). Yet this idea is neither unreal (*unwirkliches*) nor simply subjective, but real and objective; nor is it merely an "ideal" idea, that is, a goal, a should-be true; nor a "transcendent" idea as a striven-for truth; rather, it is the true congruence from which untrue being (*unwahre Sein*) and subjective thought are mere abstractions. The subject/object congruence, however, is not the simple homogeneity of Kant's schematism; it is the unity of the concept and its objectivity—not only "should" objective and subjective worlds agree in "appearance," not only "could" they be shown to agree in terms of some third thing or external criterion of truth; rather, "they are themselves the congruence of concept and reality."[2] And the reality that does not come from the concept, the concept that does not originate in objective reality, is merely subjective appearance, merely "sound and fury signifying nothing." The unity of the idea, in other words, the congruence of concept and reality, is like that of soul and body—for the idea lives in their unity and dies in their separation. And a conceptless reality or unreal concept is a kind of death: the abstract differentiation of form and content.

As simply finite then, real entities (i.e., beings as objects, and the objectivity of objects) do not concur with the idea; rather, they remain subject to a one-sided concept, that is, the concept of their being. Here the finitude of beings shows itself as a subjective judgment; and limited to the identity and difference of concept and reality, the idea remains incomplete. Objectively, however, beings are finite because they are always already in relation to their infinity. No entity simply perishes, dissolves, disappears; rather, the limit or horizon of death is far more transition and return to nature. In fact, as double, death is conceptual: on the one hand, abstract, the pure ending and decomposition of the body; on the other hand, determinate, that is, supersession in the species, taking care of life itself. In this sense, as the finite/infinite idea, the concept of the concept will first shows itself as life (*Leben*).

Yet the idea is not only the objective reality of life—for living beings also show themselves in being. At the end of the *Science of Logic:* "*being* has attained the meaning of *truth* insofar as the idea is the unity of the concept and reality; it *is,* therefore, from now on, only that which is idea."[3] Here the being of beings means not only the reality of real beings, but just as much the being of the concept. And in this way the idea is the total concept (*totale Begriff*). The concept of the concept (of being) is the idea. As subjective as it is objective, as universal as it is determinate, the idea shows itself as the idea of knowledge (*Idee des Erkennens*), of the true and the good, theory and practice, of the cognition of the concept by the concept, of being as the being of beings.

The idea, however, as the knowledge of life, does not yet know it. Previously the objectivity of the concepts of mechanism, chemism, and teleology had no idea that they were concepts; for them the idea went unnoticed, and their relation to themselves was immaterial (i.e., both unimportant and abstractly ideal). Now, objectivity as life becomes a concept, but the concept must still come to know itself as conceptual. Through the idea of knowledge, the concept of life must attain the status of the absolute idea, that is, the concept as such (*als solche*)—for only then can it be essentially conceived as true, as the self-congruence of the concept, adequacy to self. And the concept, therefore, *has* (knows) its truth only insofar as it *is* (being) the idea—for as the idea, it becomes that which it is, that is, the becoming of the concept, of the concept of the concept, the becoming-idea. Yet if the idea (and its truth) is not just the idea, then it is because it is absolute.[4]

Indeed, the relation of the concept of the concept and the concept of the concepts (i.e., of being, essence, etc.) is absolute, the absolute idea. The multiplicity of concepts stands (and stand) over and against the identity of the concept; and their difference is that through which they form the totality of the concept. The concept of the concept is the end of the *Logic;* but it is just as much its beginning—for if the concept is merely self-identical, then it is no concept at all; rather, the completion of the science of the concept as the absolute idea must be simultaneously its non-completion. The total concept, the concept of the concept and the non-concept, will show itself as a totalizing non-totality and non-totalizing totality—for completion and totality are functions of the logic of identity and difference. As conceptual, however, the concept of the concept is the identity and difference of the identity and difference of the concept with itself and its others.

The concept of the concept then is Hegel's answer to the question of the multiplicity of the concept and the concept of multiplicity—this is the idea. On the one hand, the multiplicity of the concept is reduced to the double, to the concept as two-sided: in itself and for another, identical to self and different from self, the concept of the concept and the concepts. The concept of the concept is multiple and non-multiple. On the other hand, the concept of multiplicity supersedes and takes care of transcendental multiplicity (the multiplicity that is nothing multiple) as well as empirical multiplicity (the multiplicity that is not only multiple qualities and quantities, but multiple determinations): the multiplicity of multiplicity is multiple and non-multiple, multiple multiplicity and non-multiple multiplicity. If the multiplicity of multiplicity is a concept, then its multiplicity will be absolutely two-sided—but only under the condition that it submits to the logic of identity and difference, that it presupposes a discourse of self and other, congruence and incongruence: on the one hand, a total multiplicity, an achieved and multiple multiplicity—not merely a "should be multiple"; on the other hand, a non-total multiplicity, incomplete and incongruent with itself. Do these multiplicities, however, the multiple and non-multiple multiplicity, the multiplicity of multiplicity, and so on, do they not presuppose yet another multiplicity?

The multiplicity of multiplicity, like the concept of the concept, is the idea, that is, the multiplicity of the idea and the idea of multiplicity. And the moments of this multiplicity are themselves multiple, but not simply in the sense of quantity and quality, of many in number and kind—categorizing and partitioning the moments of the concept is the most superficial of thoughts and unacquainted with truth. The counting of conceptual moments, like the counting of sheep, is the slaughter of spirit—although this remains a possibility for philosophy, a threat and promise to multiplicity:

> but to *count* the moments can be seen as altogether useless: on the one hand, that which is itself differentiated is just as much *one* (namely, the *thought* of the difference that is only one thought—as [the differentiated] is *this* differentiated element, the second relative to the first); on the other hand, however, because the thought that grasps the many in one must be dissolved out of its universality and differentiated into more than three or four distinct components . . . here, therefore, it is quite superfluous to think of numbers and counting at all, just as in other respects the mere difference of quantity and amount has no concept and says nothing.[5]

The multiple moments of the multiplicity of multiplicity, in other words, the idea of multiplicity, is itself a concept, the concept of the concept. Neither simply a number of concepts nor the concept of concepts, the idea of multiplicity supersedes and takes care of multiplicity and non-multiplicity. And this idea of multiplicity, like that of the concept, shows itself as two-sided; it can always be reduced to self and other, can always be constituted as congruence and incongruence, can always reveal and conceal itself as truth and untruth, can always be abstracted or determined as empirical and transcendental—but its truth is the relation of both, the multiple/non-multiple multiplicity of multiplicity and non-multiplicity. Yet even here (however multiple), does this multiplicity not raise the question, the possibility, the future or promise, the desire for another multiplicity, as neither simply multiple nor non-multiple?

Before this question, however, other questions: How does the multiplicity of the idea show itself as multiple, as the idea of life, the good idea and the absolute idea? What does it mean to think the multiplicity of lives and deaths, of life and death themselves? How does the good show itself as multiple, as the will to good and as wills to goods? In what way is the totality of the absolute idea, the end of the *Logic,* far more its beginning as ideas?

The Pain of Life

In the "Subjective Logic" the concept of the objective world, its objectivity, showed itself as mechanism, chemism, and teleology: first, with the physical concept, inert bodies, indifferent to themselves and each other, were conceived as moved from outside (Newtonian) forces; second, with the chemical concept, differentiated objects, irreducible to any single substance, were conceived as driven by their own characters and essences; third, with the biological concept, living beings were conceived as self-moved, as striving toward a goal, as taking themselves, their lives and deaths, as means of ultimately reproducing the species and genus. With life, all these concepts are superseded: the human being, for example, is an economy of forces acting upon bodies, and a particular gathering of substances, and a member of the genus "animal" (as identical to other animals) and the species "rational" (as different from them) with specific functions—in other words, the human being is a mechanical, chemical, teleological, living being. For Hegel the object of the *Science of Logic* in the "Doctrine of the Concept," the objectivity of this object, becomes life itself.

Not only logic, however, but all sciences have life as their object; and it is from the study of life that all particular and determinate disciplines (anthropology, psychology, etc.—as well as ontology, the study of unconditional being, *to on he on*) are abstracted. Each "life science" produces concrete knowledge of life from that which it puts into life, from its own point of view and perspective (*Ansicht*); the *Science of Logic*, however, knows its object as it essentially is, in its being and essence—for it is the science of the concept of life as life. The science of life, however, is not natural philosophy, not the science of the relation of nature and spirit; it is the study of the objective/subjective concept of life as idea. What then is life?[6]

Initially, for Hegel, life shows itself as immediate, as the natural object, or more precisely, the objectivity of the living object. Unlike mechanism, chemism, and teleology, however, life has a will of its own—and it is not simply an object; on the contrary, it acts as a subject and takes itself as origin and end. Here the subjectivity of this subject, however, of life as subject, shows itself as finite (its end is not its beginning, but its abstract limit, and death is the supersession and reality that takes care of life). Life really ends with death, but death ends just as much with life—for each is the other of each other, each has its meaning and truth in the other. Life and death are moments of the concept of both, and Hegel names this concept "spirit"—for the life of spirit is the process of living and dying, the movement that disseminates and exteriorizes itself, and thereby conceives that which is alive.

Spirit then, like an omnipresent soul, is always the spirit of life; it has its home (*oikos, Heim*) in life, in the incomprehensible secret (*unbegreifliches Ge-heim-nis*) of life itself—but a secret that, as uncanny (*un-heim-lich*), is kept by the concept: the secrecy of the secret is the concept itself, and without the concept life is inconceivable. In fact, Hegel's secret is the concept—for only with conceptual logic can the secret of life be both kept (preserved, concealed) and told (destroyed, revealed). Indeed, the secret of the secret only functions in being told—an untold secret is no secret at all, and the concept remains a secret insofar as it is omnipresent. And the secrecy of this secret must be open to all. In this way spirit can be (essentially) the true (albeit secret) meaning of life because their relation is conceptual, that is, the absolute contradiction (*absolute Widerspruch*) of the "one in multiplicity."[7] In other words, thought must follow the logic of absolute contradiction and negation in order to know spirit as life's immanent conceptual-substance—not simply its form or matter, origin or goal—but as the objectivity of life qua object and the subjectivity of life qua subject. For the *Science of Logic,* however, before life reveals itself as spirit, it shows itself as the individual, the life-process and the process of the genus.

First, life means "that which is alive in living beings," that which is originally differentiated in the objective world. Life itself, however, is not a living being; rather, it stands over and against living entities (humans, animals, plants, etc.), as that which is alive in them, but never one of them. Life is alone, pure, an individual subject, and precisely not a living object: life is not itself alive; it is that through which living individuals determine themselves as alive—for each individual realizes itself as the immediate completion of life in objective reality. Indeed, the individual completes itself by separating itself from the rest of reality via negation. In other words, it assumes its identity as a differentiated being. As the objective totality of being, however, life is only lent (*geliehen*) to the individual: living is always on borrowed time. Here the individuality of the individual as alive lies in its principle of self-determination, self-movement (*energia*), in its subjectivity or soul (*Seele*); and its objectivity is its externalization, that is, its relation to its body (*Leib*), and the outside world.

The living individual then can determine itself and relate to its objects as bodies (*Körper*) or objects (*Objekte*)—but if its life depends on connecting with others as living beings (*lebendige Dasein*), then it can no longer simply assume a mechanical or chemical inter-objective/subjective economy; rather, it must determine itself as an organism, that is, a multiplicity of members producing itself in a means/ends relation to other living beings and driven toward a given goal (achieved at their expense or at its own). Yet this is no objective teleology—for each living individual strives to fulfill its own subjective goals within a "restricted economy" of drives, an economy that is just a moment of the process of life itself. As the co-constituting circulation of products and producers, however, wherein producers of products are themselves products of their production, subjective power is always only abstracted from a "general (conceptual) economy" of forces. Here life realizes itself by producing the living individual, by cutting into and out of the objective world, by judging (*urteilen*) and delimiting. And as a determinate product, the living individual is essentially threefold: sensible (capable of receiving a multiplicity of intuitions and determining them under a principle, while producing a feeling of self), self-productive (capable of spontaneous determination, judgment and limitation on the basis of positive or negative irritation as proper to a particular species and genus), and self-preservative (capable of actually reproducing itself as a concrete living being or real totality, by defending itself against the rest of the world). In this way the subjective totality of the living individual is the concept of itself; it is life itself, but it can be that which it essentially is only over against and in relation to the world, to the external world as nothing, negated. For the world, however, the individual is equally an external other, nothing.[8]

Second, then, life shows itself as not only the living individual (with its drive to fulfill need, to supersede and take care of its other, to make it certain of itself, thereby achieving self-certainty), but as the life-process (*Lebensprozeß*). In this moment the living individual strives to determine itself as the negation of another; yet this is just as much the determination of itself as the negated of the other—the negator is the negated. Yet this self-negation, this negation of the individual's identity as negator, is not merely a loss of self, it is the process whereby the subject also preserves itself, maintains its self-identity and self-conceptualization, its sameness and its concept of self, its subjectivity. And the subject's other is, thereby, posited as equally negating and objectifying. Self-determination, in other words, is absolute negation, the contradiction of both destroying and preserving the other—not only as a subjective drive, but as the very nature of nature, the essence of life. Life means separation of the living individual from life itself whereby life comes into contradiction with itself. Life's disparity with itself, its difference from the individual, from that with which it is essentially identical, its loss of connection, is necessary for the individual to be alive. In this sense the individual's relation to the other shows itself as pain—for the identity and difference of life and the living individual is the pain of the concept, of birth, of conception itself. The individual has always already been negated (and not negated) by life, thrown out of life and into life; it is "*a*-live" and experiences its relation with that which negated it, but in order to give it life as existence. In fact, the pain of existence is that of contradiction: "one says that contradiction is not thinkable, but the fact is that in the pain of the living being it is even an actual existence."[9] To exist means to be essentially in contradiction with oneself, with others, with the world, with life itself. Each individual must negate the other in order to exist, that is, determine itself as independent—but in this negation, it finds its *existence* is no longer *its* existence; its self-determination and freedom are just as dependent upon the other, and this contradiction shows itself as "the pain of existence," a pain that each individual seeks to supersede and take care of.

With pain then the subject begins its transition to objectivity—for this feeling reconnects the living individual with the world on the level of its existence, according to a visceral ontology. And at this moment, for the individual, the world remains an object, some "thing" to be seized and worked upon (with the necessary violence of an external power), lacking in freedom and subject to the individual's concept: the world works not as cause, but as excitor, instigator of subjective action. For life, however, the individual and the world are alive, living determinations, and their internal relation is itself the life-process that pervades all beings. With the appropriation of the world, the individual begins its own end, initiates the process of its own dissolution—for its independence and freedom show themselves as dependent upon that which it appropriates. The truth of the individual's production lies in its drive to re-production, but reproduction is far more the goal of the species and genus. The individual, therefore, supersedes its particularity, takes care of its singularity, in the universality of the life-process, and posits itself as determined by the concept of its genus.[10]

Third, through the life-process, the living individual finds its own foundation in its genus (*Gattung*), in its identity with other species of living beings. Initially, however, the individual is indifferent to others; it posits itself as the center and totality of the objective world, the locus of the objectivity of all objects. The indifferent individual is certain of itself—but it is not yet true to itself, that is, it has not yet superseded itself and realized that its independence is grounded in interdependence; or more precisely, it has not yet taken care of the contradiction between itself and others. Nevertheless, with the genus, life shows itself as the true concept of the living individual and the life-process. Here life is not only the "subjectivity of the subject," not simply the moving principle of particular individuals and processes—for it is also the "objectivity of the objective" world. In this sense the genus actualizes itself in living races, in their births, reproductions, and deaths, in the destruction and preservation of individuals and individuality. And in the genus the immediacy of the living individual is superseded: individuals (abstractly) die and (concretely) live on—for individual death is the necessary process whereby differentiated and determinate living beings return to their genus, the genus that is essentially their own, that reproduces itself as individuals reproduce themselves. Death takes care of us. And the movement of the genus thereby shows itself not only as particular to it, but as the universal motion of the concept of life itself.[11]

Life then, as the one in multiplicity, means the process whereby individuals are born, reproduce, die, and live on in their genus, in the genus that is itself alive, that lives and dies with its individuals. Here the individual is double: on the one hand, finite as subject to the conditions of the objective world; on the other hand, infinite insofar as the life of the *individual* is the individual of *life*. Yet is the finite individual simply living (or dead)? Or has it not always already suffered a multiplicity of deaths and lives? Before it was born, during its "life" and after its death? Is "life" not a series of "little deaths"? Or the abstract universalization of the lives we lead? And is death not just as multiple? Or rather, is it far more that "life" and "death" are merely two ways of determining the multiplicity of states? Or do we experience a multiplicity of states—of which life and death are a somehow motivated reduction? Or is this not, more radically, itself a result of an abbreviation from a multiplicity yet unthought?

Death and the Other

> Black milk of daybreak we drink you at night / we drink you at noon in the morning we drink you at sundown / we drink and we drink you / a man lives in the house your golden hair Margarete / your ashen hair Shulamith he plays with the serpents // He calls out more sweetly play death death is a master from Germany / he calls out more darkly now stroke your strings then as smoke you will rise into the air / then a grave you will have in the clouds there one lies unconfined.
>
> —*Celan*[12]

For Hegel the secret of life and death is spirit. The secret of spirit, however, is the concept, that is, the contradictory logic through which the secrecy of the secret of life is both kept and told. And the life of spirit is essentially the movement of living and dying. Spirit, however, is never simply the universal idea of life, but always also the concrete living individual. What then does it mean for the individual to live and die? How does the *Logic* of the individual self show itself in the *Phenomenology of Spirit?* And how is this self always in relation to the life and death of an other?

On the one hand, the individual is marked by finitude; its life is a dying, a *meditatio mortis* and preparation for death, a being-toward-death, without return. As Heidegger would have it in *Being and Time:* death can be a perishing (*Verenden*) or a demise (*Ableben*); but *Dasein*'s death is always a dying (*Sterben*), that is, the way of being (*Seinsweise*) in which *Dasein* "is" always in relation to its own, irreplaceable, radically singularly life—no one can die for me, my death always belongs to me, even if you kill me, take my life, I am always the one who dies:

> *No one can take the other's dying away from him.* Of course someone can "go to his death for another." But that always means to sacrifice oneself for the Other "*in some definite affair.*" Such "dying for" can never signify that the Other has thus had his death taken away in even the slightest degree. Dying is something that every Dasein itself must take upon itself at the time. By its very essence, death is in every case mine, in so far as it "is" at all. And indeed death signifies a peculiar possibility-of-Being in which the very Being of one's own Dasein is an issue. In dying, it is shown that mineness and existence are ontologically constitutive for death.[13]

In other words, there are a multiplicity of instances in which another can stand in for me—death, however, is not one of them; rather, it is the "*possibility which is one's ownmost, which is non-relational, and which is not to be outstripped.*"[14] *Dasein* is constituted through its death, its Being-toward-the-end (*Sein zum Ende*); and when it exists, it is thrown into its mortality and finitude, through a possibility of Being that belongs to *Dasein,* that is, the possibility of no longer being-there—for death is the loss (*Verlust*) of its "there" (*Da*). It is impossible to avoid death, and this impossibility is, for *Dasein,* an absolute possibility; or rather, death is the "possibility of the absolute impossibility of Dasein."[15] *Dasein* cannot not die.

And for Hegel as well, the individual must die: our finite existence (*endliche Existenz*) implies a death without return, exchange, or recompense, unidirectionality, abstract negation of life. Yet for a phenomenologic of death, at least three problem areas might arise with the analysis of *Being and Time.* First, Heidegger claims to ground ontic-existentiell facticity in ontological-existential analysis—the latter, however, is far more abstracted out of the former, and then set up as its truth. As the possibility of impossibility, death can only "be" determined as *Dasein*'s Being-toward-the-end, in relation to non-Being, to the undying and undead (and later even Heidegger comes to a similar conclusion; cf. *PLT*). The non-relationality, the death that "be-longs" to *Dasein* is itself always also relational, that is, in relation to *Dasein*'s other ways of being, to others, and to life itself. The analysis of *Dasein* appears tied to a psychology or anthropology of consciousness—for death is neither the end of mechanical or chemical process, nor the *telos* of the genus. Second, Heidegger's emphasis on "life as death" and "death as death" is the one-sided forgetting of "death as life" and "life as life." *Dasein*'s finitude presupposes the concept of simple limit, pure end; but this is just as much the beginning of some other life-process. And *Dasein*'s Being-toward-the-end is just as much its Being-toward-the-beginning—Heidegger's thesis shows its reversibility: life, as the beginning of *Dasein*, is *Dasein*'s way of Being. And if death has been imported into life, then life must also be exported to death. Third, Heidegger cannot think *Dasein*'s death as an end, an indifferent limit, without already presupposing the concept of death as transition. Even if Heidegger thinks the relation of possibility and impossibility (and herein *Dasein*'s death is a contradiction, *sic*, Hegelian to the core), he cannot determine death as end (and *Dasein* as finite) without its other: death is the end (of what?) of life; it is finite only in relation to its other. At its logical conclusion, however, "death as end" is itself an end; the limit is limited: in order to be a limit, death must have a limit. Death can only be a possibility for *Dasein*, if the impossible becomes possible—and this is possible only if death itself is this becoming, that is, the relation of life (as *Dasein*'s Being-toward-the-end) and death. The end is only possible because it is always also a beginning. For Hegel then Heidegger's analysis of *Dasein* would remain superficial, one-sided, without synthesis or concept.

A *Phenomenology* of the individual, on the contrary, allows the end of life to show itself essentially as it is, that is, as the becoming of life. On the one hand, death is a simple end, abstract negativity (*abstrakte Negativität*): violent death awaits those living in a state of nature, a Hobbesian war of all against all, a lawless existence where life follows a logic of kill or be killed, eat or be eaten—pure finitude is always also part of every death. As a godly human, even Jesus must die a "natural death"; as a human God, he dies a human death—and this is not simply the death of Jesus' body, of some empty shell or material vessel (although it is that as well), but the natural, abstract, one-sided ending of life. In fact, Jesus *must* die a human death in order to embody the contradiction of life and death, in order to become the concept of spirit itself—for here, "God himself is dead."[16]

Death then as abstract negation is a daily occurrence: for at every instant cells, plants, humans, individuals, and so on are dying, themselves never to return. Yet if from birth onward death is the individual's destiny, then it is neither because it simply belongs to the definition of a mortal being, nor because time runs out, nor because some kind of motor breaks down—rather, death is inevitable because we are determined only insofar as we are always already torn out of totality, constituted out of universality: the individual's death is the emergence of spirit (*Hervorgehen des Geistes*). And a natural death follows from life's imbalance (between individual and universal): birth constitutes an original illness (*ursprüngliche Krankeit*), implants a germ of death (*Keim des Todes*) in each of us. The restoration of equilibrium is the just execution of our fate—hence, the cock Socrates owes Asclepius, the god of healing, for the cure of death, not only for the release of the soul from corporal constraints, but also for the ad-justment, the paying of a debt. And in this sense, death is universal justice (cf. *Phaedo*). Yet if we can imagine our deaths, or empathize with the other's death on an abstract level, then we become accustomed to the "possibility of the absolutely impossibility" of death; it becomes "something normal" or "nothing special." As life and death are normalized, the particularity of death is reduced to a mere habit (*Gewohnheit*), its universality to a platitude: everyone dies. And this zombie state of everyday death may very well be our forgetting of spirit.[17]

Nevertheless, for Hegel death is abstract, but also determinate negation, that is, supersession of the individual in the universal—for this is the circular economy that takes care of life itself. And the concept of death as abstract/determinate is a contradiction: both a finite death, a negation without return or recognition, a line (or more multiply, a pencil of lines), a pure event; and a transition into another, infinite continuation in the circle of genus and spirit. For the *Logic*, however, contradiction is not simply to be resolved; the speculative response is not merely to chose between sides and fight it out—for that is the logic of war, of blood, a blood logic, or bloody logic, but contradiction is the truth. And if philosophy is unable to think death as contradiction, then it is far more the fault of philosophers. The difficulty of death remains that thought must not forget the concept's two sides: it both is and is not—for only the movement of contradiction, the becoming of their identity and difference, is true. The contradiction of death, if it is to be contradictory itself, must be thought as a movement; the name of this movement is life. In this sense death is alive, a call to life (*Geruch zum Leben*). Life means *one* process (*Ein Prozeß*), the unity of living and dying—this one process, however, this living whole, is only "a" process.[18]

In fact, the whole of life becomes painfully clear in Hegel's *Phenomenology* of death. Here self-consciousness takes the double-form of "Lordship and Bondage"—the twofold doubling, however, is itself many-sided and of many-meanings (*vielseitig, vieldeutig*). For the lord, on the one hand, lordship means risking life (and death) in the struggle for recognition and determinately negating the other; not simply to the point of extermination (*Vernichtung*), but to the point of securing its independence in relation to the bondage of another consciousness, to a bondsman who maintains an immediate relation to a thing, who works in order to produce an object of the lord's desire. The freedom of lordship (and the pure enjoyment of the desired object—the movement of abstract or non-determinate negation, unidirectional destruction of the thing) is possible only in relation to both the other and the thing. And bondage here, on the other hand, means remaining chained to the desire for the object—for the bondsman desires the object just as much as the lord, and interest implies dependence, not freedom. If the lord, however, does not work, but enjoys the fruits of another's labor, then this (supposedly) independent consciousness shows itself as far more dependent, indebted to the bondsman as the source of the desired object.[19]

The thing, however, is not the main object of the life and death struggle; on the contrary, the lord seeks recognition—but this is precisely that which the bondsman cannot supply: "for authentic recognition the moment is lacking, wherein what the lord does to the other he also does to himself, and what the bondsman does to himself he also does to the other."[20] In a one-sided and unequal economy of recognition, the lord will never be satisfied with the bondsman's recognition; and if the testimony of this witness is always in doubt, then self-certainty can never be achieved; truth remains an "ought" to be true. In the fight to become an independent consciousness, the lord remains dependent on the bondsman for both access to the object of desire and (albeit inauthentic) recognition—lordship is the inverse, therefore, of that which it wants and wants to be.

Bondage, too, however, will show itself as the opposite of itself. The (supposedly) dependent consciousness is independent: work transforms the bondsman into the master (*Meister*) and possessor of nature. First, by working on the thing, consciousness becomes independent of desire, trans-cends, stands over and against the object (*Gegen-stand*): serving the lord, the bondsman works through his dependence upon nature, or rather, upon life itself, upon "the multiple self-differentiating expanse, singularity and complexity of life."[21] The bondsman comes to himself, gains a feeling of self, the power to realize projects, the mastery and repression of desire necessary for constructing objects, the ability to delay gratification in order to form things that are not immediately (abstractly) consumed (although that as well), but that also have some independence and self-sufficiency. And if life is multiple, then it is no surprise that the actions of the bondsman on life, his life's work, are multiple themselves, a multiple activity (*vielfache Tun*). Second, confronting the possibility of death at the hands of the lord, the bondsman has faced the inevitability of his own abstract negation—the encounter with the lord is far more the encounter with the Lord. In this existential experience, the bondsman has not simply felt afraid of the lord, of a particular person, thing, position, or force, but has been shaken to his very being and essence. The bondsman's encounter with death makes explicit that which was only implicit, namely, that life itself, the *mysterium tremendum,* is a movement toward death. With the blink of an eye (*Augenblick*)—and just in time, for the time of death is time for death—the bondsman is threatened by dissolution, infected by the absolute fear of death. The bondsman experiences the flux of everything fixed; and in this moment, death becomes the very essence of existence. From then on, death clings to the bondsman—for life is essentially death. The fear of death, the "possibility of the absolute impossibility," becomes the bondsman's own; he takes over his own death from the lord (and the Lord)—and this fear is the "beginning of wisdom."[22]

If the wisdom of bondage, however, begins with the fear of death, then it ends with self-certainty (*Gewißheit seiner selbst*)—yet this certainty is no longer that of the "I" or "ego" of Cartesian consciousness, a pure and immediate intuition of self. On the contrary, for Hegel, the pure instant of the *cogito* forgets that it has a past, a history, a procedure out of which (and through which) it has been constituted (and that it has a future, the possibility of a self-certainty to come that, for the *Phenomenology,* lies in the concept of its relation to that which it is not). In the *Meditations* the process of doubt is the *cogito*'s history. The pure (being and thinking of the) "I"—and this holds against Fichte as well—does not spring full-blown from the head of Zeus; on the contrary, it results from abstraction, condensation, analysis or distillation. Descartes, nevertheless, threatened by madness (in *Med I*), finds his sought-after certainty in an "I" that puts forward or conceives of itself, in the testimony offered by the witness—but at least two sets of questions emerge: Hegel's and Nietzsche's. First, Hegel: How can the "I" determine itself without any other whatsoever? And has it not always already been derived from its relation to the world? Is being not always in relation to nothing? Is the existence/thought of the "I" not always already in relation to a non-"I"? That makes the process of doubt possible in the first place? For is the pure certainty of the "I" not always already compromised? Second, Nietzsche: Why should I believe this witness? Just because Descartes attests to its veracity? Who is this doubter, affirmer, denier, senser, willer? Even further, what is the being, thinking and "I" to which Descartes refers? As Nietzsche writes: "the belief in the immediate certainty of thought is just another belief, and no certainty! We . . . protect ourselves against the [*sic,* Descartes's] dogmatic thoughtlessness of doubt. 'We must doubt better than Descartes!' "[23]

Regardless, even if self-consciousness successfully (abstractly) negates its other, thereby proving that it does not depend upon another for its certainty, for its essence and existence, its multiplicity, then it fails to acquire that which it seeks, the desired recognition of its independence—the death of one is the death of the other. Self-consciousness falls into a dead unity (*tote Einheit*), indifference of difference, pure identity, because it has destroyed that other upon which it depends for its opposition, negation, resistance, for its very self. Contrary to the modern philosophical tradition from Descartes to Kant, the "I" cannot determine itself alone, neither its certainty nor its existence, neither its thinking nor its being; rather, like the freedom and power of self-determination, it needs an other in order to come to itself, to recognize that it thinks and is—and the pure self-posited self-consciousness is always already a result. If the other is dead, self-consciousness can neither affirm nor deny its self-certainty, can neither cede to nor resist the truth of life—for this other would be treated as a mere thing represented in the form of thingness (*Gestalt der Dingheit*).[24]

The self-certainty of bondage then is the mediation of lord and bondsman, self and other. Previously self-consciousness was not itself; it had lost itself and its mind—a kind of madness struck and it was out of itself (*außer sich*), a double-being. Split into two self-consciousnesses, it found itself as an other—this other, however, was only itself. Now, self-consciousness doubly supersedes itself as double: it supersedes its other in order to become that which it essentially is. Self-consciousness doubly returns to itself: it gets itself back and comes to its senses—but if it can return to itself, then it is just as much because another self-consciousness gives self-consciousness back to itself. The gift of self, via recognition, is presented to self-consciousness by another, and it can only accept the gift by letting the other go, letting it be other, freeing it to be the giver of the gift—a forced giving is no giving at all, an unfree giver cannot give. The threefold doubling appears as the simple action of one, lone self-consciousness; in truth, however, the act of one is just as much the act of an other. Through the concept of recognition (*Begriff des Anerkennens*), two self-consciousnesses come into relation with one another (mutual and unequal), a relation that preserves and destroys their identity-with and difference-from each other. Life itself is determined as a double-threat to self-consciousness: the other that is itself and the other that is an other. Becoming certain of itself, however, each self-consciousness must negate the other—for I am, only if the other is not. Each self-consciousness risks its life in order to become that which it essentially is, and to raise its self-certainty to the level of truth. By risking life itself, in a life and death struggle, self-consciousness proves that it is free, independent, self-sufficient, purely for itself (*für sich*).[25]

Indeed, for Hegel the self-certainty of bondage is a function of the history of self-consciousness; and the key to this history is the other—for the certainty of self is the certainty of the other; history means history of an other, history of the other, an other history, "not my-story, but his-story." Initially each self-consciousness seeks the (abstract) negation of the other, the death of that which is (for it) inessential. Situating its self-certainty in itself in order to become master of its own fate, each cannot accept that its being, its freedom and independence, is essentially dependent upon another. The essence of self-consciousness presents itself as the other of self-consciousness. The other, however, is self-consciousness itself; and their relation is one not only of essence (possession, having, genitive, of), but also of being. The action of self-consciousness is to go out of itself, to test its mettle, to become that which it essentially is, namely, the concept of its relation to the other. Self-consciousness sees itself in the other; it sees a pure abstraction (*reine Abstraktion*) of itself over and against itself, and it does not like what it sees—for it sees only a skeleton of itself, a sign of its own death, a presentation of itself as an other.

Hegel is very precise here: in the presentation (*Darstellung*) of the other, "self-consciousness" sees only "consciousness (*Bewußtsein*)"—the self (*Selbst*) of self-consciousness (*Selbst-Bewußtsein*) has already been negated. Presentation is here already representation: self-consciousness shows not itself to itself, but a non-self, a consciousness without reflection, a uni-directional projection. Consciousness is what self-consciousness makes it—and it is no wonder that here truth remains merely one-sided, the dissatisfaction of subjective self-certainty. That which should be presented (namely, that which self-consciousness is) is left out of the presentation. The other then is the pure non-presentation of non-self-consciousness. As the product of self-consciousness, the other is no other at all; or rather, it is an other that is both other and not-other.[26]

The wisdom of bondage then, as the transformation of fear into knowledge, as life qua movement toward death, has its history in the conceptual relation of self-consciousness to the other. For Hegel the self-certainty of the bondsman is only possible in relation to the lord as other; and it is for this reason that the *fear* of the Lord (*Furcht des Herrn*) is just as much the fear of the *Lord*. By letting the other go free, letting it be purely/non-purely other, immediately and mediately other, the bondsman learns that fear belongs just as much to bondage as to lordship—fear is the essence of their relation; fear is the concept of our relation to the other. Yet what is this other that consciousness fears? What is it in the bondsman that terrifies the lord and the Lord? What makes us panic upon seeing the other in ourselves? And what is the horror of the other as other?

Hegel writes: "the other is multiple (entangled and existent) consciousness"—and this is what we fear.[27] The multiplicity of the other is that which terrifies self-consciousness; the multiplicity of the bondsman is what horrifies the lord. The fear of one, however, is the fear of the *other* (and the *fear* of the other). The fear of death shows itself to be essentially fear of the other—and the other is essentially multiple. Yet first, what is the multiplicity of the other? And second, what is therein to fear?

(1) For Hegel the other of self-consciousness is multiple in two ways: in its existence (in itself) and in its relations (with and for another), in its entanglements and its being, in its being entangled and entangled being. First, consciousness is multiply entangled because its entanglement (*Befangenheit*) itself is multiple: the other is caught in a web of interests, tied up and sutured into a network of prejudices and biases; and as interested it presents itself as bashful, diffident, awkward, and so on. Second, consciousness is multiple since being (*Sein*) is itself multiple: pure being is abstracted from the multiplicity of ways in which the other is, and its ways of being (*Seiendheit*) are abstracted from its entanglements. If the other "is" multiply and is multiply "entangled," however, then it is because it is a twofold multiplicity (its existence and essence, that it is and how it is), is itself twofold: consciousness is entangled with itself, with its interests, prejudices, embarrassments, and it is entangled with those of self-consciousness. The other's multiplicity is re-doubled, but the doubling of the double only serves to represent its multiplicity as non-multiple, as double. Consciousness is not self-consciousness because it does not reflect upon its own multiplicity, upon that which allows it to be and be that which it is; it does not understand what its multiplicity means (or how to think, be, struggle, risk, multiply)—the other does not know what it means to be other. In other words, multiplicity lies at the core of Hegel's concept of the other; its true essence and existence are themselves multiple—but it is a multiplicity that is always as non-multiple as it is multiple.

The multiplicity of the other then re-emerges in the form of the bondsman. Here death binds itself to the bondsman and thereby frees consciousness for life. In fearing the Lord, the bondsman need no longer fear the lord—for the latter cannot take from the bondsman that which the former has given. The life and death of the bondsman always belong to him. Even if the lord kills the bondsman, his death remains his own. The essence (*Wesen*) of life is death, and consciousness has taken this truth (this negativity), upon itself (*an ihr selbst*). The bondsman knows death in a way that the lord does not, that is, as twofold: the possibility of abstract and determinate negation. And he knows life as the lord cannot, namely, as the contradiction of both in the concept of life. On the one hand, the bondsman knows that his life is a living/dying, a continual abstract negation without return that is essentially its own; but on the other hand, he also knows that life (as the contradiction of life and death) supersedes his own living/dying. And the bondsman knows this double-truth because he experiences the possibility of the absolutely impossible, because (staking his life in the life-and-death struggle) he shows himself to himself as himself—he becomes that which he essentially is and he is essentially this becoming. That which the bondsman risks, however, as the lord's other, is not simply its life or existence; on the contrary, insofar as existence is always already abstracted from the multiple ways of being entangled or interested, the bondsman risks the very multiplicity that characterizes existence and essence. The multiplicity of the multiplicities (of the bondsman's entanglements and ways of existing) are at risk—and if the bondsman knows the possibility of death, then it is because he knows the multiplicity of life. The bondsman's wisdom is no longer merely that of consciousness, but of self-consciousness, of the multiplicity that is our own.

(2) The second question now: What is to fear in multiplicity? For Hegel, fear enters into the relation of self-consciousness and the multiple other when consciousness is presented in the form of "Lordship and Bondage." Here the bondsman and the lord, as others of each other, are multiple (entangled and existent) self-consciousnesses. The fear of the multiple other then is not simple of the *other,* of the multiplicity that is the other—for this other consciousness is only purely other for a moment, and then it is impurely other, that is, bondsman and lord are dependent/independent of/upon one another; rather, the "fear of the multiplicity of the other" is a "fear of a multiplicity that is just as much one's own." And if multiplicity is terrifying, then it is because it multiplies the very logic of self and other, lord and bondsman, to the point where they themselves become that which is to be feared; or more specifically, to the point where their multiplicity becomes multiple, a multiple multiplicity. The fear of the multiple other is the fear of multiplicity itself.

For Hegel, however, multiplicity always shows itself in a double (non-multiple) representation, always determines itself in a twofold representation. In the *Phenomenology* the historicity of the concept, the life of the idea, is presented in two (and only two) figures of lord and bondsman, in self-consciousness as split into itself and its other, in the two ways to die (abstractly or determinately). And in the *Logic* the idea of life is that of absolute contradiction, originally divided (*ur-teilen*) into life or death, the living or dying, soul or body (or some combination of the two) of the individual within the life-process and its continuation in its genus, the concept of life itself. In both cases, the life of life, that which is alive in life, is essentially twofold. The multiplicity of life (of the other and bondsman), is no multiplicity at all; or more specifically, its multiplicity is presented and represented within non-multiplicity, with a double concept that is itself multiple and non-multiple.

The wisdom of bondage, however, confronting the multiplicity of life, demands a more multiple logic and a more multiple phenomenology. Logically the absolute contradiction of life can be solved (and/or not) in the concept of the "one in multiplicity"; it can be destroyed and/or preserved—but simultaneously questions arise: What remains of multiplicity if it is conceived as contradiction? What is multiple about the two-sided concept? Why this solution and not another? Is it not possible to think the multiplicity of life as multiple? The processes of life and death can be resolved by superseding them in one process, taking care of them in the wholeness of life—but this implies its own supersession: Hegel's terminology implies that a *totality* is always only *a* totality. As processes, life becomes no longer simply the pain of living or the pleasure of dying; on the contrary, pleasure and pain, life and death, are unable to account for the multiplicity of living and dying, pleasure and pain, themselves. More questions arise: How can the multiplicity of life and death, of lives in process, be thought? What happens to the priority of death, as *Dasein*'s possibility of absolute impossibility, if death is far more deaths? If my finitude is not simply my ownmost, but is always only possible in relation to an other or others, that is, if my death is an event for a multiplicity of others as a multiple event? And not merely for me or them, not for individuals, but for a multiplicity of beings? Or if death has always already happened? If I am always in the process of dying a series of small deaths (*les petites morts*)? And if my death does not end my life, that is, if I continue to live in others, in the genus, work, memory, mourning, or a multiplicity of other ways? Or if living and dying are far more activities, ways of becoming, irreducible to being or not-being here or there?

Indeed, if life and death became multiple, and their multiplicity became multiple as well, then (even for phenomenologic) the life of the individual would become multiple, a multiplicity of consciousnesses and consciousness as multiple. And the other would mean far more others, an other that is always also multiple—and not just. What does it mean for the individual to determine itself not simply in relation to an other, but to the other as others and the others as others? What becomes of the self-other couple, the identity and difference of their essences and existences?

And of the double-logic on account of which (self-)certainty determines itself, the *dia-logic* through which consciousness (as two-sided) negates the other (as two-sided)? For when the multiplicity of the other is re-presented in the *Gestalt* of the bondsman, when it is reduced, abstracted, distilled as the lord's servant, then it negates its own multiplicity in order to act, contracts the multiplicity of work into a work. As Hegel himself insists, "this multiple activity has now contracted into the simple positing of differences."[28] Here a logic of identity and difference is abstracted from the multiple logics of action—and it calls itself "truth." Yet what if action, if the whole world of work, were itself to become multiple? Or rather, to show itself as always already multiple? Would each activity of consciousness not become activities? And would truth not become truths? In other words, would the introduction of multiplicity into the economy of truth not break down the logic of identity and difference? And in a situation where it appears necessary to function according to the logic of self and other, true and false, yes and no, guilt and innocence, right and wrong, is the most necessary of necessities not to function? When thought seems like the most impractical of practices, is it not the most practical to practice neither theory nor practice? When the demand to simply act or not to act becomes most critical, is the most demanded of demands not to neither to act nor to not act, but rather to multiply the simplicity of demand itself? And to multiply this multiplicity? And not just?

If so, then it is no surprise that the question of multiplicity asserts itself in Hegel's presentation of the multiple other and self, the bondsman and lord, death and life—for the double-*Logic* of life and death, on the one hand, always only abstracts from the multiplicity of living and dying (while calling itself "true" under the sign of self and other, lordship and bondage), and the secret of life itself lies unexamined. And on the other hand, the *Phenomenology* always only presents work, action and truth as twofold, and the multiplicity of the other lies unthought. Indeed, contradiction is painful because it contradicts multiplicity, or rather, because it contracts multiplicity under a double-sign, a two-sided concept, life/death, self/other, like all the philosophemes of western philosophy, because it articulates them according to the logic of identity and difference of identity and difference, or presents them as the contradiction and non-contradiction of contradiction and non-contradiction. Multiplicity, therefore, does not contradict Hegel—for that would remain simply conceptual; rather, it multiplies phenomeno-logic to the point where the double-concept (of life) shows itself as itself: non-abstraction is itself secretly abstract. The questions then that need to be asked no longer concern just life and death, self and other, but multiplicity, the multiplicity of multiplicities, and not just—for it is becoming "manys."

The Will to Truth

As the concept of the concept, the idea has shown itself as the objectivity of the object, as a living being, the life-process, and the genus. Here life is the expression of the idea, its becoming real, actual, objective. Yet life is also the life of the subject; or more precisely, it is the subjectivity of the subject, that which "has" the idea of itself—and finds, as well, that the idea "has" it. The objectivity of life was determinate for a "way of being"; now, life's subjectivity follows a "way of having," of having not merely thoughts, but knowledge—for this is the promise of philosophy (i.e., to provide true knowledge). And the idea is not only the idea of life; it is also the knowledge that it is life, the idea of cognizing (*Idee des Erkennens*) that expresses itself as an analytic-synthetic judgment of truth, and a will that wants to know this truth.

For critical idealism and the metaphysics of the soul, however, knowledge is the process of subsuming experience under a concept (or concepts) that is itself transcendentally pure and independent of experience. Here a pure subject is deduced or abstracted from experience as the condition of the possibility of experience. Yet insofar as I must make use of the "I" in order to judge myself, I cannot have an unmediated thought, knowledge, intuition, or concept of myself—the circular problem of self-consciousness is a critical difference between Hegel and Kant:

> a relationship through which, in immediate empirical self-consciousness, the absolute, eternal nature of self-consciousness and the concept manifests itself, and manifests itself for this reason, that self-consciousness is just the *existent* pure *concept,* and therefore *empirically perceptible,* the absolute relation-to-itself that, as a separating judgment, makes itself its own object and is solely this process whereby it makes itself a circle. A stone does not have this *inconvenience;* when it is to be thought or judged it does not stand in its own way; it is relieved from the burden of making use of itself for this task; it is another, outside of it, that must take the trouble.[29]

In other words, for Hegel self-consciousness (and its "way of thinking") is essentially circular. In truth, the concept of the concept can never be simply conceptual, never a mere immediate intuition of simple natures (cf. Descartes, *Regulae* XII) or the idea—the concept stands in its own way, just as we block ourselves from ourselves; and we must separate ourselves from ourselves in order to be and know ourselves as ourselves. In fact, the "I" that thinks anything, itself or its object, stands in its own way and must follow a detour, *dérive,* or trip—and it can follow this way because it is already a result of the way, of self-transcendence and return, of having gone over into its other and circling back to itself. If the "I," however, only thinks itself, then it never "knows," never arrives at knowledge of the object as it is in itself, never fulfills the promise of philosophy: thought remains subjective, but knowledge (taking the inconvenient way (*Gang*) of the "I think" to its logical conclusion, becoming conceptual) knows the identity and difference of the identity and difference of subjectivity and objectivity.

Knowledge then, not merely thought, is the subject of the history of the concrete sciences of spirit: (1) in the "science of natural spirit," psychology and anthropology interrogate the empirical self in order to ascertain "where it resides," and thereby to differentiate humans from animals, while procuring for the former the status of "rational animal"; but this means that subjectivity must be located in the pineal gland or atom, or today by neuro-physiology via PET scans somewhere in the cerebral cortex—and spirit sinks into materialism; (2) in the *Phenomenology of Spirit,* wherein spirit is no longer a mere object because it reflects back to itself, negates the immediacy of its being as object and becomes an object for itself as subject, as the consciousness that returns to itself as self-conscious, as the self-certain "I" (I negate, therefore, I am)—yet here, self-consciousness, as pure relation-to-self, takes itself for the truth of everything and posits its subjective certainty as objective while forgetting that its relation to self depends upon another, upon the other that no longer stands over and against consciousness; (3) in the "science of spirit as such [*als solche*]," wherein feelings, representations, and thoughts, in fact, the entire multiplicity of spiritual determinations. are taken as spirit's own—yet here spirit is only finite and completed, the totality of its moments as immediately given, and the other of spirit is forgotten; (4) in the *Science of Logic,* which has the idea of spirit itself for its object as the "last" science, the final supersession that takes care of all other material and formal sciences (not as merely the study of form, not the abstract negation of matter, *Stoff,* nature, etc.), and the "first" science insofar as it is from logic that the others result as abstractions—here the idea of spirit finally becomes both subjective and objective: subjective because (like the "I") it has not yet realized itself as absolute, although its object is the idea of the true and it seeks the identity and difference of concept and reality, although it takes reality as immediately given according to so-called conceptual determinations and finds in its object only that which it puts into it; and objective because it is concretely real and comes to know itself as the truth of the objective world.

A system of science then, for Hegel, is possible through the inconvenient circle by which consciousness comes to know itself. The truth of consciousness's circling, however, is just as much the way of the idea: "*thought, spirit, self-consciousness,* are determinations of the idea insofar as it has itself as its object; and its *determinate-being*, i.e., the determination of its being, is its own difference from itself."[30] In this way the self-differentiated idea is (1) the objectivity of the object (as a genus) and (2) the subjectivity of the subject (I think); and their relation is not simply one of feeling or thought, but of knowledge and cognition (*Erkennen*)—this is the idea's "way of truth," its going out of itself, destroying itself, going under, in seeking itself, its identity and reality in its difference. And it is because the idea shows itself as a subjective determinate concept of itself that it can give reality to the objective world, to the immediate appearance and experience of being.

The circular way of the idea, therefore, from itself and to itself, to the concept of itself, shows itself as a subjective drive (*Trieb*): standing in its own way, the idea is driven to a contradictory relation with its object. Knowledge (and any relation whatsoever, e.g., those of intuition, imagination, representation, etc.) of the object is supposed to be knowledge of another, of the difference between subject and object; but it remains merely knowledge of itself, solipsistic self-satisfaction. Synthetic knowledge a priori is possible because the object is never an objective world in itself; rather, it is always only for the subject, subjective objectivity. If, in the object, the subject sees only itself, that which it puts into the world, then it is because it remains true to itself, self-identical, self-identifying. And the truth of the subjective concept is as indifferent to the object as it is in itself—its value is inconsequential. The drive to knowledge, however, to the determination of the object in cognition, must far more look for the object's self-determination—for only in relation to another, can the subject be itself, determine its subjectivity, approach its concept of subjectivity and the concept of the concept. The idea then drives toward objective truth, theoretical correspondence, the congruence of the concept with reality as it is in itself—not only as it is for me, or for the subjective idea: the drive for truth becomes the drive *of* truth (*Trieb der Wahrheit*).[31]

Here Kant and Hegel part company: the former maintains the thing in itself as the limit of subjective philosophy; the latter drives further, to objective truth as the realization of the concept, relation with the "real thing," with actuality. For Kant the subjective idea, the form of the thing (space and time as forms of intuition, the categories, etc.), is always the subject's own (*das seinige*). The "negation" of the world and the thing in itself must be presupposed in order for metaphysics to be raised to the status of a science. The truth expressed in subjective conceptual judgments, however, in a neutral synthesis of concept and thing as appearance, a simple identity of subject and object, is not the unifying truth of speculative thought—and all attempts to formalize thought into a machinelike trinity of thesis/antithesis/synthesis show themselves as superficial and unphilosophical. The *Logic,* therefore, thinks not simply the formal/instrumental reason of technological progress, not only the external synthesis of indifferent concepts and objects, but also their internal/conceptual connection.

Still, initially, the subjective idea posits its object as foundational for knowledge. Kant's object must be given in appearance in order for it to be possible in experience; the manifold must present the matter of intuition to our forms of intuition (*CPR,* A 19). This kind of knowledge finds its limit in the subject: the task of the critical police of pure reason is to trace out the horizon of the subjective idea as the fate of human reason, "burdened by the questions transcending all its powers."[32] In this sense Kant is the thinker of human finitude (*Endlichkeit*)—for only then are a priori synthetic judgments possible.

For Hegel, however, Kant's truth, in truth, has not yet come to truth (*noch nicht zur Wahrheit gekommen*). The subjective idea runs up against two contradictions: first, the finitude of the subject, posited as the horizon of knowledge, is the limit of philosophical reflection on the world; the subject, however, cannot be the criterion of knowledge of the object—a Copernican revolution in reverse—rather, the object must be that which is known insofar as it shows itself as itself; second, intuition of that which is given, of an indeterminate immediacy, the manifold, abstract, pure being, so that we can determine it as an object, is supposed to be found by us—but the "givenness" of the given is already a determination, and the indeterminate is far more determined.[33]

Actual cognition, however, can be satisfied with neither an application of subjective concepts to subjective objects nor superficial intuition of mere appearances; rather, it must become the reception and apprehension of the object as given. Kant's problem of the thing in itself drops away: the thing is the object, and knowledge is true knowledge. Synthetic judgments a priori and metaphysics as a science are possible only if we come to know the world as it is. Two kinds of knowledge (analytic and synthetic), therefore, are possible as movements from the "actually unknown" to the "actually known," or more specifically, the relation of both, the concept of the unknown and the known.

First, analytic cognition (*analytische Erkennen*) follows the principle of identity: the connection of concept and object is the bringing together of that which is already together. Difference is excluded, and the other is no other at all. Analytic knowledge, however, is a conceptual (not simply representational) determination. As the development of that which is already in the object, analysis permits the object to be known conceptually—for this is not yet the concept of itself, but conceptual knowledge of another. Analysis, however, is not the simple extraction or dissection of that which was never put into the object; on the contrary, that which presents itself (or is posited as the object of analysis) is far more a finished product determined as immediate, as prior to subjective mediation—analysis is only possible on the basis of an always already completed synthesis. If knowledge is analytic, then it knows that which has been synthesized—for knowing is the immanent movement of given differences, of found conceptual determinations. And if knowledge is a mere mechanical operation, a putting together of indifferent units, an external connection of things into a trivial identity, a superficial reduction of qualitatively unequal objects to equal quantities, then it is not knowledge, but the simple task (*Aufgabe*) of expressing a tautology, the thoughtless act of a computational machine, the doing of that which must to be done. With a non-thinking machine, however, the very advantage of analytic knowledge is lost, namely, the construction is immediately derived from the task and understood (in and for itself) as construction, but the analytic construction is a construction of constructions; its concepts are determined before its determination. Analysis extends knowledge, and extension is a differentiated determination of thought. Analytic knowledge, in other words, is the immediate identity of concept and object that extends thought to grasp (*Auffassen*) that which is.[34]

Synthetic cognition, however, second, seeks to conceptualize (*Begreifen*) the object's different determinations (as well as the knower's own difference from that which is known) in a necessary unity. And the difference between analytic and synthetic is that between abstract identity and relation, between being and reflection. The relation of concept and object, however, remains external: "the sun warms the stone" is a necessary determination of an object—but only as an appearance for me, a subject.[35] Synthetic knowledge then can be a definition, a division, or a theorem.

In definition (*Definition*) an individual is identified or classed under a (universal) genus and a (specifically different) species; it is the descriptive representation of individuality as universality—"but definition reduces [the] wealth of the multiple determinations of the observed determinate-being to a simple moment."[36] Knowledge here, as the recognition of subjective concepts in the object, is doubly arbitrary: first, with respect to content, that is, the object submits to a subjective definition; second, with respect to form, that is, a characteristic is pulled out from the multiplicity of qualities and set up as determinative. Yet if the essence of a being is derived from experience or statistical calculation, then its necessity is unnecessary, an only probable, wishful, promised, habitual, or regulative necessity—as if the earlobe and brain could mark the physical essence of human beings; or as if the earlobless and acephalic, the deformed and deviant, would signify the inhuman. Indeed, the truth of definition cannot simply lie in its immediate identification of a being, but in its ability to differentiate beings.[37]

Yet that through which definition determines (both itself and its object) in the first place is not a definition, but a division (*Einteilung*)—for a universal genus must show itself as applicable to particular species, and the species must be capable of submitting to genera. In general, the movement from universal to particular is that of the system of science, of natural science, the *Science of Logic* and systematic (although not yet speculative) thought: definition becomes individual, and a multiplicity of definitions belong to the multiplicity of objects. As systematic, therefore, scientific knowledge recognizes the "belonging-togetherness" of the object and its multiplicity, and the "caring relation" of objects and their definitions. Systematic thought, however, is not the (natural) intuition of objects in themselves. Scientific knowledge begins by positing simple, abstract determinations (being, nothing, etc.) and develops into concrete relations of multiple determinations: as the simplest, the universal is first in the order of science; and it seeks to know the complexity of concrete reality as last—but this is a scientific "bad infinity." Speculative thought, on the contrary, begins with the end, with concrete multiplicity, and allows it to show itself as itself. Initially tools of scientific systematicity, instrumental reason and technological progress, both definition and division are the "business" of knowledge (*Geschäft des Erkennens*); they are driven by a "will to comparison": division demands that the discovered material (individuals) fall into particular species, and it seeks therein the universal determinations of a genus (that can then serve as the ground for the multiplication of species). Here science is not guided by reflection: if a new species is found or exterminated, then the genus is altered; if a new individual is discovered, then the species is expanded—and the hermaphrodite exposes the arbitrariness of division. In fact, the conceptless drive to know can never think speculatively. Division can only separate species from one another.[38]

The work of connecting living beings then, individual animals, of unifying nature and life, is left to the theorem (*Lehrsatz*). Whereas definition only contained a universal determination of the individual, and division only its particular difference from others, the theorem is the concept of the object, and the idea of the individual—but not yet the idea itself, that is, the concept of the concept. The theorem is the actual synthesis of the object, the necessary relations of its real determinations in identity and difference with its concept (and the concept of both). As such, the theorem is in need of proof—for otherwise, it remains a mere subjective claim, an assertion of self-evidence that remains contingent upon the one who asserts it, a one-sided testimony that remains bound to the witness who gives it certainty.[39] The theorem, therefore, is two-sided, the relation of the real determinations of the concept, the conception and expression of the whole content of the object, of universality and particularity in the individual.[40]

The Pythagorean theorem, for example, is the definition of the concept of the triangle; its determinations (axioms) alone, however, are only results abstracted from the theorem and related in an external way. The proof is the mediation and interconnection (synthesis) of the theorem's axioms—although for those unaware of its goal, it appears as mere artifice, a meaningless construction—it shows the necessity of its (albeit subjective) synthesis. Still, geometrical proofs are inappropriate for speculative philosophy: as a science of magnitude, geometry's synthesis is merely formal, quantitative, (apparently) abstracted from quality; and its object (i.e., spatial determinations of mathematical objects) is a conceptless unity, already pre-produced for its ends. Geometry is the sublime science of empty spaces, the beautiful dissection of bloodless bodies and colorless corpses, the silencing of all other interests. If philosophy follows the example of the pure science of geometry, seeks to attain the lifeless certainty of mathematics, then it remains an important activity of intuition, but not of knowing; a question for an unsensing sensibility, a finite science that dogmatically fixes a body of theorems and logical laws, and then holds up its unchanging and immobile truth, as the truth—in this gesture, however, it assures its death as tautology. For Hegel the proof of the philosophical theorem supersedes the necessity of the mathematical model—for its movement is also infinite, an infinite becoming. The concept of the theorem is necessary, but insofar as it is not yet (also) free, it is not yet the idea: synthetic and analytic knowing cannot yet know the concept of the concept.[41]

Taken together then, analytic and synthetic cognition provide a method for knowing life. Here the idea of the true (*Idee des Wahren*) is the idea of life; or, the object of knowledge (and the objectivity of the object) is the knowing subject (and the subjectivity of the subject), and they show themselves as the identity and difference of their identities and differences. The *Science of Logic,* however, is not yet truly speculative—the true idea is not yet the truth (*Wahrheit*)—for it has not yet become self-conscious, not yet come to know its own role in knowing.

In other words, with the idea of the true, philosophy stands in the way of itself. And scientific method is not enough to provide speculative knowledge; on the contrary, something completely different is needed, namely, the desire to know. Left unproved, a theorem's necessity is no necessity at all; rather, the "will" to necessity must also characterize the *Logic*. And the subject must want to know the truth of the object, if knowledge is to be possible (or actual) at all. Between the idea of necessary and true knowledge and the absolute idea stands the will to truth, and the idea of wanting (*Wollen*) itself—for the will to *truth* is just as much a *will* to truth.[42]

Indeed, the idea has shown its conceptual necessity in the theorem's philosophical synthesis, but its necessity has not yet become its freedom—and if freedom is that which the concept lacks, in all its necessity, then it is no wonder that knowing must "drive" through necessary knowledge in order to know itself. The act of knowing, the drive and will to truth, must find itself outside of itself—for the drive is always a drive toward a goal: "thinking" is always a "doing"; theoretical philosophy is always practical philosophy. In other words, the subjective idea is itself an action, and theory is a practice; and for this reason, the *Logic* turns from the idea of the true to that of the good (*Idee des Guten*).

Previously, as knowledge, the idea stood over and against its object (as an insurmountable other); as practice, however, it is no longer merely subjective—it becomes objective. The act of thinking is no longer simply ideal—for as an act, it is just as real. As good, the idea loses its superficial ideality and becomes immediately real. The practice of knowing concretely, therefore, demanded by the concept in order to determine itself as real, is for the good: every action tries to be well done; every thought, well thought. If the deed is good in itself, however, then it seeks to be universalizable, objectively good (although the drive to do good remains subjective, an immediate idea of the will, self-determination of that which is good). The idea of the good is here limited by objective reality, and it is finite; that is, its achievement is its end, its realization is its death. If theory is identical to practice, then (like means and ends) its destiny is finitude; if knowing is doing, then the concept of the good does not need to realize itself in order to become objective—for it is always already true. And the realized good is doubly limited: (1) insofar as goods are multiple, the achievement of one is the refusal of the others, of other goods for other subjects; (2) insofar as each good determines itself in relation to evil, well done is opposed to poorly done.

The realization of the good itself then, the universal good, the good that is not merely subjective and finite, remains a "should be good"—for although I "may" act according to the categorical imperative so that the maxim of my will "could be" valid, always and everywhere, as a principle of universal legislation, it never "is" so. Kant's practical idea of the good lacks an understanding of itself, that is, the reflexivity of self-consciousness that would show its theoretical moment to it: that which is good in the good act is the good itself, the theoretical idea of the good. The good act is never alone; rather, it implies its other and essence, the good, in order to be that which it is. The practical good takes the idea of the good as nothing. And practice, failing to realize its relation to theory, forgetting that it is always also theoretical, cannot even be practical. The means/ends economy of goods is a retreat to bad infinity, to a good act that can never be accomplished, to a deed that can never be determined as having been done—this logic is the forgetting and disappearance of both goods and the good, of their identity and difference. The objective concept of the practical idea is constricted by its own perspective, its own will to be practical. Only by reflecting on its own pragmatism can it practice its theory. And if the individual pragmatic act cannot be universalized, then it cannot be realized; its theory remains a subjective directive.[43]

If the drive to the idea of the good, however, is not to be simply repeated, but superseded; it must become the absolute idea, the concept of the good truth and the truth of the good. Here the individual subject (with all its means and ends, theories and practices) is no longer merely subjective and individual; rather, it becomes objective and universal as well. The idea of the true (epistemology) and the good (ethics) are united and realized in the practical idea and the objective world shows its inner ground—for it is essentially the absolute idea.

With the "idea of cognition," Hegel has once again broken with a formal, trinitarian *Logic*—for this moment has only two moments: the idea of the true and the idea of the good (or in the *Encyclopedia,* cognizing and wanting). The difference of theory and practice is the identity of cognition: knowing is truly wanting and wanting the truth, and there is no third. And the absolute idea will be reduced to a single moment, itself, the concept of itself, the concept of the concept. The moment of the supersession of all differences is approaching. The *Logic* is drawing to a close. Hegel is taking care of everything. The end is here, and multiplicity seems to be nowhere.

The End of Multiplicity

With the absolute idea, multiplicity appears to have come to an end; it is nowhere to be found and nothing at all. The theoretical and practical ideas have been synthesized; life and cognition have been totalized; subject and object have been united. First, the absolute idea shows itself as *an* idea, that is, as the idea of the concept, and the concept of the idea

(*Begriff der Idee*). Second, this concept is essentially, however, the concept of the concept; it reflects on itself as itself. Yet third, the idea becomes the idea of the idea; it is the idea of itself, and the idea of this idea, the idea that thinks itself (*sich selbst denkende Idee*); its idea is its own (*seine eigene*)—and "all else is error, confusion, opinion, striving, caprice and transitoriness."[44] If the idea's complete totality (*vollendete Totalität*) is its own, then it can be considered absolute, and it must be thought in a system of totality (*System der Totalität*).

At the end of the *Logic* then a series of questions opens up: What does Hegel mean with the end? In what way has the end of logic been reached? How can the end be thought? To what extent is the end multiple? And what is the multiplicity of this multiplicity? What here is multiple? For better or for worse, however, this series of questions cannot simply be addressed serially; rather, insofar as the "what," the "way," the "how," and the "extent" of philosophy are co-constitutive, they must also be answered simultaneously: the answer to one determines the range of possible responses to the others—or more precisely, they must be addressed neither synchronically nor diachronically, but multi-chronically, even multi-dimensionally, and not just.

First then, the end is the end of the *Logic*. The end of a book is a historical event: the last word of Hegel's text (i.e., *findet*) happens, and the *Science of Logic* is purely finite. Here the end is immediately given and present to anyone who witnesses it—and "no one witnesses for the witness."[45] Second, however, in order for the end to happen, for the event to be an event, for it to be read as an objective happening, for being to be given, the reader must already have the ability to receive it, to think it; that is, thought must be able to represent the event even before it happens. Here representation precedes presentation as its condition of possibility. The representation of the end, however, does not simply imply that the event of the end depends upon a subject or reader; on the contrary, it means that the end itself, the happening of the last word, is itself always already a representation. The real shows itself as that which it should not be: the end is supposed to happen, the book is supposed to come to a real end, but the end is the very opposite of itself, the negation of the real. The original end is no longer original; every presentation is a representation, and there is always a witness for the witness, namely, the witness—or even further, there are only witnesses. Yet third, if the immediate and real end is essentially a representation, then as such, it is a presentation. And representation, the negation of the real, is itself negated. For Hegel, however, the truth of presentation and representation lies in their relation (from which they can be abstracted), in the concept of the end.[46]

As a concept then, the absolute idea is both a presentation and a representation; it both presents a representation and represents the presence (of itself). The end of the *Logic,* however, is the beginning. Hegel writes: "the absolute idea alone is *being.*"[47] Here the "Doctrine of the Concept" circles back to the very first moment of the "Doctrine of Being"—but the absolute idea is no longer simply an "indeterminate immediacy." On the one hand, the difference between being and the absolute idea shows itself as the developmental history of logical moments (or as a gallery of images at the end of the experience of consciousness' education): if *Logic* can put the infinite progress of science and history to an end, then it is because the absolute idea supersedes and takes care of all previous moments by both destroying and preserving them. On the other hand, the absolute idea is that from which being was abstracted, that source, origin or *logos* (and truth) from which the *Science of Logic* began. The end, therefore, is a double-end and the beginning, a double-beginning—for the concept moves in a circle (although not just), and the dialectic is a circle of circles (*Kreis von Kreisen*). In this sense, the *Logic* both ends and does not end: (1) as finite, the absolute idea supersedes all previous moments, contains and takes care of an infinity of determinations within itself; (2) as infinite, however, the absolute idea is that which continues to make possible, to allow and permit, life to appear as new, show and reveal itself, by opening itself to its other, taking care of its future, by freeing itself from itself, superseding even its own totality and infinity.[48]

When defining the absolute idea, however, Hegel does not stop with being; on the contrary: "the absolute idea alone is *being,* imperishable *life, self-knowing truth* and is *all truth.*"[49] Here the absolute idea is multiple: it is being, life, truth, and all truth—and these are not simply identical, not merely to be equated with each other or reduced to each other. The absolute idea, however, is not only multiple—for it also "has" a multiplicity of predicates (as it has a variety of ways to express itself in logic, nature, art, religion, natural science), but even more important, because in a speculative sentence "is" no longer means "being" or "essence"—but "concept," the "concept of the concept." And "to be" means "to conceive." In this moment all the relations between the idea and being, life and truth, show themselves as conceptual. The *Logic* then ends with the conceptual multiplicity of the absolute idea, a multiplicity (which as merely double) is no multiplicity at all; or rather, is both multiple and non-multiple.

10

Metaphysics of Multiplicity

Identity and Difference

> *Earl of Kent:* Come, sir, arise away! I'll teach you differences: away, away! If you will measure your lubber's length again, tarry; but away! Go to; have you wisdom? so.
>
> —*Shakespeare*[1]

Now, after the beginning and end of the *Science of Logic*, it is possible to go back (or forward) to its core, to its essence. Being and the absolute idea *is* the same—for their relation is conceptual. The concept means identity and difference of identity and difference. But what do we mean with identity? And with difference? And with the relation of both? What is their logic and discourse? To what extent do they serve as the limit of a certain somehow motivated philosophy of identity and difference (so popular today)? And how do they seek to think multiplicity as double, that is, by denying, refusing, repressing, forgetting, or remembering, in a certain way, to take care of multiplicity as multiple? How do they make it possible to think multiplicity as multiple and non-multiple by never thinking multiply? And to what extent are they the touchstones of the metaphysics of multiplicity? Not the way out, but the way in to metaphysics itself?

For Heidegger, for example, multiplicity must be thought within the history of metaphysics (in the language of onto-theology) according to the ontological difference between Being and beings. In response, thought attempts to hear the difference between that which is the same (*Selbe*) and that which is identical (*Gleiche*), the harmony (*Ein-klang*) in the unity (*Ein-heit*) that is not simply identity, to hear the event or happening of difference when listening into the essence of identity. In order to hear (*vernehmen*) the language of identity, thought questions or interrogates (*vernehmen*) the way in which identity is determined by difference, but also mis-takes (*ver-nehmen*) that which has been taken for already resolved—for the re-solution of the problem of identity and difference is no solution at all. The ontological difference's irresistibility, the movement of its resolution, dissolution, and reposition, is the essence of metaphysics itself. And if metaphysics always reposes the *same* question, the identical problem differently, then it is because it has already (reflexively or not) adopted the discourse of identity and difference.

Indeed, for Heidegger identity marks the philosophy of difference, and the Hegelian logic of being and non-being (as the fate of the history of western metaphysics) completes a certain return to its origin in Parmenides, to a specific set of presuppositions: difference is branded upon identity. Between identity and difference, a circular reciprocity appears, an intimate relation of belonging, complimentarity, or interfacing. Identification is differentiation, and vice versa. The philosophy of difference begins with the discovery, or re-discovery, of the role that difference plays for identity; but this beginning is just as much its end—for here, difference returns to embrace identity, take care of it and finish it off. Yet if difference and identity are strapped together, and not simply indifferent, alien, independent, then it is because identity just as much as difference marks the philosophy of identity and difference. In other words, with the identity and difference of identity and difference, as the "*determinate original-ground of all activity and self-movement,*" Hegel's concept breaks the exclusive hold that the law of identity exercised over thought.[2]

Speculative logic then means that identity's power over difference must be re-configured—and the logic of the philosophy of difference implies a specific discourse of identity and difference. Here difference is constituted (tautologically) by the logic itself, by a differentiated discourse that contains difference as constitutive. No longer mere "expression," the relation between logic and discourse becomes circular (although not equal or reciprocal). On the one hand, discourse is the place where logic necessarily materializes; on the other hand, logic can only formulate in a particular discourse—like spirit, logic without expression is illogical: "the power of spirit is only as great as its expression, its depth only as deep as it dares to spread out and lose itself in its exposition."[3] Logic without expression is empty, expression without logic is blind.

Within the logics and discourses of metaphysics then, multiplicity is thought under the twin sign of identity and difference: identity grounds difference, difference founds identity. First, the "discourse of identity" seeks to ground multiplicity as difference, to assure, legitimate, or legislate a single essence, a self-same and secure metaphysics, a system of the sciences: for example, multiplicity contained or gathered within identity, as its other, itself, its origin; as a part, side, component, constituent, condition of difference, as its source, and so on. Yet here the question of multiplicity as such never becomes a question; rather, the logic of identity and difference finds in the philosophy of difference its most sophisticated avatar.

Second, the "discourse of difference" is not a simple reversal of identity (although it may be that as well), but rather, difference is found and founded in identity, intertwined with its other. A discourse of difference, for example, could account for an identity (that is, immediate particularity, individuality, singularity, and always also universal), because the concept is the movement (*Bewegung*) between/of the difference between/of particular universality and universal particularity—for the concept of their difference is more (*mehr*) than a word, always also "more," that is, an expression of mediation, the transition and becoming-other (*Anderswerden*) of universality/particularity. In this sense, speculative difference is no longer a discourse wherein a predicate or accident is attached (via being qua copula, identification) or detached (via nothing, *negatio,* differentiation) from a self or subject; rather, to think speculatively means "to move." And Hegel's discourse of difference thinks the movement of thought because it is thought in motion; it can say what it means and mean what it says because it also (just as well) does not say what it means and does not mean what it says, because as concept it is and is not the movement of both. In other words, the contradiction of meaning and expression is solved insofar as it is both solved and not solved, remains in motion as a contradiction that is dissolved as insoluble.

In a discourse of identity then, multiplicity is reduced to an effect, product, system, addition, supplementation, pluralization, construction, and so on. With a discourse of difference, multiplicity is contained within the double-movement of the two-sided concept (subject and substance as a displacement of the logic of subject and predicate) wherein that which is meant is both said and not said. With a discourse of identity, language expresses what is meant; but with a discourse of difference, identity cannot say what it means. A discourse of multiplicity, of multiplicity as such, however, thinks multiplicity qua multiple, takes up where identity and difference leave off, but ends by falling back under the philosophy of identity and difference, not only because it conceives its objects in their identity and difference, but also because the language with which it thinks those objects is identical to and/or different from that of identity and difference—and also because it presupposes the identity and/or difference between objects and methods.

Under the signs of identity and difference, then, the possibility of multiplicity remains a possible impossibility. From being to the absolute idea, multiplicity never seems to be able to extricate itself from the logic and discourse of the concept. Yet making Hegel into a straw man, a simple philosopher of identity, a mere one-sided idealist, a caricature of himself, leaves the full force of dialectic intact, conceals the metaphysical prejudices even more seamlessly in philosophical trappings. Only by thinking how the *Logic* and *Phenomenology*, subject and substance, idealism and materialism, infinity and finitude, both determine and do not determine the horizon of speculative thought's multiplicity can the always only two-sided concept of multiplicity be interrogated and multiplied. If the philosophy of identity and difference is as much a refusal as an acceptance of multiplicity, then in order for thought to become multiple, a logical shift is necessary; in order to think multiply, a certain transformation of desire must occur, and the logic of acceptance/refusal must itself become multiple. Here not only is multiplicity thought as multiple—for it is also thought as identity and difference, and not just. Yet what would philosophy become if multiplicity no longer simply submitted to the reductions, abstractions, constraints of identity and difference? Can thought approach this multiplicity as multiple, that is, not only, but also, as multiple, a multiplicity of multiplicities—and not just? And then how could philosophy think, read, write, speak, and so on?

Thought and Being

For Hegel, Parmenides is the thinker of thought's self-production, of the thinking that is identical with thought, that is, with itself and its being. Here philosophy shows itself as one-sided idealism, as essentially metaphysical (not prior to metaphysics) insofar as it thinks truth as being: "there still remains just one account of a way, that it is."[4] Being is a non-created, imperishable, whole, of one genus (*mounogenes*, one *Geschlecht*), unshaken and without end—and as such it is not an indeterminacy to be reduced by some sort of exterior categories; rather, it is self-limiting, necessarily self-determining, and self-determined. If Parmenides' goddess indicates a twofold path, then it is because truth as being delimits itself via its other, through negation, the non-being that is not:

> come now, and I will tell you (and you must carry my account away with you when you have heard it) the only ways of inquiry that are to be thought of. The one, that [it/being] is and that it is impossible for [it/being] not to be, is the path of persuasion (for it attends upon truth); the other, that [it/being] is not and that is needful that [it/being] not be, that I declare

> to you is an altogether indiscernible track: for you could not know what is not—that cannot be done—nor indicate it.[5]

Parmenides' rejection of nothing, however, of that which is not, his refusal to think negation in general, means that he cannot think concrete limit, finitude, delimitation, determination. Being, in other words, is neither indeterminate immediacy, pure non-determination, bound-less, nor is it mediated via negation; rather, it is self-determined absolute necessity, that is, the necessity that being is, and that being is the true.[6]

Hegel, then, like Parmenides, thinks the sameness of the relation of thought and being. Parmenides writes: "the same thing is there to be thought and is why there is thought. For you will not find thinking without what is, in all that has been said."[7] And Hegel translates: "thinking and that for the sake of which the thought is, is the same."[8] Here with the grammatical error, the use of third person singular instead of plural, of "is" rather than "are," Hegel thinks "the *is*" (*das Ist*), that is, the being that makes out the sameness of thinking and being (and that for the sake of which thought is)—for sameness is the relation of two identical beings, thought and being.

Hegel marks the difference between forms of the verb "to be" grammatologically (not terminologically, as in Heidegger's difference between sameness and identity), that is, by the glitch in the structural laws of language, by the inadequacy of grammar as expression for the work of thought. If Parmenides, therefore, could think neither thought nor being as determinate, then it is because he refused negation, and contradiction as mediation—for in order for thought and being to be the same, they must also be different. For Hegel, however, Parmenides must be read within the history of one-sided idealism: not sensible beings, but the thought of them is their being—this is the opposite of materialism.[9] Thought and being *are* in relation to being, but being is only an idea.

Hegel's solution then to the problem of Parmenides' idealism is the concept. Here the relation between being and thought is displaced by that of subject and substance:

> In general, thereby, as expressed above, substance is in itself subject, all content is its own reflection into itself. The subsistence or substance of a being is its self-identity; for its non-self-identity would be its dissolution. Self-identity, however, is pure abstraction; but this is *thinking*. When I say "*quality*," I say the simple determinateness; through quality one being is distinguished from another, or is a being; it is for itself, or it subsists through this simplicity with itself. But thereby, it is essentially *thought*.—Conceptualized herein is the fact that being is thought; and this

> is the source of that insight which usually eludes the usual non-conceptual talk about the identity of thought and being.[10]

The truth of identity, in other words, is no longer merely one-sided; rather, it is the concept of contradiction that thinks the identity and difference of being and thought under the sign of substance and subject. For Hegel, in order to take care of Parmenides, the basic laws of logic, of identity (that being is, means that it is itself, A is A, A = A), of non-contradiction (being cannot simultaneously be and not be, A and not-A, it is or it is not), of the excluded middle (being is either A or not-A, they are logically exclusive, and there is no third), must be superseded. For Parmenides logic is the force that holds thought back from the "way of seeming," from the illusion that something can not-be, from thinking "that which is not." Logical impossibility, therefore, forms the limit of what Parmenides can think, and not think (i.e., that which is not, that which does not exist, that which has no being, that which is not the same as being). And the logic of being (ontology), and of being's self-identity, prohibits (to this day) the opening of philosophy to another logic, discourse, or way of thinking.

Being and Essence

The essence of identity and difference can no longer be thought in a way that simply belongs to the history and logic of being; on the contrary, it must be thought as their contradiction. Yet if the "Doctrine of Essence" begins with the concept of identity and ends with contradiction, then it is (once again) only because the beginning is the end—and in a multiplicity of ways: (1) as the immediate identity of identity and difference without difference; (2) as the sameness and difference of original beginning and returning beginning; (3) as the final cause, goal, *telos* that determines the development; (4) as the beginning from which its moments are disseminated; (5) as the mediation of both beginning and end. In other words, the circle is not merely an image of dead totality or eternal life, not only the identity of start and finish; rather, in circling, the circle shows itself as multiple.

In fact, the "Doctrine of Essence" should perhaps be found at the end of the *Logic*'s circle from the "Doctrine of Being" to the "Doctrine of the Concept"—for here lies the essence of the concept. Initially the essence (*Wesen*) of being is identity. On the one hand, for the *science* of logic, identity is temporally later but essentially (*wesen-tlich*) earlier than being. The term "to be," as a verb, a time-word (*Zeitwort*) "has preserved essence in the past participle [*gewesen*] of the verb *to be;* for essence is past—but timelessly past—being."[11] When it appears in the text, essence has already been; it is past. On the other hand, for speculative thought, the past of being is neither past, present, nor future, but essence—and not in the sense of infinite essence, purely without a time, timeless, but as a-temporal. Yet the time of essence is not the essence of time: time is the other of space, only a moment of the concept of motion, an abstraction from the double-sidedness of place.[12] Nevertheless, with the past participle, language preserves (and destroys) the moments of thought in the progression of thought from being to essence (to the absolute idea), takes care of them in the self-movement of being out of itself and back to itself. Here, on the one hand, for scientific one-sided thought, being is a provisional (*vorläufig*) beginning, and to be superseded—but this supersession comes back to itself in the end; it is taken care of by the truth of being for science. On the other hand, for speculative thought, the verbs of a given language contain (and hence, can express or conceive of) the essence of being. In this way, the *Logic* is always scientific/speculative and temporal/essential—and if language has a double role to play, then it lies in the always already double-entendre of the logical concept in motion.

Likewise in the *Phenomenology* then, the "now" (and "this"), exemplifying the immediacy of sense-certainty (that does not yet think "time and space"), is not the now—for the now is no longer at precisely the moment when it is now; it is far more a not-now, a having-been: "'*now*'; it has already ceased to be in being shown; the *now* that *is,* is another now than the one shown, and we see that the now is just this: already when it is, to be no more."[13] The essence of being now is its negation, the no-longer-now, will-be-now, not-now, non-being, nothing: "but what has been is, in fact, *no essence; it IS not,* and it was with being that we were concerned."[14] Within the scientific narrative, therefore, the essence of now, the no-longer-now (past, *ge-wesen*) and the not-yet-now show themselves *after* the immediate being of the now; the not-now is a later stage in the education of consciousness from the simple now to its negation and back to the now. In truth, however, the now is a result of the particular multiplicity of nows gathered as a simple now: "*showing* is, therefore, itself the movement that expresses what the now, in truth, is; namely, a result, or a multiplicity of nows held-together; and the showing is the experience that now is a *universal.*"[15] The essence of the now is multiplicity, and the now that appears as immediate is always already mediated, constituted by nows. Prior to being immediately now, and before the past of no-longer-now (or the future of not-yet-now), nows within nows are essentially multiple—and in this sense, the nows are scientifically latter, but essentially prior to the now.

Here, the now's immediacy means presence, the being present of that which is essentially no-longer, non-being, non-presence, or not-yet-present. Being, as being present now (and here), is being only in the past (or future; and there). Yet when and where being is present here and now, it is not present. The essence of presence is non-presence—but the speculative truth of both is that from which they are constituted as results, that which is essentially prior to them, is the movement that produces them, namely, their becoming one another that marks the supersession of being as presence or non-presence, that takes care of the concept of present non-presence and non-present presence. And the certainty of the sense of here, now, and being is itself a result, abstraction, construction, distillation.

In the *Logic* then, it is no surprise that the essence of being is as "here" as it is "now," as spatial as it is temporal—and just as much essentially a-spatio-temporal. The truth of being is essence means that behind being lies something else, something completely different: "Being is the immediate. Since knowing wants to recognize the true, that is, what being is *in and for itself,* it does not stop at the immediate and its determinations, but penetrates through it on the supposition that *behind* this being there is yet something other than being itself, that this background makes out the truth of being."[16] Science drives toward the logic behind the mask; its progress to the essence of being is its process, the unfolding in opposition, the production of its own content as itself—but it sees only the spatial "behind" of being. For speculative thought, however, "behind" is precisely not simply spatial; rather, identity is behind being as its cause, ground, foundation (*Hinter-grund*), reason, support, as its essence, that which is between or lies at (and is) the bottom. In this sense, essence gets to the bottom of things by determining how logic takes care of being. And the space of identity, like its time, is doubled—for scientifically speculatively, essence *is* and *is "behind"* being; it is the truth that lies behind as both "past or having been" and "future or still to come," as that which both lags, delays, or defers being and simultaneously promises to be, to become that which it is, as that which "may have been" and "may be."

If identity then, shows itself as the essential space/time of being, it is because being is essentially presence, shows itself as present (*an-wesen-d*), presences as essence (*Wesen*). "To be" means "to be present" (*wesen*), to be doubly present—here and now, there and then. The presencing of essence and being is reciprocal: being is present scientifically before/behind and essence is present speculatively as before/behind. It is not surprising, therefore, that the language of being is the language of essence—for essence is also presence, that is, that which is present in being as its truth. Identity is doubled, therefore, a double-identity: (scientific-speculative) essence and being, and as such identity means presence.

Between the "Doctrine of Being" and the "Doctrine of Essence" then a conceptual relation shows itself: on the one hand, the determinations of essence are identical to those of being (and those of the concept) insofar as they function via negation of an other in the return to self and will be taken as the sum total of all realities (*Inbegriff aller Realitäten*); on the other hand, they are different insofar as their "character and nature" are specific to essence and are precisely not those of being (or the concept). And essence is the transition from being to the concept of the concept; it is the negation of being that will find the truth of its movement in the absolute idea's self-dissemination.[17]

Difference of Identity

In the *Logic* then identity becomes explicit as an essentiality or determination of reflection; it takes up the position of being, but it is no longer an immediate indeterminacy—rather, it is a specific form of mediated indeterminacy. The difference between being and identity (between the first moment of the "Doctrine of Being" and that of the "Doctrine of Essence") is an essential difference, a difference of essence—for being and identity are both identical and different; they are conceptually related. What difference then does identity make?

For Hegel identity initially shows itself as "simple self-relation, pure *identity*."[18] And it takes the form of a sentence (*Satz*): positively stated as "*everything is identical with itself,* A = A"; and negatively as "A cannot at the same time be A and not A."[19] The subject of the sentence (formula, proposition) for identity is "everything"; and to this subject, the predicate of identity, of itself, is ascribed. Predication, however, is the more general act of connecting a category with a being. The determination of a being as itself, therefore, is one determination among many, one law of thought or category of reflection among a multiplicity: everything is everything, but it is also of a particular quality and quantity; it also is (has being), and so on. In fact, the predicate of identity is never alone: if everything is identical, then it must also have a multiplicity of determinations. Predication is essentially multiple, and identity is a product, the result of a reduction or abstraction that takes place via the negation that lies at the core of identity's constitution. Any single determination of being is essentially a transition into its opposite: "the *several propositions* which are set up as *absolute laws-of-thought* are, therefore, more closely considered, *opposed to one another,* they contradict one another and mutually supersede themselves [or take care of each other]."[20] The expression of logical law functions via opposition, mutual exclusion, negation: for example, the assumption of the law of identity rules out difference; non-contradiction means that the acceptance of difference is the rejection of identity. In determining identity, in other words, that which is negated is just as necessary as that which is determined—one only functions with the other, relative, with respect to an other as that through which it can even begin to determine itself: "both present themselves with equal necessity and, as immediate assertions, are at least equally correct."[21]

The formula for identity then has its determining force in the relation, in the copula, that operates between subject and predicate (unlike the judgment that has its force in the predicate). The difference between a formula and a judgment appears in the difference between verb and participle: the verb "to be" is the connection between subject and predicate (the rose *is* without "why"—Angelus Silesius); however, when it is transformed into a participle (being), the emphasis is displaced to the predicate (being *red,* the rose is without "why"). As a formula, identity needs a subject, a being, everything, something that can be determined; it must have a particular quality, namely identity with self—but this is the non-speculative sense of identity that remains merely subject and not also substance; simply subjective and not also objective. Being is no longer a real predicate (Kant), but it is not yet essence. And identity means self-identity, without relation to an other, without the mediation of opposition, indifference to subject and object alike—and this will be its downfall, that is, the contradiction that drives essence out of itself into the concept.

Indeed, for Hegel, with the immediacy of pure being ("*only being is, and nothing is really nothing*") Parmenides marks the first expression of abstract identity (and its contradiction) in the western philosophical tradition.[22] At the core of this identity, however, the necessity of difference lies un-thought: identity without difference is empty, difference without identity is blind—and only the concept of both is their truth. Speculation will show that the thought of contradiction lies in the essential being of identity and difference. Yet first, identity must be considered as it appears, as abstract.

In the *Science of Logic* then, the truth of being is posited as self-identity, the disappearance of all otherness in pure self-sameness: "to be" means "to be self-identical." In this way, however, identity is not identical with being—for it has being as its history and is, therefore, no longer simply immediate—rather, it is the moving process of its own reflection:

"to be" means "to be reflexive." And identity means the immediacy of reflection with itself. Here the essence of identity is produced from and in identity itself, by reflecting itself to itself; yet the origin or source of its production, the other through which it constructs itself, the being to which it owes its existence, is forgotten, repressed, concealed. Thinking this identity, however, does not mean thinking the interweaving of identity and some other, the interconnecting or binding of identity to some difference; nor does it mean tearing or abstracting identity out of some connection that it already has with difference—for identity is not merely next to, outside of, before or after itself; their relation is more intimate, and identity means the self-difference of identity itself and the self-identity of difference. The concept of identity, in other words, is the movement, transition, process, the becoming of both; it is the identity and difference of identity and difference, the identity that negates and supersedes, originates in and takes care of, but also produces and conceives being. And here difference is far more non-identity, no difference at all, the difference that does not differentiate, that makes no difference, that is indifferent; it is difference as a mere tool through which identity determines itself, an indifferent other of identity. Difference is other, therefore, at this moment, only insofar as it serves the purposes of identity, submits to its role as non-identity, as the mirror in which identity sees itself for itself, show itself (its essence) to itself. In this sense identity's reflection comes from itself, is repelled from itself, is internal- or self-repulsion (*Abstoßen*); but this reflection is repulsive (*abstoßend*)—for in it identity sees only its own reflection, only the boring, infinite re-presentation of itself. Identity is identity only insofar as it is not difference, insofar as its difference is its own, only in itself; and difference is difference only if it is not identity. And identity is determined as identical only insofar as it is different from difference, the negation of its other that is its own negation, but difference is the true essence of identity since identity is identity be-cause of difference, the difference that is its cause and ground. Thus, identity is only a moment of its own self-constitution, of the dialectical movement, the process of reflection through difference that returns it to itself, to the identity and difference of its identity and its difference.[23]

The logic of identity then is founded upon the law of identity (A = A) that functions via the exclusion of difference: identity and difference are different—but this means that identity is a difference, namely, different from difference. An identity that denies the difference that is essential to it, or that it contains within itself, is no identity at all, but only the one-sided determination of a merely formal, abstract, incomplete truth, the simple identicalness of identities. The truth of identity, therefore, is the "*unity of identity with difference.*"[24] But unity here is not mere oneness, simple abstract identity, A = A, a tree is a tree; rather, in unity, identity is essentially separate from difference—for unity means its opposite as well, separation.[25]

Since predication then conceals the essential difference of identity, another discourse must be mobilized to think identity's difference, and the essence of identity as the unity and separation of identity and difference. A philosophical leap is required. As in the *Phenomenology*, speculative thought expresses itself in a *Satz*, that is, sentence, proposition, formula, the movement, that is itself the leap (*Satz*) from predicative judgment to speculation:

> Formally, what has been said can be expressed thus: the general nature of the judgment or proposition, which involves the distinction of subject and predicate, is destroyed by the speculative proposition, and the proposition of identity which the former becomes contains the counter-thrust against that subject-predicate relationship.—This conflict between the general form of a proposition and the unity of the concept which destroys it is similar to the conflict that occurs in rhythm between meter and accent. Rhythm results from the floating center and the unification of the two. So, too, in the philosophical proposition the identification of subject and predicate is not meant to negate the difference between them, which the form of the proposition expresses; their unity, rather, is meant to emerge as a harmony. The form of the proposition is the appearance of the determinate sense, or the accent that distinguishes its fulfillment; but that the predicate expresses the substance, and that the subject itself falls into the universal, this is the *unity* in which the accent dies away.[26]

Predicative identity, in other words, claims to make an assertion with identity (a plant is a plant); but it is self-contradictory: the predicate, which should be different from the subject, is identical to it—nothing has been said when something should have been said. For speculative thought, therefore, being, essence and concept cannot be thought as predicates—not only because they are not real predicates (Kant), but because they are not just predicates, because predication cannot do them justice. The predicative form is inadequate to the expression of speculative truth, fundamentally unprepared for the thought of the identity and difference of identity and difference.

And not only language, but predicate logic fails to be speculative as well. The law of identity that is supposed to be the solitary ground of all logic and the assurance of truth, the first fundamental proposition implied in every experience and the foundation of every claim, is no longer alone; rather, it shows itself to be always already integrated with the law of difference: the tree is a tree and not a non-tree; A is A and not B, C, D. Since logic then abstracts from concrete identity, and from the experience of identity and difference, it cannot ground empirical identity—identity is nothing identical. Indeed, identity is more than simply identity; it includes that which it negates, that other through which it determines itself.

Speculative thought, therefore, expresses identity as a movement (*Satz*), or set of movements, sets of sets, movements of movements. Taken alone, in itself, the (positive, A = A) law of identity is the result of an abstraction or reduction (from the concept of identity that thinks it with difference). By taking identity as such, for the moment, the *Logic* commits a necessary injustice, an injustice that permits science to function, to build arguments, produce systems, construct truth, and subsequently to order empirical reality. For speculative thought, however, identity is more than just identity: it (at least, for Hegel) doubly exceeds itself insofar as it is itself only in relation to its other. First, the "more" (*das Mehr*) of identity is the difference revealed in every assertion of identity: "a tree is a tree" includes the negation of that which is not a tree, assumes difference (the non-tree, another entity) in the determination of the tree.[27] Second, the "more" is that which is completely different from the identical—neither the identification of identical things, nor the things themselves as identical, but the concept of identity that is the truth of both, the concept from which both have always already been abstracted. In fact, the "more" of identity "means" that what is meant cannot be said and that what is said cannot be meant: meaning is the experience that another is meant, as that which is meant.[28] The "more," therefore, must be rethought if the essence of identity is to be thought—that which has been subtracted from identity must be returned to it, added once again, recaptured or recapitulated. In this sense, difference is the supplement of identity, the lost other that identity re-calls to itself.

Yet identity does not appear by subtracting difference from the concept of identity and difference. And subtracting identity from difference ($n - 1$) will never reveal difference as such. On the contrary, the procedure of subtraction only exacerbates abstraction, only reduces the complexity of thought further—less is not "more." Identity is not a frame, veil, or abstract category that has been added to difference in order to contain, structure, and control it; rather, it is the result or end product of scientific logic. Speculative thought, therefore, returns the "more" of identity to it—for in the expression of identity, difference is always already there. Yet is identity as such not only the subtraction of difference, of an other, but of others, of a multiplicity of "mores"? Is the concept of identity only "one" more? How does the speculative proposition, so adept at thinking the double, the identity and difference of identity and difference, think multiplicity? How can addition (or subtraction) think multiply without indifference? Or is a completely different method necessary? A means for thinking not simply identity as the relation of identity and the identical, and not merely their difference or differal but that which (perhaps, to employ—for the moment—the usual subterfuge of transcendental philosophy) makes them possible, although not necessary? And what does it mean to think multiplicity as the contradiction of identity and difference? And not just as contradiction?

For Hegel these questions can be addressed only in relation to the negative expression of identity, the law of non-contradiction (A is not simultaneously A and not-A) that takes the "more" of identity as the negation of the negation: A and not-A are different, but are both determinations of the identical A. Here identity is thought as the relation of differences, as containing difference within itself; yet this is both the solution to the problem of identity and its non-solution, its dissolution—for if identity and difference fall under the sign of identity, then it is because the essence of identity does not only mean identity; rather, it means difference as well. Difference, in other words, is just as much the speculative solution to the problem of identity and difference as is identity—the meaning of this solution, however, the concept of difference itself, must also be differentiated.

Identity of Difference

In the *Science of Logic* the differentiation of difference is tripartite: absolute, diverse, opposition. Absolute difference is the other of the identity of identity and difference, the essential difference of identity and difference, difference as difference, in and for itself. Yet as such, difference is just difference, simply in relation to itself; it is the difference of A and not-A that no longer thinks (subtracts, $n - 1$, or represses, reduces) their identity. In absolute difference, non-identity is ex-pressed. In this moment, however, expression is inclusion—difference thinks differences in one and the same difference. Like identity before it, difference only sees itself, its own reflection, and can only contain its other (identity) within itself, only think the essence of different beings in (deference to) terms of difference. As such, difference is identity; not itself, but its other. And difference shows itself to be double: both itself and its other, the difference of difference and identity is its identity.[29]

If "absolute difference," however, is self-identical difference as the identity of identity and difference, then "diverse difference" is its other, its negation, that is, difference as the difference of identity and difference.

And diverse difference is double: on the one hand, as the difference of identity, it is the difference of indifferent differences; on the other hand, like Leibnizian monads, each difference is indifferent to all others because each is self-identical, self-reflective, each is the identity (as ground and element of its solipsistic difference) of indifferent differences—the former is "likeness" (reflection in itself); the latter, "unlikeness" (external reflection). Here each difference is indifferent to its relation of likeness or unlikeness to other differences. Differences are related not by the differences themselves, but via the medium of an external third (like God or reason), through the back and forth of comparison wherein each maintains its indifference—even to the difference of the other. In this way the third party, which is supposed to relate differences to one another, ends by separating them even more. With comparison, differences that are supposed to be connected (through the relation of the "insofar as" the two "sides of," or the "with respect to") are actually separated. In other words, through a third party, like and unlike differences are denied their identities and differences.[30]

Nevertheless, as the opposite of identity, difference can be expressed propositionally: "*all things are different,* or *there are no two things like each other.*"[31] Yet this law of diversity cannot mean that a thing is like no other thing (the indeterminate multiplicity of pluralism or relativism), since then it is also not like itself (A is not A); rather, difference here means self-identical, but different from all others (determinate diversity). Two things are not just one number—for they are different, incomparable, insofar as they are determined; their determination, however, as different (in the sense of unlike), is their likeness and identity. Taken to its logical conclusion, difference shows its relation to identity: if all things are different, then they are simultaneously like and unlike, identical and different—like insofar as they are all "things," "beings," that they are and are ones (Aristotle), like all the other things; unlike insofar as they are two different things (*ex hypothesi*).

As Leibniz knew, however, the logical conclusion of diverse difference is absolute multiplicity (*absolute Vielheit*). Indeed, as the other of Spinoza's (one/identical) universal substance, Leibniz thinks the individual monad as fundamental principle. Monads are the mark of determinate diversity—on the one hand, each monad is an individual, unique, independent (all monads are qualitatively different):

> there are no two *indiscernible individuals.* A nobleman with the spirit of my friends, in speaking with me in the presence of Madame l'Electrice in the garden of Herrenhausen, believed that he could well find two leaves entirely alike. Madame l'Electrice challenged him, and he ran around for

> a long time searching in vain for them. Two tastes of water, or of milk, seen under the microscope will be found to be discernible. It is an argument against the atoms, which are not less opposed than the void, according to the principles of true Metaphysics.[32]

In other words, the principle of individuation (*principe d'individuation*), along with the principle of sufficient reason (*Raison suffisante, nihil est sine ratione*), revolutionizes metaphysics by thinking original multiplicity.

On the other hand, all monads are monads, that is, ideally identical. Monads are not empty Epicurean atoms but determinate, substantial forms (like Aristotelean *entelechies*)—their difference is neither merely that of different spaces or times, nor that of external comparison from some philosophical consciousness or subject; rather, their *difference* is *their* difference, difference in themselves via their internal principle (*principe interne*). As Hegel insists: "not only do we differentiate the animal through its claws, but it differentiates itself essentially thereby, defends itself, preserves itself. If two things are different merely insofar as they are two, then each is *one;* however, in itself, *two* makes not a relation, but the determinate difference in itself—that is the main thing."[33] Monadic difference then is immanent determination; that is, their difference lies in the way in which they essentially contain all others within themselves as reflected—Spinoza's *omnis determinatio est negatio* is internalized. Difference is thereby not only that (*daß*) totality exists in each monad, but how (*wie*) it exists and is reflected. Since monads are different, no relation or transition between them is possible (hence, the necessity of pre-established harmony); however, their indiscernibility is their identity—their reflective self-determination identifies them as monads, reveals their essence. The indifference of monads to other monads is their difference: monadic essence is self-determination via exclusionary reflection—the difference of each, its discernibility, is its identity: externally all monads are monads, all are subject to the continuity of one pre-established harmony, all are a number (one); internally, each is self-identical, their individuality as essential self-determination, determination of self as negation of an other that is within itself, an other that is merely the reflection of an other.[34]

Leibnizian multiplicity then is not simply multiple, an external number of monads; on the contrary, it is determinate insofar as it is simultaneously internal. Multiplicity here cannot maintain its separation from its other, its distance from identity—for it is multiple as many ones. The paradigm of metaphysics shifts from original identity to original multiplicity, to a multiplicity of identities, multiple identities. And the *Monadology* is metaphysically schizophrenic with respect to the structure of self-determining discernibles. Yet monads can be self-identical because they are in relation to others, to that from which they are different, unlike—determinate difference is constituted by both likeness and unlikeness, identity and difference.

And for Hegel, following Leibniz, the logical conclusion of the question of difference is determinate multiplicity. Can multiplicity, however, be multiple if it is determinate? Is multiplicity multiple if it is only *determinate* multiplicity? If it falls under Spinoza's law of *omnis determinatio est negatio,* if it submits to the fundamental principle of negation? Is the double-logic of negation (or of affirmation) adequate to multiplicity? What would it mean for determination to become multiple?

Regardless, for Hegel (thinking against Leibniz), two things are never (completely) different—non-determinate multiplicity is merely a moment, and determinate multiplicity means that all things are simultaneously unlike and like, that all beings are essentially self-oppositional. Perspectives, sides, with respect to . . . , insofar as . . . , are superficial subterfuges deployed in order to avoid thinking opposition as such, to simply displace the problem to the subjective or objective, internal or external, realm. The essence of speculative difference, in the *Science of Logic* as well as in the *Phenomenology,* is the thought of opposition (*Gegensatz*).

Indeed, with the concept of opposition, the logic of difference comes to completion: unity is essentially diversity, identity is essentially difference. Here the difference between reflective identity/difference and its expression as likeness/unlikeness is the difference of both, and their identity. Each side of the likeness/unlikeness opposition is a moment of the other, contained and not contained in the other: on the one side, likeness is posited as the likeness of likeness and unlikeness; on the other side, unlikeness is posited as the unlikeness of likeness and unlikeness—and the former is positive positing; the latter, negative positing. They posit the difference of their different moments, therefore, as differently determined; and thereby they have each other in themselves as moments. Each is itself insofar as it is double, namely itself and its other, being itself and not-being itself; and each is independent, self-positing in relation to itself, and dependent, self-positing by virtue of an other, self-constituted by negation of another.[35]

In fact, the moments of opposition are paradigmatic for the entire discourse of difference. First, positive and negative are opposed to one another: they are inseparable, negative reflections of each other within the relation—each is what the other is not, that is, each is insofar as the other is. Second, positive and negative are insofar as the other is not—negation reflects them back to themselves, and they are interchangeable. Finally, "positive and negative is, *thirdly,* not only something posited, not merely an indifferent something, but their *positedness*, or the *reference to other in a unity* which *they are not themselves*, is *taken-back* into each."[36] Here, once again, Hegel's grammatical failure is the failure of grammar—for in the language of the concept, in the expression of speculative thought, positive and negative *are* not the same, they *is* the same. Each is itself (different) only in their relation: they are independent, indifferent to each another, non-oppositional; and simultaneously, dependent, co-constituting, that is, negating, excluding, opposing one another. In this sense the concept of opposition thinks the opposition and non-opposition of opposition and non-opposition.

With the discourse of identity and difference then, each is (in and for) itself only in their relation; they imply one another as opposed-non-opposition and non-opposed-opposition. On the one hand, oppositional differences are one, identical: for example, arithmetically, $+y-y=y$; geographically, an hour's distance east and west result in the same position; economically, liabilities and assets equalize or cancel each other out. On the other hand, differences are different, two, double: plus is plus, minus is minus: east is east, and west is west; a quantum of money means subsistence for the worker and profit for the capitalist.[37]

Hegel's discourse of difference qua opposition then thinks the difference of identical and differential difference—and the concept of difference is the identity and difference of both. Yet it also thinks the concept of opposition as the (opposing/non-opposing) relation of opposed differences and their oppositionality. Here opposition is not only the opposition of oppositionals, but also the opposition of oppositionality and that which is opposed. In other words, the concept of opposition relates both oppositional differences to each other (east and west) and oppositionality to that which is opposed (direction to east/west). And in this sense opposition is neither what Heidegger would call ontic nor ontological; rather, it is the relation of both as identical and different—for "to be opposite" means "to be different." How then does the concept of difference show itself as the essence of being?

Difference in Difference

The essence of the question of being is the question of essence—for the essence of being is not being, but the other of being, namely, essence. In order to think the essence of being, therefore, a particular logic is necessary; and within this logic, the question of being, of what something is, is the question of identity and difference. Being is not, however, the solution to the meaning of identity and difference, it is far more the problem; and in order to think that problem, Hegel turns to the logic of the contradiction (*Widerspruch*) of identity and difference.

Indeed, for its part, difference shows itself as the relation of two predicates, things, beings, entities, as different, that is, as moments of their absolute difference from one another—but as the difference of their identity and difference, and not as their identity. As diverse difference, difference is indifference of differences or multiple identities. With contradiction, however, differences show themselves as essentially conceptual, that is, double: on the one hand, they are different only through one another, relative to each other as dependent moments, in relation (*ratio*) via the identical ground (*ratio*) that forms their difference; on the other hand, they are indifferent to one another, exclude each other insofar as they are independent, self-subsistent determinations-of-reflection—in other words, they contradict one another.[38]

The logic of contradiction then, may be understood in terms of positive and negative. Initially positive and negative determinations are indifferent to one another. Here each is related to the other only insofar as it has their contradiction as its own: for instance, for the positive, the negative is that which is not positive, that through which the positive is positive—but not as an other of the positive; rather, as the negative contained within the positive, the negative (nothing) that belongs to the (being of the) positive. Exclusion is inclusion; the negative is negative only as the negative of the positive—or it is no negative at all. The negative is positive, however, it is also negative; each is the other insofar as they reflect one another—their truth is the process of reflection, and also their contradiction. Difference is only implicitly able to resolve the opposition of identity and difference, unity and separation: "for it is the *unity* of sides which are, only insofar as they are *not one*—and it is the *separation* of sides which are, only as separated *in the same relation*."[39] In an explicit contradiction, however, positive and negative not only exclude one another and make each other into a reflection or likeness of themselves—they exclude themselves as well. In applying the law of identity, for example, positive is positive insofar as it is not negative; but as non-negative, positive is no longer merely positive—for it is that which is excluded from the negative. An excluding positive becomes an excluded negative; and the contradiction that belonged to the positive shows itself as the contradiction of the negative—they are *one* reflection. Similarly (although not identically, i.e., identity with a difference), negative excludes positive as its unlikeness, the negative of the negative—but negative is itself negative, and an unlikeness of positive. In this sense the identity of each is their non-identity; each is identical with itself in opposition to its self-identical other—for in the process of reflection, positive and negative mutually exclude one another insofar as they include one another as likenesses/un-likeness.[40]

Negative and positive contradictions then are the same—and in this sense, their (positive/negative) contradiction is "null"; it is the unity in which their independence is destroyed, exterminated, abstractly negated, the identity in which difference disappears, an indifference or zero-point where positive and negative are perfectly interchangeable. Here translation between identary and differential discourses appears to be perfect. However, the null is only one side of the concept of contradiction wherein positive and negative are superseded, wherein their different identities remain/do not remain, exist/no longer exist, are posited and taken care of by the double-movement of their becoming one another. The essence of positive and negative shows itself in a reflective relation that returns them to themselves; each is independent-dependent through a self-negation. The double-structure of contradiction, therefore, of the dependence-independence of things, beings, predicates, and so on, means that all opposites (positive and negative, light and darkness, good and evil), are subject to the "logic of the null," a zero-sum logic that is simultaneously plus and minus: truth, for example, is no longer simply correspondence (identity) of concept/thought/subject and object/thing/substance—for it is just as much their negation, their non-correspondence (difference), and "without this knowledge, not a single step can really be made in philosophy."[41] Thus, with the concept of contradiction, "*the positive and negative is the same.*"[42]

Contradiction then ends by falling into nullity, the indifference of identity and difference; yet this fall is only a moment: the concept of contradiction will show itself as ground or cause (*Grund*). And in the reflective process, essence shows itself as ground because the contradiction of positive and negative is also (but not only) an oppositional relation, that is, a relation of indifference, of mere identity: "the resolved contradiction is therefore ground, essence as unity of the positive and negative."[43] In other words, ground is essence because only through that which essence is also not (i.e., reflection), can it become that which it is, as well. In the *Science of Logic* essence and ground *is* the same.

Logic of Contradiction

The *Logic* then implies a threefold, speculative re-interpretation of the logic of identity and difference: with relation to the law of identity, the law of the excluded middle, the law of non-contradiction. First, the law of identity becomes the law of identity and non-identity—for identity never only concerns identity; A is never only equal to itself. Rather, identity is "more" than identity; it is determined only through the negation of difference (and differences) that it contains within itself. Here, insofar as identity is connected to and separated from difference, the concept of both makes out the speculative logic of identity and difference.

Second, the law of the excluded middle is supposed to mean that all predicates either apply or do not apply to a given subject (X is either A or not-A; something is sweet, green, square, etc., or not), and there is no third. Yet the subject, indifferent to its having or not having a specific predicate, is already a third—a dead something, the excluded middle, is not excluded; rather, it is far more included in order that a predicate can be ascribed or not-ascribed to a subject. Predication thereby is never simply a question of either/or, but of either/or and both/and. Even further, the law of the excluded middle presupposes the identity of a subject that is already doubled, that is, more than a third: the being that is either sweet or not-sweet is not simply itself; it is just as much non-being, nothing, or rather, the becoming of both. In this sense the law of the excluded middle no longer functions for speculative logic—with respect to the other of the law of identity, the subject that is both A and not-A, there is a middle. Something never shows itself as the subject of a single, abstract predicate: a being is never just sweet or not-sweet—for it also contains a multiplicity of other predicates. Speculative thought means that a subject is more than simply the sum of its predicates. And the "etc." (*usf.*) reveals that predication according to the law of the excluded middle is already a result, abstraction: negation can determine a subject with multiple predicates, but negation and/or affirmation are already reduced from the particular ways in which a being has any specific predicate, that is, is sweat, green, square, and so on. A singular something is never just sweet or not-sweet; rather, it shows itself as a multiplicity of predicates from which sweet is abstracted and then judged to be present or absent, positive or negative. The logic of the excluded middle, however, insofar as it thinks only two ways of being/not-being or having/not-having, makes all things into dead things. Speculative logic, on the contrary, thinks beings in their multiplicity.[11] Yet the questions remain: Can the *Science of Logic,* insofar as its dialectic satisfies itself with the two and only twofold concept, think multiple predication? Can its form of judgment (S is and is-not P, S and P *is* the same, etc.) allow the thing to show itself as itself, in all its multiplicity? Can Hegel think not only the identity of identification and identities, and not simply the difference of differentiation and differences, and not merely their contradictory relation, but also the multiplicity from which they have been abstracted, produced, created, constructed, differentiated, distilled, reduced?

Regardless, the law of non-contradiction becomes, third, the law of contradiction: "*all things are in themselves contradictory*."[45] And the law of non-contradiction is an a posteriori, subjective reflection—for self-contradiction is the essence of being, and the root of all self-movement. Life, for instance, means that which contains the force of self-contradiction within itself as the origin of self-movement. As contradiction, therefore, beings are simultaneously here and not-here, are and are-not in the same place—space and time are no longer pure forms; rather, they are contaminated: the essence of being is to be here and not-here, be present and non-present, necessarily and contingently, maybe and definitely. The essence of being is contradiction: the little word "is," found everywhere, in every sentence, proposition, formula, movement, moment, is always already in relation to its negation, to "is not." Contradictory determinations are always double: parent and child, male and female, up and down, left and right, and so on, are negations only relative to one another, simultaneously differentiated from one another as indifferent and identical to each other as interdependent.[46]

Speculative thought, then, thinks contradiction qua contradiction—and resolution as a moment therein. The kind of reflection that is rich in spirit (*geistreiche Reflexion*) grasps and asserts both the moments of contradiction and the transition between them. Thinking reason (*denkende Vernunft*) reduces multiplicity to the essential difference of opposition, and then to contradiction. Picture-thinking hates contradiction (as nature abhors a vacuum) and therefore seeks resolution; speculative thought, however, realizing that contradiction belongs to nature itself, and that resolution is merely one-sided, seeks the concept. In this way contradiction is not an error, imperfection, or defect; it is far more the essence of being itself. In other words, every determination, being, thing, and so on, is both inherently self-contradictory and "contradiction resolved"—for the concept is neither an idea nor a thing, but the moving relation of both.[47]

The laws of the logic of identity and difference then can be re-articulated: identity/non-identity, the excluded/included middle, non-contradiction/contradiction. Identity and difference have shown themselves in a conceptual relation—they are self-identical, pure, independent, indifferent to one another, in and for themselves; and self-differentiated, contaminated, dependent, concerned with another, in and for each other. The essence of being is doubled as the identity and difference of identity and difference; and as contradiction resolved, the relation between the "Doctrine of Essence" and the "Doctrine of Being" is also doubled—for speculative thought is the thought of the double qua double.

Difference, therefore, is not multiplicity—for thinking-reason reduces multiplicity to one side of a doubled-concept. Multiplicity appears only under the condition that it is subsumed under (classical or, here, Hegelian) logical laws, under the twofold signs of opposition or contradiction. Multiplicity qua multiplicity can be neither determined nor thought as such: it cannot be determined if all determination is negation; it cannot be thought if all thinking is conceptual, that is, two-sided, not multi-sided. Leibniz's attempt to think multiplicity falls back into identity as identities, that is, many *ones,* the metaphysical schizophrenia of multiple identities. Multiplicity, however, is neither many things, nor the manyness or multipleness of those things, nor some combination or permutation of the same—for as such it cannot be thought according to the logic of identity and difference. Multiplicity as multiple requires another logic, a multiple logic, multi-logics. Here a phenomeno-logic of multiplicity, by which a thing shows itself as itself, joins Aristotelian metaphysics as the study of being qua being. In this sense multiplicity as multiplicity is not yet "manys," but it is perhaps the first loosening of the hold that the discourse of identity and difference holds over philosophy.

Logics of Multiplicity

Now, the logic of multiplicity qua multiple may be articulated. The law of identity (A = A) is itself a product of what Nietzsche calls "an abbreviation-process,"[48] the concentration of forces or "will to power"—and the abbreviation of the abbreviation, not from its other, difference, negation (not-A), but from multiplicity. Before a being is self-same, identical with itself, it is not simply different from itself, the negation of itself; rather, it is also "more" than itself, many more: A is B, C, D, before it is just A. The law of identity must not simply be replaced by the law of non-identity (for example, by a principle of individuation that is itself no longer multiple, by multiple identities); it must be re-read as multiplicity. Neither the logic that expresses itself as "S is P," nor the speculative sentence that thinks "S as P and not-P," are appropriate for multiple predication; rather, S is not even S (nor not-S)—for S is always also multiple. Multiplicity is the truth of identity, and multiple predication may thereby be articulated within the logic of identity and difference as a formula. In this way multiplicity may enter into the logic of the concept of being, of the relation of beingness and beings, the (ontological) difference between being and beings, between onto-logical and ontic-logical discourses. Identity is an abbreviation that takes care of multiplicity, and judgment is its subsumption under logical laws—but the law of identity does not belong to the logic of multiplicity. The problem then is not "if" reduction occurs, and the goal is not to demonstrate "that" subsumption is possible; rather, it is the question: How can reduction be multiple, and how can subsumption be multiplied? Or rather, how can reduction and subsumption themselves become multiple? And not just?

Regardless, in a logic of multiplicity, the law of identity means that all identities are multiplicities, and the multiplicities themselves are multiple. Identity resolves the problem of multiplicity by translating multiplicity as identity, or multiple identities—for resolution itself belongs to the logic of identity and difference; and its result or version of multiplicity, within the context of its rules, laws, logic, within its own horizon or limit, may be no other. The logic of identity and difference, like metaphysical thought itself, always remains a possibility for multiplicity—but its necessity has come undone, and the force of its truth has imploded, collapsed, folded, broken down.

With the logic of multiplicity then, a thing is no longer just a thing. Before the thing can be identical with itself, it must be itself—and the thing is not only itself. Initially multiplication appears as double: internally, the thing is a multiplicity of parts, of sections, nodes, modes, and so on; externally, it is *not* all other beings. Within the thing, the relations between the relations, between parts, are themselves multiple and (external) determination is multiple negation. Determination here shows itself to be the question of being as existence: the thing is or is not, or is and is not insofar as affirmation of existence is negation of existence. Yet multiplication means that determination is not reduced to affirmation/negation; rather, it is multiplied in an attempt to take account of the thing in a multiplicity of relations, a multiplicity prior to identary abbreviation. And the logic of multiplicity means that the double is already a reduction, and the thing as multiple cannot be merely internal/external. The multiplication of identification is neither static (a fixed canon or set of logical laws) nor active (a movement of thought)—for static/active is not multiple; rather, it is a multiplicity of processes, the multiplications of identity. And this multiplication is not a return (or non-return) to an original multiplicity, but a metamorphosis of multiplicity itself, a re-articulation of thought limits and judgment mechanisms. The thing is no longer just a thing or not a thing; it is a multiplicity, it is things, things that are themselves things. And the question of multiplicity is here that of finitude, of the possibility of infinite multiplication: Is the thing infinite? Or a finitude that contains its infinity within itself? Or that will find its infinity outside itself? Or is the thing as multiple far more neither finite nor infinite? And do these questions themselves return to a logic of identity and difference?

In fact, the logic of multiplicity is neither finite nor infinite nor finite/infinite; rather, its time and space are multiple. And questions of finitude or infinity belong to another discourse and another desire, in other words, to metaphysics as a philosophy of identity, as a philosophy of difference, to the abbreviation of multiplicity. In the logic of multiplicity, therefore, the law of identity is replaced by the law of multiplicity—but this law precisely does not mean "all things are multiple"; rather, it means that all things are multiple, identical, differentiated, and "more." Yet the "more" here is not infinite (or finite)—it is the mark of the law of multiplicity; it means that predication and logical formulation (e.g., "everything is x") are inadequate to "multiple mores," that the subject itself is also "mores"; and it means the discourse of identity and difference is inappropriate for multiple languages, the multiplicity of language, and the language of multiplicity. In this sense the law of multiplicity is not just the law of multiplicity—for it is always also "more."

The logic of multiplicity, however, is not simply a rearticulation of things—for multiplicity is not merely a thing—it also rethinks the status of thoughts. Ideas or concepts themselves are always "more" than is identified and differentiated; they are always in relation to that other that they negate in order to constitute their identity, always an abbreviation of multiplicity, and always also multiple in themselves. But multiplicity is not simply an idea—for the logic of multiplicity implies the multiplication of the very difference between thoughts and things. Here multiplicity is no longer either ideal or real, concept or object, subject or substance—or some avatar of both—it is the multiple multiplicity that exceeds them.

The law of the excluded middle, then, is no longer exclusive/inclusive. If predication is multiple, then a thing is always in relation to a multiplicity of predicates, and there is always a third, that is, the already multiple subject, subjects. Predication no longer means either/or nor both/and—for these belong to the logical reductions of identity and difference. As multiple, the thing cannot be thought as either being or not-being a particular quality, as having or not-having a predicate within itself, its borders, as part of its self-identity. The question of the excluded middle shows itself to be the question of limitation, of the process of containment. Here, multiplicity means that the law of the excluded middle cannot think the "etc." For the logic of multiplicity, although a thing's predicates can be reduced to identities and/or differences, they may also be multiple. The discourse of multiplicity is not the language of exclusion/inclusion; rather, the predicative relation itself becomes multiple. The subject-object relation is no longer a choice between either having (a predicate) or being (a thing) since the relations between subject and object are multiple: a thing is, has, thinks, writes, smells, speaks, and so on. The multiplicity of time-words or verbs is the clue to the multiplicity of predication. And the law of predication via the inclusion/exclusion of the middle has been transformed by the logic of multiplicity into the law of multiple-predication—and this law is not just the law of multiplicity, for it is always also "etc." Even further, the law of multiplicity means not only that things are multiple, and not simply that they are both multiple and non-multiple, but that their multiplicity always exceeds identity and difference, and subject-object predication. The law of multiplicity, however, means that the essential multiple-ness of the "etc." of things, the multiplicity that is no-thing multiple, is multiple as well. And it means that the multiplicity of the multiple is always also a limitation of multiplicity itself.

The law of non-contradiction then, as well, is not the law of contradiction, but the law of multi-diction, of multiple expression. Speaking is not just "for" or "against" oneself (nor both), neither contradiction nor its resolution: all things are neither contradictory nor non-contradictory. Life is not a question of movement, nor is death a problem of stasis; space and time are not pure-contaminated, here/not-here, now/not-now, present/absent. For the discourse of multiplicity, laws of language, like those of logic, become multiple. If the "single" is the mark of the logic of non-contradiction, and the "double" (*-entendre,* -movement, -bind, -sides, -concept, etc.) that of the logic of contra-diction, then the "multiple" is that of the logic of multi-diction. The law of non-contradiction has found its twin (its other and, thereby, itself) in the law of contradiction—they form two sides of the law of contra-non-contra-diction; yet before the double-choice presents itself, prior to judgment and formal logic, diction is multiple. The law of multi-diction needs a multiple language: the discourse of poly-linguism. The inadequacies of predication or formal logic become once again apparent with respect to the "more" and the "etc.," the "multi—no longer double—diction." For the logic of multiplicity, the law of contradiction (and non-contradiction) as the law of multi-diction—is not just the other, negation, refusal, denial, rejection, that is, double, of the law of contra/non-contradiction—for it is always also "multiple." The logic of contradiction has opened the possibility of logics, and diction here means not just speech, or writing, or expression—or language as a totality; rather, it is all those and more, multiplied.

The law of diction means that multiplicity is prior to identity and difference, but neither in a spatio-temporal sense, nor as essence (ground, cause, reason, origin, or source) for being, nor in some conceptual combination of both; rather, it is prior in the sense of "priority" as "import-ance." The logic of multi-diction is only multiple if multiplicity, taking priority, imports meaning, significance, value, to identity and difference as well. Multiplicity articulates (*legein, dicare*) the multi-justice (*poly-dikē*) that lies prior to the logical laws of multiplicity, but it is also that which makes its actions (and the justice of its actions) more multiple than multiplicity itself—for multiplicity is the kind of justice that complicates the very difference between that which is identified as justice and law, and then complicates both the complication and the complicator, that complicates the entire logic of complication. Multiplicity, in other words, is that which lies prior to both justice and the laws of logic.

Becoming Multiple

Now, with the logic of multiplicity, it is possible to return to the origin of metaphysics, to Parmenides' fragment: "for the same: thought to be and to be."[49] Here, for Hegel, being is only in relation to non-being—and the sameness of being and thought is conceptual, that is, the identity and difference of identity and difference. Heidegger therefore maintains that Parmenides is an outstanding example of pre-onto-theological thought: identity and difference stand out; original difference is resolved insofar as it is maintained by the question of the Being of beings. In other words, Parmenides' question is that of the *identity* of being and the *being* of identity. Yet to question Parmenides within the circle of the philosophy, logic, and discourse of identity and difference is to read against multiplicity. And it is only with multiplicity, through a shift in both discourse and logic, that the fragment may be read multiply.

Indeed, for Parmenides, the relation between being and thinking is that of "sameness." Sameness, however, is itself multiple: *auto* means "same"; "self," "myself," "oneself," "alone" (i.e., with oneself), "together with" (that which belongs to oneself); "he, she, it" (personal pronoun); but also that which is natural, just or right for something, that which belongs to it; the ideal or essential; that which is exactly, precisely, or just something, simply or merely; or as emphasis (e.g., the very x), etc. The multiplicity of meanings mark the "etc." of the relations, the multi-diction that lies prior to thinking and being, the "relations" that can always be reduced to a mere relation, always gathered, superseded, distilled, negated, etc., in a "relation," but that always also remains possibly multiple, multiply possible, a possibility that is possibilities.

Not only does *auto*-relation then show itself as multiple, as *auto*-relations, but thinking and being themselves think and are multiple: they each are "more" than just themselves; thinking does more than just think; being does more than it is. The more of thinking means that thinking is not just thinking: the thing that thinks is the thing that doubts, conceives, affirms, denies, wants, does not want, imagines, senses (Descartes). In other words, thinking is a multiplicity of activities (verbs) and an "etc." The "more" of definition is always multiple—not just double, two-sided, positive and negative, affirmation/negation, revealing/concealing, etc. Thinking is never alone; rather, it is always also in relation to eating, sleeping, drinking, etc. Definition, therefore, can be defined as the framing (re-framing or framing-up) that takes care of multiplicity within the logic and discourse of identity and difference. For the logic of multiplicity, however, definition is multiple definition and poly-predication: thinking multiply is the kind of thinking that lies prior to its reduction to thinking/non-thinking, before the abstraction to thinking as reasoning. And thinking is one verb or action among many, among many that are also many; and here predicative discourse is no longer adequate to thinking this many.

Parmenides then thinks thinking (*noein*) and being (*estin*) as multiple. And thinking means seeing, discerning, remarking, perceiving, reasoning; but also intending, meaning, implying, giving sense to; contriving, devising; and indicating and resolving. The meanings of thinking are all there, present, in the fragment; that is, they all have being. And being means existing, being present, being real, living; being possible or lawful; belonging, being one of a group, gathering, being a part, property or mark, having; being present at a certain time and place. Hence, a multiplicity of meanings once again. And the multiple senses of being may all be thought, seen, discerned, and so on.

Yet even more important: being also means some, for example, some-things, some-times—that is, being means many (*estin hos, eisin hoi; est qui, sunt qui*). The "some" of a being is not "a" being; rather, it is beings. Parmenides's fragment, therefore, also means "for the same: thought to be many and to be many, thinking and many are the same, thinking is many." Yet if being and thinking are multiple and these multiplicities are themselves multiple, and not just, then Parmenides very well may be the first thinker of manys in the history of western philosophy.

The logic of multiplicity makes possible the thinking and being of thinking and being as multiple, makes multiplicity into a possibility, into possibilities, possibilities that are neither endless nor un-endless nor both—for they are made possible by the multiplicity that lies before them. No longer subject to the discourse of identity and difference, becoming multiple, Parmenides emerges as a thinker of multiplicity. The fragment becomes fragments (not in the sense of pluralization, but as multiple), shattered meanings that can always be reduced once again, broken down to the logic of identity and difference, that can take its place in the philosophy of identity and difference; however, the possibility of thinking the fragments as multiple also remains possible, remains possibilities. Yet if the grammar and discourse of multiplicity as simply multiple, as just multiple, is just a possibility, then the philosophy of identity and difference is still a possibility for thought and being; but it is no longer a necessity. Demonstrating "that" discourse and logic are multiple is essential, but it is also important to show "how" they are multiple (and not just)—or rather, how they are manys (and not just "that" and "how").

"Some" questions remain: What is the effect of re-reading the history of philosophy no longer as onto-theology, but as multiple? How is it possible that the "manys" of philosophical thought lie within the history of metaphysics? If the logic of multiplicity, as marked by the "etc.," "more," and "multiple" (not identical/single or differential/double), is itself multiple, then what does it mean to speak, think, write, etc. with a grammar and discourse of multiplicity, with discourses and languages? What are the problems, solutions, and re-solutions of poly-linguism, of thoughts and beings in many languages? Is a philosophical "tower of Babel" inevitable? Is a common language, a universal mathematics or theoretical "Esperanto" necessary? Or can multiplicity become (or is it already) manys? And to what extent must some justice of multiplicity lie at the core of manys?

Conclusion

Problem of Multiplicity

The investigation has shown "that" and "how" philosophy has thought multiplicity. In even the most (apparently) non-multiple of thinkers, multiplicity plays a critical role. Here Hegel marks a certain horizon: on the one hand, the thinking of multiplicity opens up to the logic of multiplicity, to its identity and difference, its contradiction and non-contradiction; on the other hand, it closes off multiplicity under the sign of the double-bind of the concept, the double—and only double—entendre. And this is the problem of multiplicity itself, the problem that may be more of a problem at the end than it was at the beginning. Yet if multiplicity is only a problem, then it is not yet problems; and if it is not yet problems, then it is because it is not only multiplicity—rather, multiplicity shows itself as multiplicities, the becoming multiple of problems, many problems and many multiplicities. Even further, these problems and multiplicities show themselves as multiple: no longer multiple identities or differences, but multiple multiplicities. To stop here, however, to be satisfied with the superficial production, construction, constitution, of multiplicities, is not enough—for the exclusion, negation, of all that is non-multiple (or its inclusion, affirmation) falls away from questions and multiplicities themselves. The problems remain those of multiplicities, of questioning, thinking, reading, speaking, writing, multiply; and of the multiplicity of these multiplicities, that is, multiplicities that are multiple, but not just multiple, that are just as much identities, differences, and so on.

In this sense the multiplicity that is both multiple and non-multiple is the concept of multiplicity; but a multiplicity that is not just multiple and non-multiple might be called "manys." Here and now, however, "manys" is just a name, a name signifying nothing, or worse; it may be some-thing, or somethings. Hence, multiplicities "are" not yet "manys"; they cannot yet be, think, speak, write, and so on, in many ways.

To follow these ways is to think along many paths, with many logics, to speak in many tongues, polyglottal, to write in many hands, to hear polyphonies (not just—but also—the syn-chronism of sym-phonies), and so on. The ways of the western philosophical tradition must be "abandoned"—for however multiple they appear, their fear of an uncontrolled and uncontrollable multiplicity holds them back from "manys." To abandon, however, is not to negate, exclude, refuse, destroy, and it is neither positive nor negative, nor both; rather, it means to surrender, to give up control, relinquish power, and thereby to open up to other ways of doing philosophy. That which is a-band-one-d are the ways of thinking (and one band of thinkers, like a route of wolves—that is, never a pack) that seeks to bind multiplicity together, to hold, preserve, or subjugate it under the sign of that which is no longer multiple: pluralized identities, subjects, predicates, definitions, relations, moments, modes; differences between quality and quantity, existence and essence, being and nothing, finitude and infinity, life and death, modes of possibility or impossibility; or multiplicities that determine themselves precisely by excluding or including identities or differences, and that thereby return to whence they came.

A certain sur-render-ing then, to multiplicity as such, renders it multiple—and these multiplicities, the ways of thinking multiplicities as multiple. And in this sense the surr-end-er may be a certain end—but one that neither signifies a new beginning, nor a return to an old beginning. Indeed, since its ways are infinitely mutable as long as it remains within the discourse of identity and difference, that is, never comes to pose the questions of multiplicity as multiple, the end of metaphysics is not a dead end; rather, the end is not just an end—it is more than an end (a *sûr*-rend and *surr*-end), also a beginning, middle, and so on. The abandoning of the pathways of metaphysics, therefore, means thinking off-*piste,* writing without the grammar of the tradition, listening for the multiplicity of languages that are always also in play, speaking without signposts and laws. The end of metaphysics is the beginning of multiplicity—but their relations are multiple, and not just that of beginning to end. If the questions of multiplicities then cannot be posed within the limits of metaphysics, they can also not be posed from a without—both within and without are always already metaphysical determinations that assume the logic and discourse of a philosophy of identity and difference. For metaphysics, to think multiply is either to think in the wrong way, to be off the track, on a *Holzweg,* or it is to not think at all. In other words, metaphysical multiplicity is always already co-constituted with non-multiplicity (identity, difference, etc.); they are in a relation of modes, substantives, predicates, and so on.

Metaphysics is one of many of ways of thinking—for thinking can also mean thinking multiply. And philosophy is never just thinking. At this moment then, philosophy must enter an uncharted wilderness, where a foreign tongue and the very lack of signposts, of demarcated paths, imply many paths, and where the relations between the nature of questioning are also multiple. Indeed, multiplicities are not anathema to philosophy; rather, they are already in play—the question is whether they can be heard, seen, tasted, and so on (and not as either sensation or thought, nor as both—but rather in the multiplicity from which this "identity and difference" is a result, abstraction, distillation, construction, determination).

As the investigation has shown, through the shift to a certain logic of contradiction, Hegel supersedes the understanding of multiplicity as superficial pluralization. And by both leaving behind and not leaving behind, forgetting and remembering, destroying and preserving, the *Logic* takes care of multiplicity qua predicate and substantive. No longer strapped to a one-sided version of multiplicity as either mode or relation, object or subject, pure or impure, in itself or for another, Hegel is able to think multiplicity as doubly identical, doubly differential, doubly multiple. Here multiplicity has multiple meanings: universal particularity, a kind (way, quality) of becoming that shows itself in the moments of being and not-being multiple, a quantitative relation of an identity and multiple identities, the relation between qualitative and quantitative multiplicities, and so on. And these meanings, insofar as they maintain their particularity and independence, are not simply dependent on one universal or fundamental meaning (like the absolute idea of multiplicity)—for the concept of multiplicity in Hegel is just as much as such (*an sich*), multiple, as it is (for) another, non-multiple; it is the identity and difference of the identity and difference of both.

It is, however, still possible to maintain, employing the "usual subterfuge" (or "usual suspects"), that these ways of thinking multiplicity (as identical, different, etc., and as multiple, as another and as such), have as their condition of possibility a prior multiplicity (not a prior identity, difference, and so on—since that is the traditional pathway of metaphysics), that is, "multiplicities," an original multiplicity from whence multiplicity, identity, difference, and so on emerge or are constituted. Or that their origin comes after them; that is, that prior to multiplicity are pure multiplicities from which they have been abstracted, produced, constructed, reduced, distilled, abbreviated, and so on—for they can show themselves, appear as given, be present or absent, "gone" multiple, because they have multiplicities not as their end (whereto), but as their *telos* (wherefore). Here a certain version of history is presupposed, but whether linear (scientific, prior, certainty of the "here and now") or circular (speculative, priority, truth of the concept), the historical movement of multiplicity means that space and time are merely moments, that both type of movements are superseded and taken care of in dialectic. Yet with Hegel's historicization of multiplicity, the doubles of linear/circular, a priori/a posteriori, space/time, cause/effect, ground/result, possibility/actuality, are superseded or "taken care of" as well. In this sense the "usual subterfuge" can no longer be deployed; and another way of thinking must emerge if the double-entendre of the concept of multiplicity is to be heard. Yet to what extent is this double-movement not capable of thinking multiplicity multiply if it does not itself go multiple? And what would it mean for thought to go multiple?

The problem of multiplicity, in other words, is that all this remains within the metaphysical arch of thought (however identical, different, etc., and multiple) that stretches from the Greeks to us—and as such, it cannot go multiple. Yet even for metaphysics, multiplicity cannot be pluralization since addition of more of the same or different will never produce multiplicity. Nor can multiplicity simply be defined since any single definition is no longer multiple, since definition (determination) follows a logic of identity and difference, of *negatio;* and it cannot be multiply defined because this multiplicity remains a mystery; and it cannot be indefinite—for this is only an evasion of the problem, or worse, a hidden definition that is no longer multiple, that returns and acquiesces to the difference of definition/non-definition. Multiplicity cannot be (or be expressed by, thought through, understood as) a simple substantive or predicate (real or universal) because the logic of predication means that there is only the difference between subject and object, a difference overcome through the identity of a copula. And it cannot be a modality because the bind of possibly/actually, necessarily/contingently, as/not as multiple, whether it adds or does not add anything to a being (object, substantive, thing, idea—and this too is a return to a predicative, i.e., non-multiple) remains a mere double-bind. Nor can multiplicity be a relation between two qualities, quantities, substantives, predicates, or relations: if the copula just unites differences (or identities), then it will never think multiply. Nor will any combination or permutation of these forms and matters, subjects and substances, of multiplicity ever go multiple; rather, they will far more remain stuck within the metaphysical wheel that can only repeat with a difference, only think the double that is the same and not the same.

Metaphysics then has already anticipated the problem of and the solution to multiplicity; and it comes to its logical conclusion in Hegel's thought of multiplicity, of multiplicity and non-multiplicity—yet another multiplicity, one that is reduced, produced, denied in this twofold, remains to be thought. For Hegel, if philosophy is to ever think differently, then it must find a way that remains un-named, un-thought (or both thought and unthought), that follows the essence of metaphysics to its logical conclusion in the double-logic of identity and difference. But, to put it multiply, in a language from which the distinction or difference between metaphysics and non-metaphysics is inadequate (and not just also adequate): if philosophy goes multiple, then it thinks metaphysics as one track, one way of thinking multiplicity.

Yet for metaphysics, the problem of multiplicity is always that of being or not being multiple, of becoming or not becoming multiple, of pure or impure, finite or infinite multiplicity. Here if determination is negation—and this version of determination is itself only possible if all determination is not only negation (and also only negation)[1]—then it is dependent upon Spinoza. In this respect Hegel completes Parmenides' thought of being and nothing in becoming, and the problem of becoming multiple is taken care of by phenomenologic. Yet what if philosophical determination could mean becoming "more" multiple than multiplicity? More multiple than multiple and non-multiple multiplicity? What would it mean to think "more" multiply than the multiplicity of meaning itself? And if it is impossible to close metaphysics (for in its closure it remains open—and because the closing and opening of thinking and being is not enough), then what could the becoming multiple of thought as neither a negation nor a delimitation of metaphysics mean? What might the expansion of metaphysics to the point of neither explosion nor implosion entail? Indeed, if the production of meaning, of making sense, is only possible within the horizon of metaphysics, for metaphysics, then manys makes no sense; it is nonsense—but for a philosophy gone multiple, is this not the most non-multiple of objections?[2] And if the problem of multiplicity stretches the internal weaknesses of a system to its breaking point, then does this problem not become far more the question of the problem itself? In other words, must not the problem of multiplicity, when faced with manys, not call that which is problematic about the problem into question?

A Multiplicity of Questions

At the limit of the problem of multiplicity, the problem (and its assumed solution, or its solvable/unsolvable status) becomes problematic—and the question of multiplicity becomes a question, a multiplicity of questions. Indeed, the problem of multiplicity has shown "what" multiplicity is: multiplicity *is* multiple and *is not* multiple; or for Hegel it is the movement (that has already happened) of the multiple in the non-multiple and vice versa. The being of multiplicity, being multiple, is only a moment, a multiplicity that determines itself (negatively) with respect to a non-multiplicity. If multiplicity is only multiple, purely multiple, then it is not multiplicity, is not what it should be; it is far more nothing. The being of multiplicity is what it is not: in being multiple, it is non-multiple. The nothing of multiplicity, not-being multiple, is the answer to the question "What is multiplicity?" And multiplicity is nothing; yet in not being multiple, multiplicity is in fact something: multiplicity is multiplicity. The difference, however, between "what it is" and "how it is" remains: multiplicity is multiplicity, but it is not multiple, not thought as multiple. In fact, the question of the being/nothing, that is, becoming, of multiplicity serves to cover over the question of the multiplicity of multiplicity, of how it can be asked multiply. Only asking about being, "what it is," thought cannot think multiplicity as multiple, think multiply, cannot go multiple itself. The questions then are: How can multiplicity be thought as multiple? And how can the (onto-noetic) difference between "what" and "how" it is (is not, both is and is not) itself go multiple? How can the identity and difference of thinking (*noein*) and being (*estin*) go multiple? And not just?

In fact, the (Greek) question of the "what" of being may be posed, as Heidegger does, in terms of the Being of beings (*Sein des Seienden*), in terms of the multiplicity of the being of an entity or thing. Yet even here the questions multiply themselves: How is it that "multiplicity belongs to Being itself"?[3] What *is* its being? What does it mean to think multiplication (*Mannigfaltigung*) as the inner possibility of multiplicity itself? If multiplicity is explicitly not many, that is, neither a preponderance of determinations (*Mehrheit*), nor the everyday absorption in the multiplicity (*Vielfältigkeit*) with which we are concerned, nor a quantity or counting of ones, then what is the nature of being's multiplicity? And how is it possible that being *is* multiple? What is the being-multiple of being? If being can multiply itself, if cause can be differentiated into causes (*aitia*), then is it not because being is always also multiple? If the multiplication of entities occurs not because of a multiplicity of things, but, on the contrary, because entities always also have the possibility of multiplication, then what is (or are) the origin(s) of the multiplicity of historical events, of figures of consciousness, of things, of human beings, in fact, of all multiplicity?[4] If multiplicity belongs to being itself, then is it because being means primordial multiplication (*ursprüngliche Mannigfaltigung*)?

Or does this answer to the question of multiplicity only serve to cover over the fact that the question of multiplicity, of the multiplicity of multiplicity, has never been asked, and has never been asked multiply—for it is always only asked in terms of the difference (not the multiplicity) of multiplicity and the multiple? And if the question of multiplicity lies at the end of a metaphysical trajectory initiated by the Greeks, can we repose the question no longer simply before or after difference (and identity), but at their center? Once again then: "What *is* multiplicity"?

Indeed, at the apogee of the metaphysics of identity and difference, Hegel's answer to these questions lies in the thought of multiplicity that allows it to be multiple and non-multiple: the logic of the concept governs what multiplicity is (its being), what it is not (its nothing), what it is and is not (its becoming)—the "how" translates the "what." To be multiple means also not to be multiple. Multiplicity is multiple as a moment—for instance, when it is abstractly multiple, without returning to a unity, without being non-multiple. In the moment that it is multiple, however, multiplicity is also non-multiple—that is, the concrete truth of being multiple and not being multiple is the movement from multiple multiplicity to non-multiplicity and from non-multiple multiplicity to multiplicity, that is, their becoming one another. In other words, the answer to the question "What *is* multiplicity?" is a double-moment, a moment wherein multiplicity is both multiple and not multiple—for conceptual multiplicity is always two-sided. As multiple multiplicity, multiplicity is, in fact, multiple, multi-sided, a multiplicity of moments, objects, subjects, relations, and so on. Yet when multiplicity *is* multiple, then it only *is* (and/or is not) multiple—the being of multiplicity returns it to non-multiplicity. The question about the being of multiplicity (what is it?) presupposes a double-determination, the non-multiplicity of being and nothing (i.e., of becoming).

The multiplicity of multiplicity then shows itself as the logic of the concept, as a means of determination that thinks multiplicity as non-multiple. Just as Aristotle determined the identity of multiplicity (of a species, genus, being, etc.) via difference, just as Kant differentiated the thing in itself from the object of appearance in order to think the identity of the (now-non-manifold) manifold, Hegel (dependent upon the logic of identity and difference) determines multiplicity via negation. Multiplicity is supposed to be thought as multiple, but at the moment that it is and/or is not multiple, it is no longer multiple: the logical form of the concept delimits, distills, abbreviates its matter. The question is not if multiplicity is not multiple; rather, it is: Why it is only multiple and/or non-multiple, pure or impure, finite or infinite, is or is not (being and/or nothing, i.e., becoming)? Why is it that multiplicity can never be thought multiply? What metaphysical logic forbids multiplicity itself?

For Hegel the true answer to these questions lies in "how" the thinking of multiplicity (wherein multiplicity is multiple/non-multiple) must be in conflict with thinking multiply. If the concept of multiplicity is just multiple, then it is not multiple—thus, it is also self-same, identical. By universalizing/particularizing the logic as a contradictory way of thinking, as the law for thought, multiplicity can only be thought as multiple/non-multiple; its being is no-thing, or more concretely, the truth is that it is only multiple if it is always also non-multiple, that is, in a moving relation (becoming) with its other. In this sense the dialectic is the logical conclusion of the attempt to think multiplicity as identity and difference. Here thought and being are the same and not the same. If multiplicity is thought multiply and non-multiply; then "what" is thought is/is not multiple, and "how" it is thought is double, that is, multiply/non-multiply.

To think multiplicity as multiple, therefore, it is not enough to think multiplicity as identical, differential, multiple, and so on; rather, thought must itself go multiple. Going multiple, multiplicity is/is not (not) just multiple. Going multiple, thought multiplies multiplicity: first, as that which thinks against the non-multiple, refuses, negates, denies non-multiplicity. Second, as that which thinks against the "multiple and/or non-multiple," thinks another multiplicity because it does not follow the logic of the concept, because it cannot be reduced to the two sides of multiple/non-multiple without denying the very multiplicity that was supposed to be thought—in this way it is multiplicities, that is, the determinations of multiple, of non-multiple, of both multiple and non-multiple, neither multiple nor non-multiple, of multiplicity as multiple, as identical, as differential, as triple, fourfold, and so on. Third, the going multiple of thought shows itself as one of the two sides of the onto-noetic difference, a difference that is and is thought from Aristotle to Hegel as the subsumption of multiplicity to non-multiplicity, or rather, the permitting of multiplicity only insofar as it is and/or is not multiple and/or non-multiple. Fourth, multiple thought thinks no longer simply "for" or "against" the non-multiple; rather, as "more" multiple than affirmation and negation, it has gone multiple. Fifth, thought multiplies its relation to being in such a way that their relation itself goes multiple, and thinking and being can no longer be the same—for there is much "more" to philosophy than just ideas and things.

For the discourse of identity and difference, however, the being and thought of multiplicity means that only that which *is* can be thought, and thinking determines being as beings. Indeed, for Hegel, being as *physis* means to show itself as itself, to appear, be expressed, enter into unconcealment, be remembered. And thought can determine *physis* because it belongs to *physis*, shares in its power, *is* and is part of nature. Being is appearing; yet in order to appear, being must appear to something. Being, therefore, appears to thought, and it is what it is qua appearing only if and when it appears to thought. Without thought, being cannot appear, cannot be what it is; it remains inert, inactive, dead—and essentially not *physis*. Being can appear to thought because thought already is; and thought can think what *is* because thinking is only of that which is. Yet "thought is *physis*" also means that it only becomes what it is, has its being, in its difference, from what it thinks; just as being, for its part, only is, insofar as it takes its distance from thought. Thought and being are co-constituted in their identity and difference, their relation and non-relation. In Hegel's concept, in other words, multiplicity and thinking multiply are the same; they are in a relation of becoming, of identity and difference, that is, a relation that is multiple and no longer multiple, and that is only *a* relation, *a* double-movement.

It is always possible then for thought to fall into the non-multiplicity of as such/as another, commensurable/incommensurable with multiplicity, to think multiplicity as multiple, non-multiple, as identical, differential, and so on; but this possibility is no necessity. As with thought and being, the relation of sameness too goes multiple (*polla*). The (ontological) question of the being of multiplicity "What is multiplicity?" can also be answered multiply (identically, differentially, etc.). And if metaphysics thinks multiplicity as non-multiple, then its logical conclusion lies in thinking multiplicity as multiple, as the multiplicity of multiplicities. Yet at the end of metaphysical questioning, at the point where the question of multiplicity itself becomes a multiplicity of questions—and where these questions become that which is most questionable—at the moment when multiplicity goes multiple, another multiplicity comes into question, a multiplicity that may always be re-articulated as a metaphysical multiplicity, that may always be subsumed under a way of thinking driven by the logic of identity and difference, may always be thought simply as the relations between that which is multiple, or between multipleness and the multiple, or between multiplicity and the multiple—but a multiplicity too that may go multiple. And this "multiplicity" might be called manys.

The Unkindest Cut of Manys

Manys is the name then for a multiplicity wherein whatness and howness are no longer only separable/inseparable, independent/dependent, or co-constitutive, because their distinction goes multiple. First, if multiplicity were merely many, simply plural and multiple (*polla he polla,* or pure *plēthos*) or merely non-multiple, then they would be perfectly metaphysical; and if they were both (or neither) multiple and/or non-multiple, then they would still be metaphysical—but manys means that these possibilities are only possible. With manys, metaphysics loses its necessity, although it still asserts its interpretation of multiplicity, insists on the logic, grammar, discourse of identity and difference and multiplicity, although this way of thinking is profoundly inadequate for a thinking become too multiple for multiplicity. Indeed, the necessity of metaphysics lies in identity and difference and multiplicity—with manys, however, that which is (or presents itself as) necessary shows itself as essentially arbitrary. Even further, the very difference between necessary and arbitrary that used to mark the limitations of metaphysics, that lies (*legein*) within the metaphysical logic (*logos*) of identity and difference, multiplies itself through an allotropic and multiple translation of "lying" as "lying."

Second, if thinking and being come up against manys, then not only are they thoughts and beings, but ways of thinking and being, ways among ways, actions among acts. Manys is marked by the multiplicity of "among," being as among beings, being-with, beings among beings; thinking as thinking among, thoughts among thoughts, thinking-with (not an other, but others, others that render the self/other determination multiple)—and a becoming multiple of thinking/being as verbs, actions, participles, gerunds, among verbs, actions, participles, gerunds. The many of metaphysics shows itself as many among manys, a manys that is already many, a becoming many of many to the point where philosophizing lies not just among thinking and being, but among manys. And philosophy can no longer be restricted to an event of thought, the work of a thinking subject, the task of grounding metaphysics as a science, the freedom of individuals, can no longer be reduced to a happening of being, a letting the thing show itself as itself or as another, the revealing of that which is in truth, or of truth itself—for coming face to face with manys, philosophy acts and acts out, out of manys (although this too may very well be just an act).

Third, then, manys is the name for that which in history (and the history of philosophy) is not only many and/or non-many, not just many as such or as another; it is not only a thought/concept or/and thing/object, nor is it both (even their movement); it is the name for that which is "more" than many, a many that can no longer be approached via one and/or many interpretations. Manys is not only before or after (or contemporaneous with, temporally/spatially, and not just) the metaphysical interpretation of identity and difference: for example, constitution, creation or construction, following a metaphysical (linear/circular) understanding of time and space (history), deploying a logic of identity and difference in determining or abstracting the relation between constituted and constituter, between that which is constituted and that (transcendental *eidos* or empirical *Stoff*) out of which it is constituted (whether it is self-made or produced by another)—for this assumes the poetological difference (*poesis* as making) between "means of production" and "meaning-production," between raw material and product. The logic of constitution is itself constituted on the basis of identities and differences and multiplicitics; but as not just spatial, temporal, or multi-dimensional, the act of philosophizing may lie far closer to a story (rather than a history) of manys.

In other words then, fourth, the "s" of manys cannot signify superficial pluralization—many is already plural, and its increase will never reach manys; it does not function to maintain the continuity or discontinuity, the identity or difference, between metaphysics and the thought of its negation; rather, it marks the breakdown in grammar and language, the logical glitch, the prick in the tissue of a discourse that burns out or flags with multiplicity. Indeed, for a metaphysical interpretation of multiplicity, manys is much too many—it is taken to be a mis-take, a slip or error, a faitery or counterfeit concept, a bad neologism, funny or amusing at best, insulting and pretentious arrogance at worst, the "most unkindest cut of all." For manys, however, its "s" flags its own breakdown, its identity, difference, and multiplicity (and not just its own—for manys is not just manys) to the moment of their collapse. As Hegel's concept signifies that logic has been loosened up to the point where it can think contradiction, hear the double-entendre, the "s" of manys means that thoughts, beings, readings, words, languages, actions, philosophies have become multiple (and not just), that the full force of multiplicity has finally come into play as manys. In this way the "s" of manys marks the point that lies at the very core of metaphysics where multiplicity becomes "more" than multiple and exceeds polytropism itself, where philosophy plays a role that it has perhaps never played before.

Metaphysics and Manys

> To prefer just to be with somebody else, to engage of one's own free will in spiritual intimacy with another, that was true adultery. It had been easy enough to accept this view of morality with one's brain, thought Edwin. It was when promiscuity changed from a concept to a percept that trouble began.
>
> —*Burgess*[5]

Metaphysics then, insofar as it only thinks multiplicity or is multiple (or both), cannot become multiple, cannot multiply the philosophemes of western thought, the identities and/or differences between being and beings, being and non-being, thought and being, meaning and sense, sign and referent, idea and thing, and so on, to the point of manys. Within a metaphysical horizon, manys, strictly speaking, is not. Manys, however, can translate metaphysics into a discourse that, becoming multiple, becoming becomings, becoming manys, can reinterpret its interpretations, abbreviations, determinations (of, for example, being and nothing) as only possible––and not just, for it is actually them as well. In this way finishing the arch of criticism launched by Aristotle against Plato and the Pythagoreans, and culminating in Hegel, metaphysics raises the question of being qua beings but never takes the multiplicity of being and beings seriously. Manys, however, cannot stop there: if the meaning of being lies in manys (not just being multiple), and the being of beings *is* not simply manys––for it not only *is,* and not only *is not*—the being of beings itself becomes multiple. Here, after the loosening of philosophy from its metaphysical object (i.e., no longer just asking the question of "what is?" or "what is x?"—the question of the meaning of being), philosophy too becomes multiple. Manys, however, is multiple in a way in which metaphysics never could *be*—precisely because being means becoming multiple, and not just. The metaphysical interpretation of the multiplicity of beings, therefore, insofar as it thinks that which *is* multiple, cannot interpret manys as such, that is, that which acts in manys ways, and not only *is*—for it also thinks, writes, speaks manys (as not only a thought). Ontological and noetic investigation remain both blind and empty if they fail to pose the question (and the cost) of their own multiplicity—and if they do, then they become multiple. To be multiple or not to be multiple, to become multiple or to remain non-multiple, is not the question; rather, it is how could a translation of multiplicity, itself becoming even "more" multiple, play a role in manys?

Thinking the unthought many as many, as the multiple ways in which multiplicity can be thought, brings metaphysics to a certain logical conclusion, a completing of the metaphysical circle that appears in the form of an arch. Here metaphysics is multiple and multiplicity is metaphysical; yet the complicity in the project of "finishing off" metaphysics is also a "start," and not just. Rather than formulating another concept, version, avatar, of multiplicity, thought changes horizons, shifts to an in-comparable way of thinking, takes a direction not yet taken—for thought becomes multiple, a thinking that is not just a question of the pluralization of thought as thoughts, not simply a way of thinking, nor only that which is to be thought, nor how it is to be thought, and so on. Precisely in completing the circle of *polla,* of *polla he polla,* with the thought of multiplicity (as multiple and/or non-multiple), metaphysics is no longer just metaphysics, and no longer simply *meta-physicoi*—for it has become multiple, and not just. And this becoming multiple of metaphysics translates multiplicity itself into a "manys" that lies dormant in philosophy.

If, from its inception then, metaphysics has sought to anticipate and control the multiplicity that threatened its identity and difference, then it has been through the very logic (the *dia-logos*) of identity and difference of its identity and difference. In this sense a perfectly metaphysical circle shows itself: being and non-being, one and many, objective and subjective, gods and mortals, transcendental and empirical, phenomena and noumena, ontic and ontological, two kinds of truth (as in *Mond,* §33), *quid juris* and *quid facti,* revealing and concealing—in all this, the logic of identity and difference grounds the identity and difference of concepts on which it is supposed to be grounded. Multiplicity, therefore, is thought only insofar as it submits and does not submit to the logic of multiplicity as multiple and non-multiple—and Hegel is the philosopher of this double, of the identity and difference of identity and difference, and its truth in the dialectical concept. Yet determining the horizon or limit (however fluctuating, resilient, amorphous, or transgressed) of the metaphysical interpretation of multiplicity, completing the circle of metaphysics, is neither a negative nor positive work that must be accomplished in order to think multiply—for negative and positive are not multiple.

An interpretation of multiplicity as multiple then can do to metaphysics what the double-logic, the is/is not, being/nothing, the concept (as multiple and non-multiple), never could, namely, interpret its multiplicity as multiple. Here the logical concept is abandoned for the percept; or rather, in a polylogue with metaphysics, philosophy sees through (*per*) to that which lies at the core of dia-logue, to the multiplicity that must be per-ceived as not-just-multiple. In this sense it is no wonder that philosophy's intimate involvement with multiplicity implies the betrayal of metaphysics, and a new beginning, perhaps, no longer in wonder. Yet if the grammar, logic, and discourse of identity and difference must be cuckolded, or if metaphysics has in some motivated way been promiscuous from its very inception, then this spells the beginning of trouble for philosophy. And if an allonoetic multiplicity, a multiplicity that does not compute (since it does not belong to the order of computation), can prove so deeply threatening to metaphysical multiplicity, then is it perhaps because this trouble lies with manys?

Improvising Manys

> Verily, this human, in spite of his youth, is an expert *improviser of life* who amazes even the subtlest observer:—it seems namely, that he makes no mistake, although he continually gambles the riskiest gamble. One is reminded of those masters of musical improvisation who the listener would also like to credit with a divine *infallibility* of the hand; although, here and there they make a mistake, as every mortal does. But they are practiced and inventive, and ready in an instant to incorporate into their thematic structure the most accidental tone to which the flick of a finger or a mood has driven them, breathing a beautiful meaning and a soul into an accident.
>
> —*Nietzsche*[6]

The interpretations of metaphysics may go multiple, but manys means that they can no longer remain simply interpretations; rather, they go improvisational. The lexicon of metaphysics, however, its logic, grammar, language, and discourse, spells out the horizon of its ability to think manys. Certainly, with Hegel, metaphysical language is ex-panded—the concept (and its identity and difference) ex-pressed as the supersession that takes care of predicative logic thinks and names multiplicity as multiple and non-multiple: they is the same. The expansion of metaphysical language, however, is also its contraction—and that is the "metaphysical contract"—the delimitation also a limitation, distillation also a stilling. A becoming multiple of thought directs itself toward multiplicity as multiple, but this multiplicity is not only a thinking—for it is also a writing, reading, speaking, feeling, and so on. And it is here that manys lies in wait.

The language of multiplicity then is neither predicative, nor formal, nor conceptual—for it is languages (and not just). Here the tense of terms is no tense at all; rather, it is a tension, a multiplicity of relations that multiplies metaphysical language. Meaning lies not only in the times or aspects of words, concepts, thoughts, not only in that to which terms refer (or do not refer), but also in their multiple connections with other words, sounds, images, other experiences, thoughts, feelings, and so on. Signification becomes the process of opening up hearing to the poly-entendre of aurality, opening up seeing to anagrams and rebuses. The language of multiplicity is the becoming multiple of the identity/difference by which metaphysics differentiates thought from sensation. And in this sense no unification of mind and body is sought; rather, thinking and sensing (as well as their difference) go multiple, two among many capacities, abilities, faculties, actions, and so on—and each itself far more multiply. Thought is here, neither pure (no picture thinking) nor merely representation; rather, the becoming multiple of identity and difference means the becoming multiple of thought as well. Thinking, therefore, means (as Descartes knew) a multiplicity of activities: imagining, feeling, sweating, and so on—for is this not how thought works, before it is worked over by metaphysics? And sensation is far more sensations, feeling far more feelings, and feeling means imagining, thinking, sweating, and so on. Languages are not only the metaphysical thinking and/or feeling of multiplicity, but also the doubting, denying, knowing, ignoring, hating, wanting, of multiplicity—for language, insofar as it has always already betrayed the linguistic, is never simply language.

Any breakdown in the interpretation of meaning then, of the categories of legitimate/illegitimate, true/false, and so on, any failure to maintain control over syntax, to fix or un-fix the pathways of inference and associations in a system (dead or alive), must be condemned by metaphysics as corrupt, irresponsible, must be named an illegitimate falsity, a lie or infidelity—but manys lies in languages. And not only within, but also across languages, the becoming multiple of philosophemes signals the loosening up of metaphysics for philosophy, for philosophies, the multiplicity of languages that are not just remembered or forgotten, but that open up to that which is normally denied in the process of making sense, producing identities and differences and multiplicities. Not only expanding philosophical vocabulary or pluralizing its subjects and substances, however, languages multiplies metaphysical terms as well: manys does not mean that *logos* simply becomes *logoi;* rather, it means that it can be improvised upon as *logos,* that the metaphysical interpretation with which it has been flagged may "brake" down, and improvisations can play upon or act out a manys that lies in wait (and not just).

Manys of *Logos*

> Disaster. Witless, idiotic disaster. Because what I have in mind is an "accident" so perfectly contrived that it will be unique, spectacular, instantaneous, a physical counterpart to that vision in which it was in fact conceived. A clear "accident," so to speak, in which invention quite defies interpretation.
>
> —*Hawkes*[7]

If it is possible to think, to write, speak, hear, multiply; then philosophy too goes multiple, goes improvisational. Here the multiplicity of differences are suspended; the multiplicity of identities of meaning, expression, sense, of essence, being, of subject and object, are put in abeyance; the multiplicity of the multiple abandoned. And with the language of manys, thought and being act too multiply for metaphysics. Indeed, metaphysics is no longer simply metaphysics—for it fails to think the multiplicity that lies at its core, and *logos* is the core of metaphysics. Heraclitus writes (Frag. 50):

> οὐκ ἐμοῦ ἀλλὰ τοῦ Λόγου ἀκούσαντας
> ὁμολογεῖν σοφόν ἐστιν Ἓν Πάντα ειναι.[8]

That is:

> When you have listened not to me but to the sense [*Logos*]; so it is wise, in the same sense [*logos*], to say: *one* is all.[9]

The meanings of *logos* are already multiple: sense, meaning, word, speech, talk, reason, thought, account, and so on. Yet if *logos* comes from *legein, legō,* then it really means laying, letting-lie, letting lie together in a gathering or saying, letting-be-said, letting be as said. The word, sense, reason, account, and so on comes from that which gathers the laying-out, collects in a layout or order. Thinking *legein* as the place from whence *logos* comes (into presence), Heraclitus writes:

> Attuned not to me but to the Laying that gathers: letting the Same lie: the fateful occurs (the Laying that gathers): One unifying All.[10]

Yet the translation also means: "Belonging not to me, but to the read lying; letting the same lie: the historical presences (the reading lying): one ones all." In this way a translation of the multiplicity of each word's meanings by words with multiple meanings may very well be more "faithful" to the polyvalence of Heraclitus's Greek.

Yet the laying (and lay) of *logos* can be heard even more multiply—and here is where improvisation begins. Not only the word, reason, and so on that is gathered, nor a letting be gathered, a laying or letting-lay-together—laying is also a lying down together in bed (*lechos*), the sexual act, from the most vulgar adultery to the most biblical of sentiments; it is producing, procreating, pushing out, bringing forth and depositing, expunging, expelling; the beating or striking down of an enemy, opponent, attacker; and the laying to rest, the burying of a body; the placing of a bet or wager; the calming or allaying of fears, and the smoothing out of surfaces; it is dissemination, spreading, distributing or giving out; and the imposition or granting of a fate (*moira*), burden, blame, of appropriate recompense, punishment; or an accenting, stressing, highlighting; it is preparing and contriving a plan; an application or practice; the claiming, appropriating, asserting of a position or legal right and the submitting to justice (*dikē, Fug*); and it is being present, being there—laying is all this and more. In a multiplicity of forms of speech (noun, verb, adjective, participle, infinitive, etc.), *legein* as laying is more multiple than metaphysics thinks.

Even further: that which lays also lies—and in this way English makes explicit that which is only implicit in Greek—for "to lie," is to be prostrate, horizontal, extended, and to be vertical, stand, remain; it means to reside or dwell, dwell in and indwell, inhere; and to remain hidden, inactive, anticipating, waiting, concealed; it is to be helpless, defenseless, open to the possibility of attack; and also to extend, reach out, direct; but just as much to have a place, a position in relation to another; and to have an effect through presence, weight, position. "To lie" is "to be," to occupy a place, exist in space: lying means being.

Lying, however, must also be heard as that which is spoken or said (*legetai*). All these terms then, speaking, lying, being, and so on, go multiple. It is always possible to differentiate their meanings into those that belong to *logos* and those that do not. And here the meanings belong and do not belong to *logos*. But does *logos* not also (perhaps much more) belong to its meanings? Speaking multiply, the relation between signifier and signified are far more relations, relations between signifiers and signifieds, and relations that indicate that signification itself is not just a question of signifiers/signifieds—for they too must be rethought multiply.

No longer a question of the legitimacy/illegitimacy of etymology, of permissible or impermissible connections, avoidable/unavoidable meaning of words, signs, terms, and so on; the manys of *logos*, and of philosophy, means hearing that which may be heard, thinking that which may be thought, perceiving that which may be perceived. Does language thereby not multiply the lie of *logos* for philosophy? No longer restricted, controlled or censored by a logic of identity and difference and multiplicity, no longer a question of what must be questioned, the questions themselves multiply: Can philosophy hear *logos* as lie—and not just? What is the lie that marks the wisdom of the Greeks? The *logos* that perhaps only now, becoming too multiple for multiplicity, can be thought? Or to what extent can the manys of *logos* lie in a play of language, thought, being, becoming, and so on?

Indeed, an improvisation of philosophy means that it is possible to think *logos* multiply. For metaphysics, however, the lie of *logos* remains simply false (*pseudos*), and in this way misleading, deceitful, illegitimate, and so on. Yet thought is not only constrained by identity, difference, multiplicity; with manys, thought confronts its own uncontrollability: the difference between controlled and uncontrolled is (itself) out of control. Hearing the lie of *logos* is far from necessary (for which two thousand years of thought is only the most superficial of testimonies), but it may just be possible. And philosophy can no longer be the same, or different—for with manys, it must improvise a *logos* gone multiple.

The multiplicity of *logos* then means that another multiplicity lies at its core, a multiplicity that is multiple, but not just. With a philosophical improvisation, and a certain infidelity to metaphysics, thought plays or acts on the manys of *logos*. The injustice in justice, however, cannot think manys—for it simply returns thought to the logic of identity and difference and multiplicity. And the approach to the question of justice, that is, the question of multiplicity, lies in manys.

Now, listening not to me, but to the lie, it is wise to agree that all is one; and "according to Heraclitus, those who love wisdom must be good inquirers into *many* things indeed."[11]

Notes

Preface

1. *A Midsummer Night's Dream,* act 2, scene 2.

2. "Χρὴ εὖ μάλα πολλῶν ἵστορας φιλοσόφους ἄνδρας εἶναι" (Heraclitus, Frag. 35; emphasis added).

3. "*Gedanken ohne Inhalt sind leer, Anschauungen ohne Begriffe sind blind*" (*CPR,* B 75, cf. §23).

4. Whenever possible, I have avoided capitalizing Hegelian terms; thus, concept (*Begriff*), identity (*Identität*), spirit (*Geist*), etc.

5. "Der bacchantische Taumel, an dem kein Glied nicht trunken ist, und weil jedes, indem es sich absondert, ebenso unmittelbar auflöst,—ist er ebenso die durchsichtige und einfache Ruhe" (*PhG,* p. 35 [§47]).

6. Cf. Heidegger, *WD,* p. 4.

7. "Sein, reines Sein,—*ohne alle weitere Bestimmung*" (*WLSb,* p. 68 [82]).

8. "*Alle Dinge sind an sich selbst widersprechend*" (*WLW,* p. 286 [439; translation modified]).

Introduction

1. "εἰ πολλά ἐστιν, ἀνάγκη τοσαῦτα εἶναι ὅσα ἐστὶ καὶ οὔτε πλείονα αὐτῶν οὔτε ἐλάττονα. εἰ δὲ τοσαῦτά ἐστιν ὅσα ἐστί, πεπερασμένα ἂν εἴη. εἰ πολλά ἐστιν, ἄπειρα τὰ ὄντα ἐστίν. ἀεὶ γὰρ ἕτερα μεταξύ τῶν ὄντων ἐστί, καὶ πάλιν ἐκείνων ἕτερα μεταξύ. καὶ οὕτως ἄπειρα τὰ ὄντα ἐστί" (Frag. 3, Simplicius *Phys* 140, 28).

2. Plato, *Soph* 232a.

3. Plato, *Parm* 127d.

4. "'Ἄνδρα μοι ἔννεπε, Μοῦσα, πολύτροπον, ὃς μάλα πολλὰ / πλάγχθη, ἐπεὶ Τροίης ἱερὸν πτολίεθρον ἔπερσεν. / πολλῶν δ' ἀνθρώπων ἴδεν ἄστεα καὶ νόον ἔγνω, / πολλὰ δ' ὅ γ' ἐν πόντῳ πάθεν ἄλγεα ὃν κατὰ θυμόν, / ἀρνύμενος ἥν τε ψυχὴν καὶ νόστον ἑταίρων" (*Odyssey,* book 1, 1–5, emphasis added). "Nenne mir, Muse, den Mann, den vielgewandten, der vielfach / Wurde verschlagen, seit Trojas heilige Burg er zerstörte. / Vieler Menschen Siedlungen sah er und lernte ihr Wesen / Kennen und litt auf dem Meer viel Schmerzen in seinem Gemüte, / Um sein Leben bemüht und die Heimkehr seiner Gefährten";

trans. R. Hampe (Stuttgart: Reclam, 1979). "C'est l'Homme aux mille tours, Muse, qu'il faut me dire Celui qui tant erra quand, de Troade, il eut pillé la ville sainte Celui qui visita les cités de tant d'hommes et connut leur esprit Celui qui, sur les mers, passa par tant d'angoisses, en luttant pour survivre et ramener ses gens"; trans. V. Bérard (Paris: Société d'Édition "Les Belles Lettres," 1967).

5. "Thatsächlich die grosse Form des Lebens sich immer auf der Seite der unbedenklichsten πολύτροποι gezeigt hat" (*KGW* V, 2, 258 [*GS*, §344; translation modified]).

6. Plato, *Parm* 127e; *Rep* V, 479b.

7. "τὸ δὲ ὂν λέγεται μὲν πολλαχῶς" and "πρὸς ἕν" (*Meta,* Γ 1003a33; cf. also Δ 7; Z 1; I 3).

8. *Monadology* §16.

9. "Mannigfaltigen unserer Vorstellungen" (*CPR,* A 105; cf. B 132).

10. "Die Vielen sind aber das Eine was das Andere ist, jedes ist Eins oder auch Eins der Vielen" (*Enzy,* §98); "träge Bewegung und Aufeinanderfolge von Geistern" (*PhG,* §808).

11. "Mannigfaltigkeit gehört zum Sein selbst" (*GA* 26, §10). Cf. also *SZ,* §12, 64, 80.

12. "Le multiple, *il faut le faire,* non pas en ajoutant toujours une dimension supérieure, mais au contraire le plus simplement, à tout force de sobriété, au niveau des dimensions dont on dispose, toujours n – 1 (c'est seulement ainsi que l'un fait partie du multiple, en étant toujours soustrait). Soustraire l'unique de la multiplicité à constituer; écrire à n – 1. Un tel système pourrait être nommé rhizome" (*Mille plateaux,* p. 13 [*A Thousand Plateaus,* p. 6]). Or again: "the wasp is nevertheless deterritorialized, becoming a piece in the orchid's reproductive apparatus; but it reterritorializes the orchid by transporting its pollen. Wasp and orchid, as heterogeneous elements, form a rhizome" [la guêpe se déterritorialise pourtant, devenant elle-même une pièce dans l'appareil de reproduction de l'orchidée; mais elle reterritorialise l'orchidée, en en transportant le pollen. La guêpe et l'orchidée font rhizome, en tant qu'hétérogènes] (ibid., p. 17 [10; translation slightly modified]). Perhaps, in the end, it is the metaphor of the wasp (*guêpe*) that marks the continuity between Deleuze/Guattari and Derrida, between disemmination and deterritorialization (cf. Derrida, *La Dissémination,* pp. 337–38). See also the argument in *What Is Philosophy?* that as transcendental empiricism, philosophy is constructivist, i.e., the creation of concepts on a plane of immanence through conceptual personae (Deleuze/Guattari, p. 38 [35]).

13. "Daß sie eine Wissenschaft ist, welche nichts als die formalen Regeln alles Denkens (es mag a priori oder empirisch sein, einen Ursprung oder Objekt haben, welches es wolle, in unserm Gemüte zufällige oder natürliche Hindernisse antreffen) ausführlich darlegt und strenge beweist" (*CPR,* B viii–ix).

14. "Elle inscrit la différence dans la vie . . . la multiplicité numérique ne survenant pas comme une menace de mort à un germe antérieurement un avec soi. Elle fraye au contraire la voie à 'la' semence qui ne (se) produit donc, ne s'avance qu'au pluriel. Singulier pluriel qu'aucune origine singulière n'aura jamais précédé. . . . Si par là ils voulaient dire quelque chose, c'est qu'il n'y a

rien avant le groupe, aucune unité simple et originaire avant cette division par laquelle la vie vient à se voir et la semence d'entrée de jeu se multiplie; rien avant l'addition en laquelle la semence commence par se soustraire, avant ce que le Drame annonçait comme 'une prolifération qui n'aurait jamais commencé,' avant ce que les Logiques consignaient comme essaim de guêpes, division au travail" (Derrida, *La Dissémination,* pp. 337–38 [*Dissemination,* p. 304]).

15. "Und wenn die abendländische Philosophie bis zu Hegel über den Satz des Parmenides: τὸ ὄν τὸ ἕν trotz aller Wandlungen im Grunde nicht hinausgekommen ist, dann bedeutet das keinen Mangel, sondern einen Vorzug und das Zeichen, daß sie, trotz allem, stark genug blieb, ihre erste Wahrheit zu bewahren" (Heidegger, *GA* 33, p. 24; my translation).

16. Plato, *Rep,* IX, 587e.

17. Cf. Foucault, *Les Mots et les choses.*

18. Cf. Nietzsche (*KGW* VIII, 1, 8): "*the human being as a multiplicity of 'wills to power:' each with a multiplicity of means of expression and forms*" [der Mensch als eine Vielheit von 'Willen zur Macht:' jeder mit einer Vielheit von Ausdrucksmitteln und Formen]. Nietzsche sides, almost always, against the quantitative many (cf. *KGW* VIII, 1, 150). And if he disassociates himself from "will to power," then is it because he knows that "a/one" [*eine*] multiplicity (*Vielheit*) remains within the logic of the one/identity, the unity that is itself only an appearance, a mask, of unity? Cf. also *KGW* VIII, 1, 11, 125, 209.

19. "Am Leitfaden des Leibes zeigt sich eine ungeheure *Vielfachheit*" (Nietzsche, *KGW* VIII, 1, 104).

20. "Der Kampfplatz dieser endlosen Streitigkeiten heißt nun *Metaphysik*" (*CPR,* A viii).

21. Cf. Ingeborg Bachmann, *Simultan* (Munich: Piper, 1972), p. 18: "what a strange mechanism she was, without having a single thought in her head, she lived, submerged in the sentences of others, and must, sleepwalkerish [instinctively], with identical but contrary sentences follow immediately after, she could make, from 'to make' machen, faire, fare, hacer and delat', she could turn over each word six times in a row, she dared only not think that to make really to make, machen machen, faire faire, fare fare, delat' delat', meant, that could make her head unusable, and she must really pay attention not, one day, to be buried alive from the masses of words" [was für ein seltsamer Mechanismus war sie doch, ohne einen einzigen Gedanken im Kopf zu haben, lebte sie, eingetaucht in die Sätze anderer, und mußte nachtwandlerisch mit gleichen, aber anderslautenden Sätzen sofort nachkommen, sie konnte aus 'machen' to make, faire, fare, hacer und delat' machen, jedes Wort konnte sie so auf einer Rolle sechsmal herumdrehen, sie durfte nur nicht denken, daß machen wirklich machen, faire faire, fare fare, delat' delat' bedeutete, das konnte ihren Kopf unbrauchbar machen, und sie mußte schon aufpassen, daß sie eines Tages nicht von den Wortmassen verschüttet wurde].

22. Aristotle, *Poetics,* §4, 1448b23.

23. *The Gay Science,* §303 (*KGW* V, 2, pp. 221–22).

24. For an example of improvisation, cf. Jacob Böhme (1575–1624), esp.

Theosophia revelata, Aurora, oder Morgenrothe im Aufgang (1612). Here the movement is among terms such as qualification (*Qualificirung*) (pp. 234, 276, 291), quality (*Qualität*) (pp. 126–35, 232, 283–85), pain (*Qual, Quaal*) (p. 126), source (*Quell*) (pp. 128–43, 230–32, 248, 282), to inqualier (*inqualieren*) (pp. 227, 231, 237–38, 249–50, 276, 281), etc. The first register reads: "paiin, pahn, painn, is the documented source in the infinite and temporal nature / in the darkness, it is embarassing and is pahn / in light, soft, bearing, pleasant and is painn / in the bearing nature, mixted and is paiin" [Quaal, Quahl, oder Quall, ist das urkündliche Quellen in der ewigen und zeitlichen Natur / im Finstern peinlich und ist Quahl / im Lichte sanft gebärende erfreulich und ist Quall / in der gebärenden Natur vermischt und ist Quaal]. Cf. also "Glossary" in Böhme, *Von der Gnadenwahl,* p. 244. "Inqualirung" is explained as "the acting in and penetrating of one in the other / like the rays of the sun and stars on an herb; happens also the spiritual in spiritual things" [das hineinwirken u. dringen eins ins andere / wie der Sonnen und Sternen Strahlen in ein Kraut; geschihet auch geistlich in geistliche Dinge] (Böhme quoted in a footnote to *WLSb,* Meiner Edition, p. 459; my quite tortured translation). Hegel explains inqualifying (*Inqualierung*) as "the movement of a quality (of sourness, bitterness, fieriness, etc.) within itself insofar as it posits and establishes itself in its negative nature (in its torment) from out of an other" [die Bewegung einer Qualität (der sauren, herben, feurigen u.s.f.) in ihr selbst, insofern sie in ihrer negativen Natur (in ihrer Qual) sich aus anderem setzt und befestigt] (*WLSb,* p. 102 [114]). Cf. also Böhme, *Gnadenwahl,* pp. 15, 26, 29, 32, 38, 41, 49, 53, 55, 121, etc. Naturally, Böhme's source is the Bible, e.g., for pain (*Qual*) and smoke (*Qualm*); cf., for example, Johannas, *Apokalypse,* 14.11: "And the smoke of their pain rose up from eternity to eternity" [Und der Qualm ihrer Qual steigt auf von Ewigkeit zu Ewigkeit]; for source (*Quelle*), cf. *Psalms,* 36.10. See also *Das Buch der Sprüche,* 13.14, 14.27, 16.22, 18.4.

Chapter 1

1. "Sed quid igitur sum? res cogitans; quid est hoc? nempe dubitans, intelligens, affirmans, negans, volens, nolens, imaginans quoque et sentiens (Mais qu'est-ce donc que je suis? Une chose qui pense Qu'est-ce qu'une chose qui pense? C'est-à-dire une chose qui doute, qui conçoit, qui affirme, qui nie, qui veut, qui ne veut pas, qui imagine aussi, et qui sent)" (*Med II*).

2. "Hoc unum nihil esse certi (il n'y a rien au monde de certain)" (*Med II*).

3. "Quia postea quaerendum foret, quidnam animal sit et quid rationale, atque ita ex una quaestione in plures difficilioresque delaberer (rechercher ce que c'est qu'animal, et ce que c'est que raisonnable, et ainsi d'une seule question nous tomberions insensiblement en une infinité d'autres plus difficiles et embarrassées)" (*Med II*).

4. "Ut nihil occurrat, per quod evidentius explicetur (qu'il n'est pas ici besoin de rien ajouter pour l'expliquer)" (*Med II*).

5. "Ego sum res cogitans (je suis une chose qui pense)" and "Id est dubitans, affirmans, negans, pauca intelligens, multa ignorans, volens, nolens, imaginans,

etiam et sentiens (qui doute, qui affirme, qui nie, qui conaît peu de choses, qui en ignore beaucoup, qui aime, qui hait, qui veut, qui ne veut pas, qui imagine aussi, et qui sent)" (*Med III*).

6. "Seien wir vorsichtiger als Cartesius, welcher in dem Fallstrick der Worte hängen blieb. *Cogito* ist freilich nur *Ein* Wort: aber es bedeutet etwas Vielfaches: manches ist vielfach und wir greifen derb darauf los, im guten Glauben, daß es *Eins* sei. In jenem berühmten *cogito* steckt 1) es denkt, 2) und ich glaube, daß ich es bin, der da denkt, 3) aber auch angenommen, daß dieser zweite Punkt in der Schwebe bliebe, als Sache des Glaubens, so enthält auch jenes erste 'es denkt' noch einen Glauben: nämlich, daß 'denken' eine Thätigkeit sei, zu der ein Subjekt, zum mindesten ein 'es' gedacht werden müsse—und weiter bedeutet das ergo sum nichts!" (*KGW* VII, 3, 371).

7. "La multiplicité des règles provient souvent de l'ignorance du maître, et ce qu'on peut ramener à un seul précepte général est moins clair quand on le divise en un grand nombre de préceptes particuliers" (*Rules for the Direction of the Soul,* XVIII).

8. "La raison veut qu'on évite la multiplicité dans les hypothèses ou principes, à peu près comme le système le plus simple est toujours préféré en astronomie" (*Discours de métaphysique,* 5).

9. "Die Geschichte der Entdeckung der *Gedanken* über das Absolute, das ihr Gegenstand ist" (Hegel, *Enzy, Vorrede zur zweiten Ausgabe*).

10. "Schlimmeres könne aber einem Menschen oder einem ganzen Lande wohl nicht begegnen, als gar nicht zu existieren" ("Klein Zaches Gennant Zinnober," *Märchen,* pp. 155–56). Cf. Kant: "if cinnabar were sometimes red, sometimes black, sometimes light, sometimes heavy, if a man changed sometimes into this and sometimes into that animal form, if the country on the longest day were sometimes covered with fruit, sometimes with ice and snow, my empirical imagination would never find opportunity when representing red color to bring to mind heavy cinnabar" [würde der Zinnober bald rot, bald schwarz, bald leicht, bald schwer sein, ein Mensch bald in diese, bald in jene tierische Gestalt verändert werden, am längsten Tage bald das Land mit Früchten, bald mit Eis und Schnee bedeckt sein, so könnte meine empirische Einbildungskraft nicht einmal Gelegenheit bekommen, bei der Vorstellung der roten Farbe den schweren Zinnober in die Gedenken zu bekommen] (*CPR,* A 100). Yet is not the question of the continuity of imagination not far more that of its discontinuity? And what would the question of imagination ask, if posed as multiple, i.e., not just as one of continuity and/or discontinuity?

11. See, e.g., *Enn* VI, 7; and *Meta,* B 4.

12. "τὸ ὂν καὶ τὸ ἓν ταὐτὸν καὶ μία φύσις τῷ ἀκολουθεῖν ἀλλήλοις ὥσπερ ἀρχὴ καὶ αἴτιον" (*Meta,* Γ 2, 1003b22).

13. "τὸ δὲ ὂν λέγεται μὲν πολλαχῶς, ἀλλὰ πρὸς ἓν καὶ μίαν τινὰ φύσιν καὶ οὐχ ὁμωνύμως" (*Meta,* Γ 2, 1003a33). Or again: "being is spoken in many ways" [τὸ ὂν λέγεται πολλαχῶς] (*Meta,* Z 1, 1028a10).

14. *Meta,* Γ 10, 1003b5 and Z 1, 1028a32. Further: "while 'being' has all these senses, obviously that which 'is' primarily is the 'what,' that indicates the

substance of the thing" [τοσαυταχῶς δὲ λεγομένου τοῦ ὄντος φανερὸν ὅτι τούτων πρῶτον ὂν τὸ τί ἐστιν, ὅπερ σημαίνει τὴν οὐσίαν] (*Meta,* Z 1, 1028a13). The word *ousia,* coming from the participle (οὖσ-α) of the verb "to be," signifies the "whatness" of a being, what it is in its being, the being of a being, that which it is when it is; it is the participle form (*ousa*) of the verb "to be" (*einai*).

15. *Meta,* Z 1, 1028a31.

16. "πῶς πολλὰ τὰ πρός τι ἀλλ' οὐχ ἕν" (*Meta,* N 2, 1089b8). Owens argues, on the contrary, that "the problem of the Stagirite is to see some kind of unity among all these different forms. Unlike Parmenides, and to a lesser degree Plato, he does not commence by taking a 'one' and asking how it can be many. He is taking a 'many' and asking how it can be one. His answer is πὸρς ἕν unity" (*The Doctrine of Being in the Aristotelian Metaphysics,* p. 460).

17. "αὕτη δέ ἐστιν ἐκεῖθεν μᾶλλον ἡ ἀπορία, πῶς πολλαὶ ἐνεργείᾳ οὐσίαι ἀλλ' οὐ μία" (*Meta,* N 2, 1089b30; cf. N 2, 1089a33). Whether book N is an "integral part of the main series" of books in the *Metaphysics* does not fall within the scope of the investigation here (cf. Owens, *Doctrine of Being,* p. 436). In fact, the analysis is limited to the question of the many as it appears, and no attempt is made at a systematic or comprehensive analysis of the *Metaphysics* itself. For such an analysis see, e.g., Owens's or Jaeger's *Aristoteles.*

18. "φαίνεται δὲ ἡ ζήτησις πῶς πολλὰ τὸ ὂν τὸ κατὰ τὰς οὐσίας λεγόμενον" (*Meta,* N 2, 1089a31).

19. "φανερὸν δὲ καὶ ὅτι τὰ πολλὰ ἀντικειμένως λεχθήσεται τῷ ἑνί. τὰ μὲν γὰρ τῷ μὴ ἤ εἶναι, τὰ δὲ τῷ διαιρετὴν ἔχειν τὴν ὕλην κατὰ τὸ εἶδος, ἢ τὴν πρώτην ἢ τὴν τελευταίαν, τὰ δὲ τῷ τοὺς λόγους πλείους τοὺς τί ἦν εἶναι λέγοντας" (*Meta,* Δ 6, 1017a3).

20. Cf. *Cat,* I, 1a1–6 and *Top,* VI 10, 148a24. Univocals must be distinguished from paronyms or derivatives (i.e., words differing with respect to their case endings—for instance, the grammarian is derived from "grammar" and the brave from "bravery"); *Cat,* I, 1a12–5.

21. "τὸ δὲ ἑνὶ εἶναι ἀρχῇ τινί ἐστιν ἀριθμοῷ εἶναι" (*Meta,* Δ 6, 1016b17).

22. *Meta,* Δ 1, 1012b34.

23. "ἢ ἔστιν ἢ γίγνεται ἢ γιγνώσκεται" (*Meta,* Δ 1, 1013a18).

24. *Meta,* A 3, 983a26–b3. See also *Physics,* II 3, 194b23–35. For Schürmann the problem with the *Metaphysics* is that it imposes "upon each and every philosophical issue the schema that rightfully pertains only to the *Physics*" (*Heidegger: On Being and Acting,* p. 42).

25. "ἀρχὴ οὖν τοῦ γνωστοῦ περὶ ἕκαστον τὸ ἕν" (*Meta,* Δ 6, 1016b20).

26. Kant's definition of being as "the simple position of a thing" [bloß die Position eines Dinges] (*CPR,* B 626), thinks against Aristotle's understanding of being as a physical or empirical principle, not an abstraction, but one concrete thing, and against being as a universal predicate of things.

27. "πανταχοῦ δὲ τὸ ἕν ἢ τῷ ποσῷ ἢ τῷ εἴδει ἀδιαίρετον" (*Meta,* Δ 6, 1016b23).

28. Hegel translates Aristotle: "pure activity is before (πρότερον) potentiality, not with respect to time, but with respect to essence" [die reine Tätigkeit ist

vor (πρότερον) der Möglichkeit, nicht der Zeit nach, sondern dem Wesen nach] (*VGP* II, p. 160; my translation).

29. *Meta,* Δ 6, 1016b.

30. Cf. *Cat,* I, 1a1–6 and *Top,* VI 3, 140a34–7. ζῷον, for example is the one name of two things with incongruent definitions (animal and still life painting)—the name is identical, but the definition is different (Owens, *Doctrine of Being,* pp. 107–35). Apparently, a logic of identity and difference is the condition of the possibility of Aristotelian equivocals.

31. Cf. *Meta,* Λ 5, 1071a20.

32. As Owens writes: "Aristotle does not require terms to be limited to one precise sense. Rather, he accepts their multiple signification, and gives detailed rules for distinguishing the different things that are expressed in various ways by the same term" (*Doctrine of Being,* p. 124).

33. "οὐχ οἷόν τε δὲ τῶν ὄντων ἓν εἶναι γένος οὔτε τὸ ἓν οὔτε τὸ ὄν. ἀνάγκη μὲν γὰρ τὰς διαφορὰς ἑκάστου γένους καὶ εἶναι καὶ μίαν εἶναι ἑκάστην, ἀδύνατον δὲ κατηγορεῖσθαι ἢ τὰ εἴδη τοῦ γένους ἐπὶ τῶν οἰκείων διαφορῶν ἢ τὸ γένος ἄνευ τῶν αὐτοῦ εἰδῶν, ὥστ' εἴπερ τὸ ἓν γένος ἢ τὸ ὄν, οὐδεμία διαφορὰ οὔτε ὂν οὔτε ἓν ἔσται" (*Meta,* B 3, 998b22; cf. also A 9, 991a and *Post Anal,* 92b13).

34. "ταῦτα δὲ γίγνοιτ' ἂν τό τε ὂν καὶ τὸ ἕν. ταῦτα γὰρ μάλιστ' ἂν ὑποληφθείη περιέχειν τὰ ὄντα πάντα καὶ μάλιστα ἀρχαῖς ἐοικέναι διὰ τὸ εἶναι πρῶτα τῇ φύσει. φθαρέντων γὰρ αὐτῶν συναναιρεῖται καὶ τὰ λοιπά. πᾶν γὰρ ὂν καὶ ἕν" (*Meta,* K 1, 1059b27; translation slightly modified).

35. "τὸ γὰρ ὂν καὶ τὸ ἓν καθόλου κατηγορεῖται μάλιστα πάντων" (*Meta,* I 2, 1053b20; translation slightly modified). The question remains—and it is not only a "modern" question: to what extent does the entire science or study of being (qua being or *qua* anything) remain tied to a philosophy of the subject, of the "I" at the core of being (be-I-ng)?

36. "αἴτιον τοῦ εἶναι" (*Meta,* Δ 8, 1017b15).

37. *Post Anal,* 71a1, 72a1 and 89b32.

38. *Meta,* α 1, 993b19.

39. *Meta,* Z 1, 1028b2.

40. "τὰ δ' αἴτια καὶ αἱ ἀρχαὶ ἄλλα ἄλλων ἔστιν ὥς, ἔστι δ' ὥς, ἂν καθόλου λέγῃ τις καὶ κατ' ἀναλογίαν, ταὐτὰ πάντων" (*Meta,* Λ 4, 1070a31).

41. *Meta,* Λ, esp. 8, 1074a37.

42. *De An,* 433b15; *Meta,* Δ 7, 1017b4

43. *Meta,* Λ 6, 1071b33, 7, 1073a6.

44. *Meta,* Λ 1, 1069a30.

45. "Die Philosophie ist nicht Identitätssystem; das ist unphilosophisch" (*VGP II,* p. 163; my translation).

46. "πότερον τὸ ἓν καὶ τὸ ὄν, καθάπερ οἱ Πυθαγόρειοι καὶ Πλάτων ἔλεγον, οὐχ ἕτερόν τί ἐστιν ἀλλ' οὐσία τῶν ὄντων " (*Meta,* B 1, 996a4, cf. also A 9, 991a, and B 4, 1001a4).

47. *Meta,* Λ 7, 1072a33.

48. "πῶς γὰρ ἔσται τάξις μή τινος ὄντος ἀϊδίου καὶ χωριστοῦ καὶ μένοντος" (*Meta,* K 2, 1060a26). Cf. Zeller, *AGP,* II.

49. "ἀλλὰ μὴν εἴ γ' ἔσται τι αὐτὸ ὂν καὶ αὐτὸ ἕν, πολλὴ ἀπορία πῶς ἔσται τι παρὰ ταῦτα ἕτερον, λέγω δὲ πῶς ἔσται πλείω ἑνὸς τὰ ὄντα" (*Meta,* B 4, 1001a29; cf. Z 6, 1031a31).

50. *Meta,* Δ 10, 1018a35.

51. "τὸ μὲν οὖν ἕτερον ἢ ταὐτο διὰ τοῦτο πᾶν πρὸς ττᾶν λέγεται, ὅσα λέγεται ἓν καὶ ὄν" (*Meta,* I 3, 1054b18; translation slightly modified).

52. "τὸ δὲ διάφορον τινὸς τινὶ διάφορον, ὥστε ἀνάγκη ταὐτό τι εἶναι ᾧ διαφέρουσιν. τοῦτο δὲ τὸ ταὐτὸ γένος ἢ εἶδος" (*Meta,* I 3, 1054b25).

53. "ὅλως τε εἰ ἔστιν ἡ ἐναντιότης διαφορά, ἡδὲ διαφορὰ δυοῖν, ὥστε καὶ ἡ τέλειος" (*Meta,* I 4, 1055a22).

54. "θατέρου μὲν δὴ οὐκ ἐνδέχεται (τί γὰε μᾶλλον τοῦ μεγάλου ἢ μικροῦ); ἀμφοῖν ἄρα ἀπόφασις στερητική" (*Meta,* I 5, 1056a16).

55. *Meta,* N 2, 1089b25.

56. "τὸ γὰε τοιοῦτο γένος καλῶ ᾧ ἄμφω ἓν ταὐτὸ λέγεται, μὴ κατὰ συμβεβηκὸς ἔχον διαφοράν" (*Meta,* I 8, 1057b37).

57. "καὶ τὸ μήτε ἀγαθὸν μήτε κακὸν ἀντίκειται ἀμφοῖν, ἀλλ' ἀνώνυμον. πολλαχῶς γᾶρ λέγεται ἑκάτερον καὶ οὐκ ἔστιν ἓν τὸ δεκτικόν" (*Meta,* I 5, 1056a24; emphasis added). Cf. also Nietzsche: "*Originality.*—What is originality? To *see* something that does not yet carry a name, cannot yet be named, although it lies there before all our eyes. The way humans usually are, the name makes a thing visible at all.—The originals are for the most part also name-givers" [*Originalität.*—Was ist Originalität? Etwas *sehen,* das noch keinen Namen trägt, noch nicht genannt werden kann, ob es gleich vor Aller Augen liegt. Wie die Menschen gewöhnlich sind, macht ihnen erst der Name ein Ding überhaupt sichtbar.—Die Originalen sind zumeist auch die Namengeber gewesen] (*GS,* §261; my translation).

58. Heidegger, *ID,* p. 58.

59. Aristotle, *Post Anal,* 89b32.

60. "Älteste Unterscheidung" (Heidegger, *GA* 33, p. 25). "In fact, ὄν and ἕν are different with respect to concept but the same with respect to essence, i.e., they belong together" [zwar sind das ὄν und ἕν dem Begriffe nach verschieden, dem Wesen nach aber dasselbe, d.h. sie gehören zusammen] (*GA* 33, p. 29; my translation).

61. Aristotle, *Top,* 103b21.

62. If Heidegger is right to call Nietzsche the last of the metaphysicians then is it because, with the thought of absolute multiplicity, he completes the absoulte unity of Aristotele? Nietzsche writes: "all unity is unity *only as organisation and ensemble-play:* nothing else as the way in which a human community is a unity: therefore, *opposite* to atomistic *anarchy;* consequently, a *mastery-construction,* that *means* one, but *is* not one" [alle Einheit ist *nur als Organisation und Zusammenspiel* Einheit: nicht anders als wie ein menschliches Gemeinwesen eine Einheit ist: also *Gegensatz* der atomistischen *Anarchie;* somit ein *Herrschafts-Gebilde,* das Eins *bedeutet,* aber nicht eins *ist*] (*KGW* VIII, 1, 102).

63. "Dans les deux cas, polygamie naturelle et monogamie historique, c'est

toujours la place de l'homme qui détermine le concept la monogamie, c'est un homme et une femme, la polygamie, c'est encore un homme et beaucoup de femmes. La femme n'est jamais polygame, ni dans la nature ni dans la société kantiennes. Telle est l'apparance: en vérité la femme a toujours tout, et dans la monogamie et dans la polygamie. Dans le harem, par example, il n'y a pas de vraie multiplicité et l'homme perd à tous les coups. Les femmes se font la guerre pour restaurer le rapport monogamique et pour que l'une d'entre elles ait tout l'homme, au moins en puissance. Si bien qu'elles l'ont toutes, aucune n'en est privée, et l'une d'entre elles finit aussi par régner sur lui. Ainsi décrit, le harem n'appartient ni à la nature ni à la culture. La polygamie ne se laisse pas penser dans cette opposition. Dans la nature il n'y a pas de mariage, dans la vraie culture, c'est la monogamie. Kant qualifie de 'barbare' ce phénomène inclassable, cette société qui n'est plus naturelle et n'est pas encore morale. On doit interroger depuis cette 'perversion' l'opposition des concepts à laquelle échappe la polygamie, celle de l'homme dont parle Kant, celle de la femme dont il ne dit rien" (*Glas,* p. 146 [128]).

64. "Unendliche *gegebene* Größe" (*CPR,* B 40, B 48; cf. Heidegger, *FD,* p. 179).

65. "Jede Anschauung enthält ein Mannigfaltiges in sich, welches doch nicht als ein solches vorgestellt werden würde, wenn das Gemüt nicht die Zeit, in der Folge der Eindrücke aufeinander unterschiede: denn *als in einem Augenblick enthalten,* kann jede Vorstellung niemals etwas anderes, als absolute Einheit sein" (*CPR,* A 99).

66. "Einheit des Objects und Einheit des Mannigfaltigen im Object" (*Ref,* Nr. 5736).

67. "Die zwar ein Mannigfaltiges darbietet, dieses aber als ein solches, und zwar *in einer Vorstellung* enthalten, niemals ohne eine dabei vorkommende Synthesis bewirken kann" (*CPR,* A 99).

68. "Alsdann fiele aber auch alle Beziehung der Erkenntnis auf Gegenstände weg, weil ihr die Verknüpfung nach allgemeinen und notwendigen Gesetzen mangelte, mithin würde sie zwar gedankenlose Anschauung, aber niemals Erkenntnis, also für uns soviel als gar nichts sein" (*CPR,* A 111).

69. "Das Mannigfaltige der Vorstellung kann in einer Anschauung gegeben werden, die bloß sinnlich di. nichts als Empfänglichkeit ist, und die Form dieser Anschauung kann a priori in unserem Vorstellungsvermögen liegen, ohne doch etwas anderes, als die Art zu sein, wie das Subjekt affiziert wird" (*CPR,* B 129; translation modified).

70. "In der Anschauung, die davon unterschieden ist, kann es nur gegeben und durch *Verbindung* in einem Bewußtsein gedacht werden. Ein Verstand, in welchem durch das Selbstbewußtsein zugleich alles Mannigfaltige gegeben würde, würde *anschauen;* der unsere kann nur *denken* und muß in den Sinnen die Anschauung suchen" (*CPR,* B 135).

71. "Unermeßliche Mannigfaltigkeit der Erscheinungen" (*CPR,* A 127).

72. Heidegger argues that, for Kant, the order of space and time (like that of the categories) is that of quantity—and the manifold allows of being ordered because it is also quantitative, i.e., quantifiable material: first, for the forms of

intuition, then for the concepts of understanding. (Cf. *Kant and the Problem of Metaphysics* and *CPR*, A 20, A 77 and B 104.)

73. "Durch bloße Begriffe" (*CPR*, B xiv).

74. *CPR*, §12; cf. B 105.

75. "Einheit, Warheit und Vollstandigkeit (transcendentale Vollkommenheit) sind die requisita jeder Erkenntnis [die] respective auf Verstand, Urtheilskraft und Vernunft (zur lezteren wird apodictische Gewißheit erfordert, di. vollstandige Warheit)" (*Ref. (Unum)*, Nr. 5734).

76. "Qualitative Einheit," "qualitative Vielheit," "qualitative Vollständigkeit" (*CPR*, §12).

77. "Woraus erhellt, daß diese logischen Kriterien der Möglichkeit der Erkenntnis überhaupt die drei Kategorien der Größe, in denen die Einheit in der Erzeugung des Quantums durchgängig gleichartig angenommen werden muß, hier nur in Absicht auf die Verknüpfung auch *ungleichartiger* Erkenntnisstücke in einem Bewußtsein durch die Qualität eines Erkenntnisses als Prinzips verwandeln" (*CPR*, B 115). Kemp Smith translates *Größe* here as "quantity," but as "magnitude" in the Aesthetic.

78. For Windelband, in the *Critique*, the task of metaphysics as a science follows the "Democritean-Galilean reduction of the qualitative to the quantitative, wherein necessity and universal-validity can be found alone on a mathematical foundation" [demokritisch-galileischen Reduktion des Qualitativen auf Quantitatives, worin allein auf mathematischer Grundlage Notwendigkeit und Allgemeingültigkeit gefunden werden kann] (Windelband, *Lehrbuch der Geschichte der Philosophie*, p. 453). In the "Amphiboly of the Concepts of Reflection," for example, Kant takes Leibniz to task for maintaining that understanding could be directed immediately to objects, and for intellectualizing sensation (*CPR*, A 267/B 323, A 271/B 327). And he takes Locke to task for sensualizing intellection. Indeed, against both, Kant insists that there are always two sources of representations (understanding and sensibility), which, while quite different, "can supply objectively valid judgments of things only in *conjunction*" [nur in Verknüpfung objektiv gültig von Dingen urteilen könnten] (*CPR*, A 267/B 323). The ground of this *conjunction* is the transcendental category of quantity—for quantitative homogeneity is the condition of the possibility of the combination of heterogeneous representations. Even the comparisons of transcendental reflection in general (via the relations of identity and difference, agreement and opposition, inner and outer, determinable matter and determination by form) are only possible on the basis of quantitative categories: for example, oneness (*Einerleiheit*, not *Identität*) means one thing, not many, numerical identity (*numerica identitas*); and variety (*Verschiedenheit*, not *Unterschied* or *Differenz*) means numerical variety (*numerischen Verschiedenheit*) (*CPR*, A 263/B 319). For a reflection on the role of quantity for the *Critique of Judgment*, see Lyotard, *Lessons on the Analytic of the Sublime*, §4.

79. "Dazu kommt aber noch, daß die dritte Kategorie allenthalben aus der Verbindung der zweiten mit der ersten ihrer Klasse entspringt. So ist die *Allheit* (*Totalität*) nichts anderes als die Vielheit als Einheit betrachtet" (*CPR*, B 110–

11). "One cannot think, however, that the third category is therefore merely a derivative, and not a primary-concept of the pure understanding" [Man denke aber ja nicht, daß darum die dritte Kategorie ein bloß abgeleiteter und kein Stammbegriff des reinen Verstandes sei] (*CPR*, B 111; translation modified). This circularity will be taken up by Hegel in the structure (although—and this is a fundamental difference—not the content) of the movement of the concept (*Begriff*).

80. "Einer und derselben allgemeinen Erfahrung" (*CPR*, A 110; cf. A 107).

81. "Die durchgängige Identität seiner selbst bei allen möglichen Vorstellungen" (*CPR*, A 116). Unfortunately, the English translation of "an die Hand geben" as "to supply" loses the ambiguity and corporality of Kant's expression: with the principle of the subjective unity of the manifold, pure apperception gives intuition a hand. Thus, in the reverse direction, transcendental apperception gives intuition (and imagination) a hand by supplying the a priori "principle of the synthetic unity of the manifold" [Prinzipium der synthetischen Einheit des Mannigfaltigen] (*CPR*, A 117).

82. "Der höchste Punkt, an dem man allen Verstandesgebrauch, selbst die ganze Logik, und, nach ihr, die Transzendental-Philosophie heften muß, ja dieses Vermögen ist der Verstand selbst" (*CPR*, B 134n; translation slightly modified).

83. "Die ursprüngliche synthetische Einheit" (*CPR*, B 135) and "der ursprünglichen *synthetischen* Einheit" (*CPR*, B 137) or "ursprünglich synthetischen Einheit."

84. "Nur vom Subjekte selbst verrichtet werden kann, weil sie ein Aktus seiner Selbsttätigkeit ist" (*CPR*, B 130).

85. *CPR*, B 131, B 145.

86. "Als der Quell aller Verbindung, auf das Mannigfaltige der *Anschauungen überhaupt* unter dem Namen der Kategorien, vor aller sinnlichen Anschauung auf Objekte überhaupt geht" (*CPR*, B 154–55).

87. "Reine Verstandesbegriffe sind also nur darum a priori möglich, ja gar, in Beziehung auf Erfahrung, notwendig, weil unser Erkenntnis mit nichts, als Erscheinungen zu tun hat, deren Möglichkeit in uns selbst liegt, deren Verknüpfung und Einheit (in der Vorstellung eines Gegenstandes) bloß in uns angetroffen wird, mithin vor aller Erfahrung vorhergehen, und diese der Form nach auch allererst möglich machen muß. Und aus diesem Grunde, dem einzigmöglichen unter allen, ist dann auch unsere Deduktion der Kategorien geführt worden" (*CPR*, A 130; cf. also §16 and B 154).

88. "Der Verstand findet also in diesem nicht etwa schon eine dergleichen Verbindung des Mannigfaltigen, sondern *bringt sie hervor*, indem er ihn *affiziert*" (*CPR*, B 154–55).

89. "Die Form aller Erkenntnis der Gegenstände (wodurch das Mannigfaltige, als zu Einem Objekt gehörig, gedacht wird)" (*CPR*, A 129).

90. *CPR*, B 80.

91. *CPR*, B 136.

92. "Gedanken ohne Inhalt sind leer, Anschauungen ohne Begriffe sind blind" (*CPR*, B 75, cf. §23). And between the first and second *Critique*, pure reason

without practical reason is empty, practical reason without pure reason is blind; if reason does not act, realize itself, then it remains mere theoretical; however, if pratice is not transcendentally grounded, then it is without reason.

93. *CPR*, B 143.

94. "*Diese vermittelnde Vorstellung muß rein (ohne alles Empirische) und doch einerseits intellektuell, anderseits* sinnlich *sein*" (*CPR*, B 177; translation modified).

95. "Die Zeit, als die formale Bedingung des Mannigfaltigen des inneren Sinnes, mithin der Verknüpfung aller Vorstellungen, enthält ein Mannigfaltiges a priori in der reinen Anschauung. Nun ist eine tranzendentale Zeitbestimmung mit der Kategorie (die die Einheit derselben ausmacht) sofern gleichartig, als sie allgemein ist und auf einer Regel a priori beruht. Sie ist aber andererseits mit der *Erscheinung* sofern gleichartig, als die Zeit in jeder empirischen Vorstellung des Mannigfaltigen enthalten ist. Daher wird eine Anwendung der Kategorie auf Erscheinungen möglich sein, vermittelst der transzendentalen Zeitbestimmung, welche, als das Schema der Verstandesbegriffe, die *Subsumtion* der lezteren unter die erste vermittelt" (*CPR*, B 177–78; cf. B 70).

96. "Die Zeit ist die formale Bedingung a priori aller Erscheinungen überhaupt. Der Raum, als die reine Form aller *äußeren* Anschauung ist als Bedingung a priori bloß auf äußere Erscheinungen eingeschränkt. Dagegen, weil alle Vorstellungen, sie mögen nun äußere Dinge zum Gegenstande haben, oder nicht, doch an sich selbst, als Bestimmungen des Gemüts, zum inneren Zustande gehören, dieser innere Zustand aber, unter der formalen Bedingung der inneren Anschauung, mit hin der Zeit gehört, so ist die Zeit eine Bedingung a priori von aller Erscheinung überhaupt, und zwar die unmittelbare Bedingung der inneren (unserer Seelen) und eben dadurch mittelbar auch der äußeren Erscheinungen. Wenn ich a priori sagen kann: alle äußeren Erscheinungen sind im Raume, und nach den Verhältnissen des Raumes a priori bestimmt, so kann ich aus dem Prinzip des inneren Sinnes ganz allgemein sagen: all Erscheinungen überhaupt, d.i. alle Gegenstände der Sinne, sind in der Zeit, und stehen notwendigerweise in Verhältnissen der Zeit" (*CPR*, A 34). The change in (B 67) from "the forms of intuition" [*die Anschauungsformen*] to "form of intuition" [*die Form der Anschauung*] must be understood within the context of Kant's argument for the ideality of outer as well as inner sense: space alone is insufficient for the production of an object. The form of intuition is ideal, not in things; self-consciousness is determined by the form of time (not space) (*CPR*, B 69).

97. *CPR*, B 338n.

98. "*Beweis:* Alle Erscheinungen enthalten, der Form nach, eine Anschauung im Raum und Zeit, welche ihnen insgesamt a priori zum Grunde liegt. Sie können also nicht anders apprehendiert, d.i. ins empirische Bewußtsein aufgenommen werden, als durch die Synthesis des Mannigfaltigen, wodurch die Vorstellungen eines bestimmten Raumes oder Zeit erzeugt werden, d.i. durch die Zusammensetzung des Gleichartigen und das Bewußtsein der synthetischen Einheit dieses Mannigfaltigen (Gleichartigen). Nun ist das Bewußtsein des mannigfaltigen Gleichartigen in der Anschauung überhaupt, sofern dadurch die Vorstellung eines Objekts zuerst möglich wird, der Begriff einer Größe (*quanti*). Also ist selbst die Wahrnehmung eines Objekts, als Erscheinung, nur durch

dieselbe synthetische Einheit des Mannigfaltigen der gegebenen sinnlichen Anschauung möglich, wodurch die Einheit der Zusammensetzung des mannigfaltigen Gleichartigen im Begriffe einer *Größe* gedacht wird; d.i. die Erscheinungen sind insgesamt *Größen,* und zwar *extensive Größen,* weil sie als Anschauungen im Raume oder der Zeit durch dieselbe Synthesis vorgestellt werden müssen, als wodurch Raum und Zeit überhaupt bestimmt werden" (*CPR,* B 202–3). Heidegger argues that quality, as intensive magnitude (*intensive Größe*), is only another type or avatar of magnitude, and the science of magnitude (pure mathematics) extended over the entire field of knowledge (*mathesis universalis*) (*CPR,* B 207–8). Once again, for Heidegger, Kant understands magnitude in terms of quantity and quantification—for his term "magnitude" [*Größe*] is a translation of the Scholastic's "*quanti*" (cf. Heidegger, *FD,* pp. 158–60, 167–69, 173).

99. "*Als solche sind alle unsere Erkenntnisse zuletzt doch der formalen Bedingung des inneren Sinnes, nämlich der Zeit unterworfen*" (*CPR,* A 99).

100. *CPR,* A 129.

101. Hegel, *Enzy,* "*Vorrede zur zweiten Ausgabe.*"

102. For Nietzsche, Hegel wills *totality* (*er will* Totalität): "*Hegel's* way of thinking is not very far from *Goethe's:* one hears Goethe over *Spinoza.* Will to deification of everything and of life, in order to find *calm* and *happiness* in its viewing and fathoming; Hegel sees reason everywhere,—before reason one may *surrender* and *be content* . . . a kind of almost *joyful* and *trustworthy fatalism* that does not revolt, that does not tire, that seeks to form a totality from itself, a belief that first in totality, everything redeems itself, appears as good and justified" [Die Denkweise *Hegels* ist von der *Goetheschen* nicht sehr entfernt: man höre Goethe über *Spinoza.* Wille zur Vergöttlichung des Alls und des Lebens, um in seinem Anschauen und Ergründen *Ruhe* und *Glück* zu finden; Hegel sieht Vernunft überall,—vor der Vernunft darf man sich *ergeben* und *bescheiden* . . . eine Art von fast *freudigem* und *vertrauendem Fatalismus,* der nicht revoltirt, der nicht ermattet, der aus sich eine Totalität Alles sich erlöst, als gut und gerechtfertigt erscheint] (*KGW* VIII, 2, 107).

103. "*Was heißt Denken?* Die Frage klingt entschieden. Sie gibt sich eindeutig. Aber schon eine geringe Besinnung zeigt: die Frage ist mehrdeutig. Deshalb geraten wir auch sogleich ins Schwanken, wenn wir sie fragen. Die Mehrdeutigkeit der Frage vereitelt vollends jeden Versuch, geradezu und ohne weitere Vorbereitung auf die Antwort loszusteuern. Darum müssen wir die Mehrdeutigkeit der Frage verdeutlichen. Hinter dem Mehrdeutigen der Frage: 'Was heißt Denken?' verbergen sich mehrerlei Wege, die Frage zu erörtern" (*WD,* p. 79 [113; translation modified]; emphasis added). Note also that the verb *heißen* means to be, to be called, to call, to mean, and to be necessary, a must, *befehlen,* an order.

104. Plotinus, *Enn* III 3, 8–9.

Chapter 2

1. *Leviathan,* book I, ch. 16.

2. *Diff,* pp. 12–15.

3. "Aufgeben, wie Aufheben, doppelsinnig: a) *Auf*geben—es als verloren, vernichtet betrachten; b) [Auf*geben*]—eben damit aber zugleich es zum Problem machen, dessen Gehalt nicht vernichtet ist, sondern der gerettet und dessen Verkümmerung, Schwierigkeit zu lösen ist" (*BS,* Aphorism 52, p. 574; cf. *WLSb,* p. 103, 119 [115–16, 132]).

4. "Rien ne t'interdit plus, venant du dehors, de tromper ta famme, mais tu n'en as plus envie puisque tu l'aimes" (*Glas,* p. 44 [35; translation modified]).

5. "Sie vernichtet beide, indem sie beide vereinigt, denn sie sind nur dadurch, daß sie nicht vereinigt sind. In dieser Vereinigung bestehen zugleich beide; denn das Entgegengesetzte, und also Beschränkte, ist hiermit aufs Absolute bezogen" (*Diff,* p. 17). In the *Science of Logic* then, being and nothing are superseded (*aufgehoben*) or "taken care of" in their result, in the concept of becoming: to supersede (*aufheben*) means resolution and preservation, dissolution of being and nothing wherein their immediacy is lost (but not exterminated) and maintained—and this is the ambiguity in the term "supersession," i.e., simultaneously preserve, protect, maintain, and dissolve, cause to cease, put an end to (*WLSb,* pp. 94–95 [106–8]).

6. "Identität des Begriffs und des Seins, des Subjekts und Objekts" (*Diff,* p. 19).

7. "Durchs Analysieren entstehen nunmehr die Glieder der Einheit und einer ihr entgegengesetzten Mannigfaltigkeit" (*Diff,* p. 19).

8. "Solche Mannigfaltigkeit ist keine Philosophie" (*Diff,* p. 12).

9. "Das wahre Eigentümliche einer Philosophie ist die interessante Individualität, in welcher die Vernunft aus dem Bauzeug eines besondern Zeitalters sich eine Gestalt organisiert hat; die besondre spekulative Vernunft findet darin Geist von ihrem Geist, Fleisch von ihrem Fleisch, sie schaut sich in ihm als ein und dasselbe und als ein anderes lebendiges Wesen an Jede Philosophie ist in sich vollendet und hat, wie ein echtes Kunstwerk, die Totalität in sich" (*Diff,* p. 12).

10. "Der Begriff, den Kant in den *synthetischen Urteilen à priori* aufgestellt hat,—der Begriff von *Unterschiedenem,* das ebenso *untrennbar* ist, einem *Identischen,* das an ihm selbst *ungetrennt Unterschied* ist, gehört zudem Großen und Unsterblichen seiner Philosophie" (*WLSb,* p. 200 [209; translation modified]).

11. "Unendlich wichtige Form der Triplizität" and "formeller Lichtfunken" (*WLSb,* p. 324 [327]).

12. "Das Prinzip, das Subjekt-Objekt erweist sich als ein subjektives Subjecktobjekt" (*Diff,* pp. 6–7).

13. "Das Objekt der Wissenschaftslehre ist nach allem das System des menschlichen Wissens" (*UBW,* p. 62).

14. "Das reine Bewußtsein, die im System als absolut aufgestellte Identität des Subjekts und Objekts, eine subjektive Identität des Subjekts und Objekts ist" (*Diff,* p. 33).

15. "*Ich bin schlechthin,* di., *ich bin schlechthin,* weil *ich bin; und bin schlechthin,* was *ich bin; beides* für das Ich" (*GW,* p. 18, and pp. 11–21; *UBW,* p. 40).

16. "Das absolute Ich ist schlechthin sich selbst gleich: alles in ihm ist Ein und ebendasselbe Ich, und gehört (wenn es erlaubt ist, sich so uneigentlich

auszudrücken) zu Einem und ebendemselben Ich; es ist da nichts zu unterscheiden, kein Mannigfaltiges; das Ich ist alles, und ist Nichts, weil es *für sich* nichts ist, kein Setzendes und kein Gesetztes in sich selbst unterscheiden kann" (*GW*, p. 182).

17. "Man denkt nicht notwendig, wenn man ist, aber man ist notwendig, wenn man denkt" (*GW*, p. 20).

18. "*Ego sum, ego existo,* quoties a me profertur vel mente concipitur, necessario esse verum (Je suis, j'existe, est nécessairement vraie, toutes les fois que je la prononce, ou que je la conçois en mon esprit)" (*Med I*).

19. For a reading of Parmenides, cf. Heidegger, *EM*, pp. 88–107 [115–40].

20. "Der Akt des Selbstbewußtseins unterscheidet sich bestimmt von anderm Bewußtsein dadurch, daß sein Objekt gleich sei dem Subjekt" (*Diff*, p. 36; cf. *UBW*, pp. 42, 61).

21. "Die Identität des reinen und empirischen Bewußtseins ist nicht eine Abstraktion von ihrem ursprünglichen Entgegengesetztsein, sondern im Gegenteil ihre Entgegensetzung ist eine Abstraktion von ihrer ursprünglichen Identität" (*Diff*, p. 36).

22. "Der bloßen Reflexion erscheint diese Deduktion als das widersprechende Beginnen, aus der Einheit die Mannigfaltigkeit, aus reiner Identität die Zweiheit abzuleiten; aber die Identität des Ich = Ich ist keine *reine* Identität, dh. keine durchs Abstrahieren der Reflexion entstandne; wenn die Reflexion Ich = Ich als Einheit begreift, so muß sie dasselbe zugleich auch als Zweiheit begreifen; Ich = Ich ist Identität und Duplizität zugleich, es ist eine Entgegensetzung in Ich = Ich: Ich ist einmal Subjekt, das anderemal Objekt" (*Diff*, p. 36).

23. "Durch *unsern menschlichen* diskursiven *Verstand*" (*Diff*, p. 65).

24. *Diff*, p. 55.

25. "Müßte wenigstens Ein Satz gewiß seyn der etwa den übrigen seine Gewißheit mittheilte; so daß, wenn, und in wie fern dieser Eine gewiß seyn soll, auch ein Zweiter, und wenn, und wie fern dieser Zweite gewiß seyn soll, auch ein Dritter, us.f. gewiß seyn muß. Und so würden mehrere, und an sich, vielleicht sehr verschiedene Sätze, eben dadurch daß sie *alle*—Gewißheit, und *die gleiche* Gewißheit hätten, nur Eine Gewißheit gemein haben, und dadurch nur Eine Wissenschaft werden" (*UBW*, p. 33).

26. "Die Nation, welche sie erfinden wird, wäre es wohl werth ihr aus ihrer Sprache einen Namen zu geben; und sie könnte dann schlechthin *die Wissenschaft*, oder *die Wissenschaftslehre* heissen" (*UBW*, p. 37).

27. "Sie wäre wohl auch werth, ihr die übrigen Kunstausdrücke aus ihrer Sprache zu geben; und die Sprache selbst, so wie die Nation, welche dieselbe redete; würde dadurch ein entschiedenes Uebergewicht über andere Sprachen und Nationen erhalten" (*UBW*, p. 37n). Cf. also *Reden an die Deutsche Nation* (1808), given in Berlin during the French occupation.

28. "Die Kantische und Fichtesche Philosophie gibt als den höchsten Punkt der Auflösung der Widersprüche der Vernunft das Sollen an, was aber vielmehr nur der Standpunkt des Beharrens in der Endlichkeit und damit im Widerspruch ist" (*WLSb*, p. 123 [136]).

29. "Festgehalten als nur Negatives, *soll es sogar nicht da,* soll unerreichbar sein. Diese Unerreichbarkeit ist aber nicht seine Hoheit, sondern sein Mangel, welcher seinen letzten Grund darin hat, daß das Endliche als solches *als seiend* festgehalten wird. Das Unwahre ist das Unerreichbare; und es ist einzusehen, daß solches Unendliche das Unwahre ist" (*WLSb,* p. 136 [149]).

30. "Die absolute Identität ist zwar Prinzip der Spekulation, aber es bleibt, wie sein Ausdruck: Ich = Ich, nur die Regel, deren unendliche Erfüllung postuliert, aber im System nicht konstruiert wird" (*Diff,* p. 40).

31. "Höchste Forderung bleibt im Fichteschen System eine Forderung" (*Diff,* p. 45).

32. "Das Prinzip der Identität wird nicht Prinzip des Systems; so wie das System sich zu bilden anfängt, wird die Identität aufgegeben" (*Diff,* p. 63).

33. "*Unendliches Streben*" (*GW,* p. 179) and "Ich soll gleich Ich sein" (*Diff,* p. 7).

34. "Ohne transzendentale Anschauung könne nicht philosophiert werden" (*Diff,* p. 28).

35. *Diff,* pp. 29–30; cf. *PhG,* p. 433 [§808].

36. "Die Wissenschaftslehre enthält bloß das Nothwendige; ist dies in jeder Betrachtung nothwendig, so ist es dasselbe auch in Absicht der Quantität, dh., es ist nothwendig begränzt" (*UBW,* p. 58).

37. "Die formale Einheit des Begriffs, der herrschen soll, und die Mannigfaltigkeit der Natur widersprechen sich, und das Gedränge zwischen beiden zeigt bald einen bedeutenden Übelstand" (*Diff,* p. 59).

38. "Spinoza zum Muster genommen" (*DSP,* p. 317).

39. "Sie ergreift nicht beide Pole in sich, sondern in einer oberflächlichen Modifikation und nachbarlichen Vereinigung entschwindet ihr das Wesen beider und sie ist beiden so wie der Philosophie fremd" (*Diff,* p. 92).

40. "An diesem Anschauen des farbelosen Lichts hält die Schwärmerei fest; eine Mannigfaltigkeit ist in ihr nur dadurch, daß sie das Mannigfaltigkeit bekämpft"(*Diff,* p. 63).

41. "Die objektive Totalität und die subjektive Totalität, das System der Natur und das System der Intelligenz *ist* eines und ebendasselbe" (*Diff,* p. 71, emphasis added).

42. "Anschauung des sich selbst in vollendeter Totalität objektiv werdenden Absoluten,—in die Anschauung der ewigen Menschwerdung Gottes, des Zeugens des Worts vom Anfang" (*Diff,* p. 75).

43. "Ein System ist vollendet, wenn es in seinen Anfangspunkt zurückgeführt ist. Aber eben dies ist der Fall mit unserem System. Denn eben jener ursprüngliche Grund aller Harmonie des Subjektiven und Objektiven, welcher in seiner ursprünglichen Identität nur durch die intellektuelle Anschauung dargestellt werden konnte, ist es, welcher durch das Kunstwerk aus dem Subjektiven völlig herausgebracht und ganz objektiv geworden ist, dergestalt, daß wir unser Objekt, das Ich selbst, allmählich bis auf den Punkt geführt, auf welchem wir selbst standen, als wir anfingen zu philosophieren" (*SI,* pp. 476–77).

44. "Das absolute Prinzip, der einzige Realgrund und feste Standpunkt

der Philosophie ist, sowohl in Fichtes als in Schellings Philosophie, die intellektuelle Anschauung;—für die Reflexion ausgedrückt, Identität des Subjekts und Objekts" (*Diff,* p. 76).

45. "Einer *Kontinuität*" (*SI,* p. viii; cf. also pp. 19, 24, 34; and *DSP, Vorerinnerung*).

46. "Die Vernunft ist das Absolute" and "zu dem wahren *An-sich*" (*DSP,* §§1–3; cf. §26).

47. *DSP,* §§6, 11, 12, *Zusatz* 1.

48. "Das *Sein* gehört ebenso zum Wesen der Vernunft als zu dem der absoluten Identität" (*DSP,* §9, *Zusatz*).

49. "Indifferenz von A = A als Ausdruck des Seins und A = A als Ausdruck des Erkennens" (*DSP,* §42, *Erklärung* 2n; cf. §51).

50. "Nicht *an sich* oder vom Standpunkt der Vernunft" (*DSP,* §14, *Zusatz*).

51. "Der Grundirrtum aller Philosophie" (*DSP,* §14, *Erläuterung*).

52. "Die absolute Identität ist absolute Totalität" (*DSP,* §26; cf. 18, 20–23).

53. "*Das erste Sein,* und das Sein, das nie produziert worden ist, sondern ist" and "die Dinge oder Erscheinungen, welche uns als verschieden erscheinen, sind nicht warhaft verschieden, sondern realiter Eins" (*DSP,* §30, *Erläuterung*).

54. *DSP,* §§122–25; cf. §§40–42.

55. *DSP,* §§46–50, 93, 95.

56. "*Die Natur strebt in der dynamischen Sphäre notwendig zur absoluten Indifferenz*" (*DSP,* §109).

57. "Der Mensch ist nicht allein in der Welt, es gibt eine Mehrheit von Menschen, es gibt ein Menschengeschlecht, eine Menschheit. Wie die Vielheit der Dinge in der Natur nach einer Einheit strebt und nur in dieser Einheit sich selbst vollendet und gleichsam glücklich fühlt, ebenso auch die Vielheit in der Menschenwelt" (*SP,* p. 460).

58. "Die absolute Identität überhaupt, sofern sie nicht als seiend, sondern als Grund ihres Seins betrachtet werde" (*DSP,* §145, *Erklärung;* cf. also §153, *Erläuterung*).

59. "Zwischen dem Wesen, sofern es existiert, und dem Wesen, sofern es bloß Grund von Existenz ist" (*UWF,* pp. 69–70; cf. also p. 127).

60. "In der Schwerkraft (§54, *Anmerkung*) mußten wir zwar dem Wesen nach die absolute Identität erkennen, aber nicht als *seiend,* da sie in jener vielmehr Grund ihres Seins ist (daselbst)" (*DSP,* §93, Anmerkung 1).

61. "Das Ens begreift sowohl *Sein* als *Wesen* in sich, für welchen Unterschied unsere Sprache glücklicherweise den verschiedenen Ausdruck gerettet hat" (*WLSb,* pp. 48–49 [63]). Cf. Heidegger (*EP,* p. 31) for a consideration of the problematic politics of "the German language" and the German mission to "save Europe" and the European people "from the Asiatic [*vor dem Aisiatischen*]."

62. "In dem Geist ist das Existierende mit dem Grunde zur Existenz eins; in ihm sind wirklich beider zugleich, oder er ist die absolute Identität beider. Aber über dem Geist ist der anfängliche Ungrund, der nicht mehr Indifferenz (Gleichgültigkeit) ist, und doch nicht Identität beider Prinzipien, sondern die allgemeine, gegen alles gleiche und doch von nichts ergriffene Einheit, das von

allem freie und doch alles durchwirkende Wohltun, mit Einem Wort die Liebe, die Alles in Allem ist" (*UWF,* p. 130; cf. also p. 137).

63. "Es gibt in der letzten und höchsten Instanz gar kein andres Sein als Wollen. Wollen ist Ursein, und auf dieses allein passen alle Prädikate desselben: Grundlosigkeit, Ewigkeit, Unabhängigkeit von der Zeit, Selbstbejahung. Die ganze Philosophie strebt nur dahin, diesen höchsten Ausdruck zu finden" (*UWF,* p. 62; cf. p. 64). I translate *Grundlosigkeit* as "groundlessness" rather than as "being unconditioned" in order to make the connection to Schelling's discussion of ground (*Grund*) and cause (*Ursache*).

64. "Sein des Seienden im Ganzen" (*WD,* p. 35 [91]). "Im Gedanken der ewigen Wiederkehr des Gleichen denkt Nietzsche das, wovon Schelling sagt, daß alle Philosophie dahin strebe, nämlich für das Ursein als Wille den höchsten Ausdruck zu finden" (*WD,* p. 47 [109]). On Heidegger's use of the same/identical distinction (cf. *WD,* p. 147 [240–41]). For Heidegger's reading of Schelling, cf. *GA* 42.

65. "*Ohne* Indifferenz, dh. *ohne* einen Ungrund, gäbe es keine Zweiheit der Prinzipien" (*UWF,* pp. 127–28).

66. "Bei Hegel ist alles nichtswürdiges Grau" (*KGW* IV, 1, p. 357). In the *Case of Wagner* (§10), Nietzsche continues: "Harshly, Schopenhauer accused the epoch of Hegel and Schelling of improbity—harshly, also wrongly: he himself the old pessimist counterfeiter, had not a whit more 'probity' than his most famous contemporaries. Let us keep morals out of this: Hegel is a *taste.* . . . And not merely a German but a European taste!—A taste Wagner comprehended [conceived, conceptualized]—to which he felt equal [big enough]—which he immortalized!—He merely applied it to music—he invented a style for himself that 'meant infinity'—he became *Hegel's heir.* . . . Music as 'idea.'—/ And how Wagner was understood!—The same human type that raved about Hegel, today raves about Wagner; in his school one even *writes* Hegelian.—Above all, German youths understood him. The two words 'infinite' and 'meaning' were really sufficient: they induced a state of incomparable well-being in young men. It was *not* with his music that Wagner conquered them, it was with the 'idea' . . . the very same means by which Hegel formerly seduced and lured them!" [Schopenhauer hat, mit Härte, die Epoche Hegel's und Schelling's der Unredlichkeit geziehen—mit Härte, auch mit Unrecht: er selbst, der alte pessimistische Falschmünzer, hat es in Nichts 'redlicher' getrieben als seine berühmteren Zeitgenossen. Lassen wir die Moral aus dem Spiele: Hegel ist ein *Geschmack.* . . . Und nicht nur ein deutscher, sondern ein europäischer Geschmack!—Ein Geschmack, den Wagner begriff!—dem er sich gewachsen fühlte! den er verewigt hat!—Er machte bloss die Nutzanwendung auf die Musik—er erfand sich einen Stil, der 'Unendliches bedeutet,'—er wurde der *Erbe Hegel's.* . . . Die Musik als 'Idee'—/ Und wie man Wagnern verstand!—Dieselbe Art Mensch, die für Hegel geschwärmt, schwärmt heute für Wagner; in seiner Schule schreibt man sogar Hegelisch!—Vor Allen verstand ihn der deutsche Jüngling. Die zwei Worte 'unendlich' und 'Bedeutung' genügten bereits: ihm wurde dabei auf eine unvergleichliche Weise wohl. Es ist *nicht* die Musik, mit der Wagner sich die Jünglinge erobert hat, es ist die 'Idee' . . .

genau Dasselbe, womit sie seiner Zeit Hegel verführt und verlockt hat!] (*KGW* VI, 3, pp. 30–31; translation slightly modified).

67. "Die Furie des Verschwindens landet schließlich im Schutt" (*Fall-Sonnet with Hegel* [*Herbstsonett mit Hegel*], p. 36).

68. "Es ist Kant vornehmlich um die Verbannung der gemein-mechanischen Vorstellungsweise zu tun, die bei der einen Bestimmung, der Undurchdringlichkeit, der *für-sich-seienden Punktualität,* stehenbleibt und die entgegengesetzte Bestimmung, die *Beziehung* der Materie in sich oder mehrerer Materien, die wieder als besondere Eins angesehen werden, aufeinander zu etwas *Äußerlichem* macht;—die Vorstellungsweise, welche, wie Kant sagt, sonst keine bewegenden Kräfte als nur durch Druck und Stoß, also nur durch Einwirkung von außen einräumen will" (*WLSb,* p. 169 [181]; cf. *CPR,* "Transcendental Doctrine of Method," esp. ch. I, §1, "The Discipline of Pure Reason in Its Dogmatic Employment").

69. "Es giebt im Geistigen keine Vernichtung" (*KGW* VIII, 1, p. 320). And "Que serait un 'négatif' qui ne se laisserait pas relever?" (Derrida, "Le Puits et la pyramide," in *Marges,* p. 126 [107]).

70. *Marges,* p. 102 [88]; *Glas,* pp. 70–74 [58–63]. Cf. also *Glas,* 130 [113] and Derrida's reading of Bataille in "De l'économie restreinte à l'économie générale: Un hegelianisme sans réserve," in *L'écriture et la difference.*

71. "Cette incapacité structurelle de penser sans relève" (*Marges,* p. 126 [107]; cf. "Le Temps des adieux," p. 46).

72. *Glas,* pp. 11, 18, 51–52, 55–56, 82, 126, 134, 155–56, 211, 258 [5, 11, 41–43, 46–47, 95, 109, 116, 136–37, 188, 231], etc.

73. "Une sorte d'allergie active et organisée, organisatrice même à l'endroit de la dialectique hégélienne" ("Le Temps des adieux," p. 24). Against this erroneous (albeit *courant*) reading, Malabou, for example, argues that, for Hegel, "the essence of necessity is contingency" [l'essence de la nécessité est la contingence] (*L'avenir de Hegel,* p. 219). As Hegel writes: "[the concept] is absolute power just because it can freely abandon its difference to the shape of self-subsistent diversity, outer necessity, contingency, caprice, opinion" [er ist die absolute Macht gerade darum, daß er seinen Unterschied frei zur Gestalt selbständiger Verschiedenheit äußerlicher Notwendigkeit, Zufälligkeit, Willkür, Meinung entlassen kann] (*WLB,* p. 40 [608; translation modified]).

74. "Il n'est pas insignifiant que le concept la réduise à rien" (*Glas,* p. 52 [43; translation modified]; cf. *Marges,* pp. 123–27).

75. "Dès que la différence se détermine, elle se détermine en opposition, elle se manifeste, certes, mais sa manifestation est en même temps (c'est le temps du même comme effacement du reste de temps dans le soi-même [*Selbst*]) réduction de la différence, du reste, de l'écart C'est la thèse" (*Glas,* p. 236 [263]).

76. "Der Geist will Gleichheit, dh. einen Sinneneindruck subsumiren unter eine vorhandene Reihe: ebenso wie der Körper Unorganisches sich assimilirt" (W I 8, *Herbst* 1885–*Herbst* 1886; 2 [90]).

77. "Die Nacht, worin, wie man zu sagen pflegt, alle Kühe schwarz sind"

(*PhG*, p. 17 [§16]), and "nur über dem Tode schwebt die Einheit" (*GCS*, p. 280; cf. *Diff*, p. 92).

78. *Diff*, pp. 76–77.

79. "Das Wahre ist so der bacchantische Taumel, an dem kein Glied nicht trunken ist, und weil jedes, indem es sich absondert, ebenso unmittelbar auflöst,—ist er ebenso die durchsichtige und einfache Ruhe. In dem Gerichte jener Bewegung bestehen zwar die einzelnen Gestalten des Geistes, wie die bestimmten Gedanken, nicht, aber sie sind so sehr auch positive notwendige Momente, als sie negativ und verschwindend sind" (*PhG*, p. 35 [§47]). Here the Bacchananlian revel as the true itself must not be confused with the "revel of God" [*Taumel des Gottes*] in the moment of "Religion in the Form of Art" [*Kunst-Religion*] (*PhG*, p. 387 [§725]; cf. Derrida, *Glas*, pp. 290–91 [261–62]).

80. "Die Wunden des Geistes heilen, ohne daß die Narben bleiben" (*PhG*, p. 360 [§669]). In the *Phenomenology* self-consciousness must also negate absolutely: like a torn and repaired sock ("a darned sock better than a torn one; not so with self-consciousness" [ein geflickter Strumpf besser als ein zerrissener, nicht so das Selbstbewußtsein]), the wounds of self-consciousness also leave scars. Hegel cited by Heidegger (*GA* 5, p. 134).

81. "Das Urteil ist eine *identische* Beziehung zwischen Subjekt und Prädikat; es wird dabei davon abstrahiert, daß das Subjekt noch mehrere Bestimmtheiten hat als die des Prädikates sowie davon, daß das Prädikat weiter ist als das Subjekt. Ist nun aber der Inhalt spekulativ, so ist auch das *Nichtidentische* des Subjektes und Prädikates wesentliches Moment, aber dies ist im Urteil nicht ausgedrückt" (*WLSb*, p. 78 [72; translation modified]).

82. "Die Sprache, als Werk des Verstandes, nur Allgemeines ausspricht" (*WLSb*, p. 105 [117]).

83. "Dadurch, daß bei den Urteilen und Schlüssen die Operationen vornehmlich auf das Quantitative der Bestimmungen zurückgeführt und gegründet werden, beruht alles auf einem äußerlichen Unterschied, auf bloßer Vergleichung, wird ein völlig analytisches Verfahren und begriffloses Kalkulieren. Das Ableiten der sogenannten Regeln und Gesetze, des Schließens vornehmlich, ist nicht viel besser als ein Befingern von Stäbchen von ungleicher Länge, um sie nach ihrer Größe zu sortieren und zu verbinden,—als die spielende Beschäftigung der Kinder, von mannigfaltig zerschnittenen Gemälden die passenden Stücke zusammenzusuchen.—Man hat daher nicht mit Unrecht dieses Denken dem Rechnen und das Rechnen wieder diesem Denken gleichgesetzt. In der Arithmetik werden die Zahlen als das Begrifflose genommen, das außer seiner Gleichheit oder Ungleichheit, das heißt, außer seinem ganz äußerlichen Verhältnis keine Bedeutung hat, das weder an ihm selbst, noch dessen Bezeihung ein Gedanke ist" (*WLSb*, p. 36 [52–53]). Here Hegel's critique of classical logic, of Kantian quantitative multiplicity, is quite close to Heidegger's critique of the technical world: "sciences does not think" [Die Wissenschaft denkt nicht] (*WD*, p. 4 [8]; cf. *TK* and Schürmann's reading of Heidegger in terms of the technological question). Cf. also Derrida's connection of Hegel and Heidegger in terms of spirit in *De l'esprit*.

84. "Weil das Rechnen ein so sehr äußerliches, somit mechanisches Geschäft ist, haben sich *Maschinen* verfertigen lassen, welche die arithmetischen Operationen aufs vollkommenste vollführen. Wenn man über die Natur des Rechnens nur diesen Umstand allein kennte, so läge darin die Entscheidung, was es mit dem Einfall für eine Bewandtnis hatte, das Rechnen zum Hauptbildungsmittel des Geistes zu machen und ihn auf die Folter, sich zur Machine zu vervollkommnen, zu legen" (*WLSb,* p. 208 [216–17]).

85. "Qu'elle soit soumise à la loi de ce dont elle est la loi, voilà qui donne à la structure du système hegelien une forme très retorse et si difficilement prenable" (*Glas,* p. 139 [121; translation modified]).

86. "But who could ever distinguish a farewell from a good-bye?" [mais qui pourra jamais distinguer un adieu d'un au-revoir?] ("Le Temps des adieux," p. 45; my translation). Cf. *The Politics of Friendship.*

Chapter 3

1. "ξυνὸν δέ μοί ἐστιν ὅπποθεν ἄρξωμαι; τόθι γὰρ πάλιν ἵξομαι αὖθις" (Frag. 5).

2. "ξυνὸν ἀρχὴ καὶ πέρας ἐπὶ κύκλου" (Frag. 103).

3. "οὐκ ἐμοῦ ἀλλὰ τοῦ λόγου ἀκούσαντας ὁμολογεῖν σοφόν ἐστιν ἓν πάντα εἶναι" (Frag. 50).

4. "Alles abgeleitet aus Einem Alles verbunden in Einem. Das eine abgeleitet aus allem. Einheit des Subjekts, des Grundes und des Ganzen. Moglichkeit Wirklichkeit Nothwendigkeit. Es sind drei transzendentale criterien der Moglichkeit der Dinge überhaupt. 3 fache formale Einheit" (Kant, *Reflexionen zur Metaphysik (Unum),* Nr. 5734).

5. "Das Wesen ist die Einheit, die Wesentlichen Stücke die Warheit, alle attribute zusammen die Vollkommenheit" (*Ref,* Nr. 5734).

6. "1. Einheit aus Vielem, 2. Einheit des Vielen unter einander, 3. Vieles aus Einem" (*Ref,* Nr. 5736).

7. "Einheit des Objects und Einheit des Manigfaltigen im Object" (*Ref,* Nr. 5736).

8. "In sich zurückkehrenden Kreislinie" (*JS I,* p. 366). "Die Begründungs- und Ergründungs-Tendenz, das Philosophieren vor der Philosophie, hat nämlich endlich sich vollkommen auszusprechen gewußt, sie hat genau gefunden, um was es zu tun war; es ist die Verwandlung der Philosophie ins Formale des Erkennens, in Logik" (*Diff,* p. 81).

9. "Die Kantische Philosophie dient so als ein Polster für die Trägheit des Denkens, die sich damit beruhigt, daß bereits alles bewiesen und abgetan sei" (*WLSb,* p. 46n [62]).

10. "Enthält wesentlich nur Eine Idee" and "daß ihr Letztes ebenso wohl ihr Erstes ist" (*JS I,* p. 367).

11. "Die Bestimmung von einem Unterschied, in welchem die Unterschiedenen untrennbar verbunden sind" (*WLSb,* p. 11 [32]).

12. "Übereinstimmung des Denkens mit dem Gegenstand" and "das Wesentliche der Wahrheit, der Inhalt, außer ihr liege" (*WLSb,* pp. 29 and 28 [44]).

13. "Daß die *Logik* diesen sicheren Gang schon von den ältesten Zeiten her gegangen sei, läßt sich daraus ersehen, daß sie seit dem *Aristoteles* keinen Schritt rückwarts hat tun dürfen, wenn man ihr nicht etwa die Wegschaffung einiger entbehrlicher Subtilitäten, oder deutlichere Bestimmung des Vorgetragenen als Verbesserungen anrechnen will, welches aber mehr zur Eleganz, als zur Sicherheit der Wissenschaft gehört Merkwürdig ist noch an ihr, daß sie auch bis jetzt keinen Schritt vorwärts hat tun können, und also allem Ansehen nach geschlossen und vollendet zu sein scheint. . . . Es ist nicht Vermehrung, sondern Verunstaltung der Wissenschaften, wenn man ihre Grenzen ineinander laufen läßt; die Grenze der Logik aber ist dadurch ganz genau bestimmt, daß sie eine Wissenschaft ist, welche nichts als die formalen Regeln alles Denkens (es mag a priori oder empirisch sein, einen Ursprung oder Objekt haben, welches es wolle, in unserm Gemüte zufällige oder natürliche Hindernisse antreffen) ausführlich darlegt und strenge beweist" (*CPR,* B viii–ix).

14. "Wenn die Logik seit Aristotles keine Veränderung erlitten hat—wie denn in der Tat die Veränderungen, wenn man die neueren Kompendien der Logik betrachtet, häufig mehr nur in Weglassungen bestehen—, so ist daraus eher zu folgern, daß sie um so mehr einer totalen Umarbeitung bedürfe" (*WLSb,* p. 35 [51; translation slightly modified]).

15. "Die Logik ist sonach als das System der reinen Vernunft, als das Reich des reinen Gedankens zu fassen. *Dieses Reich ist die Wahrheit, wie sie ohne Hülle an und für sich selbst ist*" (*WLSb,* p. 34 [50; translation modified]).

16. "Wissenschaft des reinen Denkens, die zu ihrem Prinzip das *reine Wissen* habe" and "dadurch allein, daß sie zugleich als unterschiedene (jedoch nicht für sich seiende) gewußt werden, ist ihre Einheit nicht abstrakt, tot, unbewegend, sondern konkret." Here "being is known to be the pure Concept in its self and the pure Concept is known to be true being" [das Sein als reiner Begriff an sich selbst und der reine Begriff als das wahrhafte Sein gewußt wird] (*WLSb,* p. 45 [60; translation modified]).

17. *WLSb,* p. 10 [31].

18. "Die Form der inneren Selbstbewegung ihres Inhaltes" (*WLSb,* p. 37 [53]).

19. "Daß das Negative ebensosehr positiv ist oder daß das sich Widersprechende sich nicht in Null, in das abstrakte Nichts auflöst, sondern wesentlich nur in die Negation seines besonderen Inhaltes oder daß eine solche Negation nicht alle Negation, sondern die *Negation der bestimmten* Sache, die sich auflöst, somit bestimmte Negation ist, daß also im Resultat wesentlich das enthalten ist, woraus es resultiert" (*WLSb,* p. 38 [54; translation modified]).

20. "Wir unsrer menschlichen Logik nicht geneigt sind einzuräumen, dass sie die Logik an sich, die einzige Art Logik sei (wir möchten vielmehr uns überreden, dass sie nur ein Spezialfall sei, und vielleicht einer der wunderlichsten und dümmsten)" (*KGW* V 2, p. 281).

21. "Das Prinzip aller natürlichen und geistigen Lebendigkeit überhaupt"

and "Seele des Gebäudes, die Methode, die im Dialektischen lebt" (*WLSb,* pp. 40–41 [56–57; translation slightly modified]).

22. "In Besonderes neben anderem Besondern" (*WLSb,* p. 43 [59]).

23. *PhS,* §5, 40–41, 62; cf. *CPR,* B10ff.

24. "East Coker" in *The Complete Poems and Plays* (New York: Harcourt Brace, 1950), p. 123.

25. "*Sein,* sonst nichts, ohne alle weitere Bestimmung und Erfüllung" (*WLSb,* p. 56 [69]).

26. "Daß es nichts *gibt,* nichts im Himmel oder in der Natur oder im Geiste oder wo es sei, was nicht ebenso die Unmittelbarkeit enthält als die Vermittlung, so daß sich diese beiden Bestimmungen als *ungetrennt* und *untrennbar* und jener Gegensatz sich als ein Nichtiges zeigt" (*WLSb,* p. 54 [68]).

27. "Eben *weil* es hier als der Anfang ist" (*WLSb,* p. 59 [72]).

28. "Einheit von Sein und Nichts;—oder ist Nichtsein, das zugleich Sein, und Sein, das zugleich Nichtsein ist" (*WLSb,* p. 60 [73]).

29. "Einheit des Unterschieden- und des Nichtunterschiedenseins" (*WLSb,* p. 61 [74]).

30. "Daß das Vorwärtsgehen ein *Rückgang* in den Grund, zu dem *Ursprünglichen* und *Wahrhaften* ist, von dem das, womit der Anfang gemacht wurde, abhängt und in der Tat hervorgebracht wird" (*WLSb,* p. 57 [71]).

31. "Bewußtsein auf seinem Wege von der Unmittelbarkeit aus, mit der es anfängt, zum absoluten Wissen als seiner innersten *Wahrheit* zurückgeführt . . . so wird noch mehr der absolute Geist, der als die kondrete und letzte höchste Wahrheit alles Seins sich ergibt, erkannt als am *Ende* der Entwicklung sich mit Freiheit entäußernd" (*WLSb,* p. 57 [71]).

32. "*Worin das Erste auch das Letzte und das Letzte auch das Erste wird*" (*WLSb,* p. 57 [71]).

33. "Als wahrhafte Unendlichkeit, in sich zurückgebogen, wird deren Bild der *Kreis,* die sich erreicht habende Linie, die geschlossen und ganz gegenwärtig ist, ohne *Anfangspunkt* und *Ende*" (*WLSb,* p. 136 [149]).

34. "Blendende aber falsche Scheine" (*CPR,* B 435).

35. "Diese Untrennbarkeit ist ihr Begriff" (*WLSb,* p. 141 [153–54]).

Chapter 4

1. "Was das *Erste* in der *Wissenschaft* ist, hat sich müssen *geschichtlich* als das *Erste* zeigen. Und das Eleatische *Eine* oder Sein haben wir für das Erste des Wissens vom Gedanken anzusehen" (*WLSb,* p. 76 [88]).

2. "Jenes Reale in allem Realen, das *Sein* in allem *Dasein,* welches den Begriff Gottes ausdrücken soll, ist nichts anderes als das abstrakte Sein, dasselbe, was das Nichts ist" (*WLSb,* p. 101 [111–13]).

3. "Das Nichts sei nur Abwesenheit des Seins, die Finsternis so nur *Abwesenheit* des Lichtes" (*WLSb,* p. 89 [107]).

4. "Das Nichts ist am Sein noch nicht gesetzt, obzwar Sein *wesentlich* Nichts ist und umgekehrt" (*WLSb,* p. 90 [103; translation modified]).

5. *WLSb,* p. 85 [98–99].

6. *WLSb,* p. 77 [90].

7. "Was die Wahrheit ist, ist weder das Sein noch das Nichts, sondern daß das Sein in Nichts und das Nichts in Sein—nicht übergeht—sondern übergegangen ist" (*WLSb,* p. 69 [82–83]).

8. "Weil der Synthesis der Sinn von einem äußerlichen Zusammenbringen äußerlich gegeneinander Vorhandener am nächsten liegt, ist mit Recht der Name Synthesis, synthetische Einheit außer Gebrauch gesetzt worden" (*WLSb,* p. 83 [96]).

9. "Ein für allemal zugrunde liegt und das Element von allem Folgenden ausmacht" (*WLSb,* p. 72 [85]).

10. "*Das reine Sein und das reine Nichts ist also dasselbe*" (*WLSb,* p. 69; my translation).

11. "Sein und Nichts sind dasselbe" (*WLSb,* p. 95 [108]).

12. "Die Sprach, als Werk des Verstandes, nur Allgemeines ausspricht" (*WLSb,* p. 105 [117]).

13. *WLSb,* pp. 84, 93 [97, 105].

14. "Für-sich-sein und Für-Eines-sein sind also nicht verschiedene Bedeutungen der Idealität, sondern sind wesentliche, untrennbare Momente derselben" (*WLSb,* p. 147 [160; translation slightly modified]; cf. also *Enzy,* §96).

15. "Was für ein Ding"(*WLSb,* p. 147 [160]).

16. "Die *Atomistik* hat den Begriff der Idealität nicht; sie faßt das Eins nicht als ein solches, das in ihm selbst die beiden Momente des Fürsichseins und des Für-es-seins enthält, also als ideelles, sondern nur als einfach, trocken, Für-sich-seiendes" (*WLSb,* p. 157 [169; translation modified]).

17. "Die Mannigfaltigkeit ist nur eine ideelle und innere, die Monade bleibt darin nur auf sich selbst bezogen, die Veränderungen entwickeln sich innerhalb ihrer und sind keine Beziehungen derselben auf andere" (*WLSb,* p. 149 [162; translation modified]; cf. *VGP III,* p. 238).

18. "Ein unabhängiges, nur *simultanes* Werden, in das Fürsichsein einer jeden eingeschlossen" (*WLSb,* p. 149 [162]; cf. *VGP III,* p. 251).

19. "Der Leibnizische Idealismus nimmt die Vielheit unmittelbar als eine gegebene auf und begreift sie nicht als eine Repulsion der Monade; er hat daher die Vielheit nur nach der Seite ihrer abstrakten Äußerlichkeit" (*WLSb,* p. 157 [169; translation modified]).

20. *VGP III,* pp. 249, 252–53.

21. "Alle Vielheit ist in die Einheit eingeschlossen" (*VGP III,* p. 243).

22. "Daß es *mehrere* Monaden gibt, daß sie damit auch als Andere bestimmt werden, geht die Monaden selbst nichts an; es ist dies die außer ihnen fallende Reflexion eines Dritten; sie sind nicht *an ihnen selbst Andere gegeneinander;* das Fürsichsein ist rein ohne das *Daneben* eines Daseins gehalten" (*WLSb,* p. 149 [162; translation modified]).

23. "Die Monaden sind nur *an sich* oder *in Gott,* als der Monade der Monaden, oder *auch im System*" (*WLSb,* p. 149 [162; translation modified]). Hegel traces Leibniz's term "monad" back to the Pythagoreans (*VGP III,* p. 239), but his expression "monad of monads" [Monade der Monaden] (*VGP III,* p. 247) can

be found in Giordano Bruno (Jordanus Bruno Nolanus): "God is the monad of monads; namely, being of beings" [Deus est monadum monas, nempe entium entitas] (*WLSb,* p. 149n). Heidegger traces the term back even further, through Francis Mercury van Helmont, to the Greek *monas* (μονάς), i.e., simple, unity, unit, the one, individual, solitary.

24. "Aveugle et clos, mais en revanche résonnant, comme un salon musical" (*Le Pli,* p. 6; cf. pp. 143–62).

25. *GA 24,* pp. 426–27 [300–1]; cf. *GA 26,* pp. 89–90 [72–73].

26. *Mond,* §7.

27. "Autrement ce ne seroient pas même des Etres" (*Mond,* §8).

28. "Car il n'y a jamais dans la nature deux Etres, qui soit parfaitement l'un comme l'autre, et où il ne soit possible de trouver une différence interne, ou fondée sur une dénomination intrinsèque" (*Mond,* §9).

29. "Il faut que dans la substance simple il y ait une pluralité d'affections et de rapports quoiqu'il n'y en ait point de parties" (*Mond,* §13).

30. "Nous expérimentons en nous mêmes une multitude dans la substance simple, lorsque nous trouvons que la moindre pensée dont nous nous appercevons enveloppe une variéte dans l'objet Ainsi tous ceux, qui reconnoissent que l'ame est une substance simple, doivent reconnoître cette multitude dans la Monade" (*Mond,* §8; translation slightly modified).

31. "L'ame suit ses propres loix, et le corps aussi les siennes, et ils se recontrent en vertu de l'harmonie préétablie entre toutes les substances, puisqu'elles sont toutes des représentations d'un même univers" (*Mond,* §78; translation slightly modified).

32. "Das Wort Gott ist sodann die Aushilfe, die selbst nur zur Einheit führt, die nur eine genannte ist; das Herausgehen des Vielen aus dieser Einheit wird aber nicht aufgezeigt" (*VGP III,* pp. 254–55).

33. "Das Leere ist so die *Qualität* des Eins in seiner Unmittelbarkeit" (*WLSb,* pp. 152 [165]).

34. Aristotle, *Phys,* Θ 265b24; *de coelo,* Γ 300b8.

35. *WLSb,* pp. 153–56 [165–67].

36. *WLSb,* pp. 155–57 [167–69].

37. *WLSb,* pp. 157–61 [170–73].

38. *WLSb,* pp. 161–63 [173–74].

39. *WLSb,* pp. 163–66 [174–77].

Chapter 5

1. "Die Ordnung der Dinge, in die sie sich als natürliche Wirklichkeiten einstellen, ruht auf der Voraussetzung, daß alle Mannigfaltigkeit ihrer Eigenschaften von einer Einheit des Wesens getragen werde: die Gleichheit vor dem Naturgesetz, die beharrenden Summen der Stoffe und der Energien, die Umsetzbarkeit der verschiedenartigsten Erscheinungen ineinander versöhnen die Abstände des ersten Anblicks in eine durchgängige Verwantschaft, in eine Gleichberechtigtkeit aller" (*Philosophie des Geldes,* p. 23; my translation).

2. "Alle Dinge gerieten auf dieselbe Ebene, auf eine Fläche, die einem blinden Spiegel gleicht, der nicht mehr spiegelt, nichts mehr zurückwirft. Die vorherrschende Dimension wurde die der Ausdehnung und der Zahl. Können bedeutet nicht mehr das Vermögen und Verschwenden aus hohem Überfluß und aus der Beherrschung der Kräfte, sondern nur das von jedermann anlernbare, immer mit einem gewissen Schwitzen und mit Aufwand verbundene Ausüben einer Routine. All dieses steigerte sich dann in Amerika und Rußland in das maßlose Und-so-weiter des Immergleichen und Gleichgültigen so weit, bis dieses Quantitative in eine eigene Qualität umschlug. Nunmehr ist dort die Vorherrschaft eines Durchnitts des Gleichgültigen nicht mehr etwas Belangloses und lediglich Ödes, sondern das Andrängen von Solchem, was angreifend jeden Rang und jedes welthaft Geistige zerstört und als Lüge ausgibt. Das ist der Andrang von Jenem, was wir das Dämonische (im Sinne des zerstörerisch Bösartigen) nennen. Für das Heraufkommen dieser Dämonie, in eins mit der wachsenden Ratlosigkeit und Unsicherheit Europas gegen sie und in sich selbst, gibt es mannigfache Kennzeichen" (*EM*, p. 35 [46; translation slightly modified]).

3. *PhS*, p. 201 [§364].

4. *WLSb*, pp. 176–200 [187–201].

5. *WLSb*, pp. 191–93 [201].

6. "½ + ½ nicht = 1, sondern = 2" (*KGW* VIII, 1, 90).

7. "Wenn Zahlen, Potenzen, das Mathematisch-Unendliche und dergleichen nicht als Symbole, sondern als Formen für philosophische Bestimmungen und damit selbst als philosophische Formen sollen gebraucht werden, so müßte vor allem ihre philosophische Bedeutung, di. ihre Begriffsbestimmtheit aufgezeigt werden. Geschieht dies, so sind sie selbst überflüssige Bezeichnungen; die Begriffsbestimmtheit bezeichnet sich selbst, und ihre Bezeichnung ist allein die richtige und passende. Der Gebrauch jener Formen ist darum weiter nichts als ein bequemes Mittel, es zu ersparen, die Begriffsbestimmungen zu fassen, anzugeben und zu rechtfertigen" (*WLSb*, p. 321 [325]).

8. *WLSb*, pp. 206–8 [215–16].

9. "Als *Eins*, das *Zahl* ist, hat es ferner die Bestimmtheit, insofern sie *Beziehung auf Anderes ist*, als seine Momente in ihm selbst, in seinem *Unterschied der Einheit und der Anzahl*, und die Anzahl ist selbst Vielheit der Eins" (*WLSb*, p. 195 [204; translation slightly modified]).

10. *WLSb*, pp. 197–202 [206–12]; *Enzy*, §102.

11. *WLSb*, pp. 193–95 [202–4].

12. *WLSb*, pp. 201–2 [211].

13. "Extensive und intensive Größe sind Bestimmtheiten der quantitativen *Grenze* selbst, das Quantum aber ist identisch mit seiner Grenze; kontinuierliche und diskrete Größe sind dagegen Bestimmungen der *Größe an sich*, di. der Quantität als solcher, insofern beim Quantum von der Grenze abstrahiert wird" (*WLSb*, p. 208 [217; translation slightly modified]).

14. *WLSb*, p. 209 [217].

15. "*Dieses ist durch sie das, was es ist, hat in ihr seine Qualität*" (*WLSb*, p. 114 [126]).

16. "Beziehung-auf-Anderes *innerhalb ihrer selbst*" (*WLSb,* p. 209 [218]).

17. *WLSb,* pp. 210–12 [218–20].

18. "Sie sind nur dadurch unterschieden, daß die eine die Anzahl als innerhalb ihrer, die andere dasselbe, die Anzahl als außer ihr hat" (*WLSb,* p. 213 [220]; cf. also *Enzy,* §103).

19. *PhG,* §163; cf. *WLW,* pp. 359–64 [518–23].

20. *WLSb,* pp. 212–16 [220–23].

21. *WLSb,* pp. 217–18 [224–25].

22. "Le modèle énigmatique de la *ligne* est donc cela même que la philosophie ne pouvait pas voir alors qu'elle avait les yeux ouverts sur le dedans de sa propre histoire. Cette nuit se défait un peu au moment où la linéarité—qui n'est pas la perte ou l'absence mais le refoulement de la pensée symbolique pluri-dimensionnelle [—] desserre son oppression" (*De la grammatologie,* p. 128 [86]). Cf. Derrida, *The Gift of Death,* esp. pp. 88–95. Here, once again, as in *Given Time* and *Glas,* Derrida continues to oppose uni-directional (Bataille, Baudelaire, Abraham, Jesus) and circular/spiritualized economies: the former imply dissemination without return, without reserve, without a witness, non-exchange, and the absolute gift (of death, and life); the latter (e.g., Hegel) speculates on the return it will receive in the form of remuneration, interest, profit, recognition, recompense, thanks, etc., insofar as it re-inscribes the pure gift (if it is possible) in a logic of cruelty, parity, simple symmetry—an eye for an eye. Also cf. Nietzsche, *On the Genealogy of Morals,* Second Essay, " 'Guilt,' 'Bad Conscience,' and the Like.' " Of course, for Hegel the uni-directional economy, which makes the pure "gift" (of death, time or anything whatsoever) possible (if it is possible), shows itself as an aporia precisely because it has already been abstracted from a more general economy of exchange with and without return.

23. *WLSb,* pp. 218–19 [225–26].

24. "Die Vergrößerung des Quantums ist keine *Näherung* zum Unendlichen, denn der Unterschied des Quantums und seiner Unendlichkeit hat wesentlich auch das *Moment,* ein nicht quantitativer Unterschied zu sein. Es ist nur der ins Engere gebrachte Ausdruck des Widerspruchs; es soll ein *Großes,* d.i. ein Quantum, und *unendlich,* d.i. kein Quantum sein" (*WLSb,* p. 221 [228; translation modified]). Kant's conception of time, for example, as the "*self-superseding* being-for-self of the now" [selbst aufhebende *Fürsichsein des Itzt*] is for Hegel, insofar as it forgets quality (quantity's other), not even to speak of its one-side ideality, is radically deficient (*WLSb,* p. 230 [236]).

25. *WLSb,* pp. 220–33 [227–38].

26. *WLSb,* pp. 233–36 [238–40].

27. "Das Quantum, indem es unendlich ist, als ein aufgehobenes, als ein solches zu denken gefordert wird, das nicht ein Quantum ist und dessen *quantitative Bestimmtheit doch bleibt*" (*WLSb,* p. 239 [243; translation modified]). For Kant, the mathematical and transcendental concepts of infinity are identical: "the true (transcendental) concept of infinity is: that the successive synthesis of units in the measurement of a quantum can never be completed. This contains, therefore, a quantity (of given units) which is greater than any number—which

is the mathematical concept of infinity" [der wahre (transzendentale) Begriff der Unendlichkeit ist: daß die sukzessive Synthesis der Einheit in Durchmessung eines Quantum niemals vollendet sein kann. Dieses enthält dadurch eine Menge (von gegebener Einheit), die größer ist als alle Zahl, welches der mathematische Begriff des Unendlichen ist] (*CPR,* B 460 and B 460n; translation slightly modified). For Hegel, Kant's transcendental characterization of conceptual infinity remains merely subjective/psychological: if the subject alone can give meaning to an infinity (to a relation of more than/less than) that remains incomplete, a simple beyond, never to be realized or completed; then the contradiction of quantitative infinity itself is merely displaced to the subject—a displacement that has no place in speculative philosophy.

28. *WLSb,* pp. 236–39 [241–42].

29. "Über welche es—wenn sie als das Unendlichgroße—*keine größere oder*—wenn sie als das Unendlichkleine bestimmt ist—*kleinere mehr gebe* oder die in jenem Falle größer, in diesem Falle kleiner sei als jede beliebige Größe" (*WLSb,* p. 239 [243; translation slightly modified]).

30. *WLSb,* p. 248 [251].

31. Cf. *PhS,* §148ff.

32. "*Dx, dy* sind keine Quanta mehr, noch sollen sie solche bedeuten, sondern haben allein in ihrer Beziehung eine Bedeutung, *einen Sinn bloß als Momente.* Sie sind nicht mehr *Etwas,* das Etwas als Quantum genommen, nicht endliche Differenzen; aber auch *nicht Nichts,* nicht die bestimmungslose Null. Außer ihrem Verhältnis sind sie reine Nullen, aber sie sollen nur als Momente des Verhältnisses, als *Bestimmungen* des Differential-Koeffizienten *dx/dy* genommen werden" (*WLSb,* p. 251 [253]). Cf. also Hegel's reflection on the names "differentiation" and "integration" insofar as they ironically express their opposites (*WLSb,* pp. 290–91 [292]).

33. "Das Qualitative nur das ist, was es in seinem Unterschied von einem Anderen ist" (*WLSb,* p. 252 [255]).

34. "Unendlichen Größen sind daher nicht nur vergleichbar, sondern sind nur als Momente der Vergleichung, des Verhältnisses" (*WLSb,* p. 252 [255]).

35. "Die Grenze des Größen-Verhältnisses ist, worin es ist und nicht ist; dies heißt genauer, worin das Quantum verschwunden und damit das Verhältnis nur als qualitatives Quantitäts-Verhältnis und Seiten desselben ebenso als qualitative Quantitäts-Momente erhalten sind" (*WLSb,* p. 253 [255–56; translation modified]).

36. And if (displacing Heidegger's poetic ontology) mathematics = ontology, then must not every discipline be ontological? Do not all sciences determine that which can be said of being qua being? Cf. *L'être et l'événement,* esp. pp. 7–27; for Badiou's reading of Hegel, cf. pp. 181–90.

37. "Die Mathematik vermag überhaupt nicht Größenbestimmungen der Physik zu beweisen, insofern sie Gesetze sind, welche die *qualitative Natur* der Momente zum Grunde haben, aus dem einfachen Grunde, weil diese Wissenschaft nicht Philosophie ist, nicht vom Begriff ausgeht und das Qualitative daher, in-

sofern es nicht lemmatischerweise aus der Erfahrung aufgenommen wird, außer ihrer Sphäre liegt" (*WLSb*, p. 272 [273]).

38. "Bedürfnis der Philosophie" (cf. *Diff*, pp. 12–16; and Heidegger, *QIV*, pp. 380–83).

39. *WLSb*, p. 272 [273].

40. *WLSb*, p. 301 [304].

41. *WLSb*, p. 201 [210].

42. "Die arithmetische Multiplikation von Größen, die ihrer räumlichen Bestimmung nach *Linien* sind, zugleich eine Produktion des Linearen zur *Flächenbestimmung* sei; 3 mal 4 lineare Fuße gibt 12 lineare Fuße, aber 3 lineare Fuße mal 4 linearen Fußen gibt 12 Flächenfuße, und zwar Quadratfuße, indem die Einheit in beiden als diskreten Größen dieselbe ist. Die *Multiplikation* von *Linien* mit *Linien* bietet sich zunächst als etwas Widersinniges dar, insofern die Multiplikation überhaupt Zahlen betrifft, d.i. eine Veränderung von solchen ist, welche mit dem, in das sie übergehen, mit dem *Produkt ganz homogen* sind und nur die *Größe* verändern. Dagegen ist das, was Multiplizieren der Linie als solcher mit Linie hieße—es ist *ductus lineae in lineam* wie *plani in planum* genannt worden, es ist auch *ductus puncti in lineam*—, eine Veränderung nicht bloß der Größe, sondern ihrer als *qualitativer Bestimmung der Räumlichkeit,* als einer Dimension; das Übergehen der Linie in Fläche ist *als Außersichkommen* derselben zu fassen, wie das Außersichkommen des Punktes die Linie, der Fläche ein ganzer Raum ist" (*WLSb*, pp. 301–2 [304; translation modified]).

43. *WLSb*, pp. 300–3 [304–5].

44. "In dem analytischen Verfahren selbst, welches als ein bloßes *Summieren* erscheint, in der Tat schon ein *Multiplizieren* enthalten ist" (*WLSb*, p. 301 [304]).

45. "Wie lange bleibt sie noch eine Bibliothek, wenn wir ein Buch nach dem anderen herausnehmen? Wir sehen aber schon, daß nicht alle einzelnen Bücher zusammen die Bibliothek ausmachen 'Alle' summativ verstanden ist ganz verschieden von der Allheit im Sinne einer Einheit eigentümlicher Art, die zunächst nicht so leicht zu bestimmen ist" (*GA* 15, p. 39 [20; translation slightly modified]).

46. Cf. Badiou, *L'être et l'événement*, pp. 49–59.

47. *WLSb*, pp. 310–11 [314–15].

48. Here incommensurability marks qualitative difference within quantity: "this difference appears arithmetically as a purely quantitative one, that of the root and power, or whatever degree of powers it may be; however, if the expression is to be taken only quantitatively, for example, $a : a^2$ or $da^2 = 2a : a^2 = 2 : a$, or for the law of descent of a falling body, $t : a^2$, then it yields the meaningless ratios of $I : a$, $2 : a$, $\mathrm{I} : at$; in supersession of their merely quantitative aspect, the sides would have to be held apart by their different qualitative significance, as $s = at^2$, the magnitude in this way being expressed as a quality, as a function of the magnitude of another quality" [Arithmetisch erscheint dieser Unterschied als ein bloß quantitativer, [ein Unterschied] der Wurzel und der Potenz oder welcher Potenzenbestimmtheit es sei; jedoch wenn der Ausdruck nur auf das Quantitative als solches geht, zB. $a : a^2$ oder $da^2 = 2a : a^2 = 2 : a$, oder für das

Gesetz des Falles $t : a^2$, so gibt er die nichtsagenden Verhältnisse von $I : a$, $2 : a$, $I : at$; die Seiten müßten gegen ihre bloß quantitative Bestimmung durch die unterschiedene, qualitative Bedeutung auseinander gehalten werden wie $s = at^2$, wodurch die Größe als eine Qualität ausgesprochen wird, als Funktion der Größe einer anderen Qualität] (*WLSb*, p. 309 [312]).

49. In measuring a given quantity, for example, the exponent can function equally as amount or as unit, determiner or determined (*WLSb*, pp. 311–13 [315–17]; cf. also *Enzy*, §105).

50. "Der Exponent, als das bestimmende Quantum, negativ gegen sich als Quantum des Verhältnisses, hiermit als qualitativ, als Grenze gesetzt, daß also das Qualitative für sich im Unterschied gegen das Quantitative hervortritt" (*WLSb*, p. 314 [318; translation modified]).

51. "Für den Wert jeder ist die Größe der anderen unentbehrlich und damit untrennbar von ihr" (*WLSb*, p. 315 [319]).

52. *WLSb*, pp. 314–18 [317–21].

53. "Die Potenz ist eine Menge von Einheiten, deren jede diese Menge selbst ist" (*WLSb*, p. 318 [322; translation modified]). Kepler's $s^3 : at^2$ is one example of the power ratio.

54. *WLSb*, pp. 362, 280 [324, 257]. Cf. also Plotinus: "What is the one? The productive power of all things" [Τί δὴ ὄν; Δύναμις τῶν πάντων] (*Enn* III, 8:10).

55. *WLSb*, p. 361 [323].

56. "Das Problem *aller* Philosophie" (*PB*, Seventh Letter).

57. "Das Wesen der Philosophie ist häufig von solchen, die mit dem Denken schon vertrauter sind, in die Aufgabe gesetzt worden, zu beantworten, wie das *Unendliche aus sich heraus und zur Endlichkeit komme?*—Dies, meint man, sei nicht *begreiflich* zu machen. Das Unendliche, bei dessen Begriff wir angekommen sind, wird sich in Fortgang dieser Darstellung *weiter bestimmen* und an ihm in aller Mannigfaltigkeit der Formen das Geforderte zeigen, *wie* es, wenn man sich so ausdrücken will, *zur Endlichkeit* komme" (*WLSb*, p. 139 [152; translation modified]).

58. "Der Begriff von *Unterschiedenem*, das ebenso *untrennbar* ist, einem *Identischen*, das an ihm selbst *ungetrennt Unterschied* ist" (*WLSb*, p. 200 [209; translation slightly modified]).

Chapter 6

1. "Tue das nicht! versetzte der Hauptmann, der die Überzeugungen anderer nicht gern mit seinigen durchkreuzte, den die Erfahrung gelehrt hatte, daß die Ansichten der Menschen viel zu mannigfaltig sind, als daß sie, selbst durch die vernünftigsten Vorstellungen, auf Einen Punkt versammelt werden könnten" (*Die Wahlverwandschaften* [*The Elective Affinities*], p. 29; all translations are my own).

2. "Das Geistlose vielmehr, nicht der Geist" (*WLSb*, p. 325 [328; translation modified]).

3. *WLSb*, p. 327 [330].

4. "Κινδυνεύεις μέντοι λόγον οὐ φαῦλον εἰρηκέναι περὶ ἐπιστήμης, ἀλλ' ὃν ἔλεγε καὶ Πρωταγόρας. Τρόπον δέ τινα ἄλλονεἴρηκε τὰ αὐτὰ ταῦτα. φησὶ γάρ του "πάντων χρημάτων μέτρον" ἄνθρωπον εἶναι, "τῶν μὲν ὄντων ὡς ἔστι, τῶν δὲ μὴ ὄντων ὡς οὐκ ἔστιν." ἀνέγνωκας γάρ που" (151e–152a; translation slightly modified).

5. "*Alles, was da ist, hat ein Maß*" (*WLSb*, p. 330 [333; translation modified]).

6. "Töricht, von einem natürlichen *Maßstab* der Dinge zu sprechen" (*WLSb*, p. 330 [334]).

7. "Jedes Existierende hat eine Größe, um das zu sein, was es ist, und überhaupt um Dasein zu haben" (*WLSb*, p. 331 [334; translation modified]). Here Miller choses to translate *Dasein* as "exterior reality" although normally he uses "determinate being."

8. "Wenn also einem Menschen gesagt wird, du (dein Inneres) bist dies, weil dein Knochen so beschaffen ist; so heißt es nichts anderes, als ich sehe einen Knochen für *deine Wirklichkeit* an. Die bei der Physiognomik erwähnte Erwiderung eines solchen Urteils durch die Ohrfeige bringt zunächst die *weichen Teile* aus ihrem Ansehen und Lage, und erweist nur, daß diese kein wahres *Ansich*, nicht die Wirklichkeit des Geistes sind;—hier müßte die Erwiderung eigentlich so weit gehen, einem, der so urteilt, den Schädel einzuschlagen, um gerade so greiflich, als seine Weisheit ist, zu erweisen, daß ein Knochen für den Menschen nichts *Ansich*, viel weniger *seine* wahre Wirklichkeit ist" (*PhG*, p. 188 [§339; translation modified]). For an example of phrenology, cf. Cesare Lombroso (1836–1909), *Der Verbrecher (Homo Delinquens) in anthropologischer, ärztlicher und juristischer Beziehung* (Hamburg: 1894), Bd. I, pp. 163ff.; or the work of Johann Kaspar Lavater (1741–1801). Cf. also A. MacIntyre, "Hegel on Faces and Skulls" in *Hegel*, pp. 219–36.

9. *WLSb*, pp. 331–33 [335–36].

10. "Das *immanente* quantitative Verhalten *zweier* Qualitäten zueinander" (*WLSb*, p. 337 [340]).

11. *WLSb*, pp. 333–36 [336–39].

12. *WLSb*, pp. 336–41 [339–43].

13. *WLSb*, pp. 341–44 [344–47].

14. *WLSb*, pp. 345–46 [348–49].

15. *WLSb*, pp. 347–48 [349–51].

16. *WLSb*, pp. 348–52 [351–54].

17. John Hawkes, *The Blood Oranges* (New York: New Directions Books, 1970), p. 209.

18. *WLSb*, pp. 352–54 [354–56].

19. *WLSb*, pp. 354–63 [356–66]; *Enzy*, §§326–36, esp. §333.

20. "Das *Tiefe*, das der Geist von innen heraus, aber nur bis in sein *vorstellendes Bewußtsein* treibt und es in diesem stehen läßt—und die *Unwissenheit* dieses Bewußtseins, was das ist, was es sagt, ist dieselbe Verknüpfung des Hohen und Niedrigen, welche an dem Lebendigen die Natur in der Verknüpfung des Organs seiner höchsten Vollendung, des Organs der Zeugung,—und des Organs des Pis-

sens naiv ausdrückt—Das unendliche Urteil als unendliches wäre die Vollendung des sich selbst erfassenden Lebens, das in der Vorstellung bleibende Bewußtsein desselben aber verhält sich als Pissen" (*PhG,* pp. 192–93 [§346; translation slightly modified]). And further: "In many animals the organs of excretion and the genitals, the highest and lowest parts in the animal organization, are intimately connected: just as speech and kissing, on the one hand, and eating, drinking and spiting, on the other, are done with the mouth" (*PN,* p. 404).

21. *WLSb,* p. 328 [332].

22. Cf. *Symp,* 189e–193d.

23. "Jawohl! versetzte der Hauptmann: diese Fälle sind allerdings die bedeutendsten und merkwürdigsten, wo man das Anziehen, das Verwandtsein, dieses Verlassen, dieses Vereinigen gleichsam übers Kreuz, wirklich darstellen kann; wo vier, bisher je zwei zu zwei verbundene Wesen, in Berührung gebracht, ihre bisherige Vereinigung verlassen und sich aufs neue verbinden. In diesem Fahrenlassen und Ergreifen, in diesem Fliehen und Suchen glaubt man wirklich eine höhere Bestimmung zu sehen; man traut solchen Wesen eine Art von Wollen und Wählen zu und hält das Kunstwort Wahlverwandtschaften für vollkommen gerechtfertigt. . . . Wenn Sie glauben, daß es nicht pedantisch aussieht, versetzte der Hauptmann, so kann ich wohl in der Zeichensprache mich kürzlich zusammenfassen. Denken Sie sich ein A, das mit einem B innig verbunden ist, durch viele Mittel und durch mache Gewalt nicht von ihm zu trennen; denken Sie sich ein C, das sich ebenso zu einem D verhält; bringen Sie nun die beiden Paare in Berührung: A wird sich zu D, C zu B werfen, ohne daß man sagen kann, wer das andere zuerst verlassen, wer sich mit dem andern zuerst wieder verbunden habe. Nun denn! fiel Eduard ein: bis wir alles dieses mit Augen sehen, wollen wir diese Formel als Gleichnisrede betrachten, woraus wir uns eine Lehre zum unmittelbaren Gebrauch ziehen. Du stellst das A vor, Charlotte, und ich dein B: denn eigentlich hänge ich doch nur von dir ab und folge dir, wie dem A das B. Das C ist ganz deutlich der Capitän, der mich für diesmal dir einigermaßen entzieht. Nun ist es billig, daß wenn du nicht ins Unbestimmte entweichen sollst, dir für ein D gesorgt werde, und das ist ganz ohne Frage das liebenswürdige Dämchen Ottilie, gegen deren Annäherung du dich nicht länger verteidigen darfst" (*Wahlverwandschaften,* pp. 42–43).

24. "Verzeihen Sie mir, sagte Charlotte, wie ich dem Naturforscher verzeihe; aber ich würde hier niemals eine Wahl, eher eine Naturnotwendigkeit erblicken, und diese kaum: denn es ist am Ende vielleicht gar nur die Sache der Gelegenheit Gelegenheit macht Verhältnisse, wie sie Diebe macht; und wenn von Ihren Naturkörpern die Rede ist, so scheint mir die Wahl bloß in den Händen des Chemikers zu liegen, der diese Wesen zusammenbringt" (*Wahlverwandschaften,* p. 41).

25. Benjamin, "Goethes *Wahlverwandtschaften,*" pp. 253–333.

26. "Geschlechtsgeminschaft (commercium sexuale) ist der wechselseitige Gebrauch, den ein Mensch von eines andern Geschlechtsorganen und -vermögen macht (usus membrorum et facultatum sexualium alterius), und entweder ein natürlicher (wodurch seinesgleichen erzeugt werden kann) oder unnatürlicher

Gebrauch und dieser entweder an einer Person ebendesselben Geschlechts oder Tier von einer anderen als der Menschengattung" (*MS I,* §24).

27. "Die Verbindung zweier Personen verschiedenen Geschlechts zum lebenswierigen wechselseitigen Besitz ihrer Geschlechtseigenschaften—Der Zweck Kinder zu erzeugen und zu erziehen mag immer ein Zweck der Natur sein, zu welchem sich die Neigung der Geschlechter gegeneinander einpflanzte; aber daß der Mensch, der sich verehelicht, diesen Zweck sich vorsetzen müsse, wird zur Rechtmäßigkeit dieser seiner Verbindung nicht erfordert; denn sonst würde, wenn das Kinderzeugen aufhört, die Ehe sich zugleich von selbst auflösen" (*MS I,* §24).

28. "So Kant" ("Goethes *Wahlverwandtschaften,*" pp. 257–58).

29. "Der Unterschied der natürlichen Geschlechter erscheint ebenso zugleich als ein Unterschied der intellecktuellen und sittlichen Bestimmung. Diese Persönlichkeiten verbinden sich nach ihrer ausschließenden Einzelnheit zu *Einer Person;* die subjektive Innigkeit zu substantieller Einheit bestimmt, macht diese Vereinung zu einem *sittlichen* Verhältnisse,—zur *Ehe.* Die substantielle Innigkeit macht die Ehe zu einem ungeteilten Bande der Personen,—zu *monogamischer Ehe;* die Körperliche Vereinigung ist Folge des sittlich geknüpften Bandes. Die fernere Folge ist die Gemeinsamkeit der persönlichen und partikulären Interessen" (*Enzy,* §519; cf. §§513–28; see also *PhG,* pp. 247ff. [§456ff.] and *JS III,* pp. 238–40).

30. "Es keine Frage gibt, welche die Einheit der Philosophie erfragend umspannt. Den Begriff dieser nichtexistenten Frage, welche die Einheit der Philosophie erfragt, bezeichnet in der Philosophie das Ideal des Problems. Wenn aber auch das System in keinem Sinne erfragbar ist, so gibt es doch Gebilde, die, ohne Frage zu sein, zum Ideal des Problems die tiefste Affinität haben. Es sind die Kunstwerke. Nicht mit der Philosophie selbst konkurriert das Kunstwerke, es tritt lediglich zu ihr ins genaueste Verhältnis durch seine Verwandtschaft mit dem Ideal des Problems. Und zwar kann, einer Gesetzlichkeit nach, die im Wesen des Ideals überhaupt gründet, dieses einzig in einer Vielheit sich darstellen" (Benjamin, "Goethes *Wahlverwandtschaften,*" pp. 304–5). Benjamin here, very close to Heidegger, even makes the explicit connection between truth and language: "the truth will be discovered in the essence of language" [*Entdeckt wird die Wahrheit im Wesen der Sprache*] ("Goethes *Wahlverwandtschaften,*" p. 330).

31. *VA* I, pp. 203–11.

32. *WLSb,* pp. 364–65 [366–67].

33. *WLSb,* pp. 365–69 [367–71].

34. "Das Qualitative-Endliche *wird* zum Unendlichen; das Quantitative-Endliche ist sein Jenseits an ihm selbst und *weist über sich hinaus*" (*WLSb,* p. 370 [372; translation slightly modified]).

35. *WLSb,* pp. 369–70 [371–72].

36. *WLSb,* pp. 370–71 [372–73].

37. *WLSb,* pp. 371–72 [373–75].

38. "Und es kommt ganz nur darauf an, wie diese an ihm gesetzt sind" (*WLSb,* p. 374 [376]).

39. *WLSb*, pp. 373–81 [375–83].

40. *WLSb*, pp. 381–82 [383–84].

41. "Es ist einer der bisher ganz unbeachteten und in der Tat der schwersten Punkte in der Lehre vom Geiste, in der Systematisierung der Intelligenz die Stellung und Bedeutung des Gedächtnisses zu fassen und dessen organischen Zusammenhang mit dem Denken zu begreifen" (*Enzy*, §464).

42. *WLSb*, pp. 382–83 [384–85].

Chapter 7

1. "Hegel montrait ainsi que le concept n'a rien à voir avec une idée générale ou abstraite, pas plus qu'avec une Sagesse incréée qui ne dépendrait pas de la philosophie même" (*Qu'est-ce que la philosophie?* p. 16 [12]). Nevertheless, Deleuze and Guattari follow Nietzsche in criticizing the dialectic—as they understand and represent it: "Hegel has the idea of making use of the contradiction between rival opinions to extract from them suprascientific propositions able to move, contemplate, reflect, and communicate in themselves and within the absolute (the speculative proposition wherein opinions become moments of the concept). But, beneath the highest ambitions of the dialectic, and irrespective of the genius of the great dialecticians, we fall back into the most abject conditions that Nietzsche diagnosed as the art of the pleb or bad taste in philosophy: a reduction of the concept to propositions like simple opinions; false perceptions and bad feelings (illusions of transcendence or of universals) engulfing the plane of immanence; the model of a form of knowledge that constitutes only a supposedly higher opinion, *Urdoxa,* a replacement of conceptual personae by teachers or leaders of schools. The dialectic claims to discover a specifically philosophical discursiveness, but it can only do this by linking opinions together. It has indeed gone beyond opinion toward knowledge, but opinion breaks through and continues to break through. Even with the resources of an *Urdoxa,* philosophy remains a doxography" [Hegel ait l'idée de se servir de la contradiction des opinions rivales pour en extraire des propositions supra-scientifiques, capables de se mouvoir, de se contempler, se réfléchir, se communiquer en elles-mêmes et dans l'absolu (proposition spéculative, où les opinions deviennent les moments du concept). Mais, sous les plus hautes ambitions de la dialectique, et quel que soit le génie des grands dialecticiens, on retombe dans la plus misérable condition, celle que Nietzsche diagnostiquait comme l'art de la plèbe, ou le mauvais goût en philosophie: la réduction du concept à des propositions comme simples opinions; l'engloutissement du plan d'immanence dans les fausses perceptions et les mauvais sentiments (illusions de la transcendance ou des universaux); le modèle d'un savoir qui ne constitue qu'une opinion prétendue supérieure, Urdoxa; le remplacement des personnages conceptuels par des professeurs ou chefs d'école. La dialectique prétend trouver une discursivité proprement philosophique, mais elle ne peut le faire qu'en enchaînant les opinions les unes aux autres. Elle a beau dépasser l'opinion vers le savoir, l'opinion perce et continue de percer. Même

avec les ressources d'une Urdoxa, la philosophie reste une doxographie] (*Qu'est-ce que la philosophie?* p. 80 [12]). For a defense of Hegel and a refusal of Deleuze's reduction of the dialectical reduction—or more specifically, for an attempt to complicate their relation in order to show how Hegel and Deleuze are not in opposition, but form a "block of becoming"—cf. C. Malabou, "Who's Afraid of Hegelian Wolves?" in *Deleuze: A Critical Reader*, ed. P. Patton (Oxford: Blackwell, 1996), pp. 114–38.

2. *WLB*, pp. 5–6 [575–76].

3. "Ihre *Grundlage* und *Wahrheit* als die Identität, in welcher sie untergegangen und enthalten sind" (*WLB*, p. 11 [577; translation slightly modified]).

4. "Es kömmt nach meiner Einsicht, welche sich durch die Darstellung des Systems selbst rechtfertigen muß, alles darauf an, das Wahre nicht als *Substanz*, sondern eben so sehr als *Subjekt* aufzufassen und auszudrücken Zugleich ist zu bemerken, daß die Substantialität so sehr das Allgemeine, oder die *Unmittelbarkeit des Wissens*, als diejenige, welche *Sein* oder Unmittelbarkeit *für* das Wissen ist, in sich schließt" (*PhG*, p. 18 [§17; translation modified]).

5. "Begriff des Begriffes" (*WLB*, pp. 11–16 [577–82]; cf. *SI*, §2).

6. "Die Kantische Philosophie begeht hierin eine weitere Inkonsequenz, sie *entlehnt* für die *transzendentale* Logik die Kategorien als sogenannte Stammbegriffe aus der subjekiven Logik, in welcher sie empirisch aufgenommen worden. Da sie letzteres zugibt, so ist nicht abzusehen, warum die transzendentale Logik sich zum Entlehnen aus solcher Wissenschaft entschließt und nicht gleich selbst empirisch zugreift" (*WLB*, p. 44 [613; translation slightly modified]; cf. *CPR* B 106–7).

7. "Hat keine andere[n] Momente oder Bestimmungen als das Ich selbst" (*WLB*, p. 19 [585; translation slightly modified]).

8. Here Hegel's critique follows that of skeptics such as Schulze and Maimon; cf. *Aenesidemus* and *Versuch einer neuen Logik oder Theorie des Denkens*.

9. "Scheinen in Anderes" (*WLB*, pp. 22–25 [588–92]; cf. *Enzy*, §§161–62).

10. "Schon *für sich selbst die Wahrheit*" (*WLB*, p. 26 [593; translation modified]).

11. "Übereinstimmung der Erkenntnis mit ihrem Gegenstand" (*WLB*, p. 26 [593; translation modified]).

12. *WLB*, pp. 25–28 [592–95].

13. *WLB*, pp. 29–30 [596–97].

14. *WLB*, p. 31 [599].

15. "So ist jedes jener Momente so sehr *ganzer* Begriff als *bestimmter Begriff* und als *eine Bestimmung* des Begriffs" (*WLB*, p. 32 [600; translation modified]; cf. *Enzy*, §163).

16. "Das wahre Eigentümliche einer Philosophie ist die interessante Individualität, in welcher die Vernunft aus dem Bauzeug eines besondern Zeitalters sich eine Gestalt organisiert hat; die besondre spekulative Vernunft findet darin Geist von ihrem Geist, Fleisch von ihrem Fleisch, sie schaut sich in ihm als ein und dasselbe und als ein anderes lebendiges Wesen an Jede Philosophie ist in sich vollendet und hat, wie ein echtes Kunstwerk, die Totalität in sich" (*Diff*, p. 12).

17. "In dem Begriff ist die Identität zur Allgemeinheit, der Unterschied zur

Besonderheit, die Entgegensetzung, die in den Grund zurückgeht, zur Einzelheit fortgebildet In diesen Formen sind jene Reflexionsbestimmungen wie sie in ihrem Begriff sind. Das Allgemeine erweis sich nicht nur als das Identische, sonder zugleich als das Verschiedene oder *Konträre* gegen das Besondere und Einzelne, ferner auch als ihnen entgegengesetzt oder *kontradiktorisch;* in dieser Entgegensetzung aber ist es identisch mit ihnen und ihr wahrhafter Grund, in welchem sie aufgehoben sind. Ein Gleiches gilt von der Besonderheit und Einzelheit, welche ebenso die Totalität der Reflexionsbestimmungen sind" (*WLB,* p. 46 [615–16; translation modified]).

18. *This Sex Which Is Not One,* p. 28. "So sexualité toujours du moins double, est encore plurielle . . . En effet, la plaisir de la femme n'a pas á choisir entre activité clitoridienne et passivité vaginale, par example. Le plaisir de la caresse vaginale n'a pas à se substituer à celui de la caresse clitoridienne. Ils concourent l'un et l'autre, de la manière irremplaçable, à la jouissance de la femme. Parmi d'autres . . ." (pp. 27–28).

19. "Es ist die *Seele* des Konkreten, dem es inwohnt, ungehindert und sich selbst gleich in dessen Mannigfaltigkeit und Verschiedenheit" (*WLB,* p. 34 [602]).

20. *WLB,* pp. 33–35 [601–3]; cf. *Enzy,* §160.

21. "Der Unterschied, welcher wesentliches Moment des Begriffs, aber im rein Allgemeinen noch nicht als solcher gesetzt ist, enthält im bestimmten Begriff sein Recht" (*WLB,* p. 43 [612; translation modified]; cf. pp. 35–37 [604–5]).

22. *WLB,* pp. 41–43 [605–8].

23. *WLB,* pp. 37–39 [605–8].

24. "Ist somit zwar der *Begriff,* aber als *Begriffloses,* als Begriff, der nicht als solcher gesetzt ist" (*WLB,* p. 40 [609; translation modified]; cf. also pp. 41–46 [610–12]).

25. "Der Anfang, das Prinzip, oder das Absolute, wie es zuerst und unmittelbar ausgesprochen wird, ist nur das Allgemeine. So wenig, wenn ich sage: *alle* Tiere, dies Wort für eine Zoologie gelten kann, ebenso fällt es auf, daß die Worte des Göttlichen, Absoluten, Ewigen *u.s.w.* das nicht aussprechen, was darin enthalten ist;—und nur solche Worte drücken in der Tat die Anschauung als das Unmittelbare aus" (*PhG,* p. 19 [§20]).

26. "Sie meinen *dieses* Stück Papier, worauf ich dies schreibe, oder vielmehr geschrieben habe; aber was sie meinen, sagen sie nicht Wenn sie wirklich dieses Stück Papier, das sie meinen, *sagen wollten,* und sie wollten *sagen,* so ist dies unmöglich, weil das sinnliche Diese, das gemeint wird, der Sprache, die dem Bewußtsein, dem an sich Allgemeinen, angehört, *unerreichbar* ist" (*PhG,* p. 70 [§110; translation modified]).

27. "In der Ohnmacht der Natur, den Begriff in seiner Ausführung festzuhalten, liegt die Schwierigkeit und in vielen Kreisen die Unmöglichkeit, aus der empirischen Betrachtung feste Unterschiede für Klassen und Ordnungen zu finden. Die Natur vermischt allenthalben die wesentlichen Grenzen durch mittlere und schlechte Gebilde, welche immer Instanzen gegen jede feste Unterscheidung abgeben, selbst innerhalb bestimmter Gattungen (z.B. des Menschen) durch Mißgeburten, die man einerseits dieser Gattung zuzählen muß, denen andererseits aber Bestimmungen fehlen, welche als wesentliche Eigentümlichkeit

der Gattung anzusehen wären.—Um dergleichen Gebilde als mangelhaft, schlecht, mißförmig betrachten zu können, dafur wird ein fester Typus vorausgesetzt, der aber nicht aus der Erfahrung geschöpft werden könnte, denn diese eben gibt auch jene sogenannten Mißgeburten, Mißförmigkeiten, Mitteldinge usf. an die Hand: er setzte vielmehr die Selbständigkeit und Würde der Begriffsbestimmung voraus" (*Enzy,* §250, *Zusatz*).

28. "In der Natur finden sich freilich in einer Gattung mehr als zwei Arten, so wie diese vielen Arten auch nicht das aufgezeigte Verhältnis zueinander haben können. Es ist dies die Ohnmacht der Natur, die Strenge des Begriffs nicht festhalten und darstellen zu können und in diese begrifflose blinde Mannigfaltigkeit sich zu verlaufen. Wir können die Natur in der Mannigfaltigkeit ihrer Gattungen und Arten und der unendlichen Verschiedenheit ihrer Gestaltungen *bewundern,* denn die Bewunderung ist *ohne Begriff,* und ihr Gegenstand ist das Vernunftlose. Der Natur, weil sie das Außersichsein des Begriffes ist, ist es freigegeben, in dieser Verschiedenheit sich zu ergehen, wie der Geist, ob er gleich den Begriff in der Gestalt des Begriffes hat, auch aufs Vorstellen sich einläßt und in einer unendlichen Mannigfaltigkeit desselben sich herumtreibt. Die vielfachen Naturgattungen oder Arten müssen für nichts Höheres geachtet werden als die willkürlichen Einfälle des Geistes in seinen Vorstellungen. Beide zeigen wohl allenthalben Spuren und Ahndungen des Begriffs, aber stellen ihn nicht in treuem Abbild dar, weil sie die Seite seines freien Außersichseins sind; er ist die absolute Macht gerade darum, daß er seinen Unterschied frei zur Gestalt selbständiger Verschiedenheit äußerlicher Notwendigkeit, Zufälligkeit, Willkür, Meinung entlassen kann, welche aber für nicht mehr als die abstrakte Seite der *Nichtigkeit* genommen werden muß" (*WLB,* pp. 39–40 [607–8; translation modified]).

29. "μάλα γὰρ φιλοσόφου τοῦτο τὸ πάθος, τὸ θαυμάζειν. οὐ γὰρ ἄλλη ἀρχὴ φιλοσοφίας ἢ αὕτη, καὶ ἔοικεν ὁ τὴν Ἶριν Θαύμαντος ἔκγονον φήσας οὐ κακῶς γενεαλογεῖν" (*Theaet,* 155d).

30. *Enzy,* §§245–51.

31. "Das Identische different und das Differente identisch" (*Enzy,* §314).

32. "Ohnmacht der Natur setzt der Philosophie Grenzen" (*Enzy,* §250, *Zusatz*).

33. "Das Glück meines Daseins, seine Einzigkeit vielleicht, liegt in seinem Verhängniss: ich bin, um es in Rätselform auszudrücken, als mein Vater bereits gestorben, als meine Mutter lebe ich noch und werde alt Diese doppelte Herkunft, gleichsam aus der obersten und der untersten Sprosse an der Leiter des Lebens, décadent zugleich und *Anfang*—dies, wenn irgend Etwas, erklärt jene Neutralität, jene Freiheit von Partei im Verhältniss zum Gesammtprobleme des Lebens, die mich vielleicht auszeichnet. Ich habe für die Zeichen von Anfang und Niedergang eine feinere Witterung als je ein Mensch gehabt hat, ich bin der Lehrer par excellence hierfür,—ich kenne Beides, ich bin Beides" (*KGW* VI, 3, 262).

34. "ὁδὸς ἄνω κάτω μία καὶ ὡυτή" (Frag. 60).

35. *WLB,* pp. 49–51 [618–21].

36. *WLB,* pp. 194–221 [187–201]; see also *PhG,* pp. 63–70 [§§90–110].

37. "Vielheit gehört dem Sein an" (*WLB,* p. 52 [622]; cf. *WLSb,* p. 68 [82]).

38. "Mannigfaltigkeit gehört zum Sein selbst" (*GA* 26, §10; cf. *SZ,* §64, §80).

39. *WLB,* p. 52 [622].

40. "Absolute, ursprüngliche *Teilung seiner*" (*WLB*; translation modified).

41. "Die verschiedenen Sprachen neben einander gestellt zeigen, dass es bei den Worten nie auf die Wahrheit, nie auf ainen adäquaten Ausdruck ankommt denn sonst gäbe es nicht so viele Sprachen" (*KGW* III, 2, 373).

42. *Enzy,* §§458–59.

43. "Der Namen existiert als *Sprache*" (*JS I,* p. 288; cf. p. 290, and *Enzy,* §20, *Zusatz*).

44. "Die Bedeutung des Zeichens ist nur in Beziehung auf das Subjekt" (*JS I,* p. 287; cf. *Enzy,* §458, *Zusatz*).

45. "In Namen ist erst eigentlich das *Anschauen,* das Tierische, und Zeit und Raum überwunden" (*JS III,* p. 190).

46. *Enzy,* §459, *Zusatz;* cf. Derrida, "Le Puits et la pyramide," in *Marges de la philosophie,* pp. 79–127.

47. "Befestigtes Zeichen; bleibende Beziehung" (*JS III,* p. 193).

48. *Enzy,* §462.

49. "Grundbedürfnisse der Sprache überhaupt" (*Enzy,* §459, *Zusatz;* cf. §§460–64).

50. "Der existierende Begriff des Bewußtseins," "Namengebende Kraft," "Schöpferkraft" (*JS I,* p. 288).

51. "τὸ γὰρ αὐτὸ νοεῖν ἔστιν τε καὶ εἶναι" (Frag. 3). Cf. *JS III,* pp. 189–90; *Enzy,* §20, *Zusatz; PhG,* p. 70 [§110].

52. "Der Begriff kann als solcher wesentlich nur mit dem Geiste aufgefaßt werden, dessen Eigentum nicht nur, sondern dessen reines Selbst er ist" (*WLB,* p. 48 [618; translation modified]).

53. "Wenn Begriffe nun in der Weise genommen worden, daß sie solchen Zeichen entsprechen, so hören sie auf, Begriffe zu sein Ihre Bestimmungen sind nicht so ein Totliegendes wie Zahlen und Linien, denen ihre Beziehung nicht selbst angehört; sie sind lebendige Bewegungen" (*WLB,* p. 47 [617; translation slightly modified]).

54. *WLB,* p. 48 [618].

55. *PhG,* pp. 276–86 [§§508–26]; cf. *Enzy,* §411, *Zusatz.*

56. *PhG,* p. 351 [§652].

57. Cf. *Enzy,* §165.

58. "Realität des Begriffes" (*WLB,* pp. 53–59 [623–30]).

59. "Wer die *Richtigkeit* einer *Anschauung* oder *Wahrmehmung,* die Übereinstimmung der *Vorstellung* mit dem Gegenstand *Wahrheit* nennte, hat wenigstens keinen Ausdruck mehr für dasjenige, was Gegenstand und Zweck der Philosophie ist" (*WLB,* p. 65 [636; translation modified]).

60. "*Alle Dinge sind ein Urteil*" (*Enzy,* §167).

61. "*Das Einzelne ist allgemein*" (*WLB,* p. 61 [632]; cf. *Enzy,* §169).

62. *WLB,* pp. 60–64 [630–36]; cf. *Enzy,* §§170–72.

63. "Das Einzelne ist aber auch *nicht* ein Allgemeins" (*Enzy,* §173).

64. *"Das Einzelne ist ein Besonderes"* (*WLB,* p. 65 [637]).

65. *"Niemand zeugt für den Zeugen"* ("Atemwende," in *Gesammelte Werke,* Bd. II, p. 72).

66. *WLB,* pp. 64–69 [636–41].

67. Similarly, for Hegel crime negates not only a particular law, but also the universal sphere of law as law, right as right (*WLB,* p. 70 [642)].

68. *"Das Allgemeine ist allgemein"* (*WLB,* p. 70 [643]).

69. *WLB,* pp. 69–70 [641–43].

70. *"Dieses ist ein wesentlich Allgemeines"* (*WLB,* p. 72 [645]).

71. *"Einige Einzelne sind ein Allgemeines"* (*WLB,* p. 73 [645]).

72. "Sie gewinnt somit durch die vergrößerte Mehrheit der Glieder nichts an Allgemeinheit" (*WLB,* p. 75 [647]).

73. *"Was allen Einzelnen einer Gattung zukommt, kommt durch ihre Natur der Gattung zu"* (*WLB,* p. 77 [650]).

74. *WLB,* pp. 77–83 [650–57]; cf. p. 85 [658].

75. *WLB,* pp. 84–85 [657–59].

76. "Handle so, daß die Maxime deines Willens jederzeit zugleich als Prinzip einer allgemeinen Gesetzgebung gelten könne" (*KPrV,* §7; cf. *WLB,* pp. 85–86 [659–60]).

77. *WLB,* pp. 86–87 [660–61].

78. *WLB,* pp. 87–89 [661–63]; *Enzy,* §§179–80.

Chapter 8

1. John Hawkes, *Travesty* (New York: New Directions Books, 1976), p. 75.

2. "Deshalb müssen wir alle fragen und immer wieder fragen, um es zu wissen, oder auch nur, um zu wissen, warum und inwiefern wir es nicht wissen. Ist der Mensch, sind die Völker nur in dieses Weltall hineingestolpert, um ebenso wieder hinausgeschleudert zu werden, oder ist es anders? Wir müssen fragen. Es gilt sogar auf lange Zeit hinaus erst ein noch viel Vorläufigeres: Wir müssen erst wieder *lernen* zu fragen. Das geschieht allein, indem Fragen, freilich keine beliebigen, gefragt werden. Wir wählten die Frage 'Was ist ein Ding?' Es zeigt sich jetzt: Die Dinge stehen in verschiedenen Wahrheiten" (*FD,* p. 11; emphasis added).

3. Cf. *CPR,* Third and Fourth Antinomies.

4. *CPR,* B xxiii.

5. *FD,* p. 11.

6. *WLB,* p. 147 [726].

7. *WLB,* pp. 133–35 [711–14].

8. *CPR,* Third Antinomy; cf. Schelling, *UWF,* pp. 382–85.

9. *WLB,* pp. 136–38 [714–16].

10. *WLB,* pp. 137–40 [716–18].

11. *WLB,* pp. 140–42 [718–21].

12. *WLB*, pp. 142–45 [721–24]. Hegel's political analogy is explicit: this is not a Hobbesian "war of all against all" but the universal (state) fulfilling the particular (needs) of the individual (citizen); cf. *GPR*.

13. *WLB*, pp. 145–46 [724–25].

14. *WLB*, pp. 146–47 [725–26].

15. *WLB*, pp. 148–49 [727–28].

16. *WLB*, pp. 149–52 [728–31].

17. *WLB*, pp. 152–53 [731–33].

18. *WLB*, pp. 154–59 [734–40].

19. *WLB*, pp. 160–62 [740–43].

20. *WLB*, pp. 162–65 [743–46].

21. *WLB*, pp. 165–70 [745–51].

22. *WLB*, pp. 170–72 [751–54].

Chapter 9

1. *Crise de vers*, p. 244.

2. "Sie sind selbst die Kongruenz des Begriffs und der Realität" (*WLB*, p. 174 [756]; cf. *CPR* A 137/B 176ff.).

3. "*Sein* hat die Bedeutung der *Wahrheit* erreicht, indem die Idee die Einheit des Begriffs und der Realität *ist;* es ist also nunmehr nur das, was Idee ist" (*WLB;* p. 175 [757; translation modified]).

4. *WLB*, pp. 173–78 [755–60].

5. "Die Momente aber zu *zählen* kann überhaupt als unnütz angesehen werden, indem teils das Unterschiedne selbst ebensosehr nur *Eines* ist, nämlich eben der *Gedanke* des Unterschiedes, der nur Ein Gedanke ist, als er *dieses* Unterschiedne, das zweite gegen das Erste ist,—teils aber, weil der Gedanke, der das Viele in Eines befaßt, aus seiner Allgemeinheit aufgelöst und in mehr als drei oder vier Unterschiedne unterschieden werden muß . . . also hier überhaupt an Zahl und ans Zählen zu denken ganz überflüssig, wie auch sonst der bloße Unterschied der Größe und Menge begrifflos und nichts sagend ist" (*PhG*, p. 413 [*PhS*, §776; translation modified]).

6. *WLB*, pp. 179–80 [761–62].

7. "Eins in der Mannigfaltigkeit" (*WLB*, pp. 180–82 [762–64]).

8. *WLB*, pp. 182–86 [764–69] cf. *Enzy*, §218.

9. "*Wenn man sagt, daß der Widerspruch nicht denkbar sei, so ist er vielmehr im Schmerz des Lebendigen sogar eine wirkliche Existenz*" (*WLB*, p. 188 [770]).

10. *WLB*, pp. 187–89 [769–72], cf. *Enzy*, §219.

11. *WLB*, pp. 189–91 [772–74] cf. *Enzy*, §§220–21.

12. "Schwarze Milch der Frühe wir trinken dich nachts / wir trinken dich mittags und morgens wir trinken dich abends / wir trinken und trinken / ein Mann wohnt im Haus dein goldenes Haar Margarete dein aschenes Haar Sulamith er spielt mit den Schlangen // Er ruft spielt süßer den Tod der Tod ist ein Meister aus Deutschland / er ruft streicht dunkler die Geigen dann steight ihr als Rauch in die Luft / dann habt ihr ein Grab in den Wolken da liegt man

nicht eng" (*Death Fugue* [*Todesfuge*], in *Poems of Paul Celan* [*Mohn und Gedächtnis*], trans. M. Hamburger, pp. 62–65).

13. "*Keiner kann dem Anderen sein Sterben abnehmen.* Jemand kann wohl 'für einen Anderen in den Tod gehen.' Das besagt jedoch immer: für den Anderen sich opfern '*in einer bestimmten Sache.*' Solches Sterben für . . . kann aber nie bedeuten, daß dem Anderen damit sein Tod im geringsten abgenommen sei. Das Sterben muß jedes Dasein jeweilig selbst auf sich nehmen. Der Tod ist, sofern er 'ist,' wesensmäßig je der meine. Und zwar bedeutet er eine eigentümliche Seinsmöglichkeit, darin es um das Sein des je eigenen Daseins schlechthin geht. Am Sterben zeigt sich, daß der Tod ontologisch durch Jemeinigkeit und Existenz konstituiert wird" (Heidegger, *SZ,* §47), cf. Derrida, *The Gift of Death,* pp. 41–46. Cf. also *Aporias,* esp. pp. 72–80. Here Derrida argues that the possibility of the absolute impossibility of Da-sein's (being-towards-)death is always already contaminated by its necessary perishing—by deconstructing Heidegger's distinction between authentic and inauthentic, Derrida calls the entire existential analysis of *Being and Time* into question. Derrida's own aporias appear far more Hegelian than not—the articulation of the "awaiting death" [*le s'attendre à la mort*], for example, is "one example among others, one of these cases in which a strange logical figure of contradiction would take the form of an antinomy or of an aporia, of a problem of language or of logic to be resolved" [un example parmi d'autres, l'un de ces cas où une étrange figure logique de la contradiction prendrait la forme d'une antinomie ou d'une aporie, d'un problème de language ou de logique à résoudre] (p. 72 [127]).

14. "*Eigenste, unbezügliche, unüberholbare Möglichkeit*" (Heidegger, *SZ,* §50) J. Stambaugh translates it as "*ownmost nonrelational possibility not to be bypassed.*"

15. "*Möglichkeit der schlechthinnigen Daseinsunmöglichkeit*" (*SZ,* §50).

16. "Gott selbst gestorben ist" (*PhS,* §785 [*PhG,* p. 419]); cf. Nietzsche, *Gay Science,* §125.

17. *Enzy,* §§368, 370, 375.

18. *FVC,* in *Werke,* vol. I, pp. 68–69; *Enzy,* §§217, 222.

19. *PhS,* §§190–91 [*PhG,* p. 113].

20. "Aber zum eigentlichen Anerkennen fehlt das Moment, daß, was der Herr gegen den andern tut, er auch gegen sich selbst, und was der Knecht gegen sich, er auch gegen den andern tue" (*PhG,* p. 113 [*PhS,* §191; translation modified]).

21. "Die vielfache sich in sich unterscheidende Ausbreitung, Vereinzelung und Verwicklung des Lebens" (*PhG,* p. 117 [*PhS,* §199; translation modified]).

22. "Anfang der Weisheit" (*PhG,* pp. 114–15 [*PhS,* §§194–95]). Cf. *Psalms* 111:10: "The fear of the LORD is the beginning of wisdom; A good understanding have all they that do thereafter; His praise endureth for ever."

23. "Der Glaube an die unmittelbare Gewißheit des Denkens ist ein Glaube mehr, und keine Gewißheit! Wir . . . wehren uns gegen seine dogmatische Leichtfertigkeit im Zweifel. 'Es muß besser gezweifelt werden als Descartes!' " (VII 40 [25]; cf. also *BGE,* §§16, 17).

24. *PhS,* §§188–89 [*PhG,* p. 112].

25. *PhS*, §§178–87 [*PhG*, pp. 108–11].

26. *PhS*, §§187–88 [*PhG*, pp. 110–11]; cf. §196 [p. 116].

27. "Das Andre ist mannigfaltig befangenes und seiendes Bewußtsein" (*PhG*, pp. 111–12 [*PhS*, §187; translation modified]).

28. "Dies vielfache Tun hat sich nun in die einfache Unterscheidung zusammengezogen" (*PhG*, pp. 117 [*PhS*, §199]).

29. "Ein Verhältnis, wodurch sich im unmittelbaren empirischen Selbstbewußtsein die absolute, ewige Natur desselben und des Begriffes offenbart, deswegen offenbart, weil das Selbstbewußtsein eben der *daseiende*, also *empirisch wahrnehmbare*, reine *Begriff*, die absolute Beziehung auf sich selbst ist, welche als trennendes Urteil sich zum Gegenstand macht und allein dies ist, sich dadurch zum Zirkel zu machen—Ein Stein hat jene *Unbequemlichkeit* nicht; wenn er gedacht oder wenn über ihn geurteilt werden soll, so steht er sich selbst dabei nicht im Wege; er ist der Beschwerlichkeit, sich seiner selbst zu diesem Geschäft zu bedienen, enthoben; es ist ein Anderes außer ihm, welches diese Mühe übernehmen muß" (*WLB*, p. 194 [777–78; translation modified]).

30. "*Denken, Geist, Selbstbewußtsein* sind Bestimmungen der Idee, insofern sie sich selbst zum Gegenstand hat und ihr *Dasein*, di. die Bestimmtheit ihres Seins ihr eigener Unterschied von sich selbst ist" (*WLB*, p. 192 [775; translation modified]).

31. *WLB*, pp. 199–200 [783–84].

32. *CPR*, A vii.

33. *WLB*, pp. 200–2 [784–86].

34. *WLB*, pp. 202–8 [786–93].

35. *WLB*, pp. 209–10 [793–95].

36. "Die Definition reduziert aber diesen Reichtum der mannigfaltigen Bestimmungen des angeschauten Daseins auf die einfachsten Momente" (*WLB*, p. 210 [795]).

37. *WLB*, pp. 210–14 [795–800].

38. *WLB*, pp. 215–19 [800–5].

39. Cf. Descartes, *Med III*.

40. *WLB*, pp. 220–23 [806–10].

41. *WLB*, pp. 220–23 [811–18]; cf. *WLW*, pp. 408–9 [570–71], and *WLSa*, pp. 21, 24, 27–29.

42. *Enzy*, §§232–33.

43. *WLB*, pp. 231–35 [818–22]; cf. *KPrV*, §7.

44. "Alles Übrige ist Irrtum, Trübheit, Meinung, Streben, Willkür und Vergänglichkeit" (*WLB*, p. 236 [824; translation modified]). Cf. *Enzy*, §236; and Aristotle, *Meta*, 1072b20.

45. "Niemand zeugt für den Zeugen" *Atemwende*, "Aschenglorie" *Gesammelte Werke*, ed. B. Allemann and S. Reichert, vol. II (Frankfurt: Suhrkamp, 1986), p. 72; my translation.

46. Cf. *Vorlesungen über die Philosophie der Weltgeschichte* (1822/28/30), 4 vols., ed. J. Hoffmeister (Hamburg: Meiner, 1994) (*Lectures on the Philosophy of World*

History, Introduction: Reason in History, trans. H. B. Nisbet [Cambridge: Cambridge University Press, 1975]).

47. "Die absolute Idee allein ist *Sein*" (*WLB*, p. 236 [825]).

48. *Phen*, §808 *Enzy*, §§242–44. Cf. Heidegger, *ID*, p. 32.

49. "Die absolute Idee allein ist *Sein*, unvergängliches *Leben*, *sich wissende Wahrheit* und ist *alle Wahrheit*" (*WLB*, p. 236 [825]).

Chapter 10

1. *King Lear*, act 1, scene 4.

2. "*Bestimmter Urgrund aller Tätigkeit und Selbstbewegung*" (*WLW*, p. 266 [417]).

3. "Die Kraft des Geistes ist nur so groß als ihre Äußerung, seine Tiefe nur so tief, als er in seiner Auslegung sich auszubreiten und sich zu verlieren getraut" (*PhG*, p. 14 [§10]).

4. "μόνος δ' ἔτι μῦθος ὁδοῖο λείπεται ὡς ἔστιν" (Frag. 8). Hegel translates this as "but truth is only the *is*" [die Wahrheit ist aber nur das *Ist*] (*VGP I*, p. 288).

5. "εἰ δ' ἄγ' ἐγὼν ἐρέω, κόμισαι δὲ σὺ μῦθον ἀκούσας, αἵπερ ὁδοὶ μοῦναι διζήσιός εἰσι νοῆσαι. ἡ μὲν ὅπως ἔστιν τε καὶ ὡς οὐκ ἔστι μὴ εἶναι, πειθοῦς ἐστι κέλευθος ('Αληθείῃ γὰρ ὀπηδεῖ), ἡ δ' ὡς οὐκ ἔστιν τε καὶ ὡς χρεών ἐστι μὴ εἶναι, τὴν δή τοι φράζω παναπευθέα ἔμμεν ἀταρπόν. οὔτε γὰρ ἂν γνοίης τό γε μὴ ἐόν (οὐ γὰρ ἀνυστόν) οὔτε φράσαις" (Frag. 2).

6. *VGP I*, pp. 284–93.

7. "ταὐτὸν δ' ἔστι νοεῖν τε καὶ οὕνεκεν ἔστι νόημα. οὐ γὰρ ἄνευ τοῦ ἐόντος, ἐν ᾧ πεφατισμένον ἐστίν, εὑρήσεις εὸ νοεῖν" (Parmenides, Frag. 8, 34–36).

8. "'Das Denken und das, um weswillen der Gedanke ist, ist dasselbe Denn nicht ohne das Seiende, in welchem es sich ausspricht' (manifestiert, ἐν ᾧ πεφατισμένον ἐστίν, 'wirst du das Denken finden; denn es ist nichts und wird nichts sein außer dem Seienden,'" (*VGP I*, p. 289).

9. *VGP I*, p. 293.

10. "Dadurch überhaupt, daß wie es oben ausgedrückt wurde, die Substanz an ihr selbst Subjekt ist, ist aller Inhalt seine eigene Reflexion in sich. Das Bestehen oder die Substanz eines Daseins ist die Sichselbstgleichheit; denn seine Ungleichheit mit sich wäre seine Auflösung. Die Sichselbstgleichheit aber ist die reine Abstraktion; diese aber ist das *Denken*. Wenn ich sage *Qualität*, sage ich die einfache Bestimmtheit; durch die Qualität ist ein Dasein von einem andern unterschieden, oder ist ein Dasein; es ist für sich selbst, oder es besteht durch diese Einfachheit mit sich. Aber dadurch ist es wesentlich der *Gedanke*.—Hierin ist es begriffen, daß das Sein Denken ist; hierein fällt die Einsicht, die dem gewöhnlichen begrifflosen Sprechen von der Identität des Denkens und Seins abzugehen pflegt" (*PhG*, p. 39 [§54; translation modified]).

11. "Hat im Zeitwort: *Sein*, das Wesen in der vergangenen Zeit: *gewesen*, behalten; denn das Wesen ist das vergangene, aber zeitlos vergangene Sein" (*WLW*, p. 241 [389]). Hegel's thought of the relation between time and being, being and time, prefigures all of Heidegger. In the difference between time and temporality, the time-lessness of being will show itself to be just as much temporal.

And the extension of time through its preservation of the past and its direction toward the future is the other (negation) of any pretense to the priority of the "now" so endemic to a philosophy of presence. Cf. Malabou, *L'avenir de Hegel* and Derrida, "Le Temps des adieux."

12. *Enzy,* §§253–61.

13. "*Itzt;* es hat schon aufgehört zu sein, indem es gezeigt wird; das *Itzt,* das *ist,* ist ein anderes, als das gezeigte, und wir sehen, daß das Itzt eben dieses ist, indem es ist, schon nicht mehr zu sein" (*PhG,* p. 67 [§106; translation modified]).

14. "Aber was *gewesen* ist, ist in der Tat *kein Wesen; es IST nicht,* und um das Sein war es zu tun" (*PhG,* p. 67 [§106; translation modified]).

15. "Das *Aufzeigen* ist also selbst die Bewegung, welche es ausspricht, was das Itzt in Wahrheit ist; nämlich ein Resultat, oder eine Vielheit von Itzt zusammengefaßt; und das Aufzeigen ist das Erfahren, daß Itzt *Allgemeines* ist" (*PhG,* p. 68 [§107; translation modified]). The concept of now will be the supersession that takes care of the now as particular and universal, as immediate and mediated, as singular now and multiple nows; it will be a singular multiplicity and multiple singularity.

16. "Das Sein ist das Unmittelbare. Indem das Wissen das Wahre erkennen will, was das *Sein an und für sich* ist, so bleibt es nicht beim Unmittelbaren und dessen Bestimmungen stehen, sondern dringt durch dasselbe hindurch mit der Voraussetzung, daß *hinter* diesem Sein noch etwas anderes ist als das Sein selbst, daß dieser Hintergrund die Wahrheit des Seins ausmacht" (*WLW,* p. 241 [p. 389]).

17. *WLW,* p. 242 [391].

18. "Einfache Beziehung auf sich selbst: reine *Identität*" (*WLW,* p. 258 [409]).

19. "*Alles ist sich selbst gleich,* A = A" and "A kann nicht zugleich A und nicht A sein" (*WLW,* p. 258 [409]). Hegel's attack on pure identity is obviously (but not exclusively) directed at Fichtean (i.e., Kantian) subjectivism as it appears in the system of transcendental idealism. Here the "absolute I" plays the role of identity as "first, absolute, unconditional principle" (*GW,* p. 18 and *UBW,* p. 40).

20. "Die *mehreren Sätze,* die als *absolute Denkgesetze* aufgestellt werden, sind daher, näher betrachtet, *einander entgegengesetzt,* sie widersprechen einander and heben sich gegenseitig auf" (*WLW,* p. 260 [411]).

21. "Beide bieten sich mit gleicher Notwendigkeit dar und haben als unmittelbare Behauptungen wenigstens gleiches Recht" (*WLW,* p. 259 [410]).

22. "*Nur das Sein ist, und das Nichts ist gar nicht*" (*WLSb,* p. 70 [83; translation modified]).

23. *WLW,* pp. 261–62 [411–13].

24. "*Einheit der Identität mit der Verschiedenheit*" (*WLW,* p. 263 [414]).

25. *WLW,* pp. 262–63 [413–14].

26. "Formell kann das Gesagte so ausgedrückt werden, daß die Natur des Urteils oder Satzes überhaupt, die den Unterschied des Subjekts und Prädikats in sich schließt, durch den spekulativen Satz zerstört wird, und der identische Satz, zu dem der erstere wird, den Gegenstoß zu jenem Verhältnisse enthält—

Dieser Konflikt der Form eines Satzes überhaupt, und der sie zerstörenden Einheit des Begriffs ist dem ähnlich, der im Rhythmus zwischen dem Metrum und dem Akzente statt findet. Der Rhythmus resultiert aus der schwebenden Mitte und Vereinigung beider. So soll auch im philosophischen Satze die Identität des Subjekts und Prädikats den Unterschied derselben, den die Form des Satzes ausdrückt, nicht vernichten, sondern ihre Einheit als eine Harmonie hervorgehen. Die Form des Satzes ist die Erscheinung des bestimmten Sinnes oder Akzent, der seine Erfüllung unterscheidet; daß aber das Prädikat die Substanz ausdrückt, und das Subjekt selbst ins Allgemeine fällt, ist die *Einheit,* worin jener Akzent verklingt" (*PhG,* pp. 43–44 [§61; translation slightly modified]). A musical movement is also a *Satz.*

27. *WLW,* p. 264 [415].

28. *PhG,* p. 44 [§63].

29. *WLW,* pp. 264–66 [416–17].

30. *WLW,* pp. 267–70 [418–21].

31. "*Alle Dinge sind verschieden,* oder: *Es gibt nicht zwei Dinge, die einander gleich sind*" (*WLW,* p. 270 [422; translation slightly modified]).

32. "Il n'y a point deux *individus indiscernables.* Un Gentilhomme d'esprit de mes amis, en parlant avec moi en présence de Madame l'Electrice dans le jardin de Herrenhausen, crut qu'il trouveroit bien deux feuilles entièrement semblables. Madame l'Electrice l'en défia, et il courut longs-tems en vain pour en chercher. Deux goutes d'eau, ou de lait, regardée par le Microscope, se trouveront discernables. C'est un argument contre les atomes, qui ne sont pas moins combattus que le vuide, par les principes de la véritable Métaphysique" (Fourth Letter from Leibniz to Clark, *Opera philosophica,* p. 755; cf. pp. 759, 765–66, and *Monad,* §§8–9).

33. "Nicht nur wir unterscheiden das Tier durch seine Klauen, sondern es unterscheidet sich wesentlich dadurch, wehrt sich, erhält sich Sind zwei Dinge bloß dadurch verschieden, daß sie zwei sind, so ist jedes Eins; Zwei macht aber an sich kein Verhältnis aus, sondern der bestimmte Unterschied an sich, das ist die Hauptsache" (*VGP III,* p. 241).

34. *VGP III,* pp. 233–55.

35. *WLW,* pp. 272–73 [424–25].

36. "Das Positive und Negative ist *drittens* nicht nur ein Gesetztes noch bloß ein Gleichgültiges, sondern ihr *Gesetztsein oder die Beziehung auf das Andere in einer Einheit,* die *nicht sie selbst sind,* ist in jedes *zurückgenommen*" (*WLW,* p. 274 [426; translation modified]).

37. *WLW,* pp. 275–78 [427–31].

38. *WLW,* p. 279 [431].

39. "Denn er ist die *Einheit* von solchen, die nur sind, insofern sie *nicht eins* sind,—und die *Trennung* solcher, die nur sind als *in derselben Beziehung* Getrennte" (*WLW,* p. 279 [431; translation slightly modified]).

40. *WLW,* pp. 279–80 [431–33].

41. "Ohne diese Erkenntnis läßt sich eigentlich kein Schritt in der Philosophie tun" (*WLW,* p. 285 [438]).

42. Once again, the grammatical failure is the failure of grammar (to think the concept speculatively): "*das Positive und Negative ist dasselbe*" (*WLW,* p. 283 [435]).

43. "Der aufgelöste Widerspruch ist also der Grund, das Wesen als Einheit des Positiven und Negativen" (*WLW,* p. 282 [435]).

44. *WLW,* pp. 285–86 [438–39].

45. "*Alle Dinge sind an sich selbst widersprechend*" (*WLW,* p. 286 [439; translation modified]).

46. *WLW,* pp. 286–88 [439–41].

47. *WLW,* pp. 288–90 [442–43].

48. Cf. "*Eines Abkürzungs-Prozesses*" (Nietzsche, *KGW* VI, 2, 231 [*BGE,* §268; cf. also §186]).

49. "τὸ γὰρ αὐτὸ νοεῖν ἔστιν τε καὶ εἶναι" (Frag. 3).

Conclusion

1. Schelling opens up the possibility of a determination that is not negation—in fact, Spinoza's ominous *omnis* is already absent: "the saying, *determinatio est negatio,* does not in any way apply to this sort of determination, since this is itself one with the reality and concept of this essence, thus really being the essential element in this essence" [von einer solchen Bestimmtheit gilt der Spruch: *Determinatio est negatio,* keineswegs, indem sie mit der Position und dem Begriff des Wesens selber eins, also eigentlich das Wesen in dem Wesen ist] (*UWF,* p. 101 [62]).

2. "To put it quite summarily, one seeks in vain to extract the question of meaning (the meaning of time, or of anything else) as such from metaphysics, or from the system of so called 'vulgar' concepts" [il serait donc vain, disons-le sèchement et rapidement de vouloir arracher en tant que telle la question du sens (du temps ou de quoi que ce soit) à la métaphysique ou au système des concepts dits 'vulgaires'] (Derrida, *Marges,* p. 59 [51]).

3. In 1928 Heidegger explicitly posed the question of multiplicity in Aristotelian terms: "Mannigfaltigkeit gehört zum Sein selbst" (*GA* 26, §10; cf. *SZ,* §64, §80).

4. *GA* 26, §10; cf. also *SZ,* §15. For Heidegger as well, the questions multiply themselves: What are the ramifications for *Dasein* (i.e., that being which has Being as an issue for it and is defined as care [*Sorge*]), of the specific type of multiplicity (*Mannigfaltigkeit*) within itself? The multiplication that belongs to *Dasein* is primordial dissemination (*ursprüngliche Streuung*)—and this ground constitutes the inner possibility of (1) factical dispersion (*Zerstreuung*); (2) corporal, gender, sexual, racial, etc., differentiation (*Geschlechtlichkeit*); (3) curiosity as a mode of everydayness qua not-tarrying, distraction, inability-to-dwell (*Unverweilen, Zerstreuung, Aufenhaltslosigkeit*); (4) the fall into the inauthentic they-self (*das Man-selbst*) in which *Dasein* is dispersed (*BT,* §27, §36, §71). Lost in dispersion then, *Dasein* is first able to find itself: "*it loses itself in such a manner that it must, as it were, only subsequently pull itself together out of its dispersal, and think up for itself a unity in which*

that 'together' is embraced" [verliert es sich so, daß es sich gleichsam erst nachträglich aus der Zerstreuung zusammenholen und für das Zusammen eine umgreifende Einheit sich erdenken muß] (*BT,* §75; translation slightly modified). Cf. Derrida, *Geschlecht I,* p. 164. The condition for the possibility (the not-yet, future, that which is to come or may be) of ontical multiplicity lies in ontological multiplicity as metaphysical neutrality, the actual and concrete origin (*Ursprung*). Ontological difference is the way (*hodos*) in which *Dasein* is, i.e., is as gathering/disseminating (prior to ontical dispersion/re-connection) (*GA* 26, §10). The possibility of *Dasein*'s differentiation, therefore, lies in the multiplication of multiplicity, in the belonging-togetherness of multiplicity, which already resides in Being (*GA* 26, §13). *Dasein* is being-with (*Mitsein*) multiple others, not because they share an identifiable species, language, essence or community, not because they are unified under common goals, values or ideas; on the contrary, the unification is possible on the basis of the dispersion of being-with, on the dispersion that characterizes the place in which *Dasein* finds itself thrown with others. Primordial multiplication is that which allows *Dasein* to both be-with and be-there: ontical multiplicity is grounded in ontological multiplication (*GA* 26, §10). Thus, at least in the 1928 course, primordial multiplication is the origin of the difference between Being and being, the ground of the twofold distinction with which metaphysics classifies entities into ideas or things, the cause of the double-dissection of the world into the fourfold heaven and earth, mortals and gods.

5. *The Doctor Is Sick* (London: Heinemann, 1960), pp. 13–14.

6. "Wahrlich, dieser Mensch, trotz seiner Jugend, versteht sich auf die *Improvisation des Lebens* und setzt auch den feinsten Beobachter in Erstaunen:—es scheint nämlich, dass er keinen Fehlgriff thut, ob er schon fortwährend das gewagteste Spiel spielt. Man wird an jene improvisierenden Meister der Tonkunst erinnert, denen auch der Zuhörer eine göttliche Unfehlbarkeit der Hand zuschreiben möchte, trotzdem, dass sie sich hier und da vergreifen, wie jeder Sterbliche sich vergreift. Aber sie sind geübt und erfinderisch, und im Augenblicke immer bereit, den zufälligsten Ton, wohin ein Wurf des Fingers, eine Laune sie treibt, sofort in das thematische Gefüge einzuordnen und dem Zufalle einen schönen Sinn und eine Seele einzuhauchen" (*GS,* §303; translation modified).

7. *Travesty* (New York: New Directions Books, 1976), p. 23.

8. "Listening not to me but to the *Logos* it is wise to agree that all things are one" (*PP,* p. 187; cf. also *VA,* p. 209 [61]).

9. Snell translates Heidegger: "Habt ihr nicht mich, sondern den Sinn vernommen; so ist es weise, im gleichen Sinn zu sagen: *Eins* ist Alles" (*VA,* 207 [59; translation modified]).

10. "Nicht mir, aber der lesenden Lege gehörig: Selbes liegen lassen: Geschickliches west (die lesende Lege): Eines einend Alles" (*VA,* p. 226 [75]).

11. "Χρὴ εὖ μάλα πολλῶν ἵστορας φιλοσόφους ἄνδρας εἶναι καθ' Ἡράκλειτον" (Frag. 35, emphasis added).

Selected Bibliography

Altizer, Thomas J. J. "Hegel and the Christian God." *Journal of the American Academy of Religion* 59, no. 1: 71–91.

Aristotle. *The Basic Works of Aristotle.* Ed. R. McKeon. New York: Random House, 1941.

Aubenque, Pierre. *Le Problème de l'être chez Aristote.* Paris: P.U.F., 1966.

Badiou, Alain. *L'être et l'événement.* Paris: Seuil, 1988.

Beaufret, Jean. "Séminaire du Thor." In *Questions III et IV.* Paris: Gallimard, 1976.

Benjamin, Walter. "Goethes *Wahlverwandtschaften*" (1924). In Goethe, *Die Wahlverwandschaften,* pp. 253–333. Frankfurt: Insel, 1972.

Biard, J., et al. *Introduction à la lecture de la Science de la logique de Hegel.* Paris: Aubier Montaigue, 1981.

Bigelow, Pat. *The Conning, the Cunning of Being.* Tallahassee: Florida State University Press, 1990.

Böhme, Jacob. *Aurora oder Morgenröte im Aufgang.* Frankfurt: Insel, 1992.

———. *Sämtliche Schriften.* 11 vols. Stuttgart: Frommann, 1955.

———. *Von der Gnadenwahl.* Stuttgart: Reclam, 1988.

Brentano, Franz. *Von der Mannigfachen Bedeutung des Seienden nach Aristotles* (1862). Hildesheim: G. Olms, 1960. Trans. R. George as *On the Several Senses of Being in Aristotle.* Berkeley: University of California Press, 1975.

Celan, Paul. *Gesammelte Werke.* 5 vols. Ed. B. Allemann and S. Reichert. Frankfurt: Suhrkamp, 1983. Selections trans. M. Hamburger as *Poems of Paul Celan.* New York: Persea Books, 1972.

Deleuze, Gilles. *Le Pli: Leibniz et le baroque.* Paris: Minuit, 1988.

———. *La Philosophie critique de Kant.* Paris: P.U.F., 1963. Trans. H. Tomlinson and B. Habberjam as *Kant's Critical Philosophy: The Doctrine of the Faculties.* Minneapolis: University of Minnesota Press, 1984.

Deleuze, Gilles, and Félix Guattari. *Anti-Œdipe: Capitalisme et schizophrénie.* Paris: Minuit, 1972. Trans. R. Hurley, M. Seem, and H. R. Lane as *Anti-Oedipus: Capitalism and Schizophrenia.* Minneapolis: University of Minnesota Press, 1983.

———. *Mille plateaux: Capitalisme et schizophrénie.* Paris: Minuit, 1972. Trans. B. Massumi as *A Thousand Plateaus: Capitalism and Schizophrenia.* Minneapolis: University of Minnesota Press, 1987.

———. *Qu'est-ce que la philosophie?* Paris: Minuit, 1991. Trans. H. Tomlinson and G. Burchell as *What Is Philosophy?* New York: Columbia University Press, 1994.

Derrida, Jacques. "*Apories: Mourir—s'attendre aux limites de la vérité.*" In *Le Passage des frontières: Autour du travail de Jacques Derrida.* Paris: Galilée, 1993. Trans. T. Dutoit as *Aporias: Dying—Awaiting (One Another at) the "Limits of Truth."* Stanford: Stanford University Press, 1993.

———. *De la Grammatologie.* Paris: Minuit, 1967. Trans. G. C. Spivak as *Of Grammatology.* Baltimore: Johns Hopkins University Press, 1974.

———. *Marges de la philosophie.* Paris: Minuit, 1972. Trans. A. Bass as *Margins of Philosophy.* Chicago: University of Chicago Press, 1982.

———. *De l'esprit: Heidegger et la question.* Paris: Galilée, 1987. Trans. G. Bennington and R. Bowlby as *Of Spirit: Heidegger and the Question.* Chicago: University of Chicago Press, 1989.

———. *Glas.* Paris: Galilée, 1974. Trans. J. P. Leavey Jr. and R. Rand as *Glas.* Lincoln: University of Nebraska Press, 1986.

———. *La Dissémination.* Paris: Seuil, 1972. Trans. B. Johnson as *Dissemination.* Chicago: University of Chicago Press, 1981.

———. *Donner le temps.* Paris: Galilée, 1991. Trans. P. Kamuf as *Given Time: I. Counterfeit Money.* Chicago: University of Chicago Press, 1992.

———. *Ecriture et difference.* Paris: Seuil, 1967. Trans. A. Bass as *Writing and Difference.* Chicago: University of Chicago Press, 1978.

———. *Positions.* Paris: Minuit, 1972. Trans. A. Bass as *Positions.* Chicago: University of Chicago Press, 1981.

———. "Le Temps des adieux: Heidegger (lu par) Hegel (lu par) Malabou." *Revue Philosophique,* no. 1 (January–March). Paris: P.U.F, 1998.

———. *La Voix et le phénomène.* Paris: P.U.F, 1967. Trans. D. Allison as *Speech and Phenomena.* Evanston: Northwestern University Press, 1973.

Descartes, René. *Œuvres et lettres.* Paris: Gallimard, 1953.

Di Giovanni, George, and H. S. Harris. *Between Kant and Hegel: Texts in the Development of Post-Kantian Idealism.* New York: SUNY Press, 1985.

Dondeyne, Albert. "La différence ontologique chez M. Heidegger." In *Revue Philosophique de Louvain.* Louvain: 3d series, volume 5b, May 1958.

Edwards, Paul. *Heidegger on Death: A Critical Evaluation.* La Salle: The Monist, 1979.

Einstein, Albert. *Über die spezielle und die allgemeine Relativitätstheorie* (1917). Braunschweig/Wiesbaden: Vieweg, 1988. Trans. R. W. Lawson as *Relativity: The Special and the General Theory.* New York: Crown, 1959.

Fichte, Johann Gottlieb. *Grundlage der gesamten Wissenschaftslehre* (1794). Hamburg: Meiner, 1988.

———. *Über den Begriff der Wissenschaftlehre.* Stuttgart: Reclam, 1972.

Frege, Gottlob. *Funktion, Begriff, Bedeutung.* Göttingen: Vandenhoeck & Ruprecht, 1986.

Gadamer, Hans-Georg. *Hegel's Dialectic: Five Hermeneutical Studies.* Trans. P. C. Smith. New Haven: Yale University Press, 1976.

Goethe, Johann Wolfgang von. *Sämtliche Werke.* 40 vols. Ed. H. Fleig. Berlin: Deutscher Klassiker, 19.

———. *Die Wahlverwandtschaften* (1809). In *Werke. Weimarer Ausgabe.* Abt. 1, vol. 20.

Reprinted by Insel Verlag (Frankfurt, 1972). Trans. E. Mayer and L. Bogan as *Elective Affinities*. New York: Continuum, 1990.

Hegel, Georg Wilhelm Friedrich. *Encyclopedia of the Philosophical Sciences in Outline and Critical Writings*. Ed. E. Behler. New York: Continuum, 1990.

———. *Gesammelte Werke*. Hamburg: Meiner, 1968ff.

———. *Lectures on the History of Philosophy*. 3 vols. Trans. E. S. Haldane and F. H. Simson. Lincoln: University of Nebraska Press, 1995.

———. *Lectures on the Philosophy of World History*. 4 vols. Trans. H. B. Nisbet. Cambridge: University of Cambridge Press, 1975.

———. *Phenomenology of Spirit*. Trans. A. V. Miller. Oxford: Oxford University Press, 1977.

———. *Science of Logic*. Trans. A. V. Miller. Atlantic Highlands, N.J.: Humanities Press International, 1969.

———. *Werke in Zwanzig Bänden*. Frankfurt: Suhrkamp, 1986.

Heidegger, Martin. *Basic Writings*. Ed. D. F. Krell. New York: Harper & Row, 1977.

———. *Der Begriff der Zeit: Vortrag vor der Marburger Theologenschaft Juli 1924*. Tübingen: Niemeyer, 1989. Trans. W. McNeill as *The Concept of Time*. Oxford: Blackwell, 1992.

———. "Colloquium über Dialectik" (September 1952). In *Hegel-Studien*, ed. F. Nicolin and O. Pöggeler, vol. 25, pp. 9–39. Bonn: Bouvier, 1990.

———. *Early Greek Thinking: The Dawn of Western Philosophy*. Trans. D. F. Krell and F. A. Capuzzi. San Francisco: Harper, 1975.

———. *Einführung in die Metaphysik*. Tübingen: Niemeyer, 1987. Trans. R. Mannheim as *An Introduction to Metaphysics*. New Haven: Yale University Press, 1959.

———. "Europa und die deutsche Philosophie." In *Europa und die Philosophie*. Frankfurt: Klostermann, 1993.

———. *Existence and Being*. Ed. W. Brock. Trans. D. Scott, R. F. C. Hull, and A. Crick. Washington, D.C.: Regnery Gateway, 1988.

———. *Gelassenheit*. Pfullingen: Neske, 1959. Trans. J. M. Anderson and E. H. Freund as *Discourse on Thinking*. New York: Harper & Row, 1966.

———. *Gesamtausgabe*. Frankfurt: Klostermann, 1978ff.

———. *Die Grundprobleme der Phänomenologie*. Frankfurt: Klostermann, 1975. Trans. A. Hofstadter as *The Basic Problems of Phenomenology*. Bloomington: Indiana University Press, 1982.

———. *Hegels Phänomenologie des Geistes*. Frankfurt: Klostermann, 1980. Trans. P. Emad and K. Maly as *Hegel's Phenomenology of Spirit*. Bloomington: Indiana University Press, 1988.

———. "A Heidegger Seminar on Hegel's Differenzschrift." *Southwestern Journal of Philosophy* 2, part 3 (1990): 27ff.

———. *Holzwege*. Frankfurt: Klostermann, 1950.

———. *Identität und Differenz*. Pfullingen: Neske, 1961.

———. *Metaphysische Anfangsgründe der Logik im Ausgang von Leibniz*. Frankfurt: Klostermann, 1978. Trans. M. Heim as *The Metaphysical Foundations of Logic*. Bloomington: Indiana University Press, 1984.

———. *Prolegomena zur Geschichte des Zeitbegriffs.* Frankfurt: Klostermann, 1979. Trans. T. Kisiel as *History of the Concept of Time (Prolegomena).* Bloomington: Indiana University Press, 1985.

———. *The Question Concerning Technology and Other Essays.* Trans. W. Lovitt. New York: Harper & Row, 1977.

———. *Questions IV.* Translated and assembled by J. Beaufret, F. Fédier, J. Hervier, J. Lauxerois, R. Munier, A. Préau, and C. Roëls. Paris: Gallimard, 1976.

———. *Schellings Abhandlung Über das Wesen der menschlichen Freiheit.* Tübingen: Niemeyer, 1971. Trans. J. Stambaugh as *Schelling's Treatise on the Essence of Human Freedom.* Athens: Ohio University Press, 1985.

———. *Sein und Zeit.* Tübingen: Niemeyer, 1993. Trans. J. Macquarrie and E. Robinson as *Being and Time.* New York: Harper & Row, 1962. Also trans. J. Stambaugh as *Being and Time.* New York: SUNY Press, 1996.

———. *Die Selbstbehauptung der deutschen Universität und Das Rektorat 1933/34.* Frankfurt: Klostermann, 1983.

———. *Über den Humanismus.* Frankfurt: Klostermann, 1949.

———. *Unterwegs zur Sprache.* Pfullingen: Neske, 1959. Trans. P. D. Hertz as *On the Way to Language.* San Francisco: Harper & Row, 1971.

———. *Vorträge und Aufsätze.* Pfullingen: Neske, 1954.

———. *Was Heisst Denken?* Tübingen: Niemeyer, 1984. Trans. J. G. Gray as *What Is Called Thinking?* New York: Harper & Row, 1968.

———. *Zur Sache des Denkens.* Tübingen: Niemeyer, 1969. Trans. J. Stambaugh as *On Time and Being.* New York: Harper & Row, 1972.

Heidegger, Martin, and Eugen Fink. *Heraclit.* Frankfurt: Klostermann, 1970. Trans. C. H. Seibert as *Heraclitus Seminar.* Evanston: Northwestern University Press, 1979.

Henrich, Dieter. *Hegel im Kontext.* Frankfurt: 1971.

Homer. *Odyssey.* Books I and II. Trans. P. Jones. Warminster: Aris & Phillips, 1991.

Husserl, Edmund. *Ideen zu einer reinen Phänomenologie und phänomenologischen Philosophie.* The Hague: Nijhoff, 1976. Trans. W. R. Boyce Gibson as *Ideas: General Introduction to Pure Phenomenology.* New York: Collier Books, 1962.

———. *Die Krisis der europäischen Wissenschaften und die transzendentale Phänomenologie.* Hamburg: Meiner, 1982.

———. *Logische Untersuchungen.* The Hague: Nijhoff, 1984.

Hyppolite, Jean. *Genèse et structure de la Phénoménologie de l'esprit de Hegel.* Paris: Aubier, 1946. Trans. S. Cherniak and J. Heckman as *Genesis and Structure of Hegel's Phenomenology of Spirit.* Evanston: Northwestern University Press, 1974.

———. *Logique et existence.* Paris: P.U.F., 1952.

Inwood, Michael. *A Hegel Dictionary.* Oxford: Blackwell, 1992.

Irigaray, Luce. *Ce Sexe qui n'en est pas un.* Paris: Minuit, 1977. Trans. C. Porter with C. Burke as *This Sex Which Is Not One.* Ithaca: Cornell University Press, 1985.

Jaeger, Werner W. *Aristoteles: Grundlegung einer Geschichte seiner Entwicklung.* Berlin: Weidmann, 1923. Trans. R. Robinson as *Aristotle: Fundamentals of the History of His Development.* Oxford: Clarendon Press, 1934.

Kant, Immanuel. *Grundlegung zur Metaphysik der Sitten* (1785/86). Ed. K. Vorländer. Hamburg: Meiner, 1994.

———. *Kritik der praktischen Vernunft* (1788). Ed. K. Vorländer. Hamburg: Meiner, 1990.

———. *Kritik der reinen Vernunft* (1781/87). Ed. R. Schmidt. Hamburg: Meiner, 1990. Trans. N. K. Smith as *Critique of Pure Reason*. New York: St. Martin's Press, 1965.

———. *Kritik der Urteilskraft* (1799). Ed. K. Vorländer. Hamburg: Meiner, 1990.

———. *Metaphysik der Sitten* (1797). 2 parts. Ed. B. Ludwig. Hamburg: Meiner, 1986.

———. *Prolegomena zu einer jeden künftigen Metaphysik, die als Wissenschaft wird auftreten können* (1783). Ed. K. Vorländer. Hamburg: Meiner, 1993.

———. *Träume eines Geistersehers, erläutert durch Träume der Metaphysik* (1766). Ed. K. Reich. Hamburg: Meiner, 1975.

Kirk, G. S., J. E. Raven, and M. Schofield. *The Presocratic Philosophers*. Cambridge: Cambridge University Press, 1991.

Kojève, Alexandre. *Introduction to the Reading of Hegel: Lectures on the Phenomenology of Spirit*. Trans. J. H. Nichols Jr. Ithaca: Cornell University Press, 1969.

Kozu, K. *Das Bedürfnis der Philosophie: Ein Überblick über die Entwicklung des Begriffskomplexes "Bedürfnis," "Trieb," "Streben," und "Begierde" bei Hegel*. Bonn: Universität Bonn, 1988.

Krolow, Karl. *Herbstsonett mit Hegel*. Frankfurt: Suhrkamp, 1981.

Laruelle, François. *Nietzsche contre Heidegger*. Paris: Payot, 1977.

Lauer, Quentin, S.J. *Hegel's Idea of Philosophy*. New York: Fordham University Press, 1971.

Leibniz, Gottfried Wihelm von. *Discours de métaphysique*. Paris: Vrin, 1993.

———. *Monadology and Other Philosophical Essays*. Trans. P. Schrecker and A. M. Schrecker. New York: Macmillan, 1965.

———. *Opera philosophica*. Ed. R. Vollbrecht. Scientia Aalen, 1959.

Léonard, André. *Commentaire littéral de la Logique de Hegel*. Paris: J. Vrin, 1974.

Löwith, Karl. *Von Hegel zu Nietzsche*. Hamberg: Meiner, 1986.

Lyotard, Jean-François. *Leçons sur l'analytique du sublime*. Paris: Galilée, 1991. Trans. E. Rottenberg as *Lessons on the Analytic of the Sublime*. Stanford: Stanford University Press, 1994.

MacIntyre, Alastair, ed. *Hegel: A Collection of Critical Essays*. Notre Dame and London: University of Notre Dame Press, 1972.

Maimon, Solomon. *Versuch einer neuen Logik oder Theorie des Denkens*. Berlin: E. Felisch, 1794; 2d ed. 1798. Reprinted, Darmstadt: Wissenschaftliche Buchgesellschaft, 1963. Reprinted, *Werke*, vol. 5. Critical edition: C. B. Engel, ed., Kantgesellschaft. Berlin: Reuther & Reichard, 1912.

Malabou, Catherine. *L'avenir de Hegel: Plasticité, Temporalité, Dialectique*. Paris: Vrin, 1996.

Mallarmé, Stéphane. *Igitur, Divagations, Un coup de dés*. Paris: Gallimard, 1976.

Marx, Werner. *Hegels Phänomenologie des Geistes*. Frankfurt: Klostermann, 1971.

Trans. P. Heath as *Hegel's Phenomenology of Spirit.* Chicago: University of Chicago Press, 1975.

Natorp, Paul. "Thema und Disposition der aristotelischen Metaphysik." *Philos. Monastsh.* 24 (1888).

Nietzsche, Friedrich. *The Gay Science.* Trans. W. Kaufman. New York: Random House, 1974.

———. *Kritische Gesamtausgabe.* Ed. G. Colli and M. Montinari. Berlin: de Gruyter, 1967ff.

Owens, Joseph. *The Doctrine of Being in the Aristotlean Metaphysics.* Toronto: Pontifical Institute of Mediaeval Studies, 1951.

Plato. *The Collected Dialogues of Plato.* Ed. and trans. E. Hamilton and H. Cairns. Princeton: Princeton University Press, 1961.

Schelling, F. W. J. *Darstellung meines Systems der Philosophie* (1801). Originally published in *Zeitschrift für spekulative Physik,* vol. 2, heft 2. Reprinted in *Schellings Werke.* Leipzig: Eckardt, 1907.

———. *Philosophische Briefe über Dogmatismus und Kriticismus.* In *Schellings Werke.* Leipzig: Eckardt, 1907.

———. *System des transzendentalen Idealismus* (1800). Hamburg: Meiner, 1992. Trans. P. Heath as *System of Transcendental Idealism.* Charlottesville: University Press of Virginia, 1993.

———. *Über das Wesen der menschlichen Freiheit* (1809). Stuttgart: Reclam, 1964. Trans. J. Gutmann as *Philosophical Inquiries into the Nature of Human Freedom.* Chicago: Open Court, 1936.

———. *Vorlesungen über die Methode (Lehrart) des akademischen Studiums* (SS 1802). Hamburg: Meiner, 1990.

Schmitt, Gerhard. *The Concept of Being in Hegel and Heidegger.* Bonn: Bouvier, 1977.

Schulze, Gottlieg Ernst. *Aenesidemus, oder über die Fundamente der von Herrn Prof. Reinhold in Jena gelieferten Elementar-Philosophie.* N.p.p., 1792. Reprinted, *Aetas Kantiana.* Brussels: Culture et Civilization, 1969. Critical edition: Arthur Liebert, ed., Kantgesellschaft. Berlin: Reuther & Reichard, 1911. Trans. and excerpted by G. di Giovanni as "Aenesidemus or Concerning the Foundations of the Philosophy of Elements Issued by Prof. Reinhold in Jena Together with a Defence of Skepticism against the Pretensions of *The Critique of Reason,*" in *Between Kant and Hegel,* ed. G. di Giovanni and G. H. S. Harris.

Schürmann, Reiner. *Le Principe d'anarchie: Heidegger et la question de l'agir.* Paris: Seuil, 1982. Trans. C.-M. Gros with R. Schürmann as *Heidegger on Being and Acting: From Principles to Anarchy.* Bloomington: Indiana University Press, 1987.

Simmel, Georg. *Philosophie des Geldes* (1900). Frankfurt: Suhrkamp, 1994.

Simon, Josef. "Die Bewegung des Begriffs in Hegels Logik." *Hegel-Stüdien* 18 (1978).

Stekeler-Weithofer, Pirmin. *Hegels Analytische Philosophie.* Munich: Ferdinand Schöningh, 1992.

Trakl, Georg. *Werke, Entwürfe, Briefe.* Ed. H.-G. Kemper and F. R. Max. Stuttgart: Reclam, 1984.

Windelband, Wilhelm. *Lehrbuch der Geschichte der Philosophie* (1892). Tübingen: J. D. B. Mohr (Paul Siebeck), 1993.

Wolff, Michael. *Der Begriff des Widerspruchs: Eine Studie zur Dialektik Kants und Hegels.* Königstein/Ts.: Hain, 1981.

Zeller, Eduard. "'Bericht,' on Natorp's *Thema und Disposition der arist. Metaph.*" *AGP* 2 (1889).

Index

A = A formula. *See* identity
absolute, the, 58–61 passim, 68, 72–74, 77, 81; and non-absolute, 75
absolute I. *See* "I"
absolute idea. *See* idea, absolute
abstract negation. *See* negation
Aesthetic. *See* Transcendental Aesthetic
Angelus Silesius, 255
anthropology, 236
aporia, xix, xxv, 31, 39, 41; "inescapable," xv
apperception, xx, 5, 45, 49–50, 97, 103, 167. *See also* self-consciousness
Archimedian thought, 27
Aristotle and Aristotelian thought, xxvii, 47, 99, 195, 198, 260, 261, 268; logic of, xxi, 10, 14, 56, 84–85; on multiplicity, xxiv, 5, 54, 281, 282; Plato and Parmenides critiqued by, xix, 30–31, 36, 38, 42, 43–44, 61, 286; and the predicate, 54, 198; "rational animal" of, 27, 33, 143, 219, 236; *Metaphysics,* 30–44 passim
art, 154–55
Atomism, xix, xxiv, 99, 105

"Bacchanalian revel," xxi, 77, 80, 179
Badiou, Alain, 124, 127
Bataille, Georges, 75, 76
becoming, xxiii, 89, 95–96, 137, 159, 161. *See also* transition
beginning is the end. *See* circularity
Being, 91, 253; and absolute idea, 246; as being, 42, 54; "and Beings," ontological difference between, xxx, 31, 73, 246, 263, 268–69; "of beings," 29, 31, 74, 183, 204, 216, 272, 280; concept of, 139; death and, 224–25; and essence, 72, 87, 160–61, 251–54, 255; essence as negation of, 165; forgetting of question of, 14; -for-self, 98–99, 100, 105, 109, 160–63 passim, 182; Hegel's "Doctrine of," 73, 79, 98, 183, 245, (and measure) 138–41, 159–63 passim; identity and, 251, 254–56, 267–68; as individuality, 183; and logic, 94; meaning of, 98; metaphysics and, xix, 36–37; and multiplicity, xxiii–xiv, xxvi–xxvii, 5, 94–98, 162, 183, 280; and non-being, 61, 89, 106, 137, 247; is one, 16; self-determination and, 249–50; subjectivity as, 203; thinking and, 249–50, 272–74, 282–83, (Cartesian view), 64; and truth, 216; universal, 36. *See also* "one," the
Benjamin, Walter, 79, 152, 153, 154
bondage, lordship and, 226–34
Bruno, Giordano, 317n23
Burgess, Anthony, 285

Cantor, Georg, 127
categorical imperative, 242–43
causality, 205
Celan, Paul, 197, 223
chemistry, 146, 152; chemical processes/chemism, 209–11, 213–14, 216, 219; of measures, 148–50
Chinese language, 75, 187–88
circularity, 76, 82–83, 86, 90–93, 163–64, 237, 286. *See also* metaphysical arch
cognition: analytic and synthetic, 128, 238–39, 241; "idea of," 243. *See also* knowledge; thinking
communication, 191. *See also* language

concept: of being, 138; of the concept, 127, 166, 215–18, 235, 240, 241, 244; conceptual knowledge, 48–49, 50–51, 61; conceptual language, 185–93; conceptual objectivity, 203–14; Hegel's "Doctrine of," 73, 161, 164, 165–67, 170, 219, 251–52, (and absolute idea) 178, 245; of judgment, 200–1; and multiplicity, xvii, xx–xxi, 86–87, 162, 217; of number, 78, 115–18; of philosophy, 58–62; of quantity, *see* quantity; of relation, 128–32, 147; of truth, 165–68, 169; of universality, 172–73. *See also* idea
conception as negation, 181
consciousness, 49, 65, 91, 167, 189, 230–31. *See also* self-consciousness
contradiction, 68, 77, 80, 87, 92–93; law of, xxix, 267; and law of non-contradiction, 84, 259, 267, 271; life and death as, 233; logic of, 89, 264, 265–68. *See also* identity and difference
Copernicus, Nicolaus, and Copernican thought, xxvi, 10, 205, 238

death, 216, 218, 219, 223–29, 230–33, 234
deconstruction, 72, 76, 80, 81, 176
definition, 239–40, 273
Deleuze, Gilles, 9, 102, 165
Democritus and Democritian Atomism, xix, 99. *See also* Atomism
demonism, 113
Derrida, Jacques, 30, 75–77, 79–81, 294n12; quoted, 15–16, 45, 60, 120, 333n13; *Of Grammatology,* 76; *Writing and Difference,* 76
Descartes, René, and Cartesian thought, 47, 103, 156, 273, 289; *cogito* and I/ego, xx, 5, 27–28, 49, 63–64, 67, 228–29, 235; dualism, 205; metaphysical arch, 85, 100, 113; opposed, 112; *Meditations,* 28, 63–64, 101, 228
desire. *See* elective affinities; sexuality
determination, 79, 98–99, 138, 157, 204, 269; of deviance, 176; qualification/quantification and, 113, 142–43, 145; Spinozistic, 20, 90, 261, 262, 338n1. *See also* self-determination
determinism, 207
deviance in nature. *See* nature
dialectic, 55, 88, 89, 92, 249, 282; and measure, 139, 158; qualification/quantification and, 110, 113
difference, 76, 259–65; "discourse of," 248, 262–63; ontological, between Being and beings, xxx, 31, 73, 246, 263, 268. *See also* identity and difference
dogmatism, 63; dogmatic idealism, 67, 69
dualism, 63, 205

ego. *See* "I" (Cartesian)
elective affinities, 146, 148–55, 162
Eliot, T. S., 90
empiricism, 15, 46, 47, 51, 52, 64, 236; Kant's argument against, xix
Epicurus, 99, 261
essence, 71, 153; Being/beings and, 72, 87, 160–61, 165, 251–54, 255; Hegel's "Doctrine of," 73, 79, 170, 251, 254, 267–68, (transition to) 159, 161; of identity, xxvii–xxviii, 256; as negation of being, 165

Fichte, Johann Gottlieb, and Fichtean thought, 92, 120; and absolute, xx, 63–68 passim, 75, 191, 228; Hegel's reaction to, 80, 81; and subjectivism, 77, 336n19; and transcendental idealism, 55, 61–70 passim; *Doctrine of Knowledge,* 66, 67, 69; *Doctrine of Silence,* 68
formalism, 75, 207
Fraenkel, Abraham Adolf, 127
freedom, free will, 73–74, 84, 227

Genet, Jean, 76
genus/genera. *See* scientific classification
geometry, 241. *See also* mathematics
German language, 187–88
German transcendental idealism. *See* idealism
God: concept of, 70, 74, 85, 95, 101, 260; existence of, 53, 73, 76; as monad of monads, 99, 100, 102, 104; truth identified with, 165
God's will, 151–52

Goethe, Johann Wolfgang von, 138, 150, 305n102; *The Elective Affinities,* 150–54; *Farbenlehre,* 199
Guattari, Félix, 9, 165

Hawkes, John, 148, 203, 289
Hegel, Georg Wilhelm Friedrich: concept of multiplicity, xx; "Doctrines," *see* Being; concept; essence; Fichte as viewed by, 80, 81; Kant as viewed by, *see* Kant, Immanuel, and Kantian thought; language as used by, *see* language; Liebniz critiqued by, 187; "manys" of, 5 (*see also* "manys"); Nietzsche quoted on, 74, 305n102
Heidegger, Martin, 30, 44, 60, 123, 247, 301n72, 320n36, 335n11; and Being, 5, 74, 95, 225, ("ontological difference") 31, 73, 246, 263; and monads, 103, 317n23; and quantification, 112, 114, 127; and technology/science, 79, 90, 312n83; and the "thing," 204, 205, 206; *Being and Time,* 95, 224
Helmont, Francis Mercury van, 317n23
Heraclitus, 30, 92, 127, 182, 290; on inquiry, xviii, 292; pantheism of, xxi, 82
hieroglyphics, 187–88
history: Hegel's view, 115, 277–78; and science, 94–95; of western metaphysics, 154, 274
Hobbes, Thomas, 58, 190, 225
Hoffmann, E. T. A., 30
Hölderlin, Friedrich: *Hyperion,* 10
Homer, 4, 26
Hume, David, 205

"I," 167, 190, 235; absolute, xx, 63–68, 191, 228, 336n19; Cartesian, 27–28, 49, 63–64, 67, 228–29, 235–37; intuition as distinct from, 47
idea: of cognition, 243; multiplicity as, xv; of totality, 215–45. *See also* concept
idea, absolute, 178, 243–44, 245, 248–49; Being and, 246
idealism, xxi, 64, 70; aporia of, 31; dogmatic, 67, 69; German transcendental/Kantian, 55, 61–70 passim, 167, 336n19; Liebnizian, 100–1; Parmenidian, 249–50
ideality (*eidos*), 99
identity: absolute, 71, 77; abstract, 255; and being, 251, 254–56, 267–68; "discourse of," 247–48, 263; essence of, xxvii–xxviii, 256; formula for/law of (A = A), xxvii, 58, 63, 65, 70–71, 84, 101, 251–58 passim, 268; individuality as, 182, 199; multiplicity structured as, 11; reason and, 70–71; of science, 91
identity and difference, xxviii–xxx, 44, 55, 163, 246–49, 254–59, 282; contradiction of, xxix, 65, 251, 255, 264–65; indifference of, 15–17; logic of, 12–13, 19, 40, 83, 87, 267–68; metaphysics of, 281; and quantity, 114
improvisation, 25–26; of "manys," 8–9, 288–89; "philosophy as," xix; of philosophy, 292
indifference: of identity and difference, 15–17; of measure, 159–61
individuality, 170, 181–85, 197, 198, 199; the living individual, 220–23 (*see also* life)
infinity, xxiv–xxv, 11, 92, 132, 319n27; of the "ought," 67; qualitative-quantitative, 120–28, 134, 135, 136, 157–58
inquiry, Heraclitus on, xviii, 292
interpretation: of "manys," 8, 26, 283–85; metaphysics and, 22–25, 26, 288
intuition, xix, 46–47, 48, 51, 167, 178; sign as, 187; time and space and, 52–53; transcendental, 67–68
Irigaray, Luce, 171

Jesus, death of, 225
judgment(s), 78; conceptual, 200–1; multiplicity of, 194–202; subjective, 199

Kant, Immanuel, and Kantian thought, 5, 30, 172, 208, 210, 229, 242, 257, 281, 319n24; and Being, 36, 255; defines marriage, 152; and determinism, 207; Hegel's view of, 66–67, 75, 83, 166–67, 205, 209, 235, 237–38; and idealism, 61, 63; and infinity, 92, 319n27; and intuitions, xix, 178; logic as understood by, xxi, 10, 83, 84–85; and the "one," 82; schematism of,

51–52, 54, 72, 86, 216; and subjectivity, 168, 199, 336n19; and the "thing," 204, 281, 298n26; *Critique of Pure Reason,* 45–54, 62, 64, 97, 167, 206
knotted line, 155–57, 158, 162. *See also* measure(s)
knowledge, 235–36, 237–42; conceptual, 48–49, 50–51, 61; philosophy as provider of, 235
Krolow, Karl, 74

language, xvi, 66, 252; breakdown of, 23, 97, 106; Chinese, 75, 187–88; conceptual, 185–93; German, 73; Hegel's use of, xxxi, 131, 140, 149–50, 193, 233, 250, 263; judgment and, 194, 195; laws of, 271; and lies, xxxii, 291; metaphysics and, 20, 186, 288–89; of multiplicity/manys, 19, 20, 192–93, 288–91; of philosophy, 24–25, 189; problem of, xxviii; of quantification, 131; thought connected to, 75, 78. *See also* names; semantics
law of the excluded middle, 266, 270
Leibniz, Gottfried Wilhelm von, 5, 30, 47, 114, 182, 260–62, 268; critiques of, 187, 302n78; denies multiplicity, 29; and dualism, 205; pantheism of, 99; *Monadology,* 100–4, 107, 261
life, 216–17, 218, 229–30, 232–34, 261; objectivity of, 235; the pain of, 219–23. *See also* death
Locke, John, 302n78
logic: a-dialogical, 20; Aristotelian, xxi, 10, 14, 56, 84–85; classical, and thinking, 75, 78, 84–85; of contradiction, 89, 264, 265–68; Hegel's definition, 85–86; of identity, *see* identity and difference; Kantian, xxi, 10, 83, 84–85; of limit, 136–37; "of logic," 86–87; and "manys," 75, 97–98, 164; multiplicity of, 55, 88–90; of multiplicity, xxii, 82–87, 268–72; "of the null" (zero-sum), 265; *Objective,* 170, 182; philosophy as, 83–84; "of revelation," 155; science of, 87, 88, 91–92, 94–95, 140; speculative, xxviii, 10, 247, 266–67; *Subjective,* 170, 173, 183, 219; symbolic, xxvii; Transcendental, 48
logos, xxxi, 17, 33, 82, 115; double, xxx; "manys" of, 289–92; meanings of, xxxii, 290–92; *pseudo-,* xxxii, 292
lordship and bondage, 226–34
love: God as, 74; ontology of, 73
lying, xiii–xiv, xxxii, 291–92

Maimon, Solomon, 55, 327n8
Mallarmé, Stéphane, 215
manifold: of critique, 45–54; intuition of, xix–xx, 167. *See also* multiplicity
many: clue to, xix; substance of, 30–45
"manys" (*polla*), xxxi, 3–9, 13, 81, 168, 234, 275–76, 287; improvising, 8–9, 288–89; interpretation of, 8, 26, 283–85; Kant's critique of, 45; logic and, 57, 97–98, 164; of *logos,* 289–92; "many ones," 104–9, 110
marriage: Derrida on, 45; Hawkes on, 148; Kant's definition of, 152
mathematics, 75, 241; limits on, 124–26. *See also* numbers, concept of; quantity
matters, manipulation of, 13–15
measure(s): as being, 138–41, 159–61; chemistry of, 148–50; indifference of, 159–61; knotted line and, 155–57, 158, 162; measureless, 157–59; multiplicity of, 161–64; of nothing, 159–61; ratio of, 145–46; real, 144–46; specifics of, 141–44
mechanical objects/mechanism, 79, 206–9, 211, 213–14, 216, 219. *See also* technology
mediation, 138
memory, 163
metaphysical arch, xxvii, xxx, 7, 85, 100, 113, 286
metaphysics, xxxii, 277; Aristotelian, 30–44 passim, 268; and being, xix, 36–37; end of, 276; and fixing of types, 175–76; history of western, 154, 274; of identity and difference, 281; interpretation of, 22–25, 26, 288; and language, 20, 186, 288–89; and multiplicity, 12, 16–17, 25, 278–79, (manys) 7–8, 285–87, 290; origin of, 272; and pantheism, xxi, 69, 72, 82, 99, 100; of quantification, 54; in the Schools, 47; as a science, 6, 45, 205, 206, 213, 284; as way of thinking, 277

modality, multiplicity as, xvi, xvii
monads, 99–104, 107, 182, 260–62, 317n23
monogamy, 45, 148, 152–53, 155
multiplicity: Being and, *see* Being; end of, 243–45; Hegel's concept, xx; of individuality, 181–85; infinite, 120–28; of judgments, 194–202; language of, 19, 20, 192–93, 288–91; Leibniz denies, 29; of logic, 55, 88–90; logic of, xxii, 82–87, 268–72; of matters, 13–15; meaning of, 97, 184–85, 201–2, (hypothetical definitions) xiv–xvii; of measures, 161–64; metaphysics and, *see* metaphysics; problem of, xviii, xx; quality of, xxiv, 40, 109–11; of quantity, 132–34, 136–37; questions of, 54–57; serial, 147–48; shift to, 6; as such, 17–21, 56, 58, 268. *See also* "manys" (*polla*)
music, 146, 148–49
Musil, Robert, xxiii

names, 187–88, 189–90, 192; abstract nominalism, 194. *See also* language
nationalism, 66
nature (*physis*), 64, 72, 140, 175–81, 212, 282–83; deviance in, 176–78, 240; double-, 149–50
negation, xxii, xxvii, 10–11, 40, 77, 237; abstract, xx, 75, 76, 108, 147, (death as) 225–26; of being and non-being, 61, 89, 106, 165; conception as, 181; of "I," 66; of many, one as, 97–99; meaning of, 79, 80; "of negation," 60, 87, 121, 134, 157, 165; of quantity, 129, 130
Neo-Platonism, 31. *See also* Plato and Platonism
Newtonian physics. *See* physics
Nietzsche, Friedrich, 26, 30, 75, 112, 268, 319n22; quoted, 4, 21, 76, 88, 115, 185, 288, 300n62, (on Descartes) 28, 228–29, (on Hegel) 74, 305n102; *Ecce Homo,* 181
nominalism, 194. *See also* names
nothing, 250; measure of, 159–61. *See also* negation
numbers, concept of, 78, 115–18. *See also* mathematics; quantity; "one," the

objectivity, 169, 186, 215–16; conceptual, 203–14; of life, 235; of mechanical objects, 206–7; of the object, 204, 209, 213, 219, 237; *Objective Logic,* 170, 182; objective reality, 220–21, 222; teleology and, 211–14
"one," the, 5, 43; Kantian view, 82; "many ones," 104–9, 110; meaning of, 32–36; as negation of many, 97–99; "in its own self," 105–7; Parmenidian concept, 16, 39, 298n16; as quantity, 116–17
ontology, 36, 55, 56, 112, 124; Kant and, xix, 50; of love, 73; ontological difference, xxx, 31, 73, 246, 263, 268; pantheistic, 82
"ought," the, 67
Owens, Joseph, 36

pantheism, metaphysical, xxi, 69, 72, 82, 99, 100
Parmenides and Parmenidian thought, xix, 30, 92, 140, 188; and being, 64, 91, 94; identity, 247, 255; metaphysical arch, xxvii, xxx; and the "one," 16, 39, 82, 298n16; and thinking, 249–50, 251, 272, 273; and "way of truth," 5, 182
particularity, 81, 87, 88; of the particular, 173–81, 182; serial, of measure, 147
phenomenology, 10–11, 14, 81; of the absolute, 85
philosophy: becomes psychology, 186; and being, 91; concept of, 58–62; "fundamental error of," 71; Hegel's view, 279; histories of, 28–30, 62, 91; of identity and difference, 249; "as improvisation," xix; improvisation of, 292; inception of Greek, xviii; and language, 24–25, 189; as logic, 83–84; and mathematical model, 241; multiplicity of, xvii–xix, 17, 23–24, 56, 275; promise of (to provide knowledge), 235; as science or system, 62; speculative, *see* thinking; structural shift in, 9, 13; transcendental, 47, 50, 61–62, 69–70, 167
physics, 34, 105, 179; Newtonian, 208, 219; theoretical, 126
physis. See nature

Plato and Platonism, 18, 30, 100, 151, 153, 178, 197; Aristotle's critique of, xix, 30–31, 36, 38, 42, 43–44, 61, 286; and the "one," 5, 35, 39, 43; and substance, 35, 37, 38; *Republic,* 13; *Theaetetus,* 140; *Timaeus,* 11, 34, 172
Plotinus, 30
pluralization, xxxv, 4, 7, 46, 137, 140
polla. See "manys"
polygamy, 45, 151
polymorphism, 10–15 passim, 61, 150
Ponge, Francis, 172
predication, 42, 194–202, 264; defined, 118; and identity, xxviii, 71, 254–55, 257–58; law of multiple, xxix; and multiplicity, xv, 270–71; "S is P" formula, xxiii, 17, 78, 97, 266, 268
pragmatism, 243
praxis, 33
presentation and representation, 244–45
Protagoras, xxv, 140
psychology, 186, 194, 236
Pythagoreans, the, 104, 115–16, 316n23; Aristotle's critique of, xix, 30, 38, 42, 43, 44, 61, 286; Pythagorean theorem, 241

quality: measure and, 138–39, 142–46, 155–57, 159–60; and multiplicity, xxiv, 40, 109–11; qualitative determination, 113; qualitative infinity, 121–28, 134, 135, 136, 157–58; qualitative relation, 129–32, 147; qualitative transition, 134–35, 143, 158; of quantity, 112–37
quantity: concept of (quantification, quantum), xxiv–xxv, 40, 48, 75, 117–20, 132–33; measure and, 138–39, 141–46, 147, 155–57, 159–60; metaphysics of, 54; multiplicity of, 132–34, 136–37; quality of, 112–37; quantitative alteration, 158; quantitative infinity, 120–28,134, 135, 136, 157–58; quantitative ratio, 123–24, 130–32, 144; quantitative relation, 129–32; quantitative transition, 134–35; superpowers and, 112–13
Quine, W. V., 127

ratio. *See* measure(s); quantity; relation
rational animal, 27, 33, 143, 219, 236
realism, xxi, 70
reason, 59, 180; the ends of, 211–14; and identity, 70–71; law of, 71; reflective, 61; speculative, 67–68. *See also* thinking
reflection, 59–60, 61, 267; judgment of, 197–98; "negative," 67
Reinhold, Karl Leonhard, 55, 65
relation: concept of, 128–32, 147; multiplicity as, xvi; objective, 203–4; science as study of, 146. *See also* elective affinities
repulsion and attraction, 106–9, 113, 114. *See also* negation

Schelling, F. W. J., 62, 65, 75, 80, 134, 338n1; identity-philosophy, 12, 38, 69–74 passim, 77, 81; metaphysical arch, 85, 113; transcendent idealism, 55, 61; *Presentation of My System of Philosophy,* 70; *System of Transcendental Idealism,* 70
schematism (Kantian), 51–52, 54, 72, 86, 216
Scholasticism, 47
Schopenhauer, Arthur, 310n66
Schulze, Gottlob Ernst, 327n8
Schürmann, Reiner, 298n24
science, 66, 178; conceptual, 68; history and, 94–95; identity of, 91; and language, 150; life as object of, 219; linear narrative of, 90, 95; of logic, 87, 88, 91–92, 94–95, 140; of measures, 146; metaphysics as, 6, 45, 205, 206, 213, 284; "of natural spirit," 236; philosophy as, 62; "of pure thought," 86; and scientism, 25; speculative thought vs., 90, 240; as study of relations, 146; and truth, 165–66. *See also* technology
scientific classification, 175; genera and species, 33, 35–36, 40–41, 175–78, 198–99, 240
secrecy, 220
self, the. *See* "I"; "one," the
self-consciousness, 97, 229–32, 235, 236, 242–43; and the "I," 65, 167; Kantian view, 166–67; in language, 190–91. *See also* apperception
self-determination, 208, 213, 220–23, 229, 237, 249–50, 261. *See also* individuality

semantics, 22, 24–25; of "one," 32–36. *See also* language
sexuality, 45, 148, 151–55 passim, 171, 209, 290
Shakespeare, William, xiii, 246
signs, 187–88, 189. *See also* names; symbols
Simmel, Georg, 112
"S is P" formula. *See* predication
skepticism, 80–81
Socrates and Socratic thought, xxxii, 80, 172, 178, 226; and pre- Socratics, 43
space and time, 47, 51–54, 62, 90, 126, 252–53
speculative logic and thought. *See* logic; reason; thinking
Spinoza, Baruch, xxii, 30, 71, 103, 166, 198, 305n102; determination, 20, 90, 261, 262, 338n1; pantheism, xxi, 69, 72, 99, 100
spirit, 59, 68, 76; absolute power of, 179; language and, 190; life and death and, 219–20, 223–24; quantification and, 112–13, 142; "science of," 236; totality of, 69, 77
structuralism, 9–13; seduction of structure, 9–13
subjectivism/subjectivity, 62–69, 77, 236, 336n20; as a being, 203; concept of, xxvi, 215–16; of the subject, 168–71, 219, 220, 222, 235, 237; subjective judgment, 199; *Subjective Logic,* 170, 173, 183, 219; subjective psychologism, 186; subjective totality, 67, 221
substance (*ousia*), xix, 166; of many, 30–45; measure of, 140
substantive, multiplicity as, xv–xvi
superpowers, 112–13
supersession, 61, 77, 80, 86, 236, 243; conceptual, 97; of dialectic, 55; of negative, 75, 76; as totality, 60
symbols, xxvii, 115–16, 189
synthesis, 47, 69, 96; of Apprehension, 46; of reproduction and recognition, 48–59

technology: fetishism of, 25, 112; mechanical objects, 79, 207–9, 211, 213–14, 216, 219; thinking vs., 79–80, 239, 312n83. *See also* science
teleology, 86, 164, 211–14, 216, 219, 220
Theaetetus, 178
theorem, the, 240–42
"thing," the, 84, 204, 205, 206, 281, 298n26
thinking, 55–56; the act of, 242; being and, 64, 249–50, 272–74, 282–83; classical logic and, 75, 78, 84–85; conceptually, 47–48; equated with reckoning, 78; the "I" as thinking thing, 27–28 (*see also* Descartes, René, and Cartesian thought); and improvising, 26; language connected to, 75, 78; logic as "science of," 86; memory and, 163; metaphysics as way of, 277; Parmenidian view, 249–50, 251, 272, 273; speculative, 61, 89, 93, 97, 165, 195, (and identity) 167, 258–59, (and quantification) 124, 128, (vs. science) 90, 240, (and symbols) 115; technology vs., 79–80, 239, 312n83. *See also* logic; reason
time: Kant's conception of, 319n24; the "now," 252–53. *See also* space and time
totality, 49, 58–59, 83, 163; God as absolute, 74; in Hegel's terminology, 233; idea of, 215–45; law of, 71; of love, 73; objective and subjective, 67, 69, 220–21; of the spirit, 69, 77; supersession as, 60
Transcendental Aesthetic, 46, 48, 52, 62
transcendental idealism. *See* idealism
Transcendental Logic, 48
transition, problem of, 125–26, 134–36, 143, 156, 158, 209. *See also* becoming
"triplicity," 62
truth, xxi, 234; being and, 216; concept of, 165–68, 169; knowledge and, 238; languages and, 185; philosophical, 195; "way of," 5, 182, 237; the will to, 235–43

universal being, 36
universality, 83, 170; of the universal, 171–73, 197, 187
unum, verum, bonum, 47–48

Zeno, xxv, 3, 127
Zermelo, Ernst, 127